FAMILIES OF THE KING:

Writing Identity in the *Anglo-Saxon Chronicle*

The annals of the *Anglo-Saxon Chronicle* are fundamental to the study of the language, literature, and culture of the Anglo-Saxon period. Ranging from the ninth to the twelfth century, the *Chronicle*'s five primary manuscripts offer a virtually contemporary history of Anglo-Saxon England, contribute to the body of Old English prose and poetic texts, and enable scholars to document how the Old English language changed.

In *Families of the King*, Alice Sheppard explicitly addresses the larger interpretive question of how the manuscripts function as history. She shows that what has been read as a series of disparate entries and peculiar juxtapositions is in fact a compelling articulation of collective identity and a coherent approach to writing the secular history of invasion, conquest, and settlement. Sheppard argues that, in writing about the king's performance of his lordship obligations, the annalists transform literary representations of a political ethos into an identifying culture for the Anglo-Saxon nobles and those who conquered them.

(Toronto Old English Series)

ALICE SHEPPARD is an assistant professor in the Department of English at Pennsylvania State University.

ALICE SHEPPARD

Families of the King: Writing Identity in the *Anglo-Saxon Chronicle*

UNIVERSITY OF TORONTO PRESS
Toronto Buffalo London

© University of Toronto Press 2004
Toronto Buffalo London
utorontopress.com

Reprinted in paperback 2019

ISBN 978-0-8020-8984-7 (cloth)   ISBN 978-1-4875-0677-3 (paper)

Library and Archives Canada Cataloguing in Publication

Title: Families of the king : writing identity in the Anglo-Saxon chronicle / Alice Sheppard.
Names: Sheppard, Alice, author.
Series: Toronto Old English series ; 12.
Description: Series statement: Toronto Old English series ; 12 | Reprint. Originally published: 2004. | Includes bibliographical references and index.
Identifiers: Canadiana 20190142928 | ISBN 9781487506773 (softcover)
Subjects: LCSH: Anglo-Saxon chronicle. | LCSH: Great Britain – Kings and rulers. | LCSH: Great Britain – History – Anglo-Saxon period, 449–1066 – Historiography. | LCSH: Great Britain – History – Norman period, 1066–1154 – Historiography.
Classification: LCC DA150 .S54 2019 | DDC 942.01–dc23

University of Toronto Press acknowledges the financial assistance to its publishing program of the Canada Council for the Arts and the Ontario Arts Council, an agency of the Government of Ontario.

   Canada Council for the Arts   Conseil des Arts du Canada

Funded by the Government of Canada   Financé par le gouvernement du Canada

for Daniel

Contents

Acknowledgments   ix

Introduction: Reading the *Chronicle*'s Past   3

1 Writing Identity in *Chronicle* History   9

2 Making Alfred King   26

3 Proclaiming Alfred's Kingship   51

4 Undoing Æthelred   71

5 Unmaking Æthelred but Making Cnut   94

6 Writing William's Kingship   121

7 Conclusion: After Lives   144

Notes   157
Bibliography   217
Index   251

Acknowledgments

In graduate school, reading the prefaces to scholarly books was a ritual that made me laugh: I never understood how so many people (and animals) came to be involved in one thing. The proverbial boot is now on the other foot. As I reflect on the process by which this book came into being, I realize that I might have written the words, but that the book itself owes equally as much to those who in various ways have surrounded me.

My dissertation committee, Tom Hill, Andy Galloway, Jay Jasanoff, and Art Groos, allowed me to bite off more than I could chew and guided me in the skills of swallowing properly. As they have continued to be insightful resources and sharp readers after my graduation, I thank them for their double duty.

My friends and colleagues at Penn State – Carey Eckhardt, Bob Edwards, Bob Frank, Kit Hume, Liz Jenkins, Jeanne Krochalis, Mark Morrisson, and Laura Reed-Morrisson – have read and reread drafts with unfailing enthusiasm and great generosity. To my friends and family: I deeply appreciate your support and encouragement.

To my colleagues in the field – Richard Abels, Nicole Clifton, Tom Hall, Nick Howe, Paul Hyams, Tom Noble, Katherine O'Brien O'Keeffe, and Mary Ramsey – thank you for your intense commitment to this project. I must also thank George Brown, Robert Polhemus, and the library staff at Stanford University for making it possible for me to work in Palo Alto. Eloise Blanchard's unflagging energy and patient readings helped me understand the core of what I wanted to say.

Chapter 3 was initially published in *Philological Quarterly* and parts of chapters 4 and 5 were published in *Via Crucis: Essays on Sources and Ideas in Memory of J.E. Cross*. For permission to republish this work, I thank the editors. All translations are mine unless otherwise noted. The following came to hand too late to consider fully: Stephen J. Harris, *Race and Ethnicity in Anglo-Saxon Literature* (New York: Routledge, 2003); Lois L. Huneycutt, *Matilda of Scotland: A Study in Medieval Queenship* (Woodbridge, Suffolk: Boydell Press, 2003). I am grateful to Thomas Bredehoft and Catherine Karkov for allowing me to see prepublication copies of their work.

I have been fortunate to receive significant funding for this project. My thanks are to the National Endowment for the Humanities, the Andrew W. Mellon Foundation, and the Research and Graduate Studies Office at Penn State University. Their support has enabled publication and facilitated critical work with scholars at a variety of different institutions.

I would like to acknowledge my debt to Barb Porter and Miriam Skey (my editors) and to the anonymous readers at the University of Toronto Press. Their skill and professionalism has turned a typescript into a book.

I dedicate my first book to Daniel without whom it would not have been possible.

Mountain View, California
July 2004

Wait: the cats ...

FAMILIES OF THE KING

Introduction:
Reading the *Chronicle*'s Past

The difficult manuscript and textual histories of the extant versions of the *Anglo-Saxon Chronicle* are well known to both historians and scholars of Old English literature, but the ways in which they affect how we read the *Chronicle* have only recently become part of scholarly discussion. To explain why they have begun reediting the many *Chronicle* manuscripts, the general editors of the new collaborative editing project assert that it was once 'impossible to establish reliably the reading of any given version save by returning directly to the manuscripts themselves.'[1] The recent editions of four of the five primary manuscripts, MSS A, B, C, and D, have made ground-breaking texts readily available to scholar and student alike, and they have greatly facilitated the kind of study that demonstrates the *Chronicle*'s value as a source of linguistic and historical information.[2] But the new editions have not in themselves changed what have become the scholarly practices of reading the *Anglo-Saxon Chronicle*.

While textual scholars have been determining how the manuscripts are related to each other, the significance of the variations, and the date and origin of the various *Chronicle* histories, scholars of Old English literature and history have mined the annals for information about single events such as the Norman Conquest and searched for background material to more canonical literary works like the *Battle of Maldon*. These approaches have unintentionally denied the artistry and ideologies of the *Chronicle* to such an extent that the annals are frequently perceived as a collection of unrelated facts; that is, the *Anglo-Saxon Chronicle* is often seen as an unreadable text, a text without meaning or significance in its own right.

To be sure, the annals slip from frantic rhetoric – 'And always after that it grew much worse; may the end be good when God wills' – to tantalizing understatement – 'Here, in this year, there was a great slaughter of birds.'[3] But the language in which scholars discuss the work of the various annalists, an effective language of marginalization,[4] has allowed us to ignore their contribution to Old English historiography and to bypass their articulation of Anglo-Saxon identity.[5]

The discourse of Anglo-Saxon identity in the *Chronicle* focuses on the figure of the king and the ways he performs his lordship obligations. In the accounts of how Alfred, Cnut, and William won, defended, and secured their kingdoms – and the equally important history of how Æthelred lost his – the annalists fashion stories of kingdom making (or, in the case of Æthelred, disintegration) in which the king's performance of his lordship obligations creates and identifies his people. In times of political uncertainty when the borders of the land are disputed and collective identity stressed, the annalists put aside land-based notions of kingdom and identity. Idealizing and smoothing recognizable aspects of historical lordship practice into a textual lordship culture, their carefully adapted interpretations of the past suggest that the people are at once created and defined by their acceptance of the king's lordship. These narratives of royal lordship are not intended to reflect everyday practice; rather, the annals of conquest, invasion, and settlement can more properly be seen as defining or constitutive fictions in which the lordship tie of king and man is written as the identifying ethos of the *Angelcynn*, the Anglo-Saxon people.[6]

That this discourse of identity has gone unnoticed is partially an effect of the *Chronicle*'s manuscript history and textual traditions. To interpret the history of the *Chronicle*, we must take into account the fact that the histories were kept, sporadically, in different places over more than three centuries by scribes who copied entries in chunks of centuries and fragments of less than a sentence. But by focusing on this history – on the fact that the extant manuscripts are not necessarily the original accounts of the events they communicate – and on the idea that their texts have been altered to fit the circumstances in which they were written, we have allowed the problems of the manuscript tradition to dominate the critical conversation. If we persist in not interpreting the very things that make the annals difficult to read – the narrative strategies of the various annalists, the relationships of the texts to their political, cultural, and textual contexts, and the relationship of the annals to other kinds of medieval historical writing – the *Chronicle* will continue, even as scholars champion Old English prose, to be the discipline's ugly duckling.[7]

In focusing on the historiography and ideology of the *Anglo-Saxon Chronicle*, I do not mean to suggest that the annals can be approached as a single unified literary work. Such assertions cannot be supported by the manuscript and textual history.[8] But the manuscript and textual history does inform how I read the *Chronicle*'s history. Scholars usually argue, for example, that the A manuscript of the *Chronicle* is not the original compilation of the annals' history. Nonetheless, the A manuscript, together with other witnesses like Asser's *Vita Alfredi*, can help us understand the limits of the common stock – the entries up to 891 – and thus the outermost boundaries of the Alfred annals.

Similarly, the C manuscript is not the original account of the *Æthelred-Cnut Chronicle*, but the features of this text have allowed Simon Keynes to argue that the entries for 983–1022 – the entries for the majority of Æthelred's reign and the early years of Cnut's rule – were written by a single annalist writing at one time.[9] This history shapes how I read the compelling rhetoric of the Æthelred-Cnut annals. For the accounts of the Norman Conquest, I shift my focus to the actual extant manuscripts and explore the annals in the historical and cultural contexts of the monastic institutions in which scholars usually agree that the manuscripts were produced.[10]

Whether or not the annals were composed by a single individual, once they are copied into other *Chronicle* manuscripts – by however many hands it takes to copy them – large parts of the *Chronicle* appear to circulate as a text.[11] This history allows me to look for commonalities of lexicon and narrative approach in the three narrative moments that are at the heart of *Families of the King*.[12] Overall, however, I treat each narrative section as a separate text, and I locate each text in its particular historical and cultural contexts.

By insisting on the importance of context, this book develops Walter Goffart's approach to interpreting the narratives of Germanic history.[13] In a closely read examination of Gregory of Tours, Paul the Deacon, Jordanes, and Bede, Goffart notes that these historians 'were never innocent; nor should anyone wish them to be. Their portrayals were conscious and deliberate, and worthy of sustained attention for precisely this reason.'[14] Goffart works from the principle that these histories are most meaningful in their local context, arguing his point by reading the *Historia* in the light of Bede's other historical writing, the present state of Northumbrian church history and controversy, the texts contemporaneous with the *Historia*, and, most extensively, what Goffart calls 'Bede's models.'[15] By the conclusion of his study, the complexity and intertextual dimensions of the *Historia* are clear, as is the necessity for reading within textual, political, and cultural contexts.

In *Families of the King*, interpreting the entries for the reigns of Alfred, Æthelred, Cnut, and William I in their contemporary equivalents of Goffart's contexts, I show how the *Anglo-Saxon Chronicle* annals respond to the political events of their day. Instead of creating legends of ethnic origins for their respective kings – that is, instead of drawing on the extant traditions of Anglo-Saxon originary legends and migration myths[16] – the Anglo-Saxon annalists offer careful studies of their king's performance of lordship. In these accounts of the past, the king's culture of lordship comes to define the king's people.

My reading of the annalists' narrative strategies is based on a study of the political circumstances these accounts narrate and on an exploration of the annals in the context of selected contemporary works, including texts from the tradition of Carolingian mirrors for princes and historical narratives such as Bede's *Historia ecclesiastica* and Orosius's *Historiarum adversus paganos libri septem*. I interpret the annalists' representations of contemporary lordship practices in conjunction with readings of the texts most frequently cited as sterling examples of lordship ideology – *Beowulf*, the *Battle of Maldon*, and the Cynewulf-Cyneheard episode of the *Anglo-Saxon Chronicle* – and with analyses of texts such as the Anglo-Saxon laws. Finally, I explore how the *Chronicle* convention for narrating the political problems of conquest and invasion contributes to an understanding of the historiography of the *Anglo-Saxon Chronicle* and thus to the larger problem of reading the *Chronicle*. Specifically, I interpret the Alfred, Æthelred, Cnut, and William annals as identifying narratives that create and define the king, his kingdom, and the people.

At the centre of this historiography is the annalists' treatment of both the political circumstance of invasion and the contemporary theological understanding of conquest and invasion.[17] The writers of history in Anglo-Saxon England were familiar with the conventional Christian idea that conquest and invasion were the outcome of sin. This tradition is present in Alcuin, Gildas, Nennius, and Bede, and it is also relevant for the loosely associated writers of history in Alfred's time. Even as the *Chronicle* annals were being compiled, Alfred also asked for translations of Bede's *Historia ecclesiastica* and Orosius's *Historiarum adversus paganos libri septem*. Nonetheless, the annalists of the *Chronicle* make very little use of this vision of the past. Where it is present, the annalists, as in the Æthelred-Cnut annals, adapt this Christian perspective to their articulation of collective Anglo-Saxon identity. Though their various accounts are separated by many years (hundreds of years in some cases), the annalists of Alfred, Æthelred, Cnut, and William's reigns all view the contemporary military and territorial problems of conquest and invasion through the lens of the king's lordship relations.

The Alfred annalist, for example, writes the peace of Alfred and Guthrum as a triumph of the king's performance of lordship. Sin and conquest appear in the Æthelred-Cnut annals, but they are adapted to fit the annalist's overall agenda. When Æthelred loses his military engagements with the Danes, the Æthelred-Cnut annalist suggests that these military losses are a result of the king's poor lordship relations (a sin) and underscores this point by defining Cnut's accession and new kingdom as a lordship exercise.[18] By the time of the Norman Conquest, the third major threat to the Anglo-Saxons, I suggest that the practice of narrating conquest as a matter of lordship relations has become a convention that enables the William annalist to accord a local significance to the narrative of national history.

I discuss the problem of defining lordship more fully below; for the moment, however, I want to suggest that the similarities in the various annalists' approaches to analysing collective identity and narrating the past are not coincidental. They are rather a deliberate historiography that separates the *Chronicle* annalists from such historians as Bede and Orosius by providing a new understanding of the structural motif of conquest and invasion and creating a secular identity for the people whose history they relate.

Furthermore, I see the history of the Alfred, Cnut, and William annals as productive, even performative.[19] It is not merely that when compared with the briefer and more elliptical entries, the annals for the reigns of Alfred, William, Æthelred, and Cnut use extensive narratives to figure conquest and invasion as problems of the kings' respective lordships. These *Chronicle* annalists use narrative and the cultural ethos of lordship to transform a commonplace of medieval kingship theory – the idea that the welfare of the people is intrinsically linked to the well-being or sin of the king – into a way of thinking about what defines a kingdom.[20] In a clear move away from originary narratives of the distant past, the annalists of conquest and invasion trace the formation of a kingdom in the recent past. Creating extended narratives from their understanding of recent events, the annalists position lordship as a defining component of Anglo-Saxon cultural identity.

To read the *Chronicle* in this way is not to undermine the scholarly significance of the events presented in the annals. The various manuscripts are important sources of our knowledge of the Anglo-Saxon past. And without the annals' narrative, our sense of the history of Anglo-Saxon England would be significantly poorer. But precisely because some annals and some sections of the *Chronicle* are narrative, they require further examination.[21] Such an approach to the annals and analysis of their cultural function reveals how the *Chronicle* can both convey a history of Anglo-Saxon England and be more than strictly historical.

CHAPTER ONE

Writing Identity in *Chronicle* History

In a recent argument against the possibility of medieval national identity, Patrick Geary declares that ethnic nationalism is a product of the nineteenth century and suggests that in the medieval period, the 'sense of belonging to a nation did not constitute' one of the most important forms of collective identity.[1] But while the plausibility of medieval national identity is a contested and well-discussed subject, the texts themselves do suggest that some kind of group identity is possible. For example, the Anglo-Saxons refer to themselves and, indeed, are variously referred to as *Angli Saxones* (the people), *Engelsaxo* (one man), or *Anglorum Saxonia* (the country), the *gens Anglorum et Saxonum*, and *Angli* or *Anglici* (the 'Angels' meaning Anglians and others);[2] the kings of Anglo-Saxon England called themselves or were called the *Bretwalda*, the *rex Angulsaxonum, rex Angulseaxna, rex totius Britannie*, etc.[3] The many different titles with different meanings and the sheer proliferation of royal styles and group names all suggest a sense of collectivity that is simultaneously distinct from and more inclusive than the bonds of 'religion, kindred, lordship, and social stratum.'[4]

For thinking about how, in a historical sense, the Anglo-Saxons may have seen themselves collectively, I find persuasive the model of *ethnie* outlined in Anthony Smith's *The Ethnic Origins of Nations*. Smith proposes six aspects of *ethnie*: a collective name, a common myth of descent, a shared history, a distinctive shared culture, an association with a specific territory, and a sense of solidarity.[5] Smith has undertaken a historical project that attempts to explain the historical process by which actual groups of actual people came to think of themselves as nations and persuaded others to think the same way.

As articulated in this work, however, the notion of *ethnie* is not generally productive for analysing the collectivity articulated by the *Anglo-Saxon Chronicle*. To be sure, there are some important similarities between Smith's model and the identity of the annals: because they address the problems of unifying different peoples into one community that accepts a common leader and government, the entries for the reigns of Alfred, Æthelred, Cnut, and William can be seen as partially consonant with Smith's claim that 'for an *ethnie* to become a "nation," it must turn its members into "citizens." '[6] Overall, however, the identity of the annals does not exactly meet Smith's criteria. For example, Smith stresses the importance of land, but, in *Families of the King*, I argue that the identity articulated in the annals is formulated without a sense of territory. If the borders of the land are unstable, any identity associated with that land is also unstable.

More important, the identity I interpret in the *Chronicle* annals is not a historical phenomenon.[7] That is, I do not claim that the lordship ethos of the annals was ever a literal expression of a historical Anglo-Saxon identity or even one that a significant proportion of the projected aristocratic audience of the text would have claimed and used. What we know about the practice of Anglo-Saxon lordship suggests that the Anglo-Saxons drew heavily from the Carolingians; it is therefore hard to claim lordship as a uniquely defining Anglo-Saxon practice.[8] We know that the *Chronicle* manuscripts circulated, but we know very little about how the *Chronicle* was read outside the circles in which it was written.[9] It is therefore hard to make claims about the appeal of such an identity.

Because of these difficulties, I turn to the work of Homi K. Bhabha for a formulation of national identity as a kind of textual community. Writing about the importance of narration and local culture in the creation of national identity, Bhabha argues for a 'cultural construction of nationness as a form of social and textual affiliation' in which the people are both the objects of 'nationalist pedagogy' and its 'subjects.'[10] Thus historical narrative can be said to create the very people whose history it purports to relate. As the 'scraps, patches, and rags of daily life' are 'turned into the signs of a coherent national culture ... the very act of the narrative performance interpellates a growing circle of national subjects. In the production of the nation as narration there is a split between the continuist accumulative temporality of the pedagogical, and the repetitious, recursive strategy of the performative.'[11] Bhabha's focus on culture and text and the way in which they shape the people (as opposed to conveying aspects of the culture of a preexisting people) opens a new avenue for thinking about the collective identity articulated by the *Anglo-Saxon Chronicle*.

As I read the annals of the *Chronicle*, I see the identities articulated and created in the entries for Alfred, Æthelred, Cnut, and William as textual representations envisioned by and circulated within contemporary monastic communities. I stress the way in which these representations both respond to the language and formulation of communal identity in certain contemporary texts and engender similar expressions of collective identity in other works. Overall, the group or national identity of the annals is textual and textually disseminated. But this textuality does not make the identity of the annals any less compelling or meaningful to their audiences. As Bhabha has argued, national identities are a form of 'textual affiliation.'[12] In times of political upheaval and times when the borders of the land are unstable, the texts that idealize and interpret recognizable aspects of everyday culture may be the most effective ways to articulate and disseminate identity.

Because I focus on the lordship images in the annals, I do not intend my analysis to be taken as a literal assessment of contemporary lordship practice or actual historical events. Even though the annals centre on the king's lordship, it would be hard to argue that Alfred's lordship literally secured his realm, and none of the seminal modern histories of his reign see the events of his kingship in this way. It is possible to argue that Æthelred's poor lordship relations lie behind the fall of his kingdom, but, when considering the loss of the Anglo-Saxon kingdom, historians usually take into account aspects of domestic politics, the failure and success of the king's diplomacy, his use of conversion as a peace-making strategy, and the joint decision of *witan* and king to pay tribute.[13] Similarly, it need not be the case that, as the annalist implies, William the Conqueror was not a legitimate king because he could not understand the obligations of Anglo-Saxon lordship; historians have analysed the discussion of William's legitimacy in terms of land, birthright, oaths, and inheritance.[14]

All these situations are far more complicated than the accounts in the *Chronicle* would have their readers believe, yet the king's performance of his lordship ties is central to the narratives for all these kings. Thus the annalists of conquest and invasion create stories of kingdom formation that can more properly be seen as defining or constitutive fictions in which lordship is written as the identifying ethos of the Anglo-Saxon people. In other words, the annalists' accounts are pedagogical in Bhabha's terms; they teach their readers what 'makes' an Anglo-Saxon and what defines Anglo-Saxon kings and kingdoms.[15] For the *Chronicle* as a whole, then, the Alfred annalist begins a meaningful discourse of identity, and the relevance of this discourse of identity is indicated in the continuation of his approach and ideals in the work of the Æthelred-Cnut and William annalists.

Though Bhabha argues from a postcolonial position, his claim that national identity can be seen as a form of textual affiliation is already deeply inscribed – if not in that language – in a variety of medieval texts and in the criticism. As analysed respectively by Gabrielle Spiegel and Amy Remensnyder, the fictional histories of the community at Saint Denys and of other selected Benedictine abbeys of southwest France can be seen to offer their readers a common vision of the past, one in which the community itself is created by a process of interpellation as its members respond to the call, that is, the unifying ideology, of that imagined past.[16] This approach to writing imaginary narratives of history is not limited to a community defined by its faith and institutional walls nor to the late medieval period.

In a careful study of community and medieval legends of origin, Susan Reynolds has noted that foundation narratives are almost always associated with distinct 'social and political collectivities,' and that these narratives are not unique to the communities in question.[17] Nor are those communities necessarily visible by virtue of such tangible markers as a monastic house or even territory. Suggesting that medieval communities are equally a function of custom, law, government, culture, and geography, Reynolds shows that the legends of origin documented in certain histories and genealogical texts – writing that offered its audience an unlikely descent from the Trojans, Woden, Gog and Magog, or even the sons of Noah – could offer a unifying identity to a variety of sometimes competing collectivities that range from the nation-state to a royal dynasty.

In the most detailed exploration of an Anglo-Saxon myth of origins, Nicholas Howe starts where Reynolds appears to conclude – with a myth of origins that spreads across multiple genres of writing, persists across multiple centuries of culture, and thus appeals to a variety of audiences and disparate communities. At the centre of Howe's work are the ways in which the Anglo-Saxons mythologized the *adventus Saxonum*. For Howe, the problem of ancestral migration is a vital part of the Anglo-Saxon literary imagination, and it is also crucial to the ways in which the Anglo-Saxons saw themselves and interpreted their experience of crisis. Howe argues that at the moments when the Anglo-Saxons' territorial and cultural worlds seemed most unstable, they turned to a widely disseminated myth of ancestral origins – a migration myth – for a way of understanding historical and cultural change.[18] So strong is the appeal of the myth of migration that it affirms the Anglo-Saxons' communal identity and allows them to draw consolation from their place in the world.[19]

None of these studies deals with what I see as the two central aspects of the Alfred, Æthelred, Cnut, and William annals: the representations of actual events in the recent past and the ultimate performativity of the identity articulated in the annals. The Anglo-Saxon identity created in the *Chronicle* centres on the figure of the king and the ways he maintains his lordship relations; it is not formulated in the realm of the mythological, genealogical, legendary, or fabulous. Rather, in their adaptations of different lordship practices, the annalists work with representations of everyday culture.

To a certain extent, the mundane is a function of all annalistic histories. In his description of the genres of historical writing, Isidore defines the function of an annal as committing to writing those details in a particular year regarding the domestic and military, territorial and maritime affairs that are worthy of being remembered.[20] The quotidian, the domestic and military history of the annals, is clearly the subject of the *Chronicle*, but the annals of this narrative of the past are not like the static records of their annalistic ancestors, the entries of the Easter tables.[21] The annals for Alfred, Æthelred, Cnut, and William do not merely, in Isidore's terms, memorialize the notable events of each year. Neither do they simply reflect a preexisting aspect of Anglo-Saxon life. They interpret the events of the recent past, creating a new and imagined history in which the king's lordship defines his newly created *Angelcynn*.

Defining Lordship

Historians of the medieval period frequently use the word 'lordship' in such varied contexts as medieval social relations and social identity, land tenure, aspects of kingship and legal theory, obligations of military service, issues of royal protection, and the difficult social and political structures evoked in explorations of vassalage and fiefs.[22] All these areas of inquiry are linked by a common understanding of the existence of a personal and political relationship between lord and man, an acceptance of the importance of that relationship, and a realization that the lordship tie can productively illuminate other areas of medieval political and social life.

At first glance, the lordship of the *Chronicle* appears to resemble that of historical practice. The annalists depict a personal relationship between lord and man, a relationship that is contracted through carefully staged rituals of submission and oath swearing and defined by a set of structured reciprocal expectations by which the lord and man might transact gifts, protection, loyalty, and even peace. In that the annalists refer to *compaternitas* (baptismal coparental relations), use language that recalls certain fidelity oaths, and evoke aspects of lordship ritual such as the swearing of oaths and the submission ceremonies, the *Chronicle* representations of lordship seem to evoke what we know of Anglo-Saxon lordship practices. And, even though, historically speaking, the bond of lord and man is differently configured in the different reigns of Alfred, Æthelred, Cnut, and William – the differences derive from the contemporary exigencies of power, culture, and historical circumstance – all the annalists offer similar representations of conventional contemporary lordship language, lordship ceremonies, and the notion of reciprocity.

Nonetheless, the depictions of lordship in the *Chronicle* are neither consistent nor complete.[23] Though in Anglo-Saxon England, such political and social questions of land tenure and military service were part of one form of lordship practice, the *Chronicle* annalists focus only on the lordship bond of the king and his men and, in particular, on the personal aspect of that tie. And, if the annalists' representations of reciprocal lordship ties, their focus on mutual obligation, and their language of lordship look conventional, the way this lordship functions is not. The relationship of king and men as it appears in the annals of conquest, settlement, and invasion is carefully tailored to each individual narrative. In the entries for Alfred's reign, the annalist suggests that Alfred builds lordship ties with the Anglo-Saxons and that he is able to extend those ties to the Danes. This extension is possible because, according to the annalist, lordship is an important element of Alfred's royal authority and, in turn, that authority is produced anew by the king's ability to include the Danes.

In the Æthelred-Cnut annals, the story of the king's lordship centres on his inability to keep the loyalty of his men and his consequent failure to secure peace with the Danes. In the story of Cnut's succession, the annalist implies that Cnut repeats Alfred's situation in reverse: Cnut's relationship to the Danes is a kingship that the annalist presents as a lordship bond. This bond creates the possibility of lordship over the Anglo-Saxons. Similarly, the narratives of the Norman Conquest and settlement examine what happens when William exchanges this dynamic personal relationship for one centred on the land. Thus though the different lordships of these kings address different contemporary political problems, they all depend on the ideas that effective lordship involves a series of complementary reciprocities and that the lordship bond is both symbolic and productive of the king's authority.

Even as I argue that the images of lordship in the *Chronicle* do not reflect contemporary practice, I also do not wish to conflate the lordship of the annals with that of Old English heroic literature.[24] The lordless speaker of the Old English *Wanderer* misses personal contact with his lord; he dreams of embracing his lord, of kissing him, and of placing his hands and head on his lord's knees.[25] The annals are less emotional. As articulated in texts like *Beowulf*, the *Battle of Maldon*, and even the Cynewulf-Cyneheard episode of the *Anglo-Saxon Chronicle*, this mutual affectionate relationship also, potentially, has some rather severe obligations. The lord is judged by his generosity, and the man by his willingness to fight and possibly die for his lord. In *Beowulf*, *Maldon*, and the Cynewulf-Cyneheard episode, the men do die for their lords, but they do so in situations that question the necessity of their sacrifice while praising their bravery. In contrast, the annals do not reward heroism or martial prowess, and the outcome of the battles is not essential to their lordship narrative.

In essence, then, my approach to understanding the significance of lordship in the *Chronicle* is informed by the complexities of contemporary literary and historical lordship scholarship, but I stress the fact that the annalists do not convey precise reflections of literary convention or actual practice.[26] Instead, I recognize the importance of literary images of lordship and acknowledge the presence of a historical relationship that is identifiable as a lordship bond, but I analyse the textual representation of that tie in order to understand the agendas of the annals. In other words, like many medieval historians, I use the lordship relationship as a vehicle for exploring another issue: in this case, the writing of Anglo-Saxon identity and the creation of a people who are known as the *Angelcynn*.

Inventing the *Angelcynn*

Throughout the various *Chronicle* manuscripts, the annalists repeatedly use some form of the term *Angelcynn* to describe the Anglo-Saxon people.[27] The literal meaning of this term and its usage in a variety of Old English texts has occasioned much discussion.[28] In particular, scholars have tried to explore whether choosing a name like *Angelcynn* might be equated with a growing sense of nationhood. They have also sought to explain why a word that literally means 'family of *Angels*' came to be the chosen term for the people under West Saxon rule and, later, for the Anglo-Saxons themselves.[29]

My interest in the word is in the nature of the collectivity implied by the element *cynn*, a word that is often and most broadly translated as 'family' but can describe all kinds of community from 'blood family' to 'nation.'[30] While the literal definition of blood family clearly cannot apply to the whole of the *Angelcynn*, I would argue that as used in the *Anglo-Saxon Chronicle*, the *cynn* element does denote a kinship bond: it refers to the sometimes but not necessarily genealogically related members of an extended family of men, a family created by the king's lordship relations.[31] In essence, then, *Angelcynn* is not just another instance of a conventional term to describe the Anglo-Saxons: the *Angelcynn* are the people who in the face of conquest and invasion are created by the bonds of lordship and who, in Æthelred's case, are lost because of the failure of lordship ties.

In two of the texts most frequently cited as literary studies of personal lordship – the *Battle of Maldon*, and the Cynewulf-Cyneheard episode of the *Anglo-Saxon Chronicle* – family or kinship language is used to describe the tie between man and lord. The metaphor is not neutral; the language of family relationship is often invoked at moments when the lordship covenant is about to be violated, that is, when someone is about to abandon the bond of kinship that they created when they accepted the obligations of lordship. In *Maldon*, when Byrhtnoth lies dead on the field and his men hesitate, Æthelwulf reminds them of their promises and of the kinship implied by their lordship relations.[32] He even refers to their lord as a member of their family, a kinsman, a *mæg*. The same formulation of lordship relations as family relations underpins the critical moment in the Cynewulf-Cyneheard episode when the retainers of both men must choose between their lordship and blood families. Both sets of retainers respond that no kinsman is dearer to them than their now-dead lord.[33]

The mapping of the language of lordship onto the language of family relationship is made doubly significant by the renewed emphasis on lordship and lordship oaths in the late ninth century. As several scholars have noticed, the political and legal culture of Alfred's court placed a high value on lordship and loyalty,[34] and Sarah Foot, in particular, has tied the increasing usage of the word *Angelcynn* to the submission and pledging rituals of lordship.[35] But whereas Foot argues for a connection between the term and a historical Anglo-Saxon identity, I am concerned only with the way in which the Anglo-Saxon annalists write identity, using a word that, if Foot is right, the Anglo-Saxons would have recognized as being associated with the creation and articulation of a sense of collectivity. In this context, the family of the *Angelcynn* can be created by an acceptance of the obligations of lordship. Like the *familia regis* of Carolingian mirrors, the families of the king in the *Chronicle* narratives of conquest and invasion are those created by his lordship relations.[36]

The limits set by the narratives of conquest and invasion are important; even in the *Chronicle*, *Angelcynn* has many shades of meaning. The dates of the manuscripts and the way in which the texts were compiled render a single reading of the term *Angelcynn* complicated. I work from the generally accepted idea that the *Chronicle* was first compiled in the reign of Alfred; this is precisely the time when the term *Angelcynn* gained currency in other (that is non-*Chronicle*) texts as a general word for Alfred's people. This general meaning is contemporaneous with my interpretation of *Angelcynn* as the word for the people defined by the king's lordship. Given the contemporaneity of the two meanings, it is not surprising to find some blurring of the two usages in the earlier *Chronicle* entries.[37]

Prior to the Alfred annals, *Angelcynn* is used, infrequently, to describe the Anglo-Saxons, as opposed to the Britons, Picts, or Scots (443 MSS A and E and 597 MSS A, C, and E; here, however, they are separate from the West Saxons). In the entry for 787 in MSS A, C, and E, *Angelcynn* appears in the Alfred annalist's sense as the people whose land the Danes sought. In the annal for 816 in MSS C and D and (815) E, *Angelcynn* is used to describe the Anglo-Saxons' area in Rome (this usage is repeated in the entry for 875 [C] and 874 [D]),[38] and, finally, in the entry for 836 in MSS A, C, and E, it denotes the people whose land King Ecgbryht, Alfred's grandfather, was forced to flee. After these instances, that is, once the annalist begins the story of Alfred's reign – a story of invasion and potential conquest – *Angelcynn* is used more consistently to describe the people formed by what the annalist presents as Alfred's performance of lordship.

In the Alfred annals, the annalist's representation of the king's philosophy of lordship – a depiction that is neither heroic nor literal – leads directly to the creation of the *Angelcynn*. In the entry for 878, Alfred uses lordship to bind the Danes to him, establish his authority, and create a new people. In 886, these, the people formed by Alfred's lordship, are termed, for the first time, the *Angelcynn*. While the precise nature of events in London is a subject of some academic discussion,[39] the annalist states that all members of the *Angelcynn* who are not living under Danish control submitted to Alfred.[40] In this moment, the *Angelcynn* formally come into being as a people whose land has been settled by the Danes and who are harassed by the Danish army, but who are bound to Alfred by lordship obligations.

The importance of this account and the significance of its terminology are emphasized by the *Chronicle* manuscript history. The five main manuscripts of the *Anglo-Saxon Chronicle* all share a virtually identical account of the past up to around 914. This history is divided into what scholars call the 'common stock' that runs as far as 890 or 891 and a series of continuations that run to 914.[41] The continuators understand and, indeed, continue the language and ideology of lordship that I identify in the Alfred section of the common stock history. In 896, the *Angelcynn* are the people that have, 'thanks to God,' been thus far spared the worst of another round of Danish raiding[42] and when the king's death is announced, the *Angelcynn* are the people over whom the continuator says Alfred is king.[43] These annalists choose *Angelcynn* as the term by which they define the odd blend of West Saxons, Mercians, Scots, and Irish over whom Alfred reigns.[44]

The idea that lordship is definitive of an *Angelcynn*, a kingdom and people created and lost in the face of conquest and invasion, appears again in the Æthelred-Cnut annals, the second *Chronicle* engagement with Danish raiding. For example, the *Angelcynn* are again the people protected from the Danes when Æthelred successfully repeats the strategy we saw Alfred using: Æthelred contracts peace as an act of lordship, baptizes Olaf, and gives him gifts.[45] Similarly, the *Angelcynn* are the people who are not slaughtered in the 1002 St Brice's Day massacre, the people symbolized by Ulfcytel's daring swordplay in 1004, and the people most sorely harassed in 1009. At the moment when, because of his poor lordship, Æthelred symbolically loses his throne to Archbishop Ælfheah, the archbishop's people are the *Angelcynn*.[46]

Finally, the *Angelcynn* are the people whose lord is betrayed and the people who are themselves betrayed in 1016 by *ealdormann* Eadric.⁴⁷

Just as Æthelred's poor lordship leads to the loss of his people, so, the Æthelred-Cnut annalist suggests, Cnut's ideal lordship gains him a new people: an Anglo-Scandinavian people who are also known as the *Angelcynn* and who, like the Anglo-Saxons before them, are defined by their king's lordship. The idea that both Danes and Anglo-Saxons can become *Angelcynn* confirms the role of lordship in defining those who may belong to this people. As I suggested above, though Cnut wins a significant victory in 1016, he is able to do so only because, as the annalist describes it, Eadric Streona betrays his people, the *Angelcynnes þeode* (the people of the *Angelcynn*).⁴⁸

Further, even though Cnut triumphs in the military engagement, the annalist explicitly states that the Dane gains not the land but the people: 'Þær ahte Cnut sige 7 gefeht him ealle Engla þeode' (There Cnut possessed the victory and he won for himself all the Anglo-Saxon people).⁴⁹ This perspective is underscored in the account of Cnut's accession. In the *Chronicle*, one of the conventions for narrating accessions is the phrase 'feng to rice' (succeeded to the kingdom). In a careful variation of this formula, the Æthelred-Cnut annalist implies that because Cnut wins his people in 1016 all that is left for him to do in 1017 is to accede to 'eallon Angelcynnes ryce' (the whole kingdom of the *Angelcynn*).⁵⁰ And in the same way that the Alfred annalist marks Alfred's control over his kingdom in 886 as a lordship ceremony, the Æthelred-Cnut annalist shows Cnut taking control by performing acts of lordship.⁵¹

Significantly, the term *Angelcynn* does not feature in the third and final *Chronicle* narrative of conquest and invasion. Whereas the Alfred and Æthelred-Cnut annalists narrate the formation of a new people defined by their respective kings' lordship, the D and E annalists communicate the end of that identity. By the end of the Norman Conquest narratives, neither the D nor the E annalist refers to the people who occupy William's new realm as the *Angelcynn*; they are no longer defined by a personal lordship tie to their king.⁵²

Although the *Chronicle* is at the centre of *Families of the King*, implicit in my focus on lordship and the *Angelcynn* are an understanding of kingship as an office (as opposed to a birthright) and a reconsideration of the authorizing power of genealogical discourse. In the manuscripts of the *Anglo-Saxon Chronicle*, genealogical material appears at several different junctures. The A or Parker manuscript has a genealogical preface; scholars argue that a similar preface began the B text; and the material appears at significant points in the early annals. By examining the moments when the genealogies appear, most scholars now accept as ideological the highly improbable lines of descent expressed in the various recitations of the West Saxon royal genealogy and regnal table; they also interpret the noble and distinguished lineage offered in the genealogy as authorizing of the king's claim to or tenure on the throne.[53]

Anglo-Saxon succession does not necessarily proceed by birthright,[54] so the myth of the unbroken vertical descent – a myth that genealogy works to perpetuate – is not necessarily the most powerful authorizing discourse.[55] Genealogical discourse might exclude as easily as it legitimizes and includes. All the kings in this study have 'family issues' around their claims to the throne. Though he was of the royal line, Alfred disinherited the sons of his brother;[56] Æthelred, also of the royal line, was suspected of having been involved in murdering his brother;[57] Cnut, clearly not of the West Saxon royal dynasty, took Æthelred's wife;[58] and William, bastard son of Robert I of Normandy, and thus also not directly of the West Saxon royal line, claimed birthright through his relationship to Emma, Æthelred's and Cnut's wife.[59] In this context, the performative discourse of lordship and the *Angelcynn* it creates offer these kings an alternate way of retrospectively authorizing their succession.

Kingship, Salvation, and History

The distinctiveness of the annalists' history is underscored by the intellectually local but geographically distant context of the Carolingian world. The cultural and intellectual history of Anglo-Saxon relations with the Continent is rich and complex, and there are many discussions about the kinds of available evidence. For my purposes, the existence of a flow of texts and ideas between Anglo-Saxon England and Francia focuses my exploration of the annalists' historiography and their ideologies of lordship. In Anglo-Saxon England, there are no direct models for the kind of annalistic writing evidenced in the *Chronicle*, so scholars often look to the Continent. Indeed, in addition to noting the Continental palaeographical elements in the manuscripts of certain Anglo-Saxon histories, Malcolm Parkes has suggested that Grimbald of St Bertin, one of the Frankish scholars Alfred invited to his court, might have had significant influence on the compilation of the *Anglo-Saxon Chronicle*.[60]

To be sure, there are some similarities between the Anglo-Saxon annals and such important Frankish histories as the *Royal Frankish Annals*, the *Annals of St Bertin* (a continuation of the *Royal Frankish Annals*) and the work of Nithard, but they are not just a matter of form and similar narrative content.[61] Both the insular and Continental histories describe the Danish incursions in narrative forms, both mention oaths, conversion, the giving of hostages, and payment of tribute as part of the general peace making with the invaders. But the Carolingian histories are substantially different from the *Anglo-Saxon Chronicle*. The Carolingian texts are more uniformly narrative; the *Chronicle* breaks into narrative primarily during the reigns when conquest and invasion are an issue. The Carolingian texts are broad in scope. Their authors pay significant attention to ecclesiastical life and domestic political life; they muse moralistically over appropriate behaviour and even make claims about the character and personality of figures like the king.

Nonetheless, the Carolingian context is important for understanding the *Chronicle* historiography of the invasions. In their discussions of the Danish incursions, the Carolingian histories mention actions and procedures that are common to both Frankish and Anglo-Saxon lordship ritual. But, noticeably, the Frankish annalists do not explicitly present the Danish raids as tests of the bond between lord and man; neither do they see the peace making as a problem of lordship. Rather, the narratives of the Danish invasions participate in the discourse of salvation history, a discourse that I shall explore more fully below. In contrast, the annals of conquest and invasion in the *Anglo-Saxon Chronicle* consistently (but not uniformly) discuss the Danish raids with reference to lordship as a kind of leadership. Salvation historiography is present primarily in the narrative of the Æthelred-Cnut annals, and it is there to underscore the story of loss.

In the same way that the Anglo-Saxon annalists' approach to narrating their past makes judicious use of the paradigms of Carolingian histories, so they also select how their philosophy of lordship intersects with Carolingian theories of kingship. Thus, I would like to stress the way in which though present in many Old English texts from the ninth century onwards, the ideals of Carolingian kingship are mainly absent from the *Anglo-Saxon Chronicle*; I suggest therefore that the annalists place their representations of lordship in counterpoint to the discourse of Carolingian ecclesiastical kingship.

Theories of Carolingian kingship are gathered into a series of texts often known as mirrors for princes. The defining traits of the genre are somewhat vague[62] and the examples plentiful, but the most important texts for my analysis of lordship in the *Chronicle* are Pseudo-Cyprian's *De duodecim abusivis saeculi* (an insular text), Smaragdus's *Via regia*, Sedulius Scottus's *Liber de rectoribus christianis*, the *De institutione regia* of Jonas d'Orléans, and Hincmar of Rheims's *De regis persona et regio ministerio* and *De ordine palatii*. These are very different pieces of writing, but they all share a general emphasis on virtue and deeds; that is, they all assume, explicitly and implicitly, that ideal kings are virtuous, that there is a circular relationship between virtuousness and deeds, and thus that ideal kingship can be earned through deeds. This emphasis on outer action generally overwhelms inquiry into the king's interior moral qualities because it assumes that these interior qualities are made visible by action.

There are some important distinctions between the discourse of Carolingian kingship and the discourse of Anglo-Saxon cultural identity in the *Chronicle* narratives of conquest and invasion. Despite similar requirements for ideal rulership, the annalists and the writers of mirrors for princes conceptualize time and place differently; these differences are essential to understanding how their texts function. Because of their emphasis on faith, I see the Carolingian kingship texts as universal, that is, as not particular to a specific time or place. This is not to say that the mirrors do not have a certain historicity – the relationship of a text to its historical contexts. After all, the Carolingian mirrors for princes have a very powerful connection to their historical presents. They were mostly written during a period when the practice of kingship was a central concern and when succession crises and family politics fed upon each other.

In that the mirrors for princes respond to these problems by laying bare the requirements for just kingship, thus seeking to contain some of the excesses, and in that they are frequently dedicated to a named king, they can clearly be connected to a historically identifiable context. But though the precepts of an individual text may well seem applicable to a certain king, even the king to whom the text is dedicated, they are so general that they also apply to the next king and, indeed, to any king who would practise Christian kingship. They define the principles of ecclesiastical kingship for all times and all places; they systematize, regulate, order, and universalize. Thus the mirrors for princes cannot create an identity for their dedicatees, their people, or their kingdoms.

Like the Carolingian kingship texts, the annals for Alfred, Æthelred, Cnut, and William also share a certain historicity. But, unlike the Carolingian mirrors, the temporality and locality of the annals are identifying. Indeed, the specificity of the entries is established from their very first words. Virtually every entry of the *Anglo-Saxon Chronicle* begins 'Her in þissum geare ...' (Here in this year) or, more simply, 'Her ...' (Here).[63] Thus, as they are written into the *Chronicle* annals, the lordship practices of Alfred, Æthelred, Cnut, and William are not universal, systematic, or prescriptive; they are specific to the time and place of the individual kings. And, as their repetitious content organizes details into coherent expressions of culture, they are identifying.[64]

The annalists' preference for the identifying over the universalizing is not just an aspect of their chosen philosophy of leadership; the move from the universalizing to the identifying also characterizes the theory of historiography in the Alfred, Æthelred, Cnut, and William annals of the *Chronicle*. In their accounts of the reigns of Alfred, Æthelred, Cnut, and William, the annalists negotiate the transfer of power (or the threat thereof) from one king to the next. And this passage of dominion structures their texts.[65] But in addition to taking the *translatio imperii* as their subject matter, the annalists of conquest and invasion also see the transfer of power motif as fundamental to their historiography.

In itself, this is not a new insight. Medieval histories are conventionally structured around the *translatio imperii* and the way in which power passes from king to king is closely connected to the various medieval understandings of historical time.[66] In his *Historiarum adversus paganos libri septem*, however, Orosius breaks with the classical usage of the phrase and the philosophy of history it implies to develop a theory of historical causation in which natural disaster and political crisis, in particular the crisis of conquest and invasion, are directly connected to the sins of the ruler and, occasionally, those of his people.[67] The sinfulness and fall of a given empire are both a clear manifestation of divine anger and a necessary event in Christian salvation history – kingdoms rise and fall until the second coming of Christ. Thus Orosius and other writers of salvation history position sin as a mechanism of divine action and understand the ends of the various realms as lessons in Christian morality.

This philosophy of causation was well known in Britain; it is present in Gildas's *De excidio et conquestu Britannie*, Alcuin's discussion of the raids on Lindisfarne, his letter to Æthelred of Northumbria, Nennius's *Historia Brittonum*, and, to a much lesser extent, in Bede's account of the fall of the Britons in his *Historia ecclesiastica*. The same philosophy also motivates the instruction in Christian morality and practice that Bede supplies for his readers (if the Anglo-Saxons can remain moral, then the *gens Anglorum* will survive).[68] It is also a philosophy of history that, as the Old English translations of Bede and Orosius suggest, was meaningful to the history writing culture of Alfred's court.

As a whole, the *Anglo-Saxon Chronicle* shares some important aspects with these examples of salvation history. It is structured around the passage of dominion and adopts a narrative approach to the structural motifs of conquest and invasion.[69] But there the similarities end. Because salvation history explains the transfer of power in the context of theology, it is not identifying of the people whose story it tells. The ubiquity and repetitiousness of the kinds of sin universalize the stories of individual kingdoms. The various dynasties and empires are figured as types, examples of flawed reigns, or problems that the coming of Christ resolves. In essence, then, salvation history is morally instructive – it points out the various rulers' faults and makes a compelling case for the role of sin in political change – but it is not pedagogical in the performative or identifying ways articulated by Bhabha and manifested in the annals of the *Chronicle*.

This is not to say that salvation history does not have a place in the *Anglo-Saxon Chronicle*. When read as a history of Æthelred's reign, the same annals that serve as an identifying narrative for Cnut's people can also be read as salvation historiography. To rationalize the loss, these annals universalize the story of the end of Æthelred's *Angelcynn*. But the *Chronicle* narratives for William, Cnut, and Alfred are different. Instead of narrating the end of an era, they relate its beginning, and they create from their stories of battle and peace making an identifying culture for the king and his people.

In the broader context of Anglo-Saxon historical writing, the annalists offer an alternate way of understanding the significance of the present and the meaning of political change. Invasion, conquest, and settlement may well serve as the arm of an enraged God, but they need not do so. Conquest and invasion can also be interpreted as problems of government and culture, problems that right lordship resolves. In salvation historiography, kingdoms are erased from the earth in a biblical manner, but this is not the only way of understanding the passage of dominion. In the *Chronicle*, conquered and conqueror coexist under a new unifying cultural identity that is shaped by the annalists' ideology of lordship.

The identifying aspect of the *Chronicle* annals is a striking complement to the universalizing history of Orosius and to the homogenizing narrative of Bede. As the cartographical *descriptio* prefacing Bede's *Historia ecclesiastica* suggests, Britain is a geographical and religious outpost of Roman Christianity.[70] Despite the reality of Anglo-Saxon England's relationships with Rome, the inhabitants of this westerly part of the Christian world are initially inscribed into Bede's history as curiosities.[71] Bede disproves the Anglo-Saxons' alienness and accords them a Christian identity and therewith full-fledged citizenship in the Roman Christian world. In thus undoing the effects of geography and connecting the Anglo-Saxons to an ideology and series of practices, conventions, and beliefs, all of which are larger than the Anglo-Saxons or any one nation, the *Historia ecclesiastica* brings Anglo-Saxon England in from the edge of the known world and, smoothing away their peculiarities, shows how the Anglo-Saxons can be absorbed invisibly into Christian history.

The performative culture of lordship in these annals interrupts Bede's view of the Anglo-Saxon Christian world as a part of the Roman Christian family.[72] The annalists figuratively redraw the map of Bede's world by eliding the effects of geography and focusing on the king's performance of lordship. They create a new paradigm for thinking about the Anglo-Saxons' position in the world, a paradigm that is local and centred on the king. In so doing, they decentre Bede's text by showing that the church need not be the ideological and cultural core of Anglo-Saxon England. The identifying narratives for Alfred, Cnut, and William place lordship, the court, and the king in the space created by that disruption.

The consistency of this approach suggests that the *Chronicle* annals represent a vernacular historiographical tradition, a tradition that narrates conquest and invasion as tests of the king's lordship, a tradition that has the potential to create collective identity. In as far as this tradition is continued over the course of three hundred years and preserved and developed by a multiplicity of scribes, I suggest in the remaining chapters of this book that the convention of writing conquest and invasion as a matter of lordship is most productively understood as an approach to Old English vernacular historiography.

CHAPTER TWO

Making Alfred King

As a whole, the Alfred annals of the *Anglo-Saxon Chronicle* have not received the kind of attention that has so illuminated other parts of the *Chronicle*. Because these entries have primarily been read by historians focusing on Alfred and his military engagements, many modern explorations of Alfred's reign are blends of biography and military history.[1] Such studies frequently interpret the Alfred annals as an example of Alfredian dynastic and personal propaganda and ultimately present Alfred as a successful warrior whose victories lie at the foundation of what is sometimes called Greater Wessex, *Engla lond*, the home of the *Angelcynn*, and sometimes even England.[2] Alfred was, as the outcome of history shows, a good fighter and strategist, and his attainments on the battlefield should not be underestimated. But the image of *Alfred: Warrior King* – to quote the title of one recent study – is not the picture advanced by the Alfred annals.[3]

The annals for 871–8, the early entries for Alfred's reign, take up the story of the king's struggles with the Danish raiders and the threat of conquest. This is not a new topic in the *Anglo-Saxon Chronicle* or even in the world of early medieval historiography.[4] But I shall argue that the annals for Alfred's reign, and in particular the annals for his early years, begin a new kind of history that reinterprets salvation history's discourse of sin, conquest, and invasion.[5] Though in ninth-century Anglo-Saxon England the threat of conquest is strong, the annalist does not explicitly suggest that the Danish invasions are any kind of punishment for the Anglo-Saxons' sins; indeed, he does not even phrase the encounters as a struggle between Christians and pagans.[6] Instead, judiciously selecting his details, the Alfred annalist writes the narrative of Alfred's accession to the throne and the story of the battles he fights to secure his kingdom as tests of the way in which the king practises lordship.

The annalist's emphasis on Alfred's performance of lordship as opposed to his kingship is essential. Many of the texts from Alfred's reign deal with contemporary theories of kingship. Some, such as the Old English translation of Gregory's *Regula pastoralis*, place Alfred's kingship firmly within the parameters of the Carolingian Christian tradition, and others, like the laws and charters, describe what scholars believe to be some of the contemporary practices. But though we know that Alfred would, in all likelihood, have had access to the Carolingian traditions – Grimbald and the other scholars he invites to his court are part of that ideological world[7] – and though Carolingian ideas of kingship are often articulated in historical texts, the Alfred annals are a very different kind of work. Disregarding the rituals and ceremonies that together with ideas of virtue and behaviour characterize many Carolingian texts on rulership, the annalist constructs Alfred's royal authority as a product of the personal lordship bond between the king and his aristocratic retainers.[8]

Moreover, the lordship of the Alfred annals is not a reliable representation of what we know from other sources about such practices in late ninth- and early tenth-century Anglo-Saxon England. For example, we know that Alfred did connect land tenure with lordship and that he was particularly interested in questions of military service – indeed, some scholars consider Alfred's program of fort building and his military service reforms important keys to his successful defence of Wessex.[9] But, in the annals, Alfred's innovations in military service come late in his reign, and they barely feature in the narrative.[10] When the text mentions them, they are only a means of maintaining a kingdom already won.

Instead, the annalist focuses on Alfred's performance of his lordship obligations. This lordship, he suggests, is symbolized and produced by an individual and personal relationship with his men; this relationship is established and symbolized by an oath of allegiance.[11] Indeed, the Alfred annalist is so concerned with the king's lordship that though the West Saxons frequently lose the battle, the defeats seem less important to the narrative than the way the king negotiates for peace. In carefully drawn representations of these peace-making scenes, the annalist deliberately, and inaccurately, casts the king's negotiations as moments when Alfred extends his lordship to the Danes. So consistent is this focus that the annals for Alfred's early years clearly suggest that in effect, if not in reality, Alfred gains and maintains Wessex by virtue of his strong lordship relations.

It is not just that Alfred uses lordship to win his kingdom; it is also that, according to the annalist, Alfred's performance of lordship becomes an identifying ethos or culture for the new Anglo-Saxon realm. In 886, the Alfred annalist records a lordship ceremony in which he transforms the blend of West Saxons, Mercians, Anglians, and Danes who accept Alfred's lordship into the *Angelcynn*, a people defined by Alfred's lordship.[12] The power of this discourse of identity is confirmed by an accident of manuscript history.

The history that is common to the five primary vernacular manuscripts of the *Anglo-Saxon Chronicle* seems to have been compiled in multiple stages.[13] In the first, the compiler, who may or may not be the Alfred annalist, writes the history of Anglo-Saxon England from 60 BC to 891;[14] the second stage (which Janet Bately has argued is written by more than one annalist) runs from 892 to 914.[15] So compelling is the story of the Alfred annalist that the continuators of this history preserve both the Alfred annalist's linguistic preference for the term *Angelcynn* and his ideology of lordship.[16]

Indeed, the 892–3 story of Alfred's dealings with Hásteinn shows that lordship, by the closing years of Alfred's reign, is both a code of behaviour – in his treatment of hostages and generosity towards his enemy, Alfred acts according to his lordship ideals even when it is clearly not in his military or strategic interest to do so – and a collective identity for Alfred's people.[17] This account implies that Alfred's lordship should be understood as a shared public culture that the Danes cannot understand and to which they therefore cannot consistently subscribe. As such, lordship in both the Alfred annals and their continuations distinguishes the Anglo-Saxons – now designated the *Angelcynn* – and becomes the marker of a new Anglo-Saxon identity.

A Problem of Honour

In the annals for 892 and 893, the Danish raiders return to Alfred's kingdom. One of the leaders, Hásteinn (OE Hæsten), establishes a fortress at Milton while the other builds a stronghold at Appledore. But the invaders are not the only threat to Alfred's security. The Northumbrians and East Anglians violate their pledges, and, like the Danes, they too begin to harry Alfred's realm. Indeed, the annalist even claims that these Anglo-Saxons went raiding on the Danes' behalf.[18] As the annals suggest, after the ceremonial retaking of London in 886, Alfred's kingdom has been at peace; thus the Anglo-Saxons' treachery and the return of the Danish raiders seem to threaten all that Alfred has achieved. Alfred once again collects an army and begins to defend his realm, and the Anglo-Saxons eventually win a decisive victory at Benfleet, one of the places where Hásteinn has built a fortress. Thus far, the annals are straightforward; Alfred responds to a threat by taking the appropriate measures, and he is successful.

But if we read military history as the primary focus of these entries, the moment when, instead of driving home a victory, Alfred acts charitably towards his enemy and leaves his kingdom open to a second attack, makes no sense. Furthermore, the annalist does not criticize Alfred for this move; rather, he portrays Alfred as honourable and communicates the king's leniency as a matter of obligation, despite the fact that the kingdom suffers. In other words, military history cannot be the only thing that motivates the annalist's narrative of Alfred's reign.

At the core of this version of events is a more complicated philosophy of appropriate action, one that asks readers of the Alfred annals who would focus on Alfred's martial prowess to rethink the terms by which they read the account of Alfred's reign. According to the annalist, Alfred's forces take control of the situation at Benfleet: they

> gefliemdon þone here 7 þæt geweorc abræcon 7 genamon eal þæt þær binnan wæs, ge on feo, ge on wifum, ge eac on bearnum, 7 brohton eall into Lundenbyrig, 7 þa scipu eall oðþe tobræcon oþþe forbærndon oþþe to Lundenbyrig brohton oþþe to Hrofesceastre; 7 Hæstenes wif 7 his suna twegen mon brohte to þæm cyninge.

> put the army to flight and destroyed the fort and took everything that was inside it, including goods, women, and children, and they took everything to London. And they either burned or broke all the ships into little pieces and took them to London or Rochester; and they took Hásteinn's wife and his two sons to the king.[19]

Alfred's only response is to send the hostages back to Hásteinn with a gift of money because, the annalist asserts, 'hiora wæs oþer his godsunu, oþer Æðeredes ealdormonnes' (one of them was his godson and the other the godson of *ealdormann* Æthelred).[20] In other words, prior to this encounter, Alfred has negotiated peace with Hásteinn and confirmed that peace by becoming the sponsor to one of his enemy's sons at his baptism and by asking a prominent retainer to sponsor the other son. For his part, the annalist notes, Hásteinn gave surety in the form of hostages and oaths ('gislas 7 aðas'), and he accepts the gifts of money Alfred offers him.[21] In attacking the kingdom, Hásteinn has clearly violated the pledge of peace.

Why then does Alfred continue to respect the bond of *compaternitas* that he has contracted with the Danish leader?[22] It is clearly in his military interests to assume that Hásteinn has violated his oaths and punish him, but he does not do so. Even though Alfred returns Hásteinn's family with more gifts, Hásteinn is not moved; he launches two more raids, one of which is in the 'ilcan ende þe Æþered his cumpæder healdan sceolde, 7 eft oþre siþe he wæs on hergað gelend on þæt ilce rice, þa þa mon his geweorc abræc' (same district that Æthelred, his son's godfather, was to rule, and again, a second time, he was out raiding in that same kingdom when his fortress was destroyed).[23] By repeating the word 'ilce' (same), the annalist expresses incredulity at Hásteinn's behaviour, but he never once criticizes Alfred for his actions and he remains silent on Hásteinn's eventual fate. To explain this curious moment, I turn to the manuscript history of the *Anglo-Saxon Chronicle* and, in particular, to the way in which the Alfred annalist writes his account of Alfred's accession and the king's early years.

Languages of Power

In the annals for 871–8, that is, the early entries for Alfred's reign, the Alfred annalist's focus on peace-making lordship as a language of royal authority significantly affects how he narrates the actual history of the land and that of the kingdom of Wessex in particular.[24] We know, for example, that many of the peace negotiations involved some discussion of territory and boundaries, but these are not part of the annalist's text.[25] By the end of the annal for 878, it is clear that Alfred controls enough territory for a sizable realm, but the Alfred annals do not explicitly discuss how much land he acquires and when.

In the *Chronicle*, Alfred's father, Æthelwulf, divides his kingdom upon his accession in 836:[26] Æthelwulf takes Wessex for himself and gives his son, Æthelstan, the areas of Kent, Essex, Surrey, and Sussex.[27] Technically, the kingdom is reunited under Alfred – he inherits both the kingdom of Wessex and the eastern regions[28] – but in the course of his reign, Alfred loses some of this territory, regains it, and proceeds to expand his kingdom into areas not previously under West Saxon control. But this, the complicated and interesting history of Alfred's land, is simply not mentioned in the *Chronicle*, because land alone cannot tell the story of how Alfred won his kingdom, and because the annalist seeks to redefine royal authority.

In the historical scholarship, a large part of the discussion on languages of royal authority rests on a single term and its variants: *Bretwalda* (MS A of the *Anglo-Saxon Chronicle*), *Brytenwalda* (MS B), *Bretananwealda* (MS C), *Brytenwealda* (MSS D and E), and *Brytenweald* (MS F).[29] For my purposes, how the *Bretwalda*'s power is realized is more important than what the word *Bretwalda* actually designates. As implied by Bede's *Historia ecclesiastica* and as used in the *Old English Bede* and the *Anglo-Saxon Chronicle*, *Bretwalda* denotes not a ruler of a certain people, but the controller of a certain amount of land:

> 7 þy ilcan geare geeode Ecgbryht cyning Miercna rice 7 al þæt be suþan Humbre wæs, 7 he wæs se eahteþa cyning se þe bretwalda wæs – ærest Elle Suþseaxna cyning se þus micel rice hæfde, se æftera wæs Ceawlin Wesseaxna cyning ...

> And in the same year, King Ecgbryht conquered the kingdom of the Mercians and everything that was south of the Humber, and he was the eighth king who was a *Bretwalda* – the first to rule such a mighty kingdom was Ælle, king of the South Saxons, the second was Ceawlin, king of the West Saxons ...[30]

Though each king is identified by his primary kingdom, he is not defined by the people he governs; rather, his identity as *Bretwalda* lies in his control of a certain amount of territory. And, linguistically, the people are defined by the name of their lord. Ecgbryht is not king of Mercia, he is the ruler of the Mercians' territory; similarly Ælle is king not of Sussex but of the South Saxons, and Ceawlin rules not Wessex but the West Saxons.[31] The Alfred annalist works to supplement this discourse of identity and power by locating national identity in the aristocratic code of lordship and, in particular, in the new peace-making lordship of Alfred.

As many scholars have observed, claims of national identity in the Old English period are not usually written along the same axes as those in the twenty-first century.[32] Nonetheless, like other Alfredian texts, the Alfred annals do provide a clear language that tracks the creation of community – national, regional, and local. In designating Alfred's new people as the *Angelcynn*, the annalist signals how the people created in his history complement the people formed in Christian historical narratives like Bede's *Historia ecclesiastica*. As Bede uses the word, the *Angli* (Old English *Angel*) sometimes include all the Anglo-Saxons, regardless of their origins, but not the Britons, Irish, and Picts; sometimes they are the Northumbrians (technically former Anglians); and sometimes the East and Middle Anglians (later Mercians).[33] Under Bede, these people become known to the Roman Christian world as the *gens Anglorum*. By contrast, in the Alfred annals, the term by which the Anglo-Saxons become known now also refers to the political and cultural identity of those who accept Alfred's lordship.

The political nature of this designation is reinforced by the annalist's choice of Old English *cynn*, 'family.' By raising the question of descent, the Alfred annalist appears to echo a second discourse of royal authority, one that focuses on lineage. The A manuscript of the *Anglo-Saxon Chronicle* begins with a recitation of the mythical West Saxon royal genealogy and regnal list. This material appears again at significant junctures in the annals, suggesting a connection between a claimant's suitability for or right to the throne and his birthright. But Anglo-Saxon succession does not necessarily proceed by birthright;[34] thus the power of the genealogy is, as many scholars have shown, ideological.[35] A noble descent might be used to distinguish a candidate and authorize his place on the throne.

For Alfred, however, the idea of blood family was both unsettling – to claim the throne, he had to disinherit his nephews – and unhelpful: the *Anglo-Saxon Chronicle* shows that Alfred's court included Franks, Frisians, Gauls, Danes, Welsh, and Irish and that his kingdom itself embraced both West Saxons and Mercians.[36] In this court, descent is more likely a source of dissent than unity. But by insisting that all these people share an important familial connection, the Alfred annalist transforms a discourse of lineage and genealogy, that is, a discourse of blood family, into one of a social and political family. In the Alfred annals, the new family of Alfred's kingdom comprises those who no matter what their birthright are willing to accept Alfred as their lord. Alfred's *Angelcynn* are made family not by common descent, but by lordship.

Cynewulf-Cyneheard: A Mythic Example

The lordship ideals behind Alfred's *Angelcynn* do not begin with the Alfred annals. In the Cynewulf-Cyneheard episode, the annal for 755, the story of feuding factions in the West Saxon royal family is written as a story of lordship. The manuscript history of the *Anglo-Saxon Chronicle* prohibits any kind of speculation about whether the Alfred annalist is responsible for the present form of the Cynewulf-Cyneheard entry. Though the Cynewulf-Cyneheard episode and the Alfred annals for 871–91 are part of what scholars call the common stock, the unusual qualities of the Cynewulf-Cyneheard entry in the *Chronicle* and its similarities to other kinds of writing like Old Norse saga have led many scholars to suggest that the compiler of the common stock crystallizes a preexisting Cynewulf-Cyneheard tradition.[37] I propose that for the Alfred annalist, the events of the Cynewulf-Cyneheard episode are a kind of cultural myth that offers an exposition of the connection between lordship and identity, a connection that the Alfred annalist tests and reworks as he narrates the foundation of Alfred's *Angelcynn*.

The Cynewulf-Cyneheard episode begins with the deposition of one King Sigebryht for unspecified wrongdoings and, with the support of the *witan*, the accession of Cynewulf. In the same year, Sigebryht is murdered by a swineherd for killing the retainer who had been with him longest. Cynewulf's reign continues for thirty-one years without major incident – he fights many battles against the Britons – until he tries to drive out a nobleman called Cyneheard. We do not learn how Cyneheard learned of his impending exile; we see only his response: an unannounced attack on Cynewulf while, sequestered from his men, the king visits a woman. In the ensuing battle, Cynewulf is killed, and his men, arriving late on the scene, are defeated. Cyneheard offers them money and their lives, but the men die willingly with their king.

When Cynewulf's reinforcements arrive, Cyneheard attempts to stave off battle by offering them land and money if they will accept his claim to the kingdom; he shores up this offer by reporting that some of the listeners' kinsmen are with him. Cynewulf's men respond that no kinsman is dearer to them than their now-dead lord; they offer their kinsmen safe passage, but Cyneheard's men, too, respond in kind: no kinsman is dearer than their lord. Battle is joined, and Cyneheard's men, with the exception of his godson, die with him. Cynewulf and Cyneheard are buried and a brief reference is made to their common ancestry, a descent from Cerdic. Most scholars and editors of the text conclude that the meaningful part of the text finishes with the death of the protagonists.[38] In fact, the annal goes on to mention the death of Æthelbald, king of Mercia, and it concludes with a reference to his burial, some mention of his successes, and an account of the Mercian genealogy for Offa, the next king.

The vast majority of the criticism on the Cynewulf-Cyneheard annal focuses on the retainers' apparent choice of their lordship relations over family bonds.[39] While this choice is certainly part of the annal, to read it as the focal point of the entry is to underestimate one of the central tenets of Anglo-Saxon lordship. Personal lordship as articulated in poems such as the *Battle of Maldon* and *Beowulf* asks the lord and retainers to bond as a family. Thus the choice that the retainers make is not one of lordship over kin, but one of political family over blood family. Moreover, by choosing their lord and political family, the retainers effectively preserve the stability of the political order. By foregrounding lordship in this way, I understand the annal not as an uncomplicated affirmation of heroic action, but as a celebration of the lordship ethic in Wessex, a study of the politics of king making, and an exploration of West Saxon identity. This approach meaningfully includes the critically neglected Mercian closing and clarifies the curious equality – even indistinguishability – of the two protagonists.[40]

The context of Anglo-Saxon lordship culture makes the story of Sigebryht's deposition both an explanation of his unspecified wrongdoings and an examination of the connection between right lordship and a nobleman's worthiness for the throne. In the opening lines of the annal, Sigebryht is deposed but not stripped of all his authority. He continues to hold Hampshire until he demonstrates his unsuitability for the throne by abusing his lordship and killing the retainer who has been with him longest. His crime appears to remove the protections of his rank, and he is killed, in an act of vengeance, by a swineherd.[41] In this moment, the annalist underscores the link between lordship ethics and the throne. Sigebryht is isolated from the lordship culture to such an extent that he can be killed, apparently with impunity and perhaps without glory, by someone wholly outside the ranks of the nobility.

The annalist's lordship philosophy is further developed in the manner of Cynewulf's accession and the annalist's brief characterization of his reign. In Cynewulf, the annalist describes right lordship in all its aspects. The new king comes to the throne not by means of a usurping land grab, but with the consent of the *witan* in order to rectify the wrongs of Sigebryht's reign. That the *witan* supports Cynewulf suggests that his actions do not betray the ideals of lordship.[42] Though we do not know how much authority the *witan* had in electing a king, representations of this process in the *Anglo-Saxon Chronicle* suggest that members of the council gave the king oaths of loyalty as part of their consent to his lordship.[43] Cynewulf's reign is one of just lordship, and this is confirmed by the annalist's summary of his actions: Cynewulf fought many great battles against the Britons. Focusing, as it does, the reader's attention on the unifying potential of a common enemy, a full understanding of the significance of this remark depends on familiarity with the ways in which the early annals report the beginnings of West Saxon history.

From the mid-fifth century to the early seventh century, the annalist punctuates his narrative with references to the Britons and battles against them, in effect suggesting that the West Saxon kingdom is carved out from and defined by territory won from the Britons and thus that the West Saxons themselves are defined by their possession of this land, in opposition to the nation of the Britons. These references are so consistent that they become a trope of early West Saxon kingdom making.[44] In the Cynewulf-Cyneheard episode, the annalist omits this land history. We learn only that Cynewulf fought and presumably won these engagements, and although his success in war is clearly important to establishing the kingdom, the most significant part of Cynewulf's lordship is the personal bond he creates with his men, a bond that the annalist characterizes as familial and one to which he attributes the political stability of Cynewulf's reign.

Cynewulf is killed in Meretun where he has been visiting a woman. Because of the gloss, *meretrix* or 'prostitute,' given in Æthelweard's translation of the *Chronicle* into Latin, many readers are tempted to see Cynewulf's behaviour as a moral failing, but, as D.G. Scragg has pointed out, it is not necessary to read this moment through Æthelweard's eyes.[45] Æthelweard has his own agenda, which is not necessarily supported by the lexical evidence. Scragg argues that *wifcyþþe* may simply mean a meeting with his wife. Whether or not Cynewulf meets with a woman or, as Katherine O'Brien O'Keeffe has argued, a mistress, I suggest that Cynewulf's encounter functions as the catalyst for the events that showcase the lordship that defines Wessex.[46]

In this context, Cynewulf's mistake, if any, is a simple oversight that should not be overinterpreted. At a time when he has recognized a clear threat to his lordship, a threat against which he intends to act, he ignores his public position as lord to engage in private pursuits, rendering himself vulnerable by separating himself from his men. As the narrative proceeds, however, this minimal weakness causes the events that glorify Cynewulf's lordship. Two sets of men come to the king's aid. The first dies with him, declaring they have no dearer kinsman. The second comes after the king's death to avenge him (the contrast with Sigebryht is particularly sharp) even though the country is now leaderless, even though they must refuse Cyneheard's offer of money and the position of favoured retainers in the new regime. If Cynewulf's behaviour is to be faulted, it does not, in the annalist's eyes, affect his rulership. In spite of his actions, Cynewulf retains the loyalty of his men.

Here, however, the annalist's interest in lordship takes a surprising turn. The annalist acclaims Cynewulf's lordship, but his text does not specifically validate Cynewulf's position as the only lord and king of Wessex.[47] The encounter between Cynewulf and Cyneheard, between lord and *ætheling*, is structured so that it affirms the practice of lordship and its exemplification in the two men without – as we might expect in a story of heroic action – explicitly endorsing either as the rightful king.[48] Indeed, the annalist refuses to distinguish between the protagonists in order to demonstrate that Cynewulf and Cyneheard are equally worthy of the throne.[49] Both men are able to inspire in their men the kind of loyalty indicative of strong personal lordship relations, and this lordship is the qualifying trait for kingship.[50]

Such an intense focus valorizes lordship not as a phenomenon of the literary heroic world, but as a way of establishing the ideological superiority of Wessex over Mercia.[51] The annal concludes with a reminder of recent Mercian history – a history in which Mercia might well have dominated or threatened Wessex – and a recitation of the Mercian royal genealogy that reminds its readers of Mercia's power. The presence of this genealogy and the Mercian section in general explain the annalist's minimization of the function of land and concomitant insistence on the significance of lordship. Through lordship, the annalist makes an important statement about the difficult question of Mercian-West Saxon relations and the problem of West Saxon identity.

Mercia and Wessex are known to have had a complicated relationship in this period. We may read the evidence as suggesting that after Cynewulf's reign Wessex returned to Mercian control, but, as Simon Keynes has persuasively argued, the evidence does not necessarily suggest that Wessex again became – or was ever – a Mercian province.[52] It is clear, however, that disputed territory played an important part in their relationship. It is thus tempting to see a parallel between the structure of the narrative – the annalist literally embeds his account of Mercian history deep in his account of West Saxon history – and what the annalist sees as the proper relationship of the two kingdoms.[53]

But even though they are present in the *Chronicle* as a whole, the historical context and the story of this land are absent from the Cynewulf-Cyneheard narrative. Æthelbald of Mercia (716–57) was a powerful king to whom in 731, according to Bede, all the kingdoms south of the Humber were subject. His eventual successor, Offa (757–96), seems to have been equally powerful. But the transition from Æthelbald to Offa was not smooth. Beornred followed Æthelbald on the throne, yet he was unable to hold his seat. Cynewulf took advantage of this period of instability to win back some former West Saxon territory. His means were sometimes unorthodox but, for a while, successful. For example, he took land in the Hwiccian province, which by this time was in the process of being absorbed into Mercia. He even bribed two members of the archbishop of Canterbury's household to steal the title deeds of Cookham, so that he could take over the monastery and the proceeds of its estates for himself.[54] In 779, Offa defeated Cynewulf and forced him to give back some of the land. Cynewulf was able to maintain the independence of Wessex, however.[55]

This brief history of the land clearly indicates how a text claiming the superiority of the West Saxons supports the history of the Alfred annals, a history in which the narrative of the local West Saxon past becomes the narrative of the national past. The writer of the Cynewulf-Cyneheard episode suggests that though, in this period, Wessex may not have been as militarily dominant as Mercia, it triumphs over its rival in the practice of lordship within its borders.[56] The Mercian king, Æthelbald, may have held his kingdom ten years more than Cynewulf's thirty-one, but, for the annalist, length of tenure does not, in this instance, point to good rule. In Wessex, Cynewulf's and Cyneheard's men die for them, but in Mercia, Æthelbald is shown to die because his lordship relations fail.[57] He is killed by a member of his retinue and bodyguard. Æthelbald's successor, Beornred, holds the throne for less than a year. This contrasts, again, with Cynewulf's reign and, in that Beornred's successor, Offa, comes from Beornred's aristocracy, this Mercian transfer of power suggestively recalls the Sigebryht scenario with which the annal began. Moreover, Offa is not designated an *ætheling*. In other words, he is not one of the expected candidates for the throne.[58]

In this particular history, Mercia appears to lack leaders. By contrast, the annalist suggests that Wessex has a superfluity of potential kings.

The Cynewulf-Cyneheard annalist passes silently over the fact that both of Wessex's potential kings are dead by the end of the annal, and he does not mention the fact that they leave behind a power vacuum. It is sufficient that Wessex has two men who because of their practice of lordship are ideal claimants to the throne. By the end of the Cynewulf-Cyneheard episode, then, lordship has become a behavioural code that is essential to West Saxon identity; it defines a rightful king and, through him, Wessex itself.

Making and Narrating Alfred's Lordship

There is no formal relationship between the Cynewulf-Cyneheard episode and the Alfred annals. But in that the Alfred annals extend and test the ideas of that entry, I suggest that the annal for 755 might serve as a conceptual preface to the annals of Alfred's early years. However compelling the practice and ideology of lordship in the Cynewulf-Cyneheard episode might be as literary tropes, the lordship that leaves Wessex without a leader cannot serve as a model for the annalist's account of how Alfred wins and secures his throne. And because the practice of lordship in the Cynewulf-Cyneheard episode threatens the welfare of the kingdom, it cannot serve as an identifying culture for Alfred's new kingdom. Thus the Alfred annalist reworks the Cynewulf-Cyneheard philosophy of lordship to suit the political circumstances of Alfred's reign. In the Alfred annals, the focus on the king's practice of lordship masks the vulnerability of the kingdom and obscures the exact expanse of territory subject to the Danes, while detailing a cultural and political ethos by which Alfred's people are formed.

In this context, the history of the Alfred annals takes on the function of providing an identity for Alfred's kingdom, and this purpose informs the annalist's narrative strategy. For example, the annalist's focus on Alfred's form of lordship shapes how he presents the Danish raids. In the annals for 872, 873, 874, and 875, the army moves into a town or geographical area, which the annalist names. But the annalist does not allow the reader to see exactly how much of Anglo-Saxon England is under Danish occupation. With one exception (Mercia in 874), the annalist just names the places that the Danes occupy, the places to which the army moves, and the places in which the Danes encounter Anglo-Saxon resistance. He strives to keep each town as a separate entity, represented only by a place name, and refuses to draw for his readers the kind of verbal map that would point out Alfred's vulnerability. Instead, by naming only the towns, the annalist suggests that the landscape across which the army moves is merely terrain.[59]

He continues this strategy of obfuscation by not explaining the significance of the towns the army occupies. Thus though some contemporary readers of the *Chronicle* would have known whether the towns and battlefields mentioned had any political or cultural significance, this knowledge is never brought to bear on the text by the annalist himself. When, for example, in 876, the army arrives in Exeter, a major city at this time, the annalist does not explain what this means for Alfred, the kingdom, or even the people of Exeter. Exeter, despite its strategic importance to Alfred, remains a place name. If this occupation seems significant, it is only because the reader makes it so. From the narration of the annals, Exeter is equivalent to Reading, Nottingham, or any of the other town names that dot the landscape of the annalist's text.

In other words, the Alfred annalist does not allow the towns to become what Henri Lefebvre would call 'representational.'[60] This strategy is complemented by his vocabulary of defeat and victory. To describe a West Saxon defeat, the annalist remarks that the Danes 'held the field,' or 'took possession of the field.'[61] In the *Chronicle* as a whole, these phrases are virtual commonplaces, but in this context the impersonal expression gains significance. We know from other sources that victory would have given the Danes far more territory than an unnamed field – see, for example, the treaty of Alfred and Guthrum[62] – but the Alfred annalist allows only for the Danes to gain the uninterpreted place in which they defeated the Anglo-Saxons. We do not know the extent of the land involved.

Just as he disguises the territorial losses, so the annalist understates the idea that the presence of the Danes is in some way an indicator of the Anglo-Saxons' vulnerability. The Danish army moves rapidly, and by focusing on the shift from place to place instead of the gradual accumulation of territory, the annalist implies that control goes with presence; once the army leaves a place, it no longer actively controls that territory. This strategy is complemented by his decision to retain the conventional opening of the Anglo-Saxon annals: 'Her' (Here). The repeated substitution of an adverb of place for one of time has been discussed in scholarship on the syntax of the *Anglo-Saxon Chronicle*.[63] However, this conventional phrase suggests that the notion of a 'here' is important to the annalist. Despite the Danish gains and corresponding Anglo-Saxon losses, there is still a 'here,' a West Saxon kingdom. The location of 'here' remains unspecified, and I would argue that while the non-specificity of the formula is traditional, the effect is meaningful. In the annals, though territory is important, the *her* of the Alfred annals cannot be tied to a particular town, county, or region; for the annalist, Alfred's kingdom is situated in the intangible relationship of man and lord.

In order to focus on lordship, the annalist leaves underdeveloped some moments that tap into other discourses of royal authority. He does not, for example, base Alfred's right to his kingdom on a ceremony of anointing that occurred in his childhood.[64] Neither does he acknowledge the importance of Carolingian discourses of ecclesiastical kingship. Rather, the text is shaped so that the annals suggest that Alfred wins and secures his kingdom only when he transforms political alliances into familial allegiances of lordship. With this agenda to hand, the annalist writes the story of Alfred's early years, the years in which he wins his kingdom, as the story of Alfred's new lordship.

The early years of Alfred's reign cast the battles between the Anglo-Saxon and Danish armies as a series of individualized skirmishes in which loyal aristocrats heroically test one another's mettle. But, as the Cynewulf-Cyneheard episode demonstrates, bravery is an insufficient foundation for creating and sustaining a kingdom; thus, the annalist gradually moves his readers from stories of defeat to scenes of peace making. As Alfred creates treaties with the Danes, he extends his lordship to his enemies and binds his people to him.

In the annal for 871 – an annal that stands as a kind of paradigm – the opening encounter depicts *ealdormann* Æthelwulf acting loyally for his lord and king, Æthelred. After the initial opening formula, the annalist focuses his readers on the hand to hand conflict of the noble protagonists: 'Ymb .iii. niht ridon .ii. eorlas up. Þa gemette hie Eþelwulf aldorman on Englafelda 7 him þær wiþ gefeaht 7 sige nam' (About three days later two [Danish] earls rode inland. Then *ealdormann* Æthelwulf met them at Englefield and fought against them there and he took the victory).[65] Having killed Sidroc, Æthelwulf emerges as the victor in this conflict, and the importance of this victory is measured in the annalist's vocabulary. Æthelwulf 'sige nam' (took the victory) as opposed to the phrase used for Danish victories 'ahton węlstowe gewald' (took possession of the battlefield). Yet the victory itself is less important than what it implies: Alfred's brother, Æthelred, is an effective lord and king.

As he relates the remaining events of 871, the annalist examines the lordship relations of King Æthelred and Alfred, his brother; specifically, he suggests that Æthelred's lordship is so strong that it defines the figure of Alfred. In the context of the early Alfred annals and Asser's *Vita Alfredi*, the annalist's perspective is important. Asser claims that the *witan* would have supported Alfred had he wished to take the throne from his brother and the spectre of two kinsmen fighting over the throne recalls, for us at least, the dynastic dispute of the Cynewulf-Cyneheard episode.[66] But the Alfred annalist passes silently over this textual tradition and, if he is aware of such support for Alfred's accession, he ignores it in order to demonstrate Alfred's respect for his lordship obligations. Throughout the annal, with one exception, even after Alfred has become king, the annalist refers to him as Æthelred's brother or the king's brother in order to emphasize that Alfred is not a king-in-waiting but a noble brother, loyal to the lordship of his king.[67] He then takes the story of Æthelwulf as a model to demonstrate the strength of this lordship bond. Just as *ealdormann* Æthelwulf engages the Danes, so do King Æthelred and his brother Alfred. Unlike *ealdormann* Æthelwulf, however, Alfred and his brother lose, but this defeat is less significant to the annalist's account than the virtue of loyal Æthelwulf and the image of the two brothers cooperating.

So important is this principle of cooperation and so straightforward is the annalist's account that, without further examination, the ideological bias towards lordship can seem conventional. Like the earlier conflict led by *ealdormann* Æthelwulf, the Alfred annalist casts his account of the battle of Ashdown as a series of individual encounters. The Danes divide into two groups; one is led by the kings, Bacgsecg and Healfdene, and the other by the earls. Æthelred takes the kings and Alfred the earls. The brothers win, and the importance of this victory is confirmed in the list of dead Danish earls. But this account of the battle is not without its complexity.

In the version of events in his *Vita Alfredi*, Asser includes a story in which Alfred is betrayed by his brother, who inexplicably spends so long at Mass that Alfred must begin the battle alone.[68] This story is missing from the Alfred annals. The manuscript history of the *Chronicle* does not allow us to tell whether Asser was adding to his text, though this addition is unique, whether the Alfred annalist did not know of these events, or whether he was suppressing what he knew. But if, indeed, the Alfred annalist was aware of these events, including them would have changed how his readers reacted to Alfred. In Asser's version, the young king is positioned as an extraordinarily

42   Families of the King

courageous fighter. If admitted into the text of the Alfred annals, this perspective would counter the annalist's focus on lordship and cooperation.

Thus, as the Alfred annalist would have it, lordship and in particular Æthelred's lordship defines the moment of Alfred's accession. Where we would expect, given that the annalist includes the anointing anecdote, an account of the rise of a powerful king, the annalist reports: 'Þa feng Ęlfred Ęþelwulfing his broþur to Wesseaxna rice' (Then his brother, Alfred, son of Æthelwulf, succeeded to the West Saxon kingdom).[69] While 'feng to rice' is a traditional formula for describing succession in the *Chronicle*, even here the possibly perfidious Æthelred defines his brother. In his first reported action as ruler, 'Ęlfred cyning' (King Alfred) here, finally, the possessor of his title, goes on to fight (and lose) at Wilton, but this loss is less important to the narrative and the overall agenda than the way in which the annalist uses his account to suggest that Alfred continues the lordship traditions of his brother.

This focus shapes the annalist's account of Alfred's first year. In his first month, Alfred fights at Wilton and loses; the annalist remarks that 'þa Deniscan ahton węlstowe gewald' (the Danes took control of the field).[70] To minimize the devastating effects of this territorial loss and to be able to present the king positively, the annalist turns away from writing the history of the West Saxon land to writing the history of Alfred's military engagements as continuations of his brother's practice of lordship. Thus the annalist presents the battles as undertakings of the king and his thanes. In addition to the battles joined by 'Ęlfred þæs cyninges broþur 7 anlipig aldormon 7 cyninges þegnas' (Alfred, the king's brother, and [several] individual *ealdormenn* and king's thanes), nine battles were fought and '.viiii. eorlas 7 an cyning' (nine earls and one king) were killed.[71] There is no mention of territory lost or gained; rather, the annalist, metonymically capturing the two nations in their lords, then allows us to assess the year's events in terms of lords lost: '7 þæs geares wærun ofslægene .viiii. eorlas 7 an cyning; 7 þy geare namon Westseaxe friþ wiþ þone here' (And in this year nine earls and one king were slain; and [also] in this year, the West Saxons made peace with the army).[72] In this picture of Alfred's kingdom, the West Saxons continue to lose physical territory, but retain the metaphorical moral high ground in their practice of lordship.

That the West Saxons should retain some semblance of superiority is essential given the actual threat posed to their kingdom. The annal for 871 begins with what has become the traditional opening formula: a description of the Danish army's movements. This time, in particular, the Danes take Reading.[73] But the loss of control that such movements might imply remains undiscussed. Similarly, there is no overall survey of the land now under Danish control. Just two years after Alfred's accession, Northumbria and East Anglia both lose their kings, and Mercia, Alfred's neighbouring kingdom, makes peace. These events are mentioned in the *Chronicle*, but their significance is elided by the strategies discussed above and the annalist's emphasis on Alfred's practice of lordship.

So consistent is this focus that the annalist suppresses the significance of the military history for the years 874–7 by leaving uninterpreted the facts that he records. He notes the weakness of Mercia and, exploiting the similarity of lordship and peace-making rituals, the Alfred annalist observes that the Danes drive out the reigning king and establish Ceolwulf as a regent. Ceolwulf swears loyalty oaths to the Danes and gives them hostages. But while Ceolwulf and the Danes make peace in a way that evokes the ceremonies and rituals of lordship, the Alfred annalist sharply distinguishes their lordship practice from that of Alfred.

When discussing Alfred's lordship, the annalist is silent about any possible territorial implications, but the lordship of Ceolwulf and the Danes is explicitly one of land. The Danes give Ceolwulf the 'Miercna rice' (kingdom of the Mercians) and the oaths and hostages are given to ensure 'þæt he him gearo wære swa hwelce dæge swa hie [the Danes] hit habban wolden' (that it would be ready for them on whatever day the Danes wanted to have it).[74] Given that between 874 and 877 the Danish army makes significant inroads into Anglo-Saxon territory, and given that in 878 the army settles in the land of the West Saxons, the annalist's refusal to acknowledge the threat to Wessex is surprising.

Instead, the annalist uses the events of 874–7 to establish a discourse of lordship by which Alfred will be seen to claim the kingdom over which he has already been crowned king. Although historians disagree about the amount of authority actually accorded Ceolwulf, the annalist's account clearly suggests that Ceolwulf – a thane, not an *ætheling*, and thus not a likely candidate for the throne – binds himself to the Danes, as shown above, by invoking the same procedures that Alfred uses to establish peace.[75] While it is clear that Alfred cannot assert lordship over the Danes (he enters into these agreements as the weaker party), the equivalence of lordship and peace-making procedures is central to the representation of Alfred as a king whose rule is identified by the ideals of a personal lordship as opposed to a lordship of land.

This focus is highlighted by the annalist's refusal to criticize the king for his inability to contain the Danish threat. Instead, by taking advantage of the similarity of lordship and peace-making practice – both require the swearing of oaths of loyalty – the Alfred annalist portrays the Danes as unworthy of the peace they negotiate. In 876 the Danes officially make peace by giving Alfred hostages and swearing 'aþas ... on þam halgan beage, þe hie ær nanre þeode noldon' (oaths ... on the holy ring, [something] they previously would not do for any other people).[76] This extra assertion both honours Alfred and makes the Danes' duplicity all the more apparent. In 876, instead of suggesting, more neutrally, that the Danish army 'cuom' (came) or 'for' (went) to a certain place, the annalist characterizes the army's incursion into Wessex as a kind of violation. The army underhandedly 'bestẹl' (stole or perhaps slunk) past the West Saxons instead of engaging them in a battle that could be reported as the kind of individual-to-individual honourable combat seen in earlier entries. In the face of such slyness, Alfred is nonetheless honourable; he makes peace. But this moment is not as simple as it seems.

With the exception that Alfred retains control over his kingdom, the language of this peace-making ceremony closely resembles that of the annalist's report of Ceolwulf's submission. And in so far as the annalist recalls Ceolwulf's situation, he also raises the possibility that Wessex is vulnerable. Simultaneously, however, the Alfred annalist also uses the language and ideology of lordship to revoke that suggestion even as he makes it.

Friþ niman (to take peace) is the conventional Old English phrase for peace making, but in this instance, because Alfred is the grammatical subject of the verb, he gains agency and authority. The king's power is further underscored by the annalist's account of the procedure. The Danes swear oaths to the king on a holy ring (which they previously would not do for any other people).[77] The swearing of oaths binds lord and man – this is part of the Anglo-Saxons' cultural vocabulary, and it is emphasized by the annalist's use of *friþ niman* to describe Ceolwulf's connection to the Danes.

Thus the annals are slanted, and the avowal that they would do this for no other people is meant to suggest that Alfred is extending his lordship over the Danes; Alfred has leverage seen in no other king. That Alfred is actually creating an alliance and not claiming the bond of lordship is immaterial to the narrative of Alfred's lordship. The annalist seeks only to establish the importance of Alfred's lordship and he underscores the point by repeating the strategy in his entry for 877. In 877, Alfred loses yet another battle with the Danes, but, the annalist claims in a move that personalizes the text and again stresses the king's lordship, Alfred makes peace and receives as many hostages as he could wish for.[78]

With these kinds of agreements as a preface, the Alfred annalist writes his account of the year 878 as a celebration of Alfred's lordship and passes silently over the fact that once Wessex has been conquered, it has effectively succumbed to the same fate as Mercia. The annal opens dramatically with a reminder of Danish deceitfulness:

> Her hiene bestẹl se here on midne winter ofer tuelftan niht to Cippanhamme 7 geridon Wesseaxna lond 7 gesæton 7 micel þæs folces 7 ofer sẹ adræfdon, 7 þæs oþres þone mæstan dẹl hie geridon 7 him to gecirdon buton þam cyninge Ẹlfrede, 7 he lytle werede unieþelice æfter wudum for 7 on morfæstenum.

> Here in the middle of winter after twelfth night, the army stole [away] to Chippenham and they conquered the land of the West Saxons and settled it and drove many of the people across the sea, and conquered most of the others, and the people submitted to them with the exception of King Alfred. And he, in some difficulty, traveled with a small army through the woods and the moor-fastnesses.[79]

By turning the Danes into a kind of amoral Other, the annalist successfully distracts the reader from understanding exactly what Alfred has lost.[80] Not only do the Danes slip past any West Saxon defences, he claims that they occupy the West Saxon land. We do not know whether this is supposed to mean some West Saxon territory (in which case it would not be unusual) or even the whole kingdom (in which case it would be unprecedented and should have provoked some narrative reaction). But, as with the narrative strategy seen earlier, a strategy that stresses people over territory, the quantity of land involved is less important than the effect it has on Alfred's lordship. The kingdom of Wessex has been weakened: Alfred has no people. The West Saxons are driven abroad, conquered, and some submit willingly. Alfred vanishes into exile with a small force. At this moment, it appears that the king has lost his kingdom.

The appearance of loss, however, is precisely the point. The annalist does not provide any administrative details – how many people, which people, what happened to the government of the kingdom, how large is that small force – all we see is the submission of Alfred's people and the king's retreat into the fastnesses of his land. To readers familiar with Old English poetry, the loss of a people and the retreat into a barren landscape, a landscape of exile, is a meaningful step in the development of Alfred's lordship. In elegiac poems such as the *Wanderer* and the *Seafarer*, a barren landscape is part of the symbolic scenery of lordship topoi.[81] This familiar terrain casts into sharp relief the lordship discourse by which Alfred will return and regain his kingdom.

Though, of course, lordship can only be made possible by successful military engagements, Alfred's ability to implement firm lordship relations with the Danes lies at the heart of this new kingdom. The annalist returns to the narrative techniques that, in the earlier annals, hid the vulnerability of Alfred's kingdom, stressing the ways that his particular approach to time, geography, and the narration of battles heralds Alfred's lordship. Events in the *Chronicle* are often connected by time references; here, however, the annalist briefly switches to the liturgical calendar.

In this account, Alfred returns at Easter, thus connecting the resurgence of this temporal lord and king with the resurrection of the eternal Lord and King. But the annalist does not further pursue the liturgical or Christian implications; he returns to the discourse of exile and land. As the king emerges from the difficult wasteland, the geography of his journey becomes rhetorically important. Alfred rides from named place to named place, apparently winning back the *Wesseaxna lond* (West Saxon land) lost to the Danes, but we are once again not told whether these places are meaningful. Even Egbert's Stone, a monument with some probable cultural and historical significance, remains uninterpreted. As a result, the reader's attention focuses by default on the king and the way in which he binds his people to him and protects them from the Danes.

As the annalist tells it, when the people return to their king, Alfred is able to win a decisive victory, again obliging the Danes to give him hostages and swear him oaths.[82] But with the balance of power tipped in Alfred's direction, these are no oaths of alliance. The Danes, represented by their leader Guthrum, swear oaths of lordship and guarantee them with the extra surety of Guthrum's desire to receive Christian baptism.[83] The use of baptism as a means of transforming alliance into allegiance is, as Thomas Charles-Edwards has demonstrated, one of three possible and conventional diplomatic tactics. All three, though they had different meanings in Anglo-Saxon England and in Francia, were standard practices for ninth-century Christian and Scandinavian rulers, and all three – baptismal sponsorship, sponsorship at confirmation, and *compaternitas* (a tie between natural father and the godparent) – are implicated in a complicated combination of spiritual kinship and lordship relations.[84]

In some instances, what Charles-Edwards calls spiritual kinship and lordship are two aspects of the same process – even to the extent that spiritual kinship might reinforce lordship; in other situations, spiritual kinship did not necessarily imply lordship. At this particular moment, however, lordship and kinship go hand in hand. Alfred, who sponsors Guthrum at his baptism, becomes the Danish leader's godfather. This tie, founded on Alfred's victory, publicly confirms the formal transformation of the equalizing peace-making oaths of alliance into the hierarchy-building formal oaths of lordship. These oaths are then celebrated by a reenactment of one of the primary, secular lordship rituals, the honourable giving of gifts.

The idea that 878 is the moment at which Alfred wins his kingdom is supported by the language and content of the remaining annals for Alfred's reign. The entries for 879–91 differ sharply from the annals that have been the focus of this chapter. Their content is frequently Frankish, and though there continue to be regular mentions of a Danish presence on Anglo-Saxon land, the Danes are not shown posing an active threat until 885. In 885, the Anglo-Saxons put up a successful defence of Rochester by managing to hold the city until Alfred arrives; Alfred's army defeats one set of raiders in East Anglia, but on the return journey is overcome by a fresh force; and the Danes of East Anglia violate their peace.

In 886, however, these interruptions are finally settled. With a certain ambiguity, the annals of the *Chronicle* suggest that Alfred had to retake the city by force. But although this entry has occasioned much discussion, historians generally agree that Alfred did not have to conquer London again; he merely conducted a ceremonial display of his lordship there.[85] Nonetheless, the annalist states that Alfred occupied London, and he then focuses on the way in which the Anglo-Saxons respond: 'Þy ilcan geare gesette Ælfred cyning Lundenburg, 7 him all Angelcyn to cirde þæt buton deniscra monna hæftniede was' (In the same year, King Alfred took over [lit. settled] the city of London and all the *Angelcynn* who were not imprisoned by the Danes submitted to him).[86] Exploiting his laconic style in which an absence of subordinating conjunctions prevents his readers from understanding the causal relationship, if any, between the take-over and the submission, the annalist remarks that Alfred occupied London and that all the people 'who were not imprisoned by the Danes submitted to him.'

The language of this submission scene is key. The central verb is *(ge)cyrran* 'to turn' that in military contexts is used for 'to submit.'[87] Because in Anglo-Saxon England submission scenes are an important part of lordship rituals, historians characterize this as the moment when Alfred takes control of, or ceremonially displays control of, his kingdom.[88] And as he describes the submission, the Alfred annalist gives new meaning to the word *Angelcynn*.

Sarah Foot has argued that in texts emanating from Alfred's court, *Angelcynn* denotes a people associated with the oaths and ceremonies of lordship.[89] I find this argument helpful for understanding the peculiar focus of the Alfred annals. Though in the *Chronicle* as a whole, *Angelcynn* has some specific meanings, it is also generally a term for the Anglo-Saxons.[90] But with one exception, the Alfred annalist has not used *Angelcynn* as a term to describe Alfred and his men.[91] Indeed, he has deliberately avoided suggesting that the Anglo-Saxons are any more unified than their respective regional collective terms would suggest.

Throughout the early Alfred annals, the Danes are consistently termed the *Deniscan*,[92] thus suggesting that the Danes are a unified force (even though there is more than one army), but the annalist consistently separates the West Saxons from the other ethnic and political Saxon groups such as the Mercians, Northumbrians, and East Anglians. After the ceremony in London, however, all the people who accept Alfred's authority become *Angelcynn*; there is effectively no distinction between Mercian, West Saxon, and East Anglian. More precisely, since *Angelcynn* designates a people created by lordship, after the submission ritual in London, Alfred gains an *Angelcynn*, a people created by his practice of lordship. Thus drawing a clear distinction between Dane and Anglo-Saxon, the annalist affirms that lordship is at the centre of Alfred's kingdom.

Narrating Alfred's Honour

The idea that lordship defines the core of Alfred's kingdom and is the public manifestation of its identity explains the peculiar situation of the Hásteinn episode. If we read this story through the lens of military history seeking Alfred the Warrior King, the king the continuator presents seems weak and ineffective. If, however, we analyse the annals for 892–3 with an eye on the representation of the king's practice of lordship, the continuator's version of the Alfred-Hásteinn episode is very different. Given the history of the preceding annals, Hásteinn's actions transgress the culture of West Saxon lordship. In thus alienating his readers, this continuator suggests that it is impossible to integrate the Danes – and the cooperating oath-breaking East Anglians and Northumbrians – back into the community of Alfred's realm. This separation confirms the identity of the West Saxons.

That the Alfred annalist creates a compelling identity for Alfred's kingdom and people and that the continuator accepts and continues this ideology is further suggested in the continuator's use of the word *Angelcynn*. In the annal for 896, the continuator notes: 'Næfde se here, Godes þonces, Angelcyn ealles forswiðe gebrocod' (Thank God, the army had not oppressed the *Angelcynn* very much).[93] Similarly, when Alfred dies, the continuator memorializes him not as a *Bretwalda* – that is, not by the territory he controls – but as the 'cyning ofer eall Ongelcyn' (the king over all the *Angelcynn*).[94] In essence, then, both the Alfred annalist and his continuator agree that simply being Anglo-Saxon is not a sufficient criterion for being a member of the *Angelcynn*. This family is constructed and defined by acceptance of Alfred's lordship.

A New History for a New Realm

The annals for Alfred's reign are dominated by a seemingly endless list of defeats, negotiated peaces, and broken pledges; military triumphs seem occasional, and, more important, ephemeral. Even at the end of his reign, Alfred is still dealing with broken pledges and the Danish armies. The disjuncture between the annals' content and contemporary history's rhetoric of battle and nation creation should suggest that militarism is not a clear enough lens through which a reading of the annals can be focused. Moreover, militarism accounts for neither the annalist's decision to turn away from the discourse of invasion as punishment nor the comparatively consistent exploration of the struggle for security from the Danes. By contrast, a focus on the annalist's rhetoric of lordship clarifies these disparities, provides a unified way of reading the annals, and explains how the annalist's history works in the context of Alfred's court. The annalist defines Alfred's court by the king's practice of lordship and understands this court as a metaphor for Alfred's realm and his nation.

This focus on lordship is essential to understanding the historiography of the Alfred annals. To contextualize the history of the *Chronicle*, scholars often turn to the Continent in search of historiographical models. And while it is true that similar acts of lordship are mentioned in similar situations in such important texts as the *Royal Frankish Annals* and their continuation, the *Annals of St Bertin*, these histories use the discourse of sin and punishment to understand the Danish invasions. Unlike the Continental historians, the annalist does not figure Alfred's struggle as a continuation of the kind of religious historiography seen elsewhere at Alfred's court, in Orosius, and, in a milder version, Bede. This is important for understanding how the *Chronicle* works as an ideological text and manifestation of a new kind of vernacular historical writing.

Whether written by the Alfred annalist or merely copied into his text, the past conveyed in the early entries of the *Anglo-Saxon Chronicle* is very different from that of the Alfred annals. The narrator of this earlier world shows very little investment in his text, though, as Hayden White has demonstrated, literary analysis can harvest meaning from the terse descriptions of events, suppression of other events, and juxtapositions of the entries themselves.[95] By contrast, the Alfred annalist adopts a different and vigorous voice that, exchanging observation for narrative, focuses on the king's inglorious but mostly successful struggle with Danish raiders.[96] As Nicholas Howe has argued, the connection between Danish invaders, territorial loss, and sin is a well-attested part of writing the Anglo-Saxon mythical past; this link is also part of the historiographical traditions of the Continent. But although reflexes of this approach might be read into certain *Chronicle* annals, the nexus of invasion, conquest, and moral culpability is not, for the Alfred annalist, appropriate for narrativizing events in the recent past.[94] Indeed, as the following chapters will show, the annalist's consistent approach to writing the history of Alfred's early years as the story of how the king uses lordship to win and secure his kingdom is a significant new approach to writing contemporary history in the vernacular.

CHAPTER THREE

Proclaiming Alfred's Kingship

Recent work on Asser's *Vita Alfredi* has pursued two separate but complementary directions. While one set of scholars has returned to the question of authenticity, asking whether the work is a genuine ninth-century text or a forgery, the other has focused on the problem of audience.[1] Because it is written in Latin, the *Vita Alfredi* stands out from other Alfredian texts like the *Old English Bede* and *Old English Orosius*, histories that, together with the *Anglo-Saxon Chronicle*, suggest the importance of vernacular historical writing at Alfred's court. Nonetheless, the evidence overwhelmingly indicates that Asser's text is genuinely from the ninth century.[2] With regard to the question of audience, most scholars agree that Asser's life of Alfred was probably not intended to circulate at court, and many offer Asser's associates in Wales as likely readers.[3]

That these questions have dominated Asser scholarship points to one of the central difficulties of reading the *Vita Alfredi*: Asser's combination of annals from the *Anglo-Saxon Chronicle* with scenes from Alfred's life makes an appealing story. Yet because the text diverges from the Carolingian models of history and royal biography, models upon which we know Asser drew, the cultural and ideological significance of the *Vita Alfredi* has been understudied and its treatment of the collective identity articulated in the Alfred annals has gone unnoticed.[4]

In that Asser retains the Alfred annalist's particular formulation of Alfred's royal power, I suggest that he accepts the cultural function performed by the Alfred annals. In that he translates the annalist's work into Latin and into the form and ideology of ninth-century Carolingian historical biography, borrowing explicitly from well-known examples of Carolingian mirrors for princes,[5] I suggest that Asser proclaims to the Latinate Christian world the Alfred annalist's articulation of collective identity. In so doing, he authorizes the annalist's formulation of royal power as a question of lordship relations.

To explain its unusual form and content, the *Vita Alfredi* is most frequently compared to Einhard's *Vita Karoli*, but as James Campbell has pointed out, Asser's text in its combination of annals and biography also stands alongside the lives of Louis the Pious by Thegan and the 'Astronomer' (anonymous); it can even be compared to Notker of St Gall's stories of Charlemagne, Ermoul's praise poem of Louis the Pious, and Abbo's poem on the siege of Paris.[6] Further, as Anton Scharer has suggested, it is not just the form of the *Vita Alfredi* that can be said to be Carolingian. Working with texts from the mirrors for princes tradition, and specifically with the varied works of Sedulius Scottus, Scharer shows the extent to which the content of the *Vita Alfredi* can be sourced in Carolingian theories of kingship and royal power.[7] The sheer diversity of these texts does nothing to fix the form of the *Vita Alfredi* in any single known category, but it is clear that the *Vita* is a hybrid text written in the Carolingian traditions of history and historical biography and that it draws heavily from the mirrors for princes tradition.[8]

That said, Asser does not simply fold his text wholesale into a Carolingian framework. Carolingian theories of ecclesiastical kingship supply no exact precedent for the Alfred annalist's understanding of the connection between lordship and the collective identity of Alfred's people. Yet Asser retains the annalist's articulation of Anglo-Saxon identity. Further, though there are many situational similarities, especially with regard to the politics of family and succession in ninth-century Francia and ninth-century Anglo-Saxon England, Carolingian mirrors for princes turn inwards to focus on morality, virtue, and the private realm, consistently positioning the king as an example for the faith life of his subjects.[9] In these texts, a tremendous power accrues to the body and person of the king.

In the *Vita Alfredi*, Asser minimizes the importance of Alfred's person and subordinates the inward aspects of Carolingian mirrors for princes to his larger project of affirming the public dimension of the annalist's theory of lordship. But he does not reject Carolingian thinking entirely. He uses the conventional Carolingian hagiographical topos of the suffering body to undercut the fascination with the physical body in the mirrors for princes tradition.[10] His Alfred has the weak and suffering corporeality of a saint, but unlike the lives of martyrs where suffering and mutilation empower the dying Christian, Asser's Alfred is weakened, though not betrayed, by his various illnesses. So severe is his suffering that, as Asser would have it, disease intrudes upon his marital celebrations, government, military engagements, and his secular and spiritual life.[11] Indeed, Alfred's only relief in all this debilitation is that his illness is not externally disfiguring and therefore is not visible to the court.[12] But by diminishing the power of the physical, Asser refocuses his readers on the relational and communal significance of the saintlike king's body.

When the saint's body is no longer personal and private, it – like the body of the king – takes on a public dimension, representing the community, social, political, and national, of which it is part.[13] Michel de Certeau argues that 'the Life of a Saint is inscribed within the life of a group, either a church or a community. It takes for granted that the group already has an existence. But it conveys its self-consciousness by associating a *figure* with a *place* ... The text also implies a network of supports (oral transmission, manuscripts, or printed works) whose infinite development it stops at a given moment' [emphasis as printed].[14] Alfred is clearly no saint, either literally or metaphorically. But de Certeau's analysis may productively be extended to Asser's royal protagonist figure, the authority of whose reign is very much supported by a network of texts that includes the *Vita Alfredi*.

Displacing the king's struggle against the raiders from the centre of the *Chronicle* annals, Asser turns to the immediate community of Alfred's court, locating the king's power in the body political and, specifically, in Alfred's *Angelcynn*.[15] But instead of merely recording who submitted to Alfred's lordship, Asser focuses on the process of winning these men. Thus the problem at the heart of the *Vita Alfredi* is one of royal authority: how Alfred can sustain the loyalty of those who have accepted his lordship. This is a problem that the Alfred annalist does not address.

Here, Asser's adaptation of Carolingian tradition is important. Taking Solomon as their primary example, writers of texts on Carolingian ecclesiastical kingship value learning as part of the king's faith and private discipline.[16] At Alfred's court, these ideas are expressed in the Old English *Regula pastoralis*, the content of which might productively be read as an Old English mirror. But, like the Frankish mirrors for princes, the recommendations of the Old English *Regula* subordinate the political to the private, moral, and devotional.

In contrast, Asser suggests that individual learning and scholarship are insufficient as political tools for sustaining loyalty. Loyalty is built when the king takes that knowledge out of the private realm and activates it by personally teaching his men. In sum, the *Vita Alfredi* suggests that in an environment where royalty, Anglo-Saxon noblemen, and aristocratic foreigners are taught together, an environment where the traditional relationships between birth, national affiliation, and kingdom-centred loyalty are dismantled, education becomes a social and cultural institution that affirms the authority of the king by securing the loyalty of his men and thereby creating peace in his land.

Frankish and Anglo-Saxon Family Politics of Succession

Though Asser writes the story of Alfred's life, he begins with the story of Alfred's father's reign. This is in part a practical decision: Asser can now describe Alfred's birth and childhood, thereby building a more complete biography of his king. But the Æthelwulf story also performs a structural and conceptual function in the *Vita Alfredi* as a whole. Just as the Cynewulf-Cyneheard episode of the *Anglo-Saxon Chronicle* prefaces the Alfred annals and the annals respond to the political succession crisis raised by the protagonists' practice of lordship, so the story of Alfred's life responds to the issues raised in Asser's account of Æthelwulf's reign.[17] But where the Cynewulf-Cyneheard episode explores succession through the political family of those who assent to the king's lordship, the political space of the Æthelwulf section – highlighting Asser's persistent engagement with Carolingian texts and discourses of power – is that of the king's family, the relatives and members of his household with whom he shares a lordship bond.

The *Vita Alfredi* begins with a brief dedication to Alfred, a version of the West Saxon royal genealogy, and Asser's account of the reign of Æthelwulf, Alfred's father.[18] Because there is no explicit guide to Asser's organizing concerns, this genealogy sustains the *Chronicle* illusion that the kingdom passes from father to son in an unbroken succession and thus that Æthelwulf's (and, later, Alfred's) right to both the throne and the land is predicated on the authority of his lineage.[19]

In the *Anglo-Saxon Chronicle*, Æthelwulf's diplomatic and military successes confirm the distinction of his lineage. Æthelwulf's reign begins, in manuscript A of the *Chronicle*, in 836 with the transfer of power in the West Saxon kingdom from Egbert to his son, Æthelwulf.[20] (The regions of Kent, Surrey, and East and South Saxon England are passed to Egbert's other son, Æthelstan.) In the years between 839 and

851, the annalist (who may or may not be the Alfred annalist) records a series of battles against the Danes.[21] Possession of the land passes sometimes to the Danes and sometimes to the Anglo-Saxons until 851, when Æthelwulf engages the invaders at Aclea and gains a decisive victory.[22] For the annalist, this battle forms a turning point in Æthelwulf's reign. Having proven the king's worthiness on the field, he can now turn to Æthelwulf's diplomatic activities. Under 853, the annalist describes how Æthelwulf helps Burgred of Mercia defeat the Welsh, gives one of his daughters to Burgred in marriage, and takes Alfred to Rome. For the year 855, he records the last years of Æthelwulf's life. The raiders stay away from Æthelwulf's kingdom, enabling the king to travel to and remain for a year in Rome. On his return journey, the king takes Judith, daughter of Charles the Bald, the Frankish king, as his queen.[23] When Æthelwulf arrives in his kingdom, the annalist notes that his people are glad to see him again.[24] Within two years, he is dead.

This deceptively neutral account of Æthewulf's reign is set apart by its conclusion. Whereas the reign of Æthelwulf's father is summarized by a survey of land the king controls,[25] the annalist marks Æthelwulf's rule by a recitation of the West Saxon genealogy and list of ruling kings. If the Æthelwulf annals are written by the Alfred annalist, this avoidance of territory is typical of his strategy;[26] nonetheless, the annalist's recourse to genealogy highlights a significant formulation of Æthelwulf's royal authority. Rhetorically, this is a strong conclusion to an account of a successful – even exemplary – reign. Æthelwulf's successes ensure that he continues the tradition he inherits.

But the form of this genealogy requires further consideration. The several extant manuscripts in which Anglo-Saxon genealogical material appears suggest the West Saxon line of descent to Æthelwulf can be broken into several broad parts: Æthelwulf to Cerdic, Cerdic to Geat, Geat to Woden, and beyond.[27] There are, of course, variations in the manuscript details, but the tradition up to Geat is fairly stable.[28] While in the Anglian royal genealogies, biblical ancestors are common, extensions beyond Geat are unusual in early versions of the West Saxon royal genealogy, and the annalist's inclusion of biblical history is extraordinary.[29] This break with tradition and the concomitant move to connect Æthelwulf with so many powerful lineages suggest the significance of genealogical discourse. By positioning Æthelwulf as the inheritor of Anglo-Saxon England's sacred, secular, and mythological pasts, the *Chronicle* annalist uses the family relationship implied by a genealogy as the ultimate marker of royal power and individual worthiness.

Though Asser retains most of this *Chronicle* account, he interprets the figure of Æthelwulf differently. As Michael Lapidge has observed, Asser is familiar with the discourse of salvation history, a discourse that understands historical events and political change as indicators of a king's sin or – since they are often connected metonymically – as the sin of his people. And Asser works with this discourse.[30] To translate the *Chronicle* battles, Asser adopts the vocabulary of war from Orosius's *Historiarum adversus paganos libri septem*, one of the most important examples of this tradition.[31] But by retaining the overall positive assessment of Æthelwulf's reign despite the disloyalty among the king's family, Asser moves away from the traditions of this intellectual background and from one of the most popular models of writing Christian history. Æthelwulf's is a good and successful reign, and the king is generous in his dealings with the church; nonetheless, neither his virtue nor his morality is sufficient to protect the integrity of his realm.

In the midst of the *Chronicle* account, Asser introduces the story of a family conflict between the king and his son that results in the division of the kingdom. Like the *Chronicle* annalist, Asser recounts Æthelwulf's battles with the Danes, his decisive victory at Aclea, Burgred's request for help, Alfred's confirmation in Rome, and the marriage between Burgred and Æthelwulf's daughter. But according to Asser, Æthelwulf, despite his lineage, military victories, and diplomatic successes, cannot secure the loyalty of his family and hold the kingdom in a state of equilibrium. The threat of Danish occupation looms – indeed, accounts of Danish victories over other kings punctuate the narrative – but Æthelwulf is not deceived by the invaders. His throne is threatened by his son and heir, Æthelbald, and supported by coconspirators, all of whom follow the king's son.[32]

As Asser narrates these events, Æthelwulf handles the situation appropriately. The king is motivated only by a desire to protect his realm; there is no personal animus in his response. Seeing that a war between father and son would disrupt the kingdom more than the rebellion, and perhaps even cause the people to reject both of them, Asser's Æthelwulf acts swiftly, prioritizing the welfare of his kingdom as a whole over dealing with the insult to his regnal authority.[33] He gives up the western districts, the more important regions of his kingdom, and rules directly only over his eastern territories.

In the *Vita Alfredi*, by contrast, Æthelwulf does not simply accept the situation. The king uses his will (like the Frankish kings) to try to prevent the situation from happening again.[34] This disposition of the kingdom, as Asser records it, bypasses the language of royal election. Indeed, the inclusion of the will's details has textual significance, though it may not comport with historical practice. By arranging for a horizontal system of fratrilineal succession, Æthelwulf relocates the idea of power from an uninterrupted vertical line of descent and situates it, horizontally, in the group of people related by blood. While this system takes the pressure off father-son relationships, it does not prevent disloyalty among the brothers.[35] Nonetheless, the kingdom has been divided, and it remains that way until after Æthelwulf dies.

In addition to separating the *Vita Alfredi* from the conventions of Christian historiography, the narrative of Æthelwulf's exemplary character also distinguishes Asser's account from the ideals of kingship expressed in certain Carolingian mirrors for princes. These educational manuals, compiled during Charlemagne's reign and up to Asser's present, respond both directly and indirectly to the complicated contemporary politics of Frankish succession.[36] In short, the Frankish succession crises all turn on the division of the territory (if not the imperial power) between designated sons, the protagonists record the partition of the royal lands in a document, and the concomitant rebellions usually pit brother against brother and/or nephew against uncle.

As if to contain this family quarrelling, texts like Sedulius Scottus's *Liber de rectoribus christianis* and Hincmar's *De regis persona et regio ministerio* and *De ordine palatii* consistently stress the importance of the king's morality and exemplary behaviour, and, as part of that morality, they explore the difficulties of family relationships and advocate order among members of the king's household. But though Asser consistently draws on Sedulius as a lexical and conceptual source[37] and though Asser's Æthelwulf episode recalls the family politics of succession in Francia, Asser's account of Æthelwulf's reign breaks with both these traditions by minimizing the power of the king's virtue. With the connection between Christian morality and the integrity of the state now put aside, Asser asks how a king can create and sustain loyalty among members of his household and family. This question is answered in his account of Alfred's life.

Crowning a New Exemplarity

Asser negotiates the question of how loyalty among members of the king's different families can be created and sustained through the structure and metaphors of his text. His focus on Alfred's journey to royal authority and the security of his kingdom meaningfully influences where he begins to read the *Chronicle* and where he ceases to borrow from the narrative material of the annals. Asser's source manuscript is now lost, but it is likely that his text began in 60 BC and extended, like the other common stock texts, as far as 891.[38] Nonetheless, Asser ignores the prehistory of the kingdom; it is not relevant to the new focus of the *Vita Alfredi*. But he does redefine the scope of the Alfred annals. Asser's annalistic story of Alfred begins in 849, in Alfred's father's reign, and ends in 887. After 887, he focuses mainly on Alfred's domestic policy. Though this focus might be a product of Asser's now-lost source, the effect means that Asser works only with the annalist's secular narrative of lordship and kingdom making. He then places at the centre of his text a series of literal and metaphorical crownings.[39] Crowning is not, of course, a formal part of any known lordship ritual; rather, these moments help Asser mark the ways Alfred secures his kingdom.

Asser's Alfred gains his kingdom four times. Asser claims that he is first anointed by the pope, then crowned on ascension to the throne; his kingship is confirmed for a third time when all of non-Danish England submits to his authority. But when he guides his realm into the 'haven of [its] homeland,' Asser indicates that Alfred has finally earned his kingdom.[40] Though Alfred has a noble genealogy, is regarded as having been anointed by the pope, and is an effective military leader, he only becomes king of a unified realm when, at the moment of his fourth crowning, the king guides the ship of his kingdom into a safe haven and secures the loyalty of his people by teaching them.

Alfred's first 'crowning' occurs in 853, in the reign of his father. In the incident reported but not discussed in the *Chronicle*, Alfred's father sends the boy to Rome where the pope anoints him as a future king and sponsors him at his confirmation. The evidence for the historicity of this moment, its relationship to Charlemagne's anointing of his sons, and its overall significance for understanding Anglo-Saxon patterns of succession go beyond the scope of this book.[41] But the narrative of anointing is significant to both the larger structure of the *Vita Alfredi* and the theory of kingship it promotes.

Alfred's anointing distinguishes the young boy's body. In its corporeal aspect, it becomes the symbol of the future united body politic and spiritual, and the sufferings of its physical dimension are thereby minimized. Alfred is translated from his humble place as the king's youngest son and unlikely heir to a new family in which the pope is his spiritual father, and he is marked as a chosen king.[42] Why Alfred earns this status is unclear. Asser has not yet endowed his king with any specific virtues; indeed, Asser says only that 'he [Æthelwulf] loved him more than his other sons.'[43] Nonetheless, the boy's new position has startling effects. The king's favouritism appears to destroy the unity of his lordship family, prompting a rebellion from his son, Æthelbald, and members of his nobility. This rebellion ultimately leads to the division of the kingdom. By not explaining Æthelwulf's reasoning, Asser allows Alfred's first crowning to formulate the questions about the place of virtue and problems of loyalty that the other crownings will symbolically resolve.

In his account of Alfred's second crowning, Asser evokes parallel Frankish situations and draws from the Carolingian mirrors for princes to explore the problem of virtue as a defining quality of a worthy king. Whereas the Carolingian mirrors seek to install virtue in their kings, in the *Vita Alfredi*, Alfred's virtue points to the marginality of the young king's candidacy.[44] In 871, King Æthelred dies and Alfred finally takes the throne. Just prior to this coronation, Asser lingers over Alfred's virtues; he is well taught in all the secular skills of hunting, speaking, and courtly behaviour, but, most importantly for an ideal Carolingian king, he has an insatiable desire for learning.[45]

Unlike his Continental counterparts, however, Alfred is not greedy for personal power.

> Eodem anno Ælfred ... totius regni gubernacula, divino concedente nutu, cum summa omnium illius regni accolarum voluntate, confestim fratre defuncto suscepit. Quod etiam vivente praedicto fratre suo, si dignaretur accipere, facillime cum consensu omnium potuerat invenire, nempe quia et sapientia et cunctis moribus bonis cunctos fratres suos praecellebat, et insuper eo quod nimium bellicosus et victor prope in omnibus bellis erat.

> In the same year Alfred ... took over the government of the whole kingdom as soon as his brother had died, with the approval of divine will and according to the unanimous wish of all the inhabitants of the kingdom. Indeed, he could easily have taken it over with the consent of all while his brother Æthelred was alive, had he considered himself worthy to do so, for he surpassed all his brothers both in wisdom and in all good habits;

and in particular because he was a great warrior and victorious in virtually all battles.[46]

As I discussed in chapter 2, the story of Alfred and his brother is, in the Alfred annals, positive; there is no suggestion that Alfred might wish to take over his brother's realm. Alfred and Æthelred cooperate because they are bound by lordship ties; indeed, the Alfred annalist consistently refers to Alfred not as the king-in-waiting, but as a noble brother, loyal to his lord. Asser retains the focus on the two brothers but alters this scenario to Æthelred's detriment and Alfred's advantage. Adding to the facts of the *Chronicle* text, Asser suggests that the security of the kingdom and Æthelred's place on the throne are more tributes to Alfred's moral virtue than a measure of his brother's authority.

But whereas Asser clearly marks Æthelbald's rebellion against Alfred's father as a usurpation rather than a legitimate passage of dominion,[47] he also suggests that Alfred's move for the throne would have been perfectly acceptable. By emphasizing the point that the *witan* would have agreed to Alfred's accession and thus raising the concept of consent, Asser borrows from an established discourse of royal election and succession in both Francia and Anglo-Saxon England.[48] In Anglo-Saxon texts like the *Chronicle*, the consent of the *witan* functions as a formal acknowledgment of the king's lordship and acceptance of lordship obligations. In this context, the idea of consent changes usurpation into an acceptable transfer of power.[49] Nonetheless, because of Alfred's morality, Asser suggests that the future king does not succumb to the depredations seen across the sea in Francia and at home in the actions of his brother.

Yet despite Alfred's virtue, the situation upon Alfred's succession is not positive. As the new king, Alfred takes on a kingdom in which familial loyalty is so weak that, were it not for his forbearance, he could have launched, with the consent of all, a rebellion more successful than that of his brother against his father. Exploiting the conventional *Chronicle* language of accession, Asser observes that Alfred 'totius regni gubernacula ... suscepit' (took over the government of the whole realm). This phrase translates the conventional and usually neutral Old English 'feng to rice' (succeeded to the kingdom). But because it only appears four times in the *Vita Alfredi* – when Æthelbald rules the Anglo-Saxons after the death of Æthelwulf, when Æthelred becomes king, here in the second crowning, and finally in a list of Alfred's activities as king – it gains added meaning.⁵⁰ This larger context indicates that the power being transferred is just that: power. Asser does not assess the king's authority. And herein lies the problem of the second crowning. Control of the country does not guarantee absolute loyalty in the king's *familia* or, to put it in the Alfred annalist's terms, government can secure neither authority nor lordship relations.

This security Alfred achieves in his third crowning. The history of events in 886 is unclear as to whether Alfred must retake London as a result of a previous breach of the peace or whether the *Chronicle* records a symbolic lordship ceremony.⁵¹ In Asser's hands, however, the entry for the year 886 implies that with the attention of the Danish army turned elsewhere, Alfred can now cease to defend his land and begin to demonstrate his control over his kingdom.

> Eodem anno Ælfred, Angulsaxonum rex, post incendia urbium stragesque populorum, Lundoniam civitatem honorifice restauravit et habitabilem fecit; quam *suo genere* Æthe[l]redo, Merciorum comiti, commendavit servandam. Ad quem regem omnes Angli et Saxones, qui prius ubique dispersi fuerant aut cum paganis sub captivitate erant, voluntarie converterunt, et suo dominio se subdiderunt.

> In this same year Alfred, king of the Anglo-Saxons, restored the city of London splendidly – after so many towns had been burned and so many people slaughtered – and made it habitable again; he entrusted it to the care of Æthelred, ealdorman of the Mercians. All the Angles and Saxons – those who had formerly been scattered everywhere and were not in captivity with the Vikings – turned willingly to King Alfred and submitted themselves to his lordship.⁵²

Despite their prominence in the text, the new architecture and material culture of London do not transform this important place into a capital city and symbol of Alfred's power. Rather, like the Alfred annalist, Asser understands the city as a symbol of Alfred's lordship. This is emphasized in his word choice: *dominium* (lordship). But Asser also alters the *Chronicle* annal in order to reinforce this point. In the Alfred annals, Alfred entrusts London to Æthelred after he has received the submission of his people. The transfer of power is thus positioned as an act of Alfred's lordship. In the *Vita Alfredi*, Asser places the act of submission after Alfred entrusts the city to Æthelred. He thus suggests that the submission results from this display of Alfred's lordship and, in so doing, he implies that Alfred's lordship is generative. Acts of lordship beget more acts of lordship which in turn beget and secure a realm.

Even though, in the *Chronicle*, submission to Alfred's lordship is an endpoint of the text, acceptance and submission are not the centre of the *Vita Alfredi*. Asser also uses the third crowning to ask how Alfred can maintain these lordship relations. Alfred is, by now, no longer merely the ruler of the West Saxons. In solidifying his borders against the Danes, he has also expanded into most of the former Mercia: his new kingdom thus comprises two peoples with a distant history of possible mutual hostility and, for the Mercians, a recent history of enforced cooperation with the West Saxons and prior submission to an enemy the West Saxons manage to withstand.[53] By entrusting this former Mercian city and present symbol of the kingdom's rebirth to *ealdormann* Æthelred, a Mercian, Alfred demonstrates his control over the land and his desire for unity among his peoples. But the unity of this kingdom depends on strong lordship relations, and such relations are not secured by the symbolism of a capital city.

Even though Alfred will ultimately link Mercia and Wessex through marriage, literally making Mercia part of the West Saxon family, Asser highlights the vulnerability of a kingdom built on military victory and cemented by family relations by turning again to the Continent.[54] In Francia, in the same year, a usurpation by family members essentially repeats Æthelbald's rebellion, reminding the reader that when the king's own family is disloyal, he is also unlikely to maintain the loyalty of those not related to him by blood.[55] Alfred, who has disinherited the children of his brother, Æthelred, must now win and maintain the loyalty of the Mercian nobility. In Asser's hands, the king's first three crownings have suggested that royal authority is not located solely in military prowess and that the social and political bonds of lordship may require reinforcement. Indeed, when involving blood family members, lordship bonds can be peculiarly vulnerable. But nothing in Asser's reworking of the annals has thus far suggested how strong lordship relations can be created.

To focus entirely on the annals incorporated into the *Vita Alfredi* is, however, only to read half the story. Asser alternates between the well-known *Chronicle* narrative of the kingdom and his original story of Alfred's life, and it is here, in Alfred's private life, that Asser locates the solution to the public problem of the king's lordship relations. The year 866 marks the accession of Alfred's brother, Æthelred, to a kingdom beset by invaders. But instead of focusing on the danger or even on the new king, Asser interrupts the narrative, turns away from the *Chronicle* using a ship metaphor, and begins a discussion of Alfred's youth:

> Sed, ut more navigantium loquar, ne diutius navim undis et velamentis concedentes, et a terra longius enavigantes longum circumferamur inter tantas bellorum clades et annorum enumerationes, ad id, quod nos maxime ad hoc opus incitavit, nobis redeundum esse censeo, scilicet aliquantulum, quantum meae cognitioni innotuit, de infantilibus et puerilibus domini mei venerabilis Ælfredi, Angulsaxonum regis, moribus hoc in loco breviter inserendum esse existimo.

> But (to speak in nautical terms) so that I should no longer veer off course – having entrusted the ship to waves and sails, and having sailed quite far away from the land – among such terrible wars and in year-by-year reckoning, I think I should return to that which particularly inspired me to this work: in other words, I consider that some small account (as much as has come to my knowledge) of the infancy and boyhood of my esteemed lord Alfred, king of the Anglo-Saxons, should briefly be inserted at this point.[56]

The literary idea of a narrative at sea can be traced back to, among others, Cicero and Quintilian, where it heralds what the author would like to introduce as his main point.[57] Asser uses it in precisely this way. Structurally, the ship image allows him to effect a transition from chronicle to hagiographical biography. More important, Asser uses its figurative significance to move lordship, the household, and the family to the centre of his work. His narrative has proceeded, like the Alfred annals, year by year in the mode of annalistic writing. The image of the ship undercuts the text so far – indeed, Asser claims that the Alfred annals, the stories of Alfred's battles, peace making, and lordship with the Danes, blow him off course. He will now no longer allow his text to drift; he will come to port and to the point of his text. Specifically, Asser suggests that ideal lordship relations are sustained and the identity of the kingdom secured only when the king teaches those whose loyalty he commands.

A Teaching King

Asser breaks with the narrative of the Alfred annals and begins the story of Alfred's life, a story in which he prepares his discussion of the king's successful lordship relations. Alfred is an unusual child, more beloved of his parents and everyone at court than any of his brothers; he is, moreover, better looking and more skilled in the expected social and courtly graces.[58] Having acknowledged these skills, Asser lingers over the moment when Alfred learns to read.

In Asser's hands, the king's interest in reading is no fleeting childhood passion. Alfred's love of learning persists into adulthood, withstands illness, and even survives the challenges of defending and governing the kingdom: 'Cui ab incunabulis ante omnia et cum omnibus praesentis vitae studiis, sapientiae desiderium cum nobilitate generis, nobilis mentis ingenium supplevit' (From the cradle onwards, in spite of all the demands of the present life, it has been the desire for wisdom, more than anything else, together with the nobility of his birth, which have characterized the nature of his noble mind).[59] In the context of an *encomium*, such enthusiastic praise does not seem out of place. As a continuation of the Alfred annals and of the stories of invasion and battle, however, such a characterization of the future king is startling. It suggests that Alfred will be a better king because he is interested in books.[60]

Learning is a value accorded much significance in Carolingian kingship texts,[61] but for Asser, scholarship is insufficient because it is a private virtue that affects only the king. Asser's Alfred needs to unite his men and provide them with a unifying identity. In his entry for 885, adopting again the ship of the narrative metaphor, Asser interrupts his account of Alfred's fight for his kingdom at the moment when the Danes break the peace. But instead of exploring the problems this failure of diplomacy raises, he turns to an account of Alfred's married life and illnesses, concentrating eventually on the education of the king's three youngest children.[62]

The youngest son, Æthelweard, 'was given over to training in reading and writing under the attentive care of teachers, in company with all the nobly born children of virtually the entire area, and a good many of lesser birth as well.'[63] He and the other children learn to read and write both Latin and English to such an extent 'that, even before they had the requisite strength for manly skills (hunting, that is, and other skills appropriate to noblemen), they were seen to be devoted and intelligent students of the liberal arts.'[64] Asser specifies, furthermore, that Edward and Ælfthryth (the two other children) were educated so well that 'to the present day they continue to behave with humility, friendliness and gentleness to all compatriots and foreigners, and with great obedience to their father.'[65] In the context of annalistic discourse, this is unusual rhetoric: it suggests that invasion and physical security are less worthy of a reader's attention than family relationships and education. Many scholars have interpreted these scenes as part of larger studies of Anglo-Saxon literacy, but such readings fail to account for the incongruity of this material in a translation of the *Chronicle* annals and do not explain the narrative space Asser devotes to the importance of learning and teaching.

Asser's interest lies not with the children's behaviour nor even with the specifics of their curriculum, but with the effect their education has upon them. He claims that learning renders Edward and Ælfthryth completely obedient.[66] Because Edward and Ælfthryth are so obedient to their father, Alfred, unlike his father, will not have to suffer an assault on his throne spearheaded by one of his children. Thus adding a political dimension to the expected Christian moral emphasis on obedience, Asser claims that education ensures the right relationship between authority and children, father and child, and king and subject.[67]

Asser develops this point by extending the explicit connection between loyalty and the book beyond Alfred's immediate relatives to the larger political family of the realm. Indeed, Asser suggests that to ensure the security of his kingdom, Alfred personally teaches all the children of all his courtiers:

> Episcopos quoque suos et omnem ecclesiasticum ordinem, comites ac nobiles suos, ministeriales etiam et omnes familiares admirabili amore diligebat. Filios quoque eorum, qui in regali familia nutriebantur, non minus propriis diligens, omnibus bonis moribus instituere et literis imbuere solus die noctuque inter cetera non desinebat.

> With wonderful affection, he cherished his bishops and the entire clergy, his ealdormen and nobles, his officials as well as all his associates. Nor, in the midst of other affairs, did he cease from personally giving, by day and night, instruction in all virtuous behaviour and tutelage in literacy to their sons, who were being brought up in the royal household and whom he loved no less than his own children.[68]

This is a startling claim, but Asser does not pursue what it would mean for traditional ideas of royalty and succession. Instead, he focuses on reworking Carolingian ideas about education and the kingdom. Carolingian mirrors for princes emphasize wisdom as a personal virtue, but, for Asser, learning is less important than teaching. Metaphorically constructing Alfred's court as a nurturing family environment, Asser depicts his king as a teacher-parent who nourishes those around him. In this court, membership in the king's family does not require a blood connection.[69] For Asser, Alfred's blood and non-blood family members are distinguished by their willingness to learn from the king.[70]

Though educating the children may facilitate unity in the future, it does not protect the king from rebellion in the present, by the children's fathers. Asser's Alfred attracts to his court a variety of foreigners, including Franks, Frisians, Gauls, Danes, Welsh, and Irish, and he also treats them the same way that he treats his Anglo-Saxon retainers.[71] Asser claims that everyone accepts Alfred's lordship because of his distribution of alms, his generous disposition to all, and his study of things unknown.[72] In exchange for this loyalty, Asser's Alfred acts 'secundum suam dignitatem' (as befit[s] his royal status), giving wealth and authority to Anglo-Saxon and foreigner alike.[73] Such munificence, however, runs the risk of alienating a native nobility of both West Saxon and Mercian aristocrats. Asser claims that those already present at Alfred's court are guided by the king's loving lordship, but, as we have already seen, and as Asser will demonstrate again, mutual affection will not bind together the adults at court and those in the outlying provinces.

In the midst of an endorsement of Alfred's talent in the realms of architecture, aesthetics, and battle, Asser notes a problem. The material beauties of the kingdom do not compel the king's subjects to loyalty: the Anglo-Saxon people 'would undertake of their own accord little or no work for the common needs of the kingdom.'[74] Virtue is not enough. Despite the king's extraordinary gifts, his artistic and military skills do not inspire the kind of loyalty that would foster a sense of community and obligation. Thus stressing how poorly the Carolingian discourse of virtue and the traditional symbols of kingship create national community, Asser returns to the ship metaphor, posing again the question of how a king secures his kingdom:

> Sed tamen ille solus divino fultus adminiculo susceptum semel regni gubernaculum, veluti gubernator praecipuus, navem suam multis opibus refertam ad desideratum ac tutum patriae suae portum, quamvis cunctis

propemodum lassis suis nautis, perducere contendit, haud aliter titubare ac vacillare, quamvis inter fluctivagos ac multimodos praesentis vitae turbines, non sinebat. Nam assidue suos episcopos et comites ac nobilissimos, sibique dilectissimos suos ministros, necnon et praepositos, quibus post Dominum et regem omnis totius regni potestas, sicut dignum, subdita videtur, leniter docendo, adulando, hortando, imperando, ad ultimum inoboedientes, post longam patientiam, acrius castigando, vulgarem stultitiam et pertinaciam omni modo abominando, ad suam voluntatem et ad communem totius regni utilitatem sapientissime usurpabat et annectebat.

Yet once he had taken over the helm of his kingdom, he alone, sustained by divine assistance, struggled like an excellent pilot to guide his ship laden with much wealth to the desired and safe haven of his homeland, even though all his sailors were virtually exhausted; similarly, he did not allow it to waver or wander from course, even though the course lay through the many seething whirlpools of the present life. For by gently instructing, cajoling, urging, commanding, and (in the end, when his patience was exhausted) by sharply chastising those who were disobedient and by despising popular stupidity and stubbornness in every way, he carefully and cleverly exploited and converted his bishops and ealdormen, and nobles, and his thegns most dear to him, and reeves as well (in all of whom, after the Lord and the king, the authority of the entire kingdom is seen to be invested, as is appropriate) to his own will and to the general advantage of the whole realm.[75]

In this, Alfred's fourth crowning, Asser brings the ship of the text home to its port, and Alfred, with some difficulty, metaphorically secures his kingdom. The external threat of the Danes has its interior counterpart: the exhausted sailors of a reluctant aristocracy. Asser diagnoses 'vulgarem stultitiam' (popular stupidity) to be at the heart of the people's unwillingness to act 'ad communem totius regni utilitatem' (for the common needs of the kingdom). Popular stupidity, manifested as laziness, renders the people unable to see the underlying reasons for the king's commands. Prior to this, Asser has depicted learning as a private pursuit and teaching as a vocational mission. Now, he portrays his king actively and consciously employing learning as a public weapon. Alfred persuades his people to work with him by giving formal instruction ('leniter docendo'); he uses the rhetorical skills of his own education to persuade them to follow him ('adulando, hortando'); to these he adds the prerogatives of his office ('imperando' and 'acrius castigando'). It does not matter to Asser that Alfred is less than personable in his means of persuasion; it is important only that the king succeeds.[76]

Alfred, of course, does win over his people, and Asser devotes some time to the bitter lessons learned by those who doubted their king. More significant, however, is the way in which the king convinces his people to follow him. In Alfred's kingdom, the dictatorial imperative of the king is a last resort; Alfred does not use it arbitrarily. Rather, he prefers to teach those around him so that the foreigners and Anglo-Saxons – despite their different heritages, dissimilar traditional loyalties, and varying geographical places of origin – are combined into a new people defined and unified by a king who teaches.

This fourth crowning symbolizes the end of Alfred's journey to security, and the king's success is reflected in the structure of the *Vita Alfredi*. For the remainder of the text, the history of the Alfred annals and the biography are combined to form the story of Alfred's domestic policy. The *Vita Alfredi* concludes, though perhaps not intentionally, with an anecdote demonstrating how education secures justice, which in turn secures peace, and peace secures the king's authority.[77] Alfred is shown teaching and exercising the authority of his lordship, but his power is not that of a military or political leader. Though the Danish raids continue throughout Alfred's reign, they are virtually absent from the rest of the *Vita Alfredi* where Asser's focus on instruction as a domestic policy shows that the king's authority derives from his willingness to instruct.

As the king's policy takes effect, Asser notices that no one in a position of power who wanted to remain there neglected his books. Even those who could not read sought instruction. No longer is the desire for knowledge a royal quirk; rather, because learning has political and domestic value, Asser suggests that inspiring a desire for knowledge will ensure justice and thus peace. Teaching creates commonality among a loosely associated body of noblemen and blood relatives. Personal instruction from the king reinforces the bond of lordship by emphasizing the personal element of the political and social tie between king and man and, in so doing, confirms the ideological centrality of lordship in Alfred's kingdom.

In effect, then, the series of 'crownings' transforms Asser's work from a general narrative of Alfred's life and adapted account of Anglo-Saxon history into a cultural text that protects and affirms the West

Saxon identity advanced in the Alfred annals of the *Anglo-Saxon Chronicle*. In making this translation, Asser does not simply alternate between *Chronicle* material and scenes from the king's life. Because, unlike the Alfred annalist, he is not concerned with establishing Alfred's kingdom – he takes its existence as given – Asser subordinates the task of writing the political history of the kingdom to the task of narrating and remaking the Alfred annalist's ideology.

Political Teaching

In the field of Alfred studies, ideas of learning and teaching are charged. We are accustomed to connecting Alfred with ideas of wisdom and education because so many Alfredian texts emphasize education.[78] Indeed, as the anonymous writer of the Middle English *Proverbs of Alfred* suggests, learning is a defining element of Alfred's rule and, perhaps, of the king himself.[79] Yet even though the *Vita Alfredi* and the Old English translation of Gregory's *Regula pastoralis* both stress the importance of a ruler who teaches, Asser's linguistic and cultural translation of the Alfred annals and his persistent engagement with the Carolingian mirrors for princes tradition distinguish his text from other Alfredian works on education.

Of all the Alfredian texts, the Old English *Regula pastoralis* most explicitly makes teaching the job (or, more accurately, burden) of a ruler;[80] it focuses on how to instruct others in their Christian duty, the appropriate ways of encouraging a wide variety of others to live a Christian life, and the morality of seeking, using, and living in a position of authority. The notion of morality is key. In some ways, Asser presents Alfred as an ideal king in terms of the Carolingian mirrors for princes and of the more local Old English translation of Gregory's *Regula pastoralis*; he studies, teaches, is humble, and adopts an appropriate attitude towards his position of power. But, overall, Asser subordinates his focus on Alfred's morality to writing the history of how Alfred creates and maintains his kingdom. In this regard, the *Vita Alfredi* is a close and careful exposition of a suggestive comment in Alfred's *Preface to the Regula pastoralis*.

In justifying his educational program, Alfred claims that when there were many wise men throughout England, the country's kings held 'ægðer ge hiora sibbe ge hiora siodo ge hiora onweald innanbordes' (both their peace, their customs, and their authority within the borders of their nations).[81] The problem of whether learning in Anglo-Saxon

England really had declined to the degree Alfred suggests elsewhere in the *Preface* has earned much scholarly attention,[82] but scholars of Alfredian wisdom often pass this sentence by. Does Alfred literally claim a direct connection between learning and authority? The Old English *Regula* is formally unrelated to the *Vita Alfredi*, but I would suggest that the similarity of this literally improbable claim and the conceptual argument of the *Vita Alfredi* together argue for a discourse in which learning and the security of the kingdom are connected. In this discourse of learning, education is individually and morally beneficial, but it also has the cultural function of creating a unified political and social group.

As Asser thematizes teaching, he expands both the discourse of lordship found in the annalistic narratives of the *Anglo-Saxon Chronicle* and that of the Carolingian mirrors for princes tradition. He also moves away from examples of royal biography offered in Einhard's *Vita Karoli* and from the historiographical discourse of sin, invasion, and conquest found in Orosius and Bede. In the *Vita Alfredi*, Asser's Alfred goes beyond a simple adherence to the usual understandings of moral Christian leadership through private study; the security of Alfred's kingdom depends not on descent or morality, but on a king who successfully uses instruction to unify his court. According to Asser, instruction is the key to Alfred's authority.

This focus shapes the *Vita Alfredi* as a biography of the king's journey to royal authority that in turn affirms the identifying culture of Alfred's court and thus, symbolically, of his united West Saxon and Mercian kingdom. Where the Alfred annalist created a political family defined by those who accepted the king's lordship, Asser extends membership in that family to those whom the king teaches and demonstrates how personal instruction from the king holds together the family of blood relations, household members, and subjects.

CHAPTER FOUR

Undoing Æthelred

Read as a history of Æthelred II's reign, the annals from 983 to 1022 reveal a story in which the people so carefully created or identified by the Alfred annalist become another conquered population.[1] But though the annalist suggests that the king and his *witan* are to be held accountable, the idea that the king is responsible for the loss of his kingdom is not intended to be a full and objective analysis of the situation. Rather, Æthelred's accountability is essential to the annalist's narrative focus. The Æthelred-Cnut annalist proclaims, 'Ealle þas ungesælða us gelumpon þuruh unrædas þæt man nolde him a timan gafol beodon oþþe wið gefeohtan' (All these misfortunes happened to us because of poor counsel in that we wanted neither to offer them tribute in a timely manner nor to fight against them).[2] This comment retrospectively frames the preceding events as a series of disasters resulting from a poorly advised king, and it further implies that if Æthelred were simply to fight, he might have been able to stem the assaults and avert the loss of his kingdom.

Although the Æthelred-Cnut annalist's claim about counsel and fighting has become central to many modern and some medieval views of Æthelred's reign – this assessment lies at the heart of Æthelred's poor reputation and the popular pun on his name – the annalist's assertion is not to be taken literally.[3] Rhetorically, the annals advocate military engagement as the most effective course of resistance, but the *Æthelred-Cnut Chronicle* neither creates nor resolves a discussion about negotiating versus fighting. Instead, the focus on fighting and counsel associates the annals with the general intellectual milieu of the late tenth and early eleventh century and, in particular, with the exploration of royal action in Ælfric's homilies and saints' lives.[4]

In a close and careful study, Malcolm Godden suggests that in this part of Ælfric's oeuvre the question of whether a king should fight can be aligned with the genre of a particular text.[5] Ælfric's homiletic work implies that the king should not fight, but his hagiographic texts argue that the king should lead his men in battle. But because Ælfric is not the only significant thinker of the period to address these ideas, I extend Godden's conclusions to a consideration of the many different texts that discuss Anglo-Saxon kingship, finding in them a hagiographic discourse that urges the king to fight and a homiletic discourse that asks the king to negotiate.

As the majority of studies on the *Æthelred-Cnut Chronicle* suggest, the annals at first take on the qualities of a hagiographic text. Æthelred is responsible because he does not fight. But in that the annals show the king negotiating, delegating, and generally working in consultation with his *witan*, the *Chronicle* also participates in a homiletic discourse of leadership, a discourse wherein the king is to delegate the task of fighting at the request of his council. The same homiletic discourse also insists that a king must protect his people and the church. To fail at this task is what both Anglo-Saxon and Carolingian theorists of ideal kingship call an 'abuse' or sin.[6]

As the Æthelred-Cnut annalist presents the narrative of Æthelred's reign, the king's unwillingness to take the field and his decision to pay tribute do not inspire the loyalty necessary for his men to be effective in battle. Because the resulting defeats and betrayals endanger the people and the church, the annalist is able to suggest that the king has failed in his duty to protect them. He further implies that the king's shortcomings derive from his abuse of royal power and that these problems – abuses or sins – culminate in the loss of the kingdom.

Thus even though the Æthelred-Cnut annals were compiled amidst a surge in homiletic and hagiographic writing and even though the annals at times partake of both homiletic and hagiographic discourse, the *Æthelred-Cnut Chronicle* is neither strictly hagiographic nor homiletic.[7] Instead, the annalist uses the issue of fighting versus negotiating to further his historiographical project: narrating the loss of the Anglo-Saxon identity articulated in the Alfred annals.

Because the Æthelred-Cnut annalist insists on Æthelred's culpability and directly connects the king's actions to the loss of the kingdom, he places his work in the tradition of salvation history. Whatever the source of transgression leading to defeat, salvation history frames sin as a function of divine time and treats each kingdom typologically. In such histories, the identifying aspects of any national community and its ruling dynasty are treated as universal problems that salvation history resolves.[8]

The framework of salvation history makes the rhetoric of the *Æthelred-Cnut Chronicle* meaningful. Using both hagiographic and homiletic discourse, the annalist constructs Æthelred's reign as an era of disaster and political incompetence on the king's part because, in salvation history, this culpability is a necessary condition for the fall of a kingdom. In writing a salvation history, the annalist does not need his readers to focus on the specific reasons for the loss of the kingdom; he needs them only to see that sin leads to conquest. In this context, Æthelred's failures, the concomitant loss of his kingdom, and the loss of his people's identity are just part of a necessary series of precursors to the second coming.

Ostensible Facts

To focus on the genre of the annalist's historiography is to reconsider the record of the past created in the *Æthelred-Cnut Chronicle*. As preserved in the annals, the following details – details that the annalist presents as the facts of Æthelred's kingship – justify the medieval and modern assessments of Æthelred's reign as one of chaos and lack of preparation. From his accession and coronation, Æthelred appears to act according to a policy he forms with the advice of his councillors.[9] The Anglo-Saxons fight the Danes in some instances, purchase peace in others, and pay tribute when they are defeated.[10] In 1011, the annalist digresses from his history to explain, 'Ealle þas ungesælða us gelumpon þuruh unrædas' (All these misfortunes happened to us because of poor counsel).[11] Generally, the broader events of the Æthelred annals support such a reading.

In the entries for the years preceding 1011, the annalist records a variety of reactions to the Danish raids: no military response (980, 981, 982, 988, 997); defeat (991 – Maldon, 999, 1001, 1004 – Thetford, 1006 – Kennet, 1010); a military response hampered by treachery (992 – Ælfric, 993 – Fræna, Godwin, and Frythegyst, 998 – no specified leader, 1003 – Ælfric again, 1009 – Wulfnoth, 1010 – no leader would collect an army); military responses hindered by poor organization (999 – king and *witan*, 1010 – king and *witan*); peace negotiations or tribute (994 – Olaf's baptism, 1002 – king and *witan*, 1006 – king and *witan*, 1007, 1009).

To add to this catalogue of disaster, the Æthelred-Cnut annalist also implies that Æthelred's personal actions run counter to the tenets of ideal kingship and thus that the loss of the kingdom is a just retribution for the king's misdeeds. The king actively harasses his people instead of protecting them. In 986, Æthelred lays Rochester to waste and a murrain occurs;[12] in 993, he has Ælfgar, son of *ealdormann* Ælfric blinded;[13] in 999, he gets his strategy wrong with the result that the land and sea armies only oppress the people and waste their effort;[14] in 1000, Æthelred ravages Cumberland; in 1002, he orders the slaughter of the Danes living in England; in 1006, he has Wulfheah and Ufegeat blinded and *ealdormann* Ælfhelm killed; in 1009, the king goes home from the battlefield prematurely; and in 1013, Æthelred abandons his country and goes into exile.

If this survey of events is taken as a complete account of the king's manoeuvres, his weakness is easily attributed to a policy born of 'unrædas' (poor counsel) and an unwillingness to fight. And if we take the annalist at his word, it is even easier to justify the Danish Conquest. Æthelred is so corrupt and incompetent that the Anglo-Saxons deserve a new king. But the problem with focusing on the ostensible facts is that while the annalist for the most part records events that are known to have taken place, the *Chronicle* is not a full record of Æthelred's reign. Indeed, the facts of the annals obscure the ideological contexts in which the *Æthelred-Cnut Chronicle* can be read and, in so doing, they prevent the reader from realizing that the facts are carefully selected and selectively presented.

Should the King Fight: A Hagiographic Perspective

The first context in which the Æthelred-Cnut annalist places his work is that of the early entries of Æthelred's reign. The annals for 979–82, the annals of Æthelred's early years, are not formally considered part of the *Æthelred-Cnut Chronicle*, but they do establish a conceptual preface to the Æthelred-Cnut annals themselves.[15] Though the Æthelred-Cnut annalist may not have written these entries, he continues their thematic emphasis on fighting and develops the implication that a willingness to fight is an essential component of Anglo-Saxon identity. In the entries for 980–1, the unknown annalist allows the first Danish raids to pass without comment.[16] On the occasion of the third attack in 982, however, he turns from his sketch of the Anglo-Saxons' defencelessness to Continental European history. In 982, the emperor, Otto, made an expedition to southern Italy where he joined battle against an army of Saracens, who came, like the Danes, from the sea and desired, like the Danes, to plunder Christian shores. Drawing an unfavourable comparison between Otto and Æthelred, the annalist remarks that Otto, despite being hard pressed, engages the invaders in battle and heroically wins the field.[17]

Though uplifting, this account of Otto's military prowess is less than accurate. Otto did mount such an attack, but it was not in response to raiders, as the unknown annalist suggests; rather, the Saracens enjoyed the support of a Byzantine court that preferred Saracen to Western control of southern Italy.[18] Furthermore, Otto was not victorious; he suffered a humiliating defeat and seems only just to have escaped with his life. Yet the annalist constructs a genealogy that links Otto to Edward the Elder and ultimately to Æthelred himself. Given that in the *Anglo-Saxon Chronicle* genealogical discourse and recitations of the West Saxon royal descent and regnal table often serve to emphasize the legitimacy of a particular king or candidate for the throne,[19] the reminder that Otto is, albeit weakly, connected to the West Saxon royal line asks the reader to compare Æthelred's and Otto's leadership.[20]

But the unknown annalist does not actually make the unlikely literal claim that Otto would be an acceptable candidate for the throne; rather, he positions Otto as an example of a fighting king in order to suggest a connection between fighting and Anglo-Saxon identity.[21] In essence, the Otto entry functions as an instance of hagiographic discourse. Briefly, Michel de Certeau points out that saints' lives are self-conscious sociological documents in which the 'life of a Saint is inscribed within the life of a group.'[22] These texts convey their 'self-consciousness by associating a *figure* with a *place*' and allow 'unity to be reestablished at a time when the group, through its development, runs the risk of being dispersed' (emphasis as printed).[23] In other words, there is a direct link between hagiographic discourse and the generation of identities, national and local.

Otto is clearly no saint in the literal religious sense. But when the annal is read as part of a hagiographic discourse in which national identity can be separated from the figure of the king and relocated in a military leader, the annalist's use of detail makes sense. His depiction of a fighting king who is related to Edward is intended to position Otto as a worthy heir to the identity of the Anglo-Saxon kingdom.

To a certain extent, the link between fighting and Anglo-Saxon identity is a justifiable interpretation of the entries for Edward's reign.

Upon accession, Edward inherits an internal threat to his authority. When his father Alfred the Great takes the throne, he also disinherits his nephews, and Alfred is successful in preventing any rebellion on their behalf.[24] Edward is marginally less persuasive than Alfred; his cousin rebels and he must go to war to protect his realm from internal and external threats.[25] For the unknown annalist's purpose, this defence is all that matters. Edward protects his claim to the throne by overcoming an internal enemy, defends his realm from external Danish raiders, and, according to one *Chronicle* tradition, uses battle to win the submission of virtually all the Anglo-Saxons living in the geographical territory of England.[26] In a hagiographic reading of the Alfred and Edward annals, the West Saxon royal family is a family that fights to save its kingdom. It is also a royal family whose people are defined by the king's willingness to fight. Just as fighting secures Edward's throne, so it also secures Otto a place in the West Saxon ruling dynasty.[27]

To interpret the Æthelred-Cnut annalist's depiction of the king as anything other than the work of a 'bitter genius,'[28] it is necessary to understand the Otto episode and the way in which hagiographic discourse meaningfully connects the annalist's emphasis on fighting, Otto's leadership, and Anglo-Saxon identity. In the history of the *Æthelred-Cnut Chronicle*, the king is not just faulted for not fighting. As the annalist would have it, Æthelred is explicitly stripped of his heritage and his people – the *Angelcynn* – precisely because he does not fight. Thus, though the Otto episode is short, it performs a significant function for the *Æthelred-Cnut Chronicle* as a whole: it prepares the Æthelred-Cnut annalist's deliberate relocation of Anglo-Saxon identity from the king to Ulfcytel and Archbishop Ælfheah, figures who are not royal but who earn their leadership of the *Angelcynn* through their willingness to fight.

The story of fighting and identity in Æthelred's kingdom begins anew with the Ulfcytel episode. In his entry for 1004, the Æthelred-Cnut annalist uses hagiographic discourse to show how Ulfcytel, a regional leader, performs in microcosm the ideal decision-making process – he chooses to fight once tribute and negotiation have failed. Yet even though Ulfcytel and men lose a significant battle, the Æthelred-Cnut annalist positions them as emblems of an ideal Anglo-Saxon England and generators of Anglo-Saxon identity.

In 1004, the Danish leader, Swein, and his fleet arrive in Norwich:

Þa gerædde Ulfcytel wið ða witan on Eastenglum þæt hit betere wære þæt mon wið þone here friðes ceapode, ær hi to mycelne hearm on ðam earde gedydon, for ðæm hi unwæres comon, 7 he fyrst næfde þæt he his fyrde gegaderede. Þa under ðam gripe þe him betweonan beon sceolde, þa bestæl se here up of scypon 7 wendon hiora fore to Þeodforda. Þa Ulfcytel þæt undergeat, þa sende he þæt mon sceolde þa scipu tohewan, ac hi abruðan þa ðe he to þohte. 7 he ða gegaderede his fyrde digolice swa he swyðost mihte ... þa com Ulfcytel mid his werode þæt hi ðær togædere fon sceoldon; 7 hi þær togædere fæstlice fengon, 7 micel wæl ðær on ægðre hand gefeol; ðær wearð Eastengla folces seo yld ofslagen. Ac gif þæt fulle mægen ðær wære, ne eodon hi næfre eft to scipon, swa hi sylfe sædon þæt hi næfre wyrsan handplegan on Angelcynne ne gemitton þonne Ulfcytel him to brohte.

Then Ulfcytel and the councillors in East Anglia decided that it would be better if they bought peace with the army before they [the army] did too much damage to the country, for they had come unexpectedly and he [Ulfcytel] had not had the time to raise his army. Then, under cover of the truce which was supposed to be between them, the army crept inland from the ships and wound their way to Thetford. When Ulfcytel learned this, then sent a message ordering that the ships be hacked to pieces, but those whom he designated for this failed. And then he gathered his army secretly, as quickly as he could ... Then Ulfcytel and his troops arrived in order to do battle there together. And they joined battle resolutely there, and many fell dead there on both sides. There the chief men of the East Anglian people were killed. If, however, their [the Anglo-Saxons'] full strength had been there, they [the Danes] would never have made it back to their ships. As they said themselves, they had never met worse hand-to-hand fighting among the *Angelcynn* than that which Ulfcytel dealt them.[29]

Because this entry follows the vivid account of defeat and treachery in the annal for 1003, the Ulfcytel episode has commonly been understood as a structural counterpoint to the story of *ealdormann* Ælfric, who betrays the king by fleeing from the fight. Unlike the treacherous Ælfric, Ulfcytel behaves appropriately even though he loses the engagement. But even this fact is less important than the significance of his presence on the field and the way in which that presence assumes the traditions of Anglo-Saxon identity.

Like Æthelred, his king, Ulfcytel begins by pursuing a policy of negotiation and tribute, but just as for Æthelred, this strategy fails. As for Æthelred, delegation as a response to the Danish raids does not inspire loyalty in Ulfcytel's men:[30] Ulfcytel, like Æthelred, is betrayed by those he delegates to act in his stead. Unlike Æthelred, however, Ulfcytel recognizes that the circumstances now demand personal intervention, and he proceeds to make up for the failed truce by personally taking the field. Though Ulfcytel is an influential retainer, he is subject to the king. Yet by the end of the annal, the people in his jurisdiction are defined not as Anglo-Saxons in general, but as a separate people, the 'Eastengla folces' (the East Anglian people) who have their own 'ylde' (chief men). Speaking, momentarily, from the Danish perspective, the annalist suggests that, because of their loyalty and willingness to fight, Ulfcytel and the group of men bound to him in lordship come to represent the *Angelcynn*, the whole of the Anglo-Saxon people.

By invoking the idea of the *Angelcynn* and by using this particular term, the Æthelred-Cnut annalist gives new meaning to the language of Anglo-Saxon identity begun in the Alfred annals. In the hands of the Æthelred-Cnut annalist, *Angelcynn* is consistently used to describe the Anglo-Saxons as a people under siege, a people distinct from the Danish invaders, but inclusive of the Danes who lived in Anglo-Saxon England.[31] This context is particularly important because it explains how a retainer, a man whose name (Ulfcytel Snilling) suggests that he was of Danish extraction, comes to represent the Anglo-Saxons.

By applying the word *Angelcynn* to Ulfcytel's East Anglians, the Æthelred-Cnut annalist transfers the ideological weight of the word *Angelcynn* from the people of Æthelred's kingdom to the people associated with Ulfcytel. He thereby shifts the locus of Anglo-Saxon identity from the ruling dynasty of the West Saxons to the leader of the East Anglians, a formerly powerful but now relatively minor and regional group that, in the face of Danish invasions, lost its independence from Alfred's Wessex.[32] Literally, then, though the Anglians have played a small part in Anglo-Saxon national history as we find it in the *Chronicle*, the Æthelred-Cnut annalist literally 'anglicizes' Anglo-Saxon identity (or underscores the literal Anglian element of the word *Angelcynn* and thus of Anglo-Saxon identity) and, effectively, allows the Anglians to reclaim their former importance. In so doing, he strategically uses the common medieval idea of a metonymic link between king and kingdom to measure Æthelred's disconnect from his people. And, more important, the annalist shows the implications of the identity created in the Alfred annals. Because in the *Chronicle*, Anglo-Saxon identity has thus far been connected to an ethos or practice, a successful national leader and generator of national identity does not have to be a king.

With the identity of the Anglo-Saxons thus decentred, the Æthelred-Cnut annalist then returns the figure of an ideal leader from the geographical and conceptual margins of the nation to a new centre: the church. Again, however, the point is not to make a new nation of Anglo-Saxons but to underscore the king's failure to protect his people and even the church. In a pointed comparison between the king and the archbishop, the annalist suggests that if Æthelred would but resist – and resistance here does not necessarily equate to fighting, though we might assume that the archbishop and his community did literally fight back – he would be performing the obligations of his office.

In 1011, Danish raiders lay siege to Canterbury. Initially, the community resists the invaders, but they are not given the chance to continue; the Danes gain entry to the cathedral community by virtue of the 'syruwrencas' (tricks) of Abbot Ælfmær, and Archbishop Ælfheah is taken hostage and eventually killed. The death of the archbishop is an important moment in Anglo-Saxon religious culture.[33] Ælfheah's death inspires a number of texts about his life and his passion, one of which – a *vita* – contrasts the success of the resisting archbishop with the failure of the defeated and hapless king.[34] There is no evidence that the Æthelred-Cnut annalist knew any of these works, but the informal life of Ælfheah included in the annals suggests his familiarity with either an Ælfheah tradition – be it textual or oral – or the events themselves.[35] More important, the contrast between the resisting archbishop and the negotiating king suggests that the Ælfheah episode is meaningful to the Æthelred-Cnut annalist's larger agenda, and this larger context explains its prominence in a chronicle where thus far ecclesiastical events have merited only a brief mention.

Significantly, the Æthelred-Cnut annalist does not lament the loss of the archbishop as an archbishop. In this account of the events of 1011, Ælfheah represents a model of leadership that Æthelred cannot match; the annalist uses his moving story to underscore his point about the culture of leadership by which the Anglo-Saxons are identified. For the annalist, an Anglo-Saxon leader should resist. So strong is the connection between resistance and Anglo-Saxon identity that, in 1011, the Æthelred-Cnut annalist transfers legitimate leadership of the country from the king who will not fight to the archbishop who, figuratively at least, will.³⁶ After the abduction of this figurehead, the annalist comments: 'Wæs ða ræpling se ðe ær wæs heafod Angelkynnes 7 Cristendomes' (He who formerly was the head of the *Angelcynn* and of Christendom was then a prisoner).³⁷

By using the word *Angelcynn*, the Æthelred-Cnut annalist again foregrounds the problem of Anglo-Saxon identity. Archbishop Ælfheah both leads the *Angelcynn* and represents their identity. But the annalist does not make the literal claim that Ælfheah should have succeeded Æthelred. Instead, he uses hagiographic discourse to confirm the connection between resistance and Anglo-Saxon identity: a fighting leader unifies his people and his will to fight for them defines that people. As Michel de Certeau puts it, 'In hagiography, individuality counts much less than character. The same features and the same episodes are passed along from one proper name to another; from all these floating elements, like an array of words and jewels, the combinations make up a fine figure and charge it with meaning.'³⁸

In the *Æthelred-Cnut Chronicle*, the king is not sufficiently present at the narrative centre, that is, on the battlefield, for him to be 'charged with meaning.' The figure of Ælfheah replaces him. Though Ælfheah is not a likely candidate for the throne, he nonetheless performs one of the offices of kingship – resistance or, more properly, defence – and thereby bears and generates Anglo-Saxon identity. The annalist's desire for this 'meaning' or identifying quality is further underscored by the pointed inclusion of this minilife of a martyr. Again, de Certeau: 'The Life of a Saint also points to the relation that the group holds with other groups. Thus the martyrdom tale is predominant wherever the community is very marginal, confronted with the threat of extinction ...'³⁹ Even though the annalist clearly suggests that the Anglo-Saxons are in great danger, Æthelred is not present; the king does not take the field so he does not take the risks that would enable him to become a martyr and have his history written as that of a martyr. By the end of the *Æthelred-Cnut Chronicle*, Æthelred may rule the Anglo-Saxons, but, the annalist suggests, they are no longer identified with and defined by their king; this function has passed to the archbishop.

Should the King Fight: A Homiletic Perspective

The clear shift of the Anglo-Saxons' identifying symbol from king to archbishop does not mean that the king should literally take the field; rather, this particular analysis of Anglo-Saxon history is a function of hagiographic discourse, a discourse that works to preserve a unifying symbol and produce a group identity. But while the *Æthelred-Cnut Chronicle* clearly has a hagiographical aspect, it also participates in a homiletic discourse that equally as clearly suggests the king should not fight. Like Malcolm Godden, I see the homiletic and hagiographic as complementary, but not just because they differ on what might be considered appropriate royal action.[40] Rather, I emphasize the way in which homiletic discourse minimizes the specifics of what would in hagiographic discourse be an identifying ethos or culture.

By way of its precepts and instructive mode, homiletic discourse links its addressees to a preexisting set of communal conventions and, in particular, to the non-identifying traditions of Christian faith and community. Thus while homiletic texts can frequently be addressed to communities under threat – Wulfstan's *Sermo Lupi ad Anglos* is a relevant example – homiletic discourse seeks to preserve the presence of the Christian faith in that community. It is not interested in the unique identity per se of that group. For example, though the *Sermo Lupi* is technically a sermon and not a homily, it – like other examples of homiletic discourse – addresses itself to the Anglo-Saxons and thus distinguishes the Anglo-Saxons from, say, the Franks, but it does not produce a set of identifying or defining characteristics for either people. Indeed, Wulfstan exhorts the Anglo-Saxons to return to the conventions and practices of their faith, a faith that both the Anglo-Saxons and the Franks share. In this regard, homiletic discourse is universalizing and not identifying.

Homiletic discourse is present in the Æthelred-Cnut annals in the Carolingian ideals of right kingship and specifically in the annalist's strategy of polarizing fighting and negotiating. Late tenth- and early eleventh-century Anglo-Saxon discussions of kingship occur in a wide variety of genres, but I am here concerned with certain of Ælfric's homilies, his translation of the Pseudo-Cyprian *De duodecim abusivis saeculi*, and Wulfstan's *Institutes of Polity*. Though they are very different from each other, these contemporary texts all suggest that a king, in this instance Æthelred, should not fight.

This position is not a peculiarity of post Benedictine Reform Anglo-Saxon England; rather, as it appears in these works, it is an Anglo-Saxon adaptation of the Carolingian mirrors for princes tradition.[41] I stress the Continental origin of these ideas not because I am interested in the question of relations between England and the Continent in the tenth century, but because the Carolingian background links Anglo-

Saxon England and its traditions to the Continent and the larger (and, in this part of the *Chronicle* at least, largely unseen) Christian world.[42] In other words, these texts are not unique compositions that identify Anglo-Saxon kingship from its counterparts; rather, they show how Anglo-Saxon kingship can be articulated as a continuation of a clearly defined tradition of ecclesiastical thought. Homiletic discourse thus connects what appear to be Anglo-Saxon ideas to the non-identifying tradition of Christian kingship. In this world, kingship is imagined as an office with clearly specified duties. And though in certain limited and defined circumstances, an ideal Christian king may wage war, a king is not primarily a warrior.

In late tenth- and early eleventh-century Anglo-Saxon England, the idea that the king should not fight is predicated on the notion that the welfare of the kingdom depends on the well-being of the king. Hincmar, writer of a number of texts on ideal kingship, dedicates a whole chapter of his *De regis persona et regio ministerio* to a discussion of the relationship between a good king and the welfare of the people.[43] He quotes Pseudo-Cyprian's ninth abuse almost in full. It is not just that a bad king will make the people unhappy; a bad king, a king who cannot perform the *justitia regis* (royal justice), stands to see his people beset by all kinds of ills, including bad, unwise, and drunk councillors, poor harvests, and invaders.[44] In their homiletic work, Wulfstan and Ælfric tighten this formulation: 'Þurh unwisne cyning folc wyrð geyrmed for oft, næs æne, for his misræde. Þurh cynincges wisdom folc wyrð gesælig and gesundful and sigefæst' (The people are made miserable very often by a foolish king, not just once, because of his misguidance. Through a king's wisdom, the people are blessed, prosperous, and victorious).[45] This distinct formulation of the issue reworks what is for Hincmar and Pseudo-Cyprian a moral problem of wisdom and counsel into a pragmatic question of royal justice and utility.

For Ælfric and Wulfstan, a good king is a wise king, and, most important, royal wisdom depends on just councillors. It is not only that, as in Carolingian texts, the king should listen to his councillors and know how to pick good ones; it is, as Ælfric puts it in his homily *Dominica post ascensionem Domini*, the *witan*'s duty not to hide their *ræd* and 'þæs behofað se cyning þæt he clypige to his witum, / and be heora ræde, na be rununge fare' (it behooves the king to embrace his wise men and act according to their counsel, not according to whispering).[46] This wisdom differs slightly from the Carolingian concept of royal *sapientia* – in which wisdom is figured as a virtue – in that the

Anglo-Saxon homilists minimize the importance of individual study and make wisdom both a theory of government and a vision of social order.[47]

In this view of the world, the king does not fight. When constructing the king's ideal society, Ælfric uses his homily, the *Maccabees*, to establish three social estates or classes, the *laboratores*, *oratores*, and *bellatores*: those who work, those who pray, and those who fight.[48] The same distinction can also be found in his pastoral letter to Wulfstan, bishop of York, and again in the *Letter to Sigeweard* that prefaces Ælfric's translation of the *Old English Heptateuch*.[49] Ælfric and Wulfstan add the king and *witan* into this scheme of social order, devising duties for the king and his advisors. Building on this principle, Wulfstan uses his *Institutes of Polity* to discuss the duties of all classes of men, stating that the kingship depends on every member of these classes fulfilling their duties.[50] In the letter prefacing his translation of the New Testament, Ælfric, discussing ways of coping with the evil of the sixth age of the world, advises the *witan* to 'smeagan mid wislicum geþeahte, þonne on mancinne to micel yfel bið, hwilc þæra stelenna þæs cinestoles wære tobrocen, 7 betan þone sona' (consider with wise thoughts, when there is too much evil among mankind, which of the throne's supports is broken and mend it immediately).[51] In this view of government, the king and his councillors are mutually responsible for each other and jointly responsible for the well-being of the kingdom.

In this way, Ælfric asserts, a king can best bear the authority invested in him. Explicitly contradicting his saints' lives, where it is appropriate for a king to fight, Ælfric claims in his *Wyrdwriteras* fragment, a homiletic text that scholars usually read as a reflection on contemporary events, that a king should not fight. Reworking the traditional Carolingian iconography of King David as a fighting king,[52] Ælfric imagines David as a leader who shares authority: 'for þan ðe an man ne mæg æghwar beon, and ætsomne / ealle þing aberan, þeah ðe he anweald hæbbe' (for one man cannot be everywhere and bear everything at once, even though he has authority).[53] His advice is that kings like David should stay away from the battlefield lest they weaken their countries by not being available to take care of other business. Ælfric is quite explicit on this point. David's thanes turn to him, saying 'Ne scealt ðu næfre heonon forð / mid us to gefeohte, þinum feore to plyhte, / þelæste þu adwæsce Israhela leohtfæt: – / þæt wæs Dauid him sylf be ðam ðe hi sædon swa' (You shall never henceforth / go with us to battle, to endanger your life / lest you extinguish the light of

Israel: – / that was David himself about whom they spoke so).[54] That fighting endangers the kingdom is clear enough; more important, however, is the claim that risking the king risks the 'light of Israel.' While this makes literal sense for David, when it is extended as an example for contemporary Anglo-Saxon kings, Ælfric implies that the individual king is less important than the office he both represents and fills. Further, the specific religious freight of the phrase 'light of Israel' adds weight to the idea that a simple secular misdeed might, in this context, be seen as a sin.

Fighting, Negotiating, and Failing at Both

In essence, then, homiletic discourse of the late tenth and early eleventh century clearly suggests that, in most circumstances, a king should not fight; he should delegate and negotiate. And Æthelred does negotiate and delegate. But the homiletic discourse of ecclesiastical kingship also requires the king to protect his kingdom, and, according to the Æthelred-Cnut annalist, this is an obligation at which Æthelred fails. Again, the fact of the failure is less important than the annalist's representation of the king's shortcomings. The annalist uses the same homiletic discourse by which he exculpates Æthelred from fighting to cast the king's failure to protect his people as an abuse of royal power. In so doing, the Æthelred-Cnut annalist narrates the loss of the kingdom as the consequence of these, the king's sins.

The central texts are Pseudo-Cyprian's ninth abuse, a *rex iniquus* (an unjust king) and, in particular, Ælfric's translation thereof. Among other duties, a good king 'scal biwerian widewan and steopbern and stale aleggen and heordom for-beodan. and þeouas addriuan. of his erde mid alle. ... godes ministre he scal mundian efre. and fedan wrecchan. and festliche winnan wið onsiȝend-ne here. and halden his eþel' (shall defend the widows and orphans, suppress stealing, forbid prostitution, and completely drive thieves out of his land ... He shall always protect the ministers of God, and feed the poor, and resolutely struggle against the invading army and hold his homeland).[55] Ælfric's language here is very careful. 'Festliche winnan' does not necessarily imply that a king should personally lead the fight, though it does not exclude it either. Ælfric requires the king only to resist, fight, or struggle resolutely, steadily, and constantly; these things he might do with political measures without even taking the field. In other words, it does not matter how Æthelred defends his kingdom, as long as he protects his people.

Just as homiletic discourse explains the king's obligations, so it also details the consequences of failure and therewith provides the connection to salvation historiography: 'And ʒif hi forsihð þas isetnesse and þas lare; þene bið his erd ihened oft and ilome eiðer ʒe on herʒunʒe. ʒe on hungre. ʒe on cwalme. ʒe on uniwidere. ʒe on wilde deoran' (And if he rejects these instructions and these teachings; then his land will again and again be afflicted either by invasions, or by hunger, or by pestilence, or by bad weather, or by wild animals).[56] Ælfric stresses that this and the other punishments are not specific to an individual king or nation; nor even are the punishments directly related to the identity of that nation. Rather, these are the punishments that the books of Christian tradition require: 'Wite ec þe king hu hit is icweðen on boken. ʒif he rihtwisnesse ne halt. þet swa swa he is on heuene on his kine setle to-foran oðer mennen; swa he bið eft iniþered on þan neoþemeste pinan under þan unrihtwise deouele þe he er iherd and icwemde' (Let the king also take note of what the books say. If he does not hold to righteousness, just as he is lifted up on his throne before other men, so he will be cast down again to the very lowest torture under the [same] unrighteous devil that he previously obeyed and pleased).[57] Sin on the part of the king leads to the loss of the kingdom.

The history of the *Æthelred-Cnut Chronicle*, while not directly modelled on Ælfric's work, offers a similar understanding of the connection between royal authority and the security of the realm. When it becomes clear that Æthelred's strategy fails to protect his people – even though he manages to negotiate peace with Olaf, other Danish leaders do not keep the peace – the nobility becomes disheartened and disloyal.[58] For the annalist, this behaviour is reprehensible. Although he admonishes the nobles, the poor behaviour of the king's men reflects most strongly on the king. In his version of Æthelred's history, disloyalty is the logical consequence of a situation in which the king and *witan* not only fail to protect but also actively oppress the people.[59] In the terms presented by both Pseudo-Cyprian and Ælfric, this abuse leads to the loss of the kingdom.

Æthelred's Sins?

To show the extent to which Æthelred's responsibility for the loss of the kingdom is a deliberate consequence of the annalist's decision to write a salvation history, I now examine the ways in which he narrates the wrongdoing for which he holds Æthelred responsible. The Æthelred-

Cnut annalist claims that the Anglo-Saxons' misery is a consequence of the king's inability to choose the right strategy at the right time: 'Ealle þas ungesælða us gelumpon þuruh unrædas' (All these misfortunes happened to us because of poor counsel).[60] As I suggested above, if the annalist's claim is taken literally, it is easy to position Æthelred as a *rex iniquus* and hold him responsible for the loss of his kingdom. But because the Æthelred-Cnut annalist writes the history of Æthelred's reign as a salvation history, neither the annals nor the image of Æthelred, *rex iniquus*, are a full or accurate representation of the situation.

Indeed, the image of Æthelred as incompetent, 'abusive,' or both is a deliberate construction. Though, as I describe above, the annalist claims that Æthelred attacks his people, he does not include in the *Æthelred-Cnut Chronicle* the social and political contexts that would show the king protecting his subjects and competently performing the responsibilities of his office.[61] In the 990s, the annalist weaves into his narrative brief notices of royal and civil appointments, punishments for certain noblemen, treachery on the part of others, tribute payments, and the negotiations that resulted in a cessation of hostilities between Olaf and the king.[62] The history behind these events is important, but absent from the annals. As Simon Keynes has argued, when seen in the light of the politics of Æthelred's succession, the king's apparent iniquity and incompetence look very different.[63]

Similarly, to position Æthelred as an unjust king, the annalist shows him attacking his land: the annalist states that the crops are blighted and that Æthelred destroys the diocese of Rochester.[64] But this statement of fact again ignores the larger history of Æthelred's reign. Despite a flurry of activity at court as Æthelred, a young king, recovers from a succession crisis and secures his place on the throne, the annalist does not explain how the raid on Rochester – which Simon Keynes analyses as the result of political tension between the king and Ælfstan, bishop of Rochester – relates to Æthelred's position.[65] The king's political position also explains Æthelred's actions in 1000. In that entry, the annalist offers his readers an unanalysed account of the king's punishing raid on Cumberland. Without comment, this seems to be an act of tyranny, but in its political context, this is less another incident of royal injustice than an effort to discipline those in Strathclyde and the Isle of Man who in the past had helped the Danish raiders from Dublin.[66]

A similar portrayal of the king lies behind the annalist's account of the St Brice's Day massacre. In other sources, the 1002 massacre of the Danes is discussed as a problematic reaction to a conspiracy that threatened the king's life,⁶⁷ but though the threat of a conspiracy is offered as an explanation in the annals, the overall context transforms the warning into another example of *unrædas*. The annalist makes no mention of any evidence that would support the claim of a threat to the king and, without such a claim, the king's reaction to what he was told is recast as an act of self-protection that attacks members of the *Angelcynn*: 'Se cyng het ofslean ealle þa deniscan men þe on Angelcynne wæron; ðis wæs gedon on Britius mæssedæig, forðam þam cyninge wæs gecyd þæt hi woldan hine besyrwan æt his life' (The king commanded all the Danish men who were among the *Angelcynn* to be killed; this was carried out on St Brice's feast day, because the king had been informed that they wanted to deceive him and take his life).⁶⁸

Given that, for the most part, the Danes of Anglo-Saxon England lived in the Danelaw, a separate but not restricted space, the phrase 'on Angelcynne' (among the *Angelcynn*) indicates not just that the Danes were living among the *Angelcynn*, but that there were, as the Alfred annals suggest, Danish members of the *Angelcynn*.⁶⁹ The history of this term as the *Chronicle* word for the people created and protected by the king's lordship means that Æthelred's attack on members of the *Angelcynn* is horrific not just because the king attacks his subjects, but because the annalist's choice of words frames the king's order as an assault on his people and on the identity associated with that people.

A brief consideration of yet another narrative the annalist chooses to omit – the history of Æthelred's attempts to halt the Danish raids through diplomatic means – underscores the idea that Æthelred's political incompetence is a deliberate construction.⁷⁰ In 991, for example, the king draws up a treaty with Richard, duke of Normandy, dissolving hostilities between Anglo-Saxon England and Normandy and stating that neither would use their land as a base for their operations. He strengthens this agreement by marrying Emma, Richard's sister, in 1002. The annalist mentions Emma's arrival in England, but he does not discuss the treaty or the significance of the king's marriage. In the early 990s, Æthelred continues to advance and promote new families and change the environment of his court. Desiring to tighten his control over his kingdom, he appoints three new *ealdormenn*.⁷¹ The record of these appointments is also missing from the annals.

Between 1002 and 1006, the problem of coordinating the defence of his realm leads Æthelred to appoint Ulfcytel to East Anglia and Uhtræd of Bamborough to the northern regions.⁷² Again, in an effort to organize the safety of a particularly troubled region, Æthelred in 1007 reverses a twenty-year-old policy of dividing the responsibility for Mercia, placing it all under *ealdormann* Eadric's control. He pledges his daughters in marriage for the loyalty of these men.[73] But even though in the tenth and eleventh centuries marriages of princesses to nobles are rare, the annalist, removing these appointments and marriages from their political and social contexts, ignores Æthelred's attempts to use political relationships to secure his *ealdormenn*'s loyalty and ensure the defence of his kingdom.[74]

Thus while the Æthelred-Cnut annalist would have his readers believe that the damaged land, demoralized people, and what he calls treachery and cowardice are direct results of the king's personal poor strategy and his *unrædas*, his account cannot be taken as a literal record of the events of Æthelred's reign. But though this perspective does not change the outcome of the annalist's account – the Anglo-Saxons still lose their kingdom – understanding the *Æthelred-Cnut Chronicle* as an example of salvation history makes sense of the repeated claim that the king and his *unrædas* are responsible for the loss of his realm.

Salvation History and Identity

Choosing salvation history as the dominant narrative mode for the history of Æthelred's reign influences both the facts that constitute the history of the annals and the meaning of those facts. Salvation history requires the king to be held responsible for the fall of his kingdom; the annalist shapes the facts to make such a reading of his text inevitable. But salvation history also signifies in the context of the *Anglo-Saxon Chronicle* as a whole. In articulating a new identity for the Anglo-Saxons, the Alfred annals perform a function that salvation history cannot do. But, in that the Æthelred-Cnut annalist narrates the fall of the Anglo-Saxon kingdom and the relocation of Anglo-Saxon identity from the king to the archbishop and others, the conventions of salvation history are more than appropriate for his historiographical purpose. Indeed, returning to salvation history for this task reinforces the idea that the *Chronicle* annals narrating the story of a kingdom founded in the face of conquest also concomitantly articulate its identity.

The many manuscripts of Wulfstan's *Sermo Lupi* support the idea that the connection between salvation history and articulations of identity is relevant in the annalist's present. In this text, Wulfstan considers the relationship between the Danish raids and the Anglo-Saxons' sins. All five extant versions of the *Sermo Lupi* are very specific about the fact that the Anglo-Saxons are sinners, and all the versions detail the nature and local effects of their sin. But the *Sermo Lupi* is not just a catalogue of transgressions and their effects on the Anglo-Saxons. In particular, redactions I and E preserve a passage that explicitly links sin to the loss of the Anglo-Saxons' land, sovereignty, and identity:

> Ac la, on Godes naman utan don swa us neod is, beorgan us sylfum swa we geornost magan þe læs we ætgædere ealle forweorðan. An þeodwita wæs on Brytta tidum Gildas hatte. Se awrat be heora misdædum hu hy mid heora synnum swa oferlice swyþe God gegræmedan þæt he let æt nyhstan Engla here heora eard gewinnan 7 Brytta dugeþe fordon mid ealle. And þæt wæs geworden þæs þe he sæde, þurh ricra reaflac 7 þurh gitsunge wohgestreona, ðurh leode unlaga 7 þurh wohdomas, ðurh biscopa asolcennesse 7 þurh lyðre yrhðe Godes bydela þe soþes geswugedan ealles to gelome 7 clumedan mid ceaflum þær hy scoldan clypian.

> So, truly, let us in the name of God do what is needful for us; let us save ourselves as zealously as we can lest we all perish together. There was, in the time of the Britons, a learned man called Gildas. He wrote about the [Britons'] misdeeds and about how with their sins they angered God so very excessively that he finally permitted the Anglo-Saxon army to conquer their land and completely destroy the host of the Britons. And everything that he said came to pass because of robberies by the powerful, the greediness for ill-gotten property, the people's illegal acts, the unjust judgments, the bishops' laziness, and the hateful cowardice of God's preachers who all too often were silent about the truth and muttered [it] into their jaws when they should have shouted it out.[75]

The story of Gildas and the Britons is the last *exemplum* of the *Sermo* and its instructional value for reading the *Æthelred-Cnut Chronicle* is complicated. In the rhetoric of the sermon, Wulfstan offers this example in order that he and the Anglo-Saxons might not *forweorðan* (perish) together. But 'perish' here is ambiguous. On one level, Wulfstan refers to the Anglo-Saxons' afterlife; if they do not reform, they will suffer eternal damnation. But the example he gives, that of the Britons, also speaks to the survival of the Anglo-Saxons' identity as a people; it is an example taken from the discourse of salvation historiography, an example that plays on Gildas's own salvation history.[76]

Wulfstan claims that many of the Anglo-Saxons' sins duplicate those of the Britons and many are worse. But the link between the homiletic understanding of sin and the conventions of salvation historiography is more important than the sins themselves.[77] For the Britons, the wages of sin are not just the loss of their territory, but also the loss of their identity as a people. Wulfstan points out that wrongdoing allows the Anglo-Saxons to conquer the Britons' land. But he also makes a clear distinction between conquering the Britons' 'eard' (land) and the destruction of the Britons themselves. By adding the phrase 'mid ealle' to the last clause of his sentence, Wulfstan stresses the destruction of the people. While the loss of a homeland is significant in itself, the destruction of the *duguþ* (the retainers or army) has even more cultural meaning. Separating land from cultural identity, Wulfstan implies that if the retainers had survived, so might have British identity. But as it is, Gildas and his historical narrative are the only surviving icons of Britain and the Britons. The lesson for the Anglo-Saxons is not just that they should behave better – though, of course, they should – it is that sin can destroy the identity of people and nation.

Even though the manuscript history of the *Sermo Lupi* suggests a relatively wide dissemination of the text, there is no evidence that the Æthelred-Cnut annalist knew Wulfstan's work. Nonetheless, the Gildas example provides a contemporary model for explaining how the eleventh-century Æthelred-Cnut annalist narrates the transfer of Anglo-Saxon identity from the king to the conqueror. In 1013, Æthelred goes into exile and the people accept Swein as their king. But Swein's reign is not long-lived. When he dies, in 1014, the Danes elect Cnut as their king. The Anglo-Saxon *witan* interprets these events as a succession crisis and reacts by inviting Æthelred to return to the throne, but not without conditions. In response to the *witan*'s request for 'rihtlicor' (more just) rule, Æthelred promises 'þæt he him hold hlaford beon wolde 7 ælc þæra ðinga betan þe hi ealle ascunudon, 7 ælc þara ðinga forgyfen beon sceolde þe him gedon oððe gecweden wære, wið þam ðe hi ealle anrædlice butan swicdome to him gecyrdon' (that he would be a loyal lord to them, and amend each of the things that they all hated, and that everything that had been done or said against him would be forgiven, provided that they all submitted resolutely to him without any betrayal).[78]

The language of the request and the promise are significant. By the terms of ideal Christian kingship, Æthelred has been a *rex iniquus* (an unjust king), and he promises to reform if his people are faithful.[79] Suggesting that the promise is satisfactory to *witan*, people, and king, the annalist notes that Æthelred was well received. But even though Æthelred has promised to do better, the annalist, complying with the conventions of salvation history, makes it perfectly clear that he does not mend his ways. The king can thus be held responsible for the loss of the kingdom.

In 1015, Æthelred seizes the property of two powerful thanes who were deceived by Eadric; indeed, Pauline Stafford shows how the details of the annal suggest that Æthelred conspired with Eadric.[80] As the annalist narrates events, Æthelred's actions appear to precipitate rebellion and facilitate further treachery, treachery that results in the West Saxons' submission to Cnut. When Æthelred takes Sigeferth's and Morcar's property, the king's son, *ætheling* Edmund takes Sigeferth's widow against Æthelred's will, heads north, takes their land, and establishes himself as lord of their people. When Edmund and Eadric are due to fight the Danes in the North, Eadric deceives Edmund and then both he and the West Saxons submit to Cnut. In 1016, when the people explicitly ask for the king to join them on the field, Æthelred refuses.[81] From this moment on, Æthelred's people appear leaderless; the king is powerless to stop the betrayals by Eadric and incapable of gathering a force loyal enough to mount a credible defence.

Further, the annalist suggests, the culture of disloyalty survives beyond the king himself. After Æthelred's death, the kingdom passes to *ætheling* Edmund, his son. In the decisive battle, King Edmund gathers all the 'Engla þeode' (the Anglo-Saxon people) – the designation is significant for prior to this moment, the annalist states only that Edmund gathers his army, his 'fyrd.' Here, however, Edmund leads the Anglo-Saxons, but he loses. By the terms of the peace negotiations, the kingdom is divided: Edmund 'feng' (succeeded) to Wessex and Cnut to Mercia; the two kings seal the peace with hostages and oaths; and peace is purchased from the Danish army.[82]

The annalist separates the negotiations over territory and authority from the discussion of Anglo-Saxon identity. As the annalist would have it, even before Cnut takes control of the land, the identity of the *Angelcynn* passes from Anglo-Saxon hands into those of the Danes:

Þa dyde Eadric ealdorman swa swa he ær oftor dyde: astealde þæne fleam ærest mid Magesæton 7 aswac swa his cynehlaforde 7 ealre Angelcynnes þeode. Þær ahte Cnut sige 7 gefeht him ealle Engla þeode.

Then *ealdormann* Eadric did as he had done so often before; he was the first among the Magesæton [a local group] to start the flight. And in so doing, he betrayed his *cynehlaford* and all the people of the *Angelcynn*. There Cnut possessed the victory, and he won all the Anglo-Saxon people for himself.[83]

In this picture, Cnut defeats the Anglo-Saxons, but not because he is the better general; rather, the Anglo-Saxons lose because Edmund inherits and cannot undo the culture left by Æthelred. The annalist explicitly shows Eadric betraying his *cynehlaford* (lord) and then the whole of the *Angelcynn*, the Anglo-Saxon people, who in this narrative are identified by a fighting king. The importance of this loss is underscored by the way in which the annalist describes Cnut's victory. Cnut does not immediately win the land of the Anglo-Saxons – he gains the territory later – he here wins the 'Engla þeode' (the Anglo-Saxon people). And when in 1017 Cnut becomes king, having already won this people, he accedes to not just the land but to the 'Angelcynnes ryce' (kingdom of the *Angelcynn*). Thus, both linguistically and conceptually, the annalist writes the political change of conquest as a change in the bearer and generator of Anglo-Saxon identity.

Making Meaning

To read the *Æthelred-Cnut Chronicle* as a narrative of disintegration and thus as salvation history is to focus on its genre and to shift critical attention from the problems of explaining the king's dramatic loss. Simon Keynes has already argued that the many studies undertaking this task are susceptible to misinterpreting the annalist's rhetoric, and he has clearly shown the folly of taking the Æthelred-Cnut annalist literally.[84] But although Keynes sensitively demonstrates how influential the annals have been, he consistently characterizes the annalist's rhetoric as 'personal' and 'idiosyncratic,' and thus unreliable.[85] He thereby misunderstands the relationship between the annalist's flights of rhetoric and the annalist's historiographic project.

The Æthelred-Cnut annalist's facts can be shown to be inaccurate or, at least, selectively presented, but what Keynes would have us see as the annalist's foibles are echoed by contemporary figures like Ælfric and Wulfstan and are preserved, as Keynes himself notes, by such mainstream medieval historians as William of Malmesbury, John of Worcester, and Henry of Huntingdon.[86] While no one would argue for the complete historical accuracy of all or, indeed, any of these figures, to suggest that they are all historically unreliable is a misleading blanket assessment.[87] That these important writers respond to the Æthelred-Cnut annalist by preserving his quirks suggests that the question of Æthelred's responsibility and the meaning of the *Æthelred-Cnut Chronicle* are more complicated than the terms 'personal' and 'idiosyncratic' might imply.

By retaining the idea that Æthelred is somehow responsible for the loss of his kingdom, William of Malmesbury, Henry of Huntingdon, and other medieval figures see in the *Æthelred-Cnut Chronicle* what many modern historians have missed: the connection between the Æthelred-Cnut annals, Carolingian mirrors for princes, and salvation histories, narratives that understand conquest and invasion as a divine punishment for sin. Because these texts reinforce the tenets of the Christian religion, any identity they express is one of faith. This conceptualization of history, a view that was well known in Anglo-Saxon England, changes how we understand the narrative content and meaning of the *Æthelred-Cnut Chronicle* as a record for both Æthelred and Cnut.

When read as a history for Æthelred II, the annals do not function as a collective narrative that places lordship at the centre of the new kingdom and its identity. Nor do they interpret conquest and invasion positively. Rather, by assenting to the Christian theory of historical causality – political change is caused by sin – the Æthelred-Cnut annalist integrates the particular story of the loss of Anglo-Saxon dominion into the general narrative of Christianity. As salvation history, the *Æthelred-Cnut Chronicle* understands conquest and invasion as a necessary part of the divine plan. Æthelred fails because he, like all the other kings in the tradition of salvation historiography, is supposed to. What at first seems to be the story of personal incompetence is instead merely the necessary preface for the coming of the next kingdom. In the accession of Cnut, that kingdom comes.

CHAPTER FIVE

Unmaking Æthelred but Making Cnut

When read as a history of the reign of Æthelred II, the annals from 983 to 1022 explain the loss of the kingdom.[1] But this narrative does not fully account for the explicit lordship language and ideology underpinning the portrayal of Æthelred's final defeats or the representation of the Danish Conquest as a series of accessions founded on Cnut's lordship relations. When read as a history that legitimizes Cnut, however, the annals form part of a larger history of the *Angelcynn*, a people created and defined in *Chronicle* narratives of conquest and invasion by the king's performance of his lordship obligations.

As in the previous chapter, Æthelred's wrongdoing is a productive point of entry into the *Chronicle* history. In the entry for 1014, the annalist has Æthelred acknowledge his mistakes and promise to reform everything that the people dislike, provided that they are faithful to him.[2] Then balancing this faithfulness, the king promises to be loyal to his people. Conventional interpretations of the Æthelred-Cnut annals prioritize the entries that feature the king's inability to keep his promise and carry out his duties.[3] In so doing, they create an all-encompassing narrative – a salvation history – of a corrupt realm in which Æthelred is responsible for the loss of the kingdom. Such readings give the king's promise little weight.

But the promise disturbs the narrative of sin and wrongdoing. Instead of recording a Danish triumph over Anglo-Saxon chaos, the annalist uses the king's promise to form the centre of a new narrative in which Cnut defeats the Anglo-Saxons, wins their loyalty, and then asserts his lordship over a defeated people. Startlingly different from the view expounded in the Æthelred history, this new perspective on the *Æthelred-Cnut Chronicle* positions the narrative of Cnut's accession as an extension of the story of Æthelred's poor lordship ties. In essence, the annalist's focus on the ethos of lordship transforms what we are accustomed to reading as a story of rupture into one of continuity. This is not a moralizing story of corruption but a narrative in which a failure of secular lordship ties is counteracted by the creation of a new culture of shared lordship. This is the history of and for Cnut's reign.

To understand why lordship is so essential to the discourses of royal authority and post-Conquest Anglo-Scandinavian identity, I consider the relationship of the Æthelred-Cnut annals to Cnut's 1018 law code, his 1020 letter to his people, and parts of II Cnut, that is, to the legal works associated with Archbishop Wulfstan.[4] In the 1018 code that reports the peace making between the Danes and the Anglo-Saxons and establishes the laws by which they will order their society, the Anglo-Saxons are asked to be loyal to their new king.[5] As if in response, the 1020 letter promises that the king will be loyal to his new people, and chapters 69–83 of II Cnut discuss potential lordship abuses by the king.[6]

Like the Æthelred-Cnut annals, none of these texts positively defines loyalty or loyal actions for either the lord or the man.[7] Rather, the Cnut legal texts establish a discourse of Anglo-Scandinavian identity that resonates strongly with the ideology of lordship articulated in the Alfred annals. In so doing, the laws and letters create a larger, albeit unacknowledged, interpretive context for the Æthelred-Cnut annals. The work of the annalist is no longer that of an individual; rather, it is part of a widespread, official discourse of Cnut's authority and Anglo-Scandinavian identity.

Recent studies of Cnut's accession have brought out the unexpected historical importance of lordship.[8] In their explorations of the king's treatment of the Anglo-Saxon *ealdormenn*, his administrative innovations, and his choices for the new rank of earl, historians have shown how Cnut used his lordship to take and maintain governmental control over his new people. Yet those facts do not explain how Cnut conquered and settled Anglo-Saxon England, nor do they explain the annalist's presentation of the changeover of power as an exercise of lordship. Furthermore, because these studies place Æthelred's mishaps of the centre of the text, they do not produce readings that explain how the annals signify in the new Anglo-Danish kingdom.

If instead we see the legal texts' ethos of lordship as an interpretive frame, a new narrative emerges that replaces the *Æthelred-Cnut Chronicle* story of two kings, one successful and one not, with a study of lordship. In the new history, the annalist addresses the possibility that a leader might betray his people, construes the reciprocal loyalty of man and lord as fundamental to both social order and collective identity, and encourages the king to fulfil his obligations to his people. By positioning Cnut as a more dedicated and loyal king than Æthelred, the annalist's history claims the Dane as an effective continuator for and the legitimate inheritor of the people known as the *Angelcynn*.[9]

The notion of continuity is central to understanding the historiography of the Æthelred-Cnut annals. When they are read as a history for Cnut, the entries for Æthelred's reign effectively develop the ideology of lordship that the Alfred annalist began. Like the Alfred annalist, the Æthelred-Cnut annalist traces the development of the king's lordship relations by pursuing the history of the *Angelcynn*. But at the conclusion of the Æthelred-Cnut history, the *Angelcynn* are the people lost by Æthelred's poor lordship bonds and won by what the annalist presents as Cnut's acceptance of his obligation to be loyal to his people and his ability to create such loyal lordship ties. The annalist's prominent and careful stress on the story of the *Angelcynn* highlights his strategy of narrating the crisis of conquest as a problem of lordship relations. Thus, the Æthelred-Cnut annals continue the discourse of Anglo-Saxon identity and develop the Alfred annalist's approach to writing history.

Salvation History and the Unmaking of Æthelred

The narrative that holds Æthelred responsible for the loss of his kingdom begins before the account of the 1016–17 passage of dominion.[10] But for the moment, I focus only on the annals for 1014, 1015, and 1016. In these entries, the explanatory power of the discourse of salvation history breaks down. In 1014, Æthelred is recalled from exile; as he reassumes his throne, the king promises 'þæt he him hold hlaford beon wolde 7 ælc þæra ðinga betan þe hi ealle ascunudon, 7 ælc þara ðinga forgyfen beon sceolde þe him gedon oððe gecweden wære, wið þam ðe hi ealle anrædlice butan swicdome to him gecyrdon' (that he would be a loyal lord to them, and amend each of the things that they all hated, and that everything that had been done or said against him would be forgiven, provided that they all submitted resolutely to him without any betrayal).[11] The annalist claims that Æthelred and his people 'fulne freondscipe gefæstnode mid worde 7 mid wedde on ægþre healfe' (established full friendship on both sides with both words and oaths).[12] In other words, Æthelred's people agree to accept his lordship, and Æthelred agrees to fulfil his lordship obligations.

The annalist works out the ramifications of this promise in the lordship narrative. He begins in 1015 by revealing the inefficacy of the promise as a way of gaining and sustaining the loyalty of Æthelred's men. Just one year after Æthelred's return from exile, *ealdormann* Eadric invites two thanes, Sigeferth and Morcar, into his chamber, but he betrays them and they are killed.[13] The king's son, *ætheling* Edmund, takes Sigeferth's widow against Æthelred's will and proceeds north, taking possession of both men's estates and establishing himself as lord of their people.[14] When the Danes appear and both Eadric and Edmund are to lead the resistance, Eadric tries to betray Edmund, and both Eadric and the West Saxons submit to Cnut.[15] The annalist uses these events to show that, despite his promise, Æthelred cannot maintain the loyalty of his men.

The extent to which Æthelred's lordship relations are broken is revealed in a deeper consideration of the personalities involved in these betrayals. Edmund is Æthelred's eldest surviving son (of his first wife, Ælfgifu); his claim to the throne is threatened by the consecration of the king's second wife, Emma, and the concomitant strengthening of her sons' claims. Given the important part Edmund had played in Æthelred's return from exile, Pauline Stafford suggests, Æthelred would have felt threatened by the number of potential candidates for the throne.[16] This context makes sense of Edmund's actions and the detail the annalist includes. Edmund revolts against his father and heads for the North to establish a power base.[17] But this is not the story the annalist tells. His focus on lordship bonds transforms the political history of succession into an exploration of lordship as the foundation of royal authority. Thus Edmund's actions register alongside the rebellions of Æthelwold[18] and Æthelbald[19] as the product of poor family and lordship bonds, and the story of the rebellion makes a strong counterpoint to the loyalty implied by the king's promise.

Even as he pursues the narrative of poor lordship, the annalist is also careful to insist that the problem is not uniquely Æthelred's. Working against the discourse of salvation history, wherein Æthelred's poor lordship relations figure as a personal and individual weakness, the annalist systematizes the Anglo-Saxons' troubles into a culture that goes beyond the individual king. When Æthelred dies in 1016, his successor is Edmund Ironside – the very *ætheling* who disobeys his father and king in 1015 and betrays him in 1016 by ravaging Northumbria and by not fighting the Danes.[20] In other words, the Anglo-Saxons are now led by one of the symbols of Æthelred's lordship failures.

As the annalist pursues his narrative of flawed lordship, it becomes clear that Edmund will also fail at his lordship relations. When Edmund takes the throne, the annalist says only that 'ealle ða witan þa on Lundene wæron 7 seo burhwaru gecuron Eadmund to cyninge, 7 he his rice heardlice werode þa hwile þe his tima wæs' (all the *witan* who were in London and the citizens [of London] chose Edmund as king, and, for the duration of his reign, he defended his kingdom boldly).[21] In stressing Edmund's bravery and willingness to fight, the annalist appears to address what would be one of the most pressing problems of Æthelred's reign: the king's unwillingness to take the field. But his narrative then goes on to show that fighting is insufficient.

In his account of the defeat by which Edmund loses Mercia and Cnut wins the *Angelcynn*, the annalist shows that disloyalty lies behind the moment of the Danish Conquest. Though Edmund successfully wins back the West Saxons who have previously submitted to the Danes, he ultimately loses Mercia because he and his people are betrayed by *ealdormann* Eadric, the very person who helped him deceive his father:[22]

> Þa dyde Eadric ealdorman swa swa he ær oftor dyde: astealde þæne fleam ærest mid Magesæton 7 aswac swa his cynehlaforde 7 ealre Angelcynnes þeode. Þær ahte Cnut sige 7 gefeht him ealle Engla þeode.

> Then *ealdormann* Eadric did as he had done so often before; he was the first among the Magesæton [a local group] to start the flight. And in so doing, he betrayed his *cynehlaford* and all the people of the *Angelcynn*. There Cnut possessed the victory, and he won all the Anglo-Saxon people for himself.[23]

Without any subordinating conjunctions or interpretive guidance to suggest otherwise, the sheer juxtaposition of these sentences allows the annalist to imply that Eadric's betrayal of his lordship obligations leads to the Anglo-Saxons' defeat. And the annalist underscores the point by using the conventional *Chronicle* lexicon of accession ('feng to rice' [succeeded to the kingdom]), suggesting the legitimacy of the successions that follow the peace making of this battle. Though the kingdom is divided – Edmund takes Wessex and Cnut Mercia – both successions are described using the word 'feng' (succeeded). Practically, this division represents a significant loss of territory for the

Anglo-Saxons, but the Æthelred-Cnut annalist ignores the land to focus only on the quality of the lordship tie. In other words, in the annalist's hands, the Danish Conquest is narrated not as a Danish military triumph, but as a failure of Anglo-Saxon lordship.

Broken Covenants and the *Angelcynn*

At first glance, the annalist's presentation of Eadric's betrayal appears to participate in the conventional discussion of lordship bonds found in such important Old English texts and lordship sources as the laws, the *Battle of Maldon*, *Beowulf*, and the Cynewulf-Cyneheard entry of the *Chronicle*. In all these works, ideal lordship is conceptualized in the depth of a man's loyalty to his lord and disloyalty – should any occur – is envisaged primarily as a betrayal of the lord by the man.[24] But in the annals for 1014, 1015, and 1016, the annalist suggests that disloyalty can run in the other direction: from the lord to his men. Æthelred's 1014 promise asks the people to be faithful to their king. This, given the events of the previous years, is unsurprising. But then the king proceeds to promise loyalty to his people. This, given the dominant portrayal of lordship relations in the *Anglo-Saxon Chronicle* is surprising.[25] In the annalist's account, Æthelred fails to keep this promise, but the king is not alone in this failure.

As the annalist narrates the events of 1015 and 1016, it seems not to matter who the lord might be; the Anglo-Saxons' troubles consistently result from disloyal lordship. In betraying his lord, Eadric, who is himself a lord, betrays his men and, more specifically, the *Angelcynn*.[26] Further, when read in full, the annal for 1016 is so ordered that it suggests Eadric's behaviour is no singular instance of a lord betraying his men: his disloyalty is foreshadowed (if not caused) by the disloyalty of the king himself. When the people request that the king come to them, Æthelred, fearing treachery, stays away.[27] The annalist never makes a causal connection between Æthelred's and Eadric's behaviour. But the succession of deceptions and the annalist's attribution of defeat to Eadric's disloyalty reinforce the idea that poor lordship leads to the Danish Conquest. On the most literal level, the kingdom falls because the Anglo-Saxon aristocrats betray their king, but this betrayal is explained and justified by a more serious disloyalty: that of a lord to his men, that of the king to his nobles.

To claim that the Danish Conquest is narrated as the story of a series of lords who betray their men is to depart significantly from the conventional understanding of the Æthelred-Cnut annals. But neither the Eadric episode nor the account of Æthelred's behaviour can be seen as aberrations; they are both structural parts of the history. And, as structural parts, they ask the annals' readers to depersonalize the story of defeat and focus on the culture of disloyal lordship, thereby rendering visible the story of lordship among the *Angelcynn*. Observing the presence of this second narrative creates a new meaning for the Æthelred-Cnut annals that shows how they function as a history for Cnut. No longer does the *Æthelred-Cnut Chronicle* tell the story of a poor king. Rather, in a study of their defining ethos and culture, the annals now narrate the history of a people.

This change in perspective explains the narrative structure, content, and, in particular, the moments when the annalist chooses to intervene or remain silent. Like Alfred, Æthelred must also face Danish incursions, and the Æthelred-Cnut annalist initially continues the narrative strategy of not criticizing the king for making peace; thus, as in the Alfred annals, the Æthelred-Cnut annalist interprets payment of tribute and baptism as positive strategies that, when performed properly, will ensure the continued existence of the *Angelcynn*.[28] The raids begin in 980 and continue throughout the early years of Æthelred's reign.[29] In 992, *ealdormann* Ælfric betrays the Anglo-Saxons and the king, but the annalist does not explicitly criticize Æthelred; he moves instead, in the entry for 993, to a brief description of the raids. Initially, then, the annalist's approach encourages the reader to prioritize policy over tactics; Æthelred's approach is more important than winning any single encounter.

The annalist's focus on the king's policy explains the detail of his entry for 994. In this year, Æthelred uses a peace-making ceremony to build a lordship tie with one of the Danish leaders. Æthelred sends for Bishop Ælfheah and *ealdormann* Æthelweard, and together these figures lead Olaf Tryggvason to Andover where the Danes and the Anglo-Saxons make peace. Like Alfred, Æthelred sponsors the Danish leader at his baptism, effectively bringing Olaf into the community of his lordship relations.[30] Like Alfred, Æthelred performs the rituals of conventional lordship ceremonies and presents Olaf with gifts. And at the end of these rites, Olaf is able to recognize the existence of a people that, the annalist asserts, the Dane calls the *Angelcynn*. Indeed, the annalist claims that 'Anlaf behet swa he hit eac gelæste þæt he næfre eft to Angelcynne mid unfriðe cuman nolde' (Olaf promised, as he also did, that he would never again come among the *Angelcynn* in hostility).³¹ Up to 994, then, Æthelred is able to design and execute a policy that binds the raiders to him in a lordship bond. This success positions him as a worthy lord and king for the *Angelcynn*.

In the annals for 995–1001, the annalist retains his strategy, but conflicting elements of the annalist's commentary and the detail of his annals suggest that this approach is only viable when the king is successful. In 997, the Danes ravage and burn the monastery at Tavistock, taking unmentionable amounts of plunder.³² In 998, the Anglo-Saxons cannot mount an effective defence, and the annalist remarks, '7 man oft fyrde ongean hi gaderede, ac sona swa hi togædere gan sceoldan þonne wearð þær æfre ðuruh sum þing fleam astiht' (And frequently an army was gathered against them [the Danes], but always as soon as they were to do battle together, then a flight was always started there for some reason).³³ A similar situation obtains in 999: when the Kentish army flees the field, the king gathers an army that fails. The annalist explicitly states that the resulting situation further oppresses the Anglo-Saxons, wastes money, and encourages the Danes, but he does not criticize the king.³⁴ In 1000, Æthelred's own ships fail to meet him,³⁵ and observing the consequence of these failures, the annalist comments in his entry for 1001:

> 7 ðær him ferdon abutan swa swa hi sylf woldan, 7 him nan þing ne wiðstod ne him to, ne dorste scyphere on sæ ne landfyrd, ne eodon hi swa feor up. Wæs hit þa on ælce wisan hefig tyme forðam þe hi næfre hiora yfeles ne geswicon.
>
> And there they [the Danes] travelled about just as they themselves wanted, and nothing opposed them, neither the fleet on the water nor the land forces dared [offer them resistance], no matter how far inland they went. It was then in every way a grievous time for they never stopped doing their evil deeds.³⁶

Despite these events – the account shows the Anglo-Saxons to be poorly organized, perhaps even cowardly – and despite his obvious frustration, the annalist does not yet hold the king responsible. Here, Æthelred can be seen pursuing the policies that should, as the Alfred annals show, produce loyal lordship ties and in so doing strengthen the *Angelcynn*. He should not be criticized.

The tension between content and narrative strategy is resolved in the entry for 1002, the year in which the annalist shows that Æthelred's policies attack the *Angelcynn* instead of binding them to him. This transgression changes the rhetoric of the account and marks the beginning of the narrative of failed secular lordship, a narrative that ultimately justifies Cnut's accession.

In 1002, events with the Danes proceed as they have done before. The king and his councillors decide to pay tribute and arrange a truce, and Æthelred deals with the extra problem of a domestic dispute. Then, in the conclusion to his narrative, the annalist notes:

> 7 on þam geare se cyng het ofslean ealle þa deniscan men þe on Angelcynne wæron; ðis wæs gedon on Britius mæssedæig, forðam þam cyninge wæs gecyd þæt hi woldan hine beswyran æt his life 7 siððan ealle his witan 7 habban siþþan þis rice.

> And in that year, the king commanded all the Danish men who were among the *Angelcynn* to be killed; this was carried out on St Brice's feast day, because the king had been informed that they wanted to deceive him and take his life and afterwards take the lives of all his *witan* and then take this kingdom.[37]

Modern commentators on this entry usually focus on the degree to which the slaughter was or was not carried out, who was singled out, and whether the possibility of organized killing can contribute to an understanding of the administrative aspects of Æthelred's reign.[38] Specifically, Simon Keynes has explained this entry by situating the events in the context of II Æthelred, a peace treaty negotiated between Olaf and Æthelred (formulated before the former's baptism), a treaty that permits certain Danes to remain in Anglo-Saxon England.[39] In this light, Keynes argues that the likely victims were these recent settlers – traders and mercenaries – and suggests that the order was precipitated by Pallig, a Dane who fought the Anglo-Saxons, despite his pledges to the king and despite the gifts the king had given him.[40]

While the reality of the situation may remain uncertain – in the annal, Æthelred acts against unspecified Danes who could just as easily be Danes who had resided in Anglo-Saxon England for many years as they could be the traders – it is clear that the annalist's account of the king's attack is carefully drawn. The story of Pallig would add a certain logic to the massacre; it would explain the annalist's statement that Æthelred acts because he fears for his life and his throne. From this perspective, Æthelred's attack would be a just response to a treacherous violation of lordship relations. But the annalist makes no mention of Pallig (if he ever knew of him) and without this framework, his language and particular use of the word *Angelcynn* reconfigure Æthelred's decision to defend himself as an act of treachery perpetrated by the king on his people.

By invoking the concept of the *Angelcynn*, the Æthelred-Cnut annalist calls upon the history of its use in the *Chronicle* and in the Alfred annals in particular.[41] In so doing, he transforms an act of self-defence into an aggressive act of disloyalty. In previous annals, the *Angelcynn* have withstood attacks from an external enemy. Now, they are attacked from within, by the king. As the annalist describes the events of St Brice's Day, the king gives orders to kill those living 'on Angelcynne' (among, with the sense of membership in, the *Angelcynn*). What we know of Anglo-Saxon social and legal culture suggests that there were some distinctions between the Danes of the Danelaw and the Anglo-Saxons in general.[42] The annalist does not here make this distinction. By not separating the one from the other, he shows the king betraying the identifying and constitutive lordship culture of Alfred's *Angelcynn*.

As the narrative of the Æthelred-Cnut annals progresses, however, the annalist goes on to suggest that this betrayal of the king's lordship ties is neither an isolated aberration nor a moral failing peculiar to Æthelred; the *Angelcynn* are destroyed by a pattern of disloyal behaviour. Indeed, the entry for 1002 is the first of a number of entries that together show a culture of disloyal lordship in which both the king and his men are complicit. In the very next annal, the entry for 1003, the annalist observes another Anglo-Saxon loss. The defeat itself is not unusual and were it not for the Æthelred-Cnut annalist's analysis of the loss, it would not be notable in the larger history of Anglo-Saxon and Danish encounters. But the annalist spins the story so that the Danes' victory derives from the behaviour and failed lordship ties of the Anglo-Saxon leader.

In 1003, *ealdormann* Ælfric is supposed to lead the defence:

Þa sceolde se ealdorman Ælfric lædan þa fyrde, ac he teah ða forð his ealdan wrencas sona swa hi wæron swa gehende þæt ægðer here on oþerne hawede. Þa gebræd he hine seocne 7 ongan hine brecan to spiwenne 7 cwæð þæt he gesicled wære 7 swa þæt folc becyrde þæt he lædan sceolde, swa hit gecweden ys, þonne se heretoga wacað þonne bið eall se here swiðe gehindrad. Þa Swegen geseah þæt hi anræde næron 7 þæt hi ealle toforan, þa lædde he his here into Wiltune.

Then *ealdormann* Ælfric was supposed to lead the army, but he then performed his old tricks as soon as they were so close that each army could look at the other. Then he pretended that he was sick and proceeded to fake vomiting and said that he had been taken ill, and thus he betrayed the people he was supposed to lead. As the saying goes, 'When the general is cowardly, then all the army is greatly hindered.' When Swein saw that they were not resolute and that they were all scattered, then he lead his army into Wilton.[43]

In this account of the defeat, Swein reserves his attack for the moment when it becomes clear that, owing to Ælfric's behaviour, the Anglo-Saxons are no longer *anræd* (resolute), and thus, the Anglo-Saxons' defeat is predicated on Ælfric's treachery.[44] The proverb, 'When the general is cowardly, then all the army is greatly hindered,' reinforces this point. As Thomas Hill has shown, this saying is part of an axiomatic tradition that discusses the value of a leader's presence on the field.[45] But by virtue of its position between the entries for 1002 and 1004, the proverb signifies in two ways. In its most immediate context, it raises the question of whether Æthelred should lead his army. But in the context of the annals as a history for Cnut, the proverb is also part of a larger discussion of Æthelred's lordship. Just as the maxim comments on the cowardice and treachery of *ealdormann* Ælfric, so it also hints at the treachery of King Æthelred: Ælfric is a coward, because his leader and lord, Æthelred, is a coward.

The claim that Æthelred's own poor lordship lies behind Ælfric's treachery complicates our understanding of the annal for 1004. In 1004, the Danes return and the Anglo-Saxons, led by Ulfcytel, are unable to respond effectively. Like Æthelred, Ulfcytel is betrayed by the men who are supposed to follow him; unlike Æthelred, however, Ulfcytel attempts to resolve the difficulty by personally taking the field. His decision to fight is validated by the annalist's comment on the outcome of the battle. Once more, the Anglo-Saxons lose – specifically, Ulfcytel loses both the engagement and the 'Eastengla folces seo yld' (the chief men of the East Anglian people). But the annalist comments, from the Danes' perspective, 'Swa hi sylfe sædon þæt hi næfre wyrsan handplegan on Angelcynne ne gemitton þonne Ulfcytel him to brohte' (As they said themselves, they had never met worse hand-to-hand fighting among the *Angelcynn* than that which Ulfcytel dealt them).[46]

Instead of criticizing Ulfcytel for what is obviously a devastating loss, the annalist turns to the Danes. Invoking the peace making with Olaf, the Danes are once more shown recognizing the existence of the *Angelcynn*, and in a brief meta-narratorial comment, the annalist reaffirms the connection between the *Angelcynn* and their leader's performance of his lordship obligations. The *Angelcynn* are discernible to the Danes in the bravery of their fighting with Ulfcytel at their helm: this bravery is born of Ulfcytel's ability to instil unity in his remaining men. By acting upon his responsibilities, Ulfcytel demonstrates his loyalty to his king; by taking the field, he demonstrates his loyalty to his men. In this version of events, Æthelred's absence from the field is conspicuous, and the annalist underscores its effects by momentarily making Ulfcytel, a regional leader, the leader of the *Angelcynn*.[47] The defeat seems not to matter.

In the context of the *Æthelred-Cnut Chronicle* as a whole, the Ulfcytel episode serves as the last example of ideal Anglo-Saxon lordship relations. After the entry for 1004, the annalist records a culture of lordship so disloyal that those who are supposed to protect the Anglo-Saxons oppress and betray them. Moreover, the king's own faithlessness is always implied in, if not central to, this treachery. In 1006, while the Danish army 'ferde swa he sylf wolde, 7 seo fyrding dyde þære landleode ælcne hearm' (went wherever it wanted and the [Anglo-Saxon] land force did their own people every kind of harm),'[48] Æthelred deals with disloyalty among his aristocracy. When the annalist reports how Æthelred responds – the king takes Wulfgeat's property, orders Wulfheah and Ufegeat to be blinded, and has *ealdormann* Ælfhelm killed – he declines to explain the king's actions or even place them in the larger context of Æthelred's struggle to secure his position, thereby allowing deeds with a clear political context to register as unmotivated acts of betrayal.

Though in certain Carolingian texts, at least, blindings symbolize disloyalty to the king, the annalist provides no explanation for this action.[49] And without any interpretive guidance from the annalist, the king's actions hang meaningfully over the text. At the very least, the mutilations figure along with the St Brice's Day massacre as further attacks on the people.[50] Similarly, there are no explicit connections between these acts and the deceptions and betrayals that occur later in the year. Thus, the general organization of the annal colludes with the conventions of annalistic style – the various elements of the entries are mostly linked by coordinating conjunctions – to position the examples of disloyalty as a response to Æthelred's betrayal of his *Angelcynn*.

In 1009, for example, the annalist comments, 'Her on þissum geare wurdan þa scypu gearwe, ðe we ær ymbbe spræcon, 7 hiora wæs swa feala swa næfre ær þæs, ðe us bec secgað, on Angelcynne ne gewurdon on nanes cyninges dæge' (Here in this year, the ships we mentioned earlier were ready, and, as the books tell us, there were more of them among the *Angelcynn* than there ever had been before in any king's day).[51] The perspective revealed in this comment is both historical and textual; moreover, it reminds readers of the Æthelred-Cnut annals that this is a narrative told with reference to other (in all likelihood *Chronicle*) narratives of the past. This retrospective and intertextual quality in turn lends meaning to the phrase 'on Angelcynne' (among the *Angelcynn*). By asserting that the ships belong to the *Angelcynn*, the Æthelred-Cnut annalist implies that the events in 1009 do not just take place in Anglo-Saxon England; that is, they are not specifically connected with the territory of the kingdom. Rather, they take place among the *Angelcynn*, a people whose lordship culture and identity bear upon our understanding of these happenings.

With his narrative thus situated as part of the history of the *Angelcynn*, the record of betrayals and treachery takes on a different hue. The annalist remarks, 'Ac we ða gyt næfdon þa gesælða ne þone wyrðscype þæt seo scypfyrd nyt wære þissum earde þe ma ðe heo oftor ær wæs' (But then we still did not have the good fortune or honour that the sea force was of any more use to the country than it had been very often before).[52] While his choice of *gesælða* (good fortune or blessing) is easily explained by the discourse of salvation history – invocations of blessings and good fortune ask the reader to look for the presence of a divine hand and to think about the teleology of salvation history – the presence of *wyrðscype* (honour) requires some clarification. How can a matter of military success depend on honour?

In 1009, after being falsely accused to the king, Wulfnoth deserts, seizes some ships, and ravages the coast. The force designated to capture him is scattered by bad weather and then destroyed by Wulfnoth himself. When news of this unsuccessful attempt spreads, 'hit wæs þa swilc hit eall rædleas wære. 7 ferde se cyning him ham 7 þa ealdormen 7 þa heahwitan, 7 forleton þa scipo ðus leohtlice' (it was then as if everything was ill-advised. And the king, the *ealdormenn*, and the chief *witan* took themselves home, and they abandoned the ships thus lightly).⁵³ Grimly underscoring this rampant treachery, the annalist observes, '7 næs se sige na betere þe eal Angelcyn to hopode' (And the victory for which all the *Angelcynn* looked was no better than this).⁵⁴ In Old English poetic literature of lordship, honour is one of the rewards of victory, yet because they are led by a king who disrespects his lordship ties, the treachery and betrayal of the Wulfnoth episode is all the reward the people can expect; and the annalist emphasizes the poignancy of this moment by once more invoking the concept of the *Angelcynn*. While at the beginning of the entry for 1009, the *Angelcynn* are a people whose history can be told in books, now the *Angelcynn* can hope for nothing more than betrayal.

Correspondingly, betrayal is at the heart of the remaining Æthelred-Cnut annals. In the entries for 1010 and the last years of Æthelred's reign, the annalist creates a narrative in which the history of the *Angelcynn* is characterized by a series of betrayed lordship bonds. In 1010, the East Anglians – the people who in 1004 were the symbols of the *Angelcynn* – flee the field in a retreat led by Þurcytel Myranheafod (Mare's Head), and the king's authority is so weak that no 'heafodman' (captain) would gather an army.⁵⁵ The entries for 1011 and 1012 narrate an even more disturbing example of disloyalty: the death of a man the annalist terms the 'heafod Angelkynnes' (the head of the *Angelcynn*).⁵⁶ In 1011, Danish raiders lay siege to Canterbury and take Archbishop Ælfheah captive. The annalist is quite explicit about the decayed sense of obligation that results in the archbishop's death. The Danes gain entry to the cathedral community by virtue of the 'syruwrencas' (tricks) of Abbot Ælfmær.⁵⁷

The depth of these deceptions is revealed when the annalist reminds the reader that Ælfheah once saved Ælfmær's life. Moreover, by using the term *syruwrencas*, the annalist casts this betrayal as one of lordship relations. There are only two instances of Old English *wrenc* (wile, stratagem, or deceit) in the Æthelred-Cnut annals, both of which appear in the context of one man's betrayed lordship obligations. Thus the word *syruwrencas* reminds the reader of the tricks (*wrencas*) of *ealdormann* Ælfric whose behaviour in 1003 points out the futility of levying an army without a strong leader and highlights the necessity of loyal lordship bonds.⁵⁸

Further, instead of lamenting the loss of the archbishop as an archbishop, the Æthelred-Cnut annalist transforms the story of Ælfheah's martyrdom into a comment upon Æthelred's disloyalty. Whether or not the title is literally meant, by endowing Ælfheah with the title, 'heafod Angelkynnes' (head of the *Angelcynn*),⁵⁹ the annalist underscores the archbishop's loyalty to Ælfmær and implicitly compares the archbishop and the king. Ælfheah's actions and, in particular, his loyalty to Ælfmær make him a worthy leader of the *Angelcynn*. By contrast, Æthelred is clearly no worthy lord.

Though Ælfheah's death and the loss of the kingdom are in no way causally connected, the annalist's narrative of lordship creates new, conceptual links between important historical events. When Ælfheah, the symbolic head of the *Angelcynn*, dies, so will the kingdom. In the very next year Æthelred loses his realm. As the annalist recounts the events of 1013, the transfer of power from Æthelred to Swein is not a victory won on the field, but an explicit extension of the poor lordship culture described in the preceding annals. When Swein arrives at Gainsborough in 1013, the annalist details the successive submissions of the Anglo-Saxons, shire by shire. But, as signalled by the annalist's use of Old English *bugan*, these are not the submissions by which lordship relations are contracted.[60] Uhtræd and all the Northumbrians 'beah' (bowed) to Swein and when the Dane perceives that 'eall folc to him gebogen wæs' (all the people had bowed to him), he moves on.[61] The people of Oxfordshire 'beah 7 gislude' (bowed and gave hostages); only 'nolde seo burhwaru bugan' (the citizens [of London] did not wish to bow).[62] Similarly, Swein takes the submission of Æthelmær and all the western thanes (*bugan* again).[63] When finally, all the people regard him as king, the people of London 'beah 7 gislude' (bowed and gave hostages).[64] In this way, the annalist implies that in yielding to the Danes, the Anglo-Saxons are conquered, as opposed to being integrated into a new kingdom or a new people.

The Anglo-Saxons' powerlessness is complemented by the passive language in which the annalist reports the passage of dominion to Swein. Departing noticeably from the 'feng to rice' (succeeded to the kingdom) formula with which *Chronicle* annalists report the accession of a legitimate king and dispensing with any notion of an election ceremony, thereby minimizing any potential evocation of a lordship tie, the Æthelred-Cnut annalist simply says, '7 eal þeodscype hine hæfde þa for fulne cyng' (And then all the people had him as their full king).[65] In this account of the transfer of power, the *Angelcynn* are not remade by the rituals in which the new Danish king is solemnized, and the absence of lordship language is notable. In essence, then, the annals of the *Æthelred-Cnut Chronicle* are so structured that the king's disloyal lordship breeds more disloyalty; this pattern ultimately leads to the loss of the kingdom and to Æthelred's exile.

Covenants (Temporarily) Remade

Æthelred's exile is, of course, literal, but in the intertextual context asserted in the annals' narrative – 'ðe us bec secgað' (as the books tell us)[66] – the literal exile of a king doubles as a literary lordship topos. Not only are exile and lordship closely associated in Old English poems like the *Wanderer* and *Seafarer*, exile is, in the *Anglo-Saxon Chronicle* narratives of Alfred, Edward the Confessor, and Æthelred II, a necessary intermediate step before the king finally wins his kingdom.[67] In the Alfred annals, for example, Alfred goes into exile after his defeat at Athelney before returning to secure his kingdom with a victory at Edington, a victory that the Alfred annalist describes as a triumph of the king's ability to bring about lordship relations with the Danes.[68] Similarly, exile as a necessary precursor to a glorious reign features strongly in the poem commemorating Edward's death: Edward 'Engla hlaford' (lord of the Anglo-Saxons) 'wunode wræclastum wide geond eorðan, / syððan Cnut ofercom kynn Æðelredes' (dwelled on the paths of exile far and wide throughout the earth after Cnut overcame the kin of Æthelred).[69] But while, for the other kings, it is enough merely to be the lord of the people, the language in which the Æthelred-Cnut annalist describes his king's return stresses a new dimension to the lordship bond: Æthelred must be loyal to his people.

The question of a lord's loyalty shapes the language of Æthelred's return. In 1014, the Danish raiders choose Cnut as their king.[70] The annalist does not describe the Danish election procedure, but he claims that the Anglo-Saxon *witan* object to Cnut as their lord – stating that for the *witan* no lord would be dearer than their own 'gecynda hlaford' (their proper lord).[71] This suggests that for the annalist at least, the Danish election ceremony could potentially be seen as legitimate. He responds by showing Æthelred using the language and ideology of loyal lordship to reconfigure his own rule. To wit, the returning king promises the *witan* and the people that 'he him hold hlaford beon wolde 7 ælc þæra ðinga betan þe hi ealle ascunudon, 7 ælc þara ðinga forgyfen beon sceolde þe him gedon oððe gecweden wære, wið þam ðe hi ealle anrædlice butan swicdome to him gecyrdon' (he would be a loyal lord to them, and amend each of the things that they all hated, and that everything that had been done or said against him would be forgiven, provided that they all submitted resolutely to him without any betrayal).[72]

For a rhetorical charter for his reign, this promise is striking.[73] As the annalist quotes the promise, Æthelred is not seen repeating his coronation oath – this would reinsert his kingship into the discourse of ecclesiastical kingship and would thus be inappropriate to the annalist's story of loyal lordship relations. Instead, the Æthelred-Cnut annalist reinforces the point by returning to the word *cyrran*, characterizing the Anglo-Saxons' resubmission to their king as an act of lordship. In this formulation of Æthelred's new kingship, the king claims loyalty as the defining aspect of his rule. In the past he has been betrayed by his men, but he has also not been sufficiently loyal to his people. Now, if his people submit to his lordship, he will be loyal to them. In having the king make such a promise, the annalist implies that loyal lordship will enable Æthelred to make reparation for the instances of his disloyalty, justify his return from exile, define his new regime, and unite his people.

At first, it seems Æthelred successfully manipulates his lordship ties; he wins a significant victory at Lindsey. The annalist tellingly notes that Cnut, contrary to a previous agreement with the people of Lindsey, was not present at the battlefield, '7 wearð þæt earme folc þus beswicen ðuruh hine' (and thus [by Cnut's absence], the wretched people were betrayed by him).[74] Throughout the annals for 1014 and 1015, the annalist accords Cnut the title 'king,' but the story of the battle of Lindsey shows that this king will not fulfil the reciprocal obligations of Anglo-Saxon lordship.[75] Not only will Cnut not be a loyal lord, he actively betrays – *beswican* – his people.

Ultimately, however, Æthelred fails. In the new narrative of the Æthelred-Cnut annals, this is not because he is immoral or incompetent; it is because he must act in and against a culture of disloyal lordship. In 1015, *ealdormann* Eadric invites Sigeferth and Morcar, two thanes, into his chamber and betrays them by having them killed.[76] The king immediately orders Sigeferth's widow to Malmesbury. With the obstacle of Ealdgyth, Sigeferth's widow, removed, Æthelred takes all the thanes' possessions. Pauline Stafford has argued that even if Æthelred is not directly behind the betrayal, his actions at least prove his complicity. Moving against Eadric, Æthelred exiles Ealdgyth to a monastery (an action that, Stafford argues, reveals Ealdgyth's political influence).[77] Stafford has also shown how Eadric's actions might be seen as an attempt to save Æthelred from a plot.[78]

Without any interpretation or extra information from the annalist, the story suggests only that Eadric and Æthelred betray the thanes and, further, that the following series of betrayals and deceptions complements the king's disloyalty. In seizing Sigeferth's and Morcar's possessions, Æthelred shows his inability to be loyal, and Eadric and *ætheling* Edmund repay him with more disloyalty. At the end of the year, the annalist suggests that the king no longer actively leads his people: while he lies sick at Cosham, Eadric and Edmund gather their respective armies, but instead of fighting the Danes, 'ða wolde se ealdorman [Eadric] beswican þone æþeling [Edmund]' (the *ealdormann* then wanted to betray the *ætheling*).[79] The armies separate without fighting, Eadric takes forty of the king's ships for himself and submits (*bugan*) to Cnut along with the West Saxons.

This scenario of betrayal at all levels is repeated in the entry for 1016, but, in this instance, the annalist is more explicit about the king's disloyalty and the effect this betrayal has upon the people.

> Þa seo fyrd gesomnod wæs, ða ne onhagode heom ðarto buton þæt wære þæt se cyng ðær mid wære 7 hi hæfdon þære burhware fultum of Lundene. Geswicon ða þære fyrdinge, 7 ferde him ælc man ham ... [7] man sende to ðam cynge to Lundene 7 bæd hine þæt he come ongean þa fyrde mid þam fultume ðe he gegaderian mihte. Þa hi ealle tosomne comon, þa ne beheold hit nan ðinc þe ma ðe hit oftor ær dyde. Þa cydde man þam cynge þæt hine man beswican wolde, þa þe him on fultume beon sceoldon, forlet ða þa fyrde 7 cyrde him eft to Lundene.

> When the army had been assembled, then nothing could please them more than if the king were there with [them] and if they could have the help of the citizens of London. They then deserted the army, and each man took himself home ... [A]nd word was sent to the king in London, asking him to come back to the army with [any] help that he could gather. When they all came together, then it availed not one thing more than it very often had done before. When the king was informed that someone who was supposed to support him was going to betray him, then he abandoned the army and went back to London again.[80]

Though, in previous entries, the annalist has explicitly discussed military disaster by attributing responsibility for treachery and betrayal where he thought appropriate, the story of how Æthelred abandons his people remains unanalysed. From this text, it is not clear whether the annalist finds this last betrayal justified – Æthelred promises loyalty only if his people are loyal to him and here the king is threatened – or

112 Families of the King

whether he finds it inexcusable. But as it is positioned in the lengthy entry for 1016, the story of Æthelred's abandonment functions as a conclusion to the narrative of the king's failed lordship and a preface to the other betrayals in that year and, in particular, to that of Eadric who betrays his *cynehlaford* and all the people of the *Angelcynn*.[81]

Making Cnut King

Because, when they are read as a history for Cnut, the Æthelred-Cnut annals exchange a narrative of personality for one of culture, the Æthelred-Cnut annalist does not cease to emphasize lordship once Cnut has won the Anglo-Saxon people. Indeed, the annal for 1017 suggests that Cnut's lordship is definitive of his rule. The Æthelred-Cnut annalist makes no mention of Cnut's coronation, though the Dane would have been crowned by Archbishop Lyfing using the second *ordo*,[82] and though a coronation narrative would have served, as it does in other *Chronicle* annals, to legitimize the king. This absence highlights what the annalist presents as Cnut's performance of royal lordship.

In his entry for 1017, the annalist writes:

> Her on þissum geare feng Cnut kyning to eallon Angelcynnes ryce 7 hit todælde on feower, him sylfan Westsexan 7 Þurkylle Eastenglan 7 Eadrice Myrcan 7 Irke Norðhymbran. 7 on þissum geare wæs Eadric ealdorman ofslagen 7 Norðman Leofwines sunu ealdormannes 7 Æþelweard Æþelmæres sunu greatan 7 Brihtric Ælfehes sunu on Defenascire. 7 Cnut cyning aflymde ut Eadwig æþeling 7 eft hine het ofslean. 7 þa toforan Kalendas Agusti het se cynigc fetian him þæs cyniges lafe Æþelrædes him to wife Ricardes dohtor.

> Here in this year King Cnut succeeded to the whole kingdom of the *Angelcynn* and he split it into four parts. He took Wessex for himself and gave Thorkell East Anglia, Eadric Mercia, and Eric Northumbria. And in this year, *ealdormann* Eadric was killed and Northman, the son of *ealdormann* Leofwine, and Æþelweard the son of Æthelmær the Fat and Brihtric, son of Ælfheah of Devonshire. And King Cnut exiled *ætheling* Eadwig and after that had him killed. And then before 1st August, the king commanded Richard's daughter, the widow of King Æthelred, to be fetched as a wife for him.[83]

From the very first sentence, the annalist establishes lordship as the constitutive aspect of Cnut's kingship. Markedly distinguishing people and land, the annalist notes that the king gains the kingdom of the *Angelcynn*. Because the Dane has already won the people and earned the title of king, all he does here is take possession of the land that constitutes the kingdom. Further, at the moment of the Dane's accession, the annalist shows the king taking possession of his throne by securing his lordship relations with his people.[84] To those whom he deems faithful, he gives land as a symbol of their lordship bond; those whom he deems untrustworthy are eventually denied a lordship tie and are killed.[85] For the annalist, Cnut uses acts of lordship to take control of his kingdom, and the king's accession is authorized by the degree of control his lordship affords him.[86] In effect, then, unlike the transfer of power after the Norman Conquest, there is no single event that definitively marks what scholars often refer to as the Danish Conquest. Rather, Cnut 'conquers' Anglo-Saxon England through a series of accessions, each of which the annalist characterizes as an act of lordship.

The annalist's single-minded focus on lordship links the Æthelred-Cnut annals to the post-Conquest cultural milieu, the rhetoric of Archbishop Wulfstan of York, and, in particular, the language of the texts that authorize and proclaim Cnut's kingship. Studies of Wulfstan and his contributions to and influence in the new Anglo-Danish realm are becoming more and more commonplace, and while I agree that Wulfstan is a key figure, I am interested for the moment only in a thread that runs throughout the legal texts with which he can be associated.[87] In a marked difference from the positions advocated in works such as Wulfstan's homilies, his *Institutes of Polity*, and, in particular, his *Sermo Lupi*,[88] the Cnut legal texts participate in a legal discourse in which loyal lordship on the part of both man and lord defines an Anglo-Danish collective cultural identity.

The first text is Cambridge, Corpus Christi College, MS 201, a text that conveys the provisions of the 1018 Anglo-Danish peace treaty and sets out what the new king will require of his people.

Ðis is seo geræednes þe witan geræddon. 7 be manegum godum bisnum. asmeadon. And þæt wæs geworden sona swa cnút cyngc. mid his witena geþeahte. frið 7 freondscipe. betweox denum 7 englum. fullice gefæstnode. 7 heora ærran saca. ealle getwæmde.

Þonne is þæt ærest þæt witan geræddan. þæt hi ofer ealle oþre þingc ænne god æfre wurðodon. 7 ænne cristendom anrædlice healdan. 7 cnut cyngc. lufian. mid rihtan. 7 mid trwyðan. 7 eadgares lagan. geornlice folgian.

> This is the ordinance which the councillors determined and devised according to many good precedents. And that took place as soon as King Cnut, with the advice of his councillors, fully established peace and friendship between the Danes and the English, and put an end to all their former enmity.
> In the first place, the councillors decreed that, above all other things, they would always honour one God and singlemindedly hold one Christian faith, and love King Cnut with due loyalty, and zealously observe the laws of Edgar.[89]

In the first instance, all the people must cleave to Cnut. But their loyalty will not go unrewarded. The author makes Cnut himself declare that loyal lordship is one of the founding principles of his reign and, moreover, that he will practise the lordship that the Anglo-Saxons would have expected of their king. The 1020 letter from Cnut to his people asserts:

> Cnut cyning gret his arcebiscopas 7 his leodbiscopas 7 Þurcyl eorl 7 ealle his eorlas 7 ealne his þeodscype, twelfhynde 7 twyhynde, gehadode 7 læwede, on Englalande freondlice.
> 7 ic cyðe eow, þæt ic wylle beon hold hlaford.

> King Cnut greets with friendship his archbishops and his suffragan bishops, Earl Thorkell, and all his earls and all his people in England, [including those] who are worth twelve hundred in wergild and those worth two hundred, his ecclesiastics and his laymen.
> And I announce to you that I will be a loyal lord.[90]

In other words, the contract between king and people, Dane and Anglo-Saxon, is imagined as one of mutual loyal lordship. Cnut, like Æthelred, promises to be a 'hold hlaford' (loyal lord) to his people, provided that they are faithful to him. The repeated idea that the people should be faithful and the reiteration of the phrase 'hold hlaford' is important because this particular phrase is only found in texts directly concerned with structuring lordship bonds between a conqueror and his people.

In the extant Old English prose corpus, the phrase 'hold hlaford' (loyal lord) occurs only six times.[91] One example is cited above in the 1020 letter, three more are in the C, D, and E *Chronicle* accounts of Æthelred's return from exile, the fifth borrows the phrase to pattern the Norman Conquest after Æthelred's oath and the Cnut texts,[92] and the sixth and earliest instance of the phrase is in IV Edgar, a secular law code that explains how the rule of law and punishment will operate in the Danelaw. In essence, IV Edgar codifies custom, while regulating, distinguishing, and creating Anglo-Saxon and Danish cultures. In this regard, IV Edgar participates in the identifying conventions of legal discourse.

The preamble and first clause explicitly take up the problems of lordship and the king's authority:

Her is geswutelod on þisum gewrite, hu Eadgar cyningc wæs smeagende, hwæt to bote mihte æt ðæm færcwealme, ðe his leodscipe swyðe drehte 7 wanode wide gynd his anweald.
(1) Ðæt is þonne ærest, þæt him þuhte 7 his witum þæt þus gerad ungelimp mid synnum 7 mid oferhyrnysse Godes beboda geearnod wære.

Here in this writ it is explained how King Edgar was thinking about what might serve as a remedy for the sudden pestilence that was severely tormenting and injuring his people far and wide throughout his jurisdiction. (1) First, it seemed to him and his *witan* that they had earned this kind of misfortune with sin and disobedience of God's commands.[93]

Redolent of the tropes of salvation discourse, this preface positions the code's statutes as a response to a plague and implies that if the Anglo-Saxons and the Danes were to be more law-abiding, their reformed behaviour would end the illness. As a whole, the text of the code regulates the behaviour of the people, thereby containing the wrongdoing that has lead to the plague.

Unusually, however, IV Edgar holds the *witan*, and explicitly the king, responsible for the plague. In the author's hands, the king responds by articulating a new social order and political ethos: 'Ic beo eow swyðe hold hlaford þa hwile þe me lif gelæst, 7 eow eallum swyðe bliðe eom, for þy þe ge swa georne ymbe frið syndon' (I will be a very loyal lord to you for as long as I live and I am very pleased with you all, because you are so eager for peace).[94] In this moment, Edgar redefines what it means both to be his subject and to be king. When people and king are united in and defined by their mutual loyalty, the threat to the kingdom will be contained and there will be peace. Loyal lordship thus becomes a remedy for social and political ill.

Clearly, the IV Edgar promise resonates with the Cnut legal texts.[95]

In different ways, both Patrick Wormald and Dorothy Whitelock have shown how Wulfstan could have had access to a copy of IV Edgar.[96] And while technically, as Wormald has shown, IV Edgar is not a direct source for either the 1018 code (sourced in Æthelred's 1008 code and the version thereof known as VI Æthelred)[97] or the 1020 letter, both Wormald and Whitelock acknowledge the importance of IV Edgar for Cnut's legislation. Whitelock has observed that IV Edgar is written in a homiletic style and has hinted at how homiletic law might be significant for understanding Wulfstan's work.[98] And both Malcolm Lawson and Patrick Wormald have analysed the connections between Wulfstan's homiletic and legal styles.[99]

But content and style as analytical lenses do not necessarily reveal the discursive function of the laws or stress the ways in which legal texts articulate collective identity and interpellate a law-abiding person into the community. Legal discourse constitutes and identifies the community for which the laws are written. In a compelling study of medieval kingdoms and communities, Susan Reynolds writes that law, like government, trade, and custom, is simply one way of defining what she calls a 'community of the realm.'[100] But it is not just that agreeing to a certain set of laws defines a community differentially or even oppositionally. Law codes and legal discourse are formative of the community they claim to regulate in that they create a space in which a people can be imagined to live.

My understanding of how legal discourse contributes to the discourse of Anglo-Scandinavian identity is drawn from Judith Butler's reading of Pierre Bourdieu's *habitus*, the 'embodied rituals by which a given culture produces and sustains belief in its own "obviousness"':[101]

> To the extent that Bourdieu acknowledges that this *habitus* is formed over time, and that its formation gives rise to a strengthened belief in the 'reality' of the social field in which it operates, he understands social conventions as animating the bodies which, in turn, reproduce and ritualize those conventions as practices. In this sense, the *habitus* is formed, but it is also *formative*: it is in this sense that the bodily *habitus* constitutes a tacit form of performativity, a citational chain lived and believed at the level of the body. The *habitus* is not only a site for the reproduction of the belief in the reality of a given social field – a belief by which that field is sustained – but it also generates *dispositions* which 'incline' the social subject to act in relative conformity with the ostensibly objective demands of the field (emphasis as printed).[102]

Though intended for a very different project, Butler's description explains how legal discourse operates. In that law structures what a person might and might not do and defines what is and what is not acceptable, law codes define part of the *habitus*. The dictates of the law are lived and believed at the level of the body, and the notion of what is lawful generates the kind of disposition that inclines a subject to conform. By stating what it means to be law-abiding, law codes construct the Anglo-Saxon subject, furthering and implementing a discourse of identity.[103]

In IV Edgar, Edgar commends the Danes' eagerness for peace and promises, in exchange, that he will be a 'hold hlaford' (loyal lord) to them for the rest of his life. In this moment, the writer of IV Edgar constructs ideal relations between the Danes and their Anglo-Saxon king as a question of loyal lordship and shows how lordship can now give both Dane and Anglo-Saxon a common identity through the presence of a king who is a loyal lord of his people.

This context of IV Edgar explains both the reference to Edgar's laws in the 1018 peace code and the cultural significance of the phrase 'hold hlaford' in the Cnut legal texts. As the Cnut texts articulate the idea of mutual loyalty between lord and man, they contribute to a new vision of the Anglo-Danish kingdom. By invoking Edgar's era in the defining texts and founding cultural charters of Cnut's reign,[104] the Cnut texts suggest that Cnut's rule will similarly be one of peace. As king, Cnut responds to the potential for royal wrongdoing and allays the Anglo-Saxons' fears by invoking a familiar self-image. Under Cnut, both Dane and Anglo-Saxon are defined by their loyalty to the king and the king's loyalty to the people. Loyal lordship has become the identifying political ethos of Anglo-Scandinavian England.

Both the discourse of mutual loyalty in secular lordship and the implication that the king can be a disloyal lord persist well into Cnut's reign, and their survival suggests the power of the discourse of Anglo-Danish identity they represent. So important is the idea that a lord can betray his men that chapters 69–83 of II Cnut deal with lordship abuses, and, in particular, abuses by the king. Pauline Stafford has pointed out the 'parallels in conception and content' between these sections of Cnut's legislation, the coronation charter of Henry I, and *Magna Carta* itself.[105] She goes on to suggest that these sections of II Cnut might well echo the concerns of the lost secular section of VIII Æthelred, issued on the occasion of his return from exile, whereupon he promises to be a 'hold hlaford' to his people.[106]

She also links this informal promise with the more formal idea of the coronation oath.[107]

Whether or not Stafford is right, her arguments acknowledge several important aspects of the 'hold hlaford' promise. As a rhetoric of lordship, the language of mutual loyalty establishes a new kind of contract, a secular, political, and cultural ethos by which the people and the king's authority are constituted. The repeated invocations of mutual loyalty link the reigns of Æthelred and Cnut, and, together with the other statutes of the Cnut legal texts, this promise defines the new Anglo-Danish kingdom and forms part of its identifying culture. Cnut's promise does not itself bring about a new culture at the moment it is uttered – if, indeed, Cnut ever did make this vow himself. Rather, authorized by his letters and affirmed by the content of his laws, the claim that the king took such an oath marks a cultural and political ethos that enables the founding of a new Anglo-Danish people.[108]

Narrating Cnut's Kingship

The discourse of identity that portrays the Danes as keepers of the ideal of mutual loyalty is sufficiently influential that twenty-five years after Cnut's accession, it is taken up by a Flemish monk who was writing in either Anglo-Danish England or on the Continent.[109] The Latin narrative of the *Encomium Emmae Reginae* is devoted to the praise and life of Queen Emma, wife of Æthelred and Cnut. Yet the text self-consciously begins not with Emma, but with the story of Swein and the years leading up to the Danish Conquest.[110] This prehistory is no unimportant prelude to the queen's own story, however; it occupies two of three books. The encomiast concentrates on the ways in which the central figures of Cnut's and Æthelred's reigns are bound to each other. Though like the Anglo-Saxons, the Danes experience crisis at moments of succession and in father-son relationships, the Danes, unlike the Anglo-Saxons, are able to overcome these difficulties through loyalty.[111]

The narrative of loyalty between Danish lords and their men begins with an act of disloyalty; the encomiast asserts that Swein's father was envious of his son and disinherited him.[112] The fact that the king is at fault is underscored by the desertion of his army and his concomitant defeat. The encomiast goes on to suggest that acts of loyal lordship define Swein's reign. The encomiast notes that, having taken over his father's throne, Swein is so good to his men that they would do anything for him.[113] This picture of ideal lordship ties is disrupted, momentarily, when the encomiast reports Thorkell's disloyalty to his king. Sent by the king to avenge the death of the king's brother, Thorkell has conquered southern England and lives now as an ally of the Anglo-Saxons.[114] Swein's men, certain that they could profit by the steadfastness of their king's lordship, suggest that Swein should invade England and take back the authority and land that has been taken from him by an act of disloyalty. Swein agrees, his son Cnut reluctantly agrees, and the decision to conquer is taken.[115] With the Conquest now figured as the act of a loyal king seeking to maintain the loyalty of his men, the narrative of the military engagements ensues. Though the encomiast reports the first battle, he professes disinterest in the narrative of war and returns instead to his theme of royal loyalty.[116]

Unlike his father, Swein is sufficiently loyal to leave his kingdom to his son, Cnut. When the Anglo-Saxons resist, Cnut returns to Denmark to consult with his brother; the encomiast lingers over the scenes of reciprocal brotherly loyalty.[117] These scenes are contrasted with what the encomiast acknowledges are the potentially conflicting and disloyal motives of Thorkell. When the invasion finally gets underway, Thorkell acts explicitly to demonstrate his loyalty to his lord, and his consistent and explicit desire to honour Cnut contrasts with the disloyalty of Eadric and Edmund.[118] When peace has been negotiated and the Danes and Anglo-Saxons are settled, the encomiast praises Cnut for his wisdom to love those who were faithful to Edmund and hate those who were disloyal to their lord.[119] According to this narrative of the Conquest, the Danes bring to Anglo-Saxon England a culture of reciprocal loyalty and establish it as the governing and defining ideology of the new realm.

That the encomiast should so explicitly write the story of the Conquest as the story of loyal lordship attests to the influence of the discourse of identity and practice of historiography in which the Æthelred-Cnut annalist participates. By narrating what could otherwise be seen as a military conquest as a transfer of power that enables the Anglo-Saxons to return to the identifying culture of their ancestors, the Æthelred-Cnut annalist forestalls an interpretation of the Danish Conquest as a disruption in Anglo-Saxon history and Old English historiographical practice. The narrative of Cnut's accession facilitates the continuation of a defining culture of lordship and the *Æthelred-Cnut Chronicle* itself continues the narrative techniques and rhetorical practice of the Alfred annals.

Equally as important, the narrative of the Danish Conquest and Cnut's accession serves as a conceptual and historiographical model for the D manuscript account of the Norman Conquest.[120] While historians of the Norman Conquest often remark upon the ways in which the Normans sought to continue Anglo-Danish institutions and copied the Danes' techniques of settlement, they tend to see the writing of the Conquest as an articulation of nascent English nationalistic sentiment.[121] The strategic reappearance of the king's promise to be a 'hold hlaford' (loyal lord) suggests, however, that the narrative of William's accession and the Anglo-Saxons' submission might more productively be read as a continuation of the discourse of identity begun in the Alfred annals and adapted in the *Æthelred-Cnut Chronicle*.

CHAPTER SIX

Writing William's Kingship

The *Angelcynn* do not survive the Norman Conquest, but the story told in the D annals suggests that the defeat at Hastings is not the sole cause of their demise.[1] Even prior to narrating the coming of the Normans, the story of the Anglo-Saxons is one of a people who, though separated by their ethnic collective terms and distinguished by their geographic histories, are united in denying their lordship obligations. These details significantly alter our understanding of the ensuing D conquest narrative: the William annalist suggests that the reasons for the loss of Anglo-Saxon lordship culture lie among the Anglo-Saxons themselves and portrays the Norman Conquest as a series of events that foreclose any return to the discourses of identity and ideal lordship articulated earlier in the Alfred and Æthelred-Cnut annals.[2] And this particular perspective leads to an account in which the actions William takes to secure his new kingdom are given a new and more sinister significance.

In the William annalist's hands, the annals of the Conquest and early years of William's reign, the entries for 1065–80,[3] recount the end of Anglo-Saxon lordship culture and the consequent loss of the Anglo-Saxon identity associated with that culture.[4] Once the Anglo-Saxon nobles surrender and the king is crowned, the annalist follows the king: William shows his power by building castles and other defensive structures on the land that he has ravaged, even as his poor lordship relations lead to rebellion.[5] For the William of the D text, land and buildings – as opposed to a lordship bond with his men – are the seat of his royal authority and the identifying symbols of his new people.

Even as the annalist uses these details to condemn the king, the overall narrative works to preserve the lordship culture and identity that

William fails to renew. Thus the significant attention given to William's scorched earth policy serves both to criticize the king and to link the annals to Anglo-Saxon lordship discourse. In Old English poems such as *Deor*, the *Ruin*, the *Wanderer*, and the *Seafarer*, poems that mourn the loss of lordship, the protagonist speaks of or from a ruined, barren landscape that symbolizes his now broken bond with his lord, and his compelling descriptions of this destroyed territory metonymically evoke the image of a country without a lord.[6] Such poetry neatly encapsulates what the William annalist presents as the Anglo-Saxons' situation. Ruled by a king who refuses to keep his promise of good lordship,[7] the Anglo-Saxons now inhabit a barren space in which they mourn the identity given them by the varying representations of the king's lordship tie.

The story of William and the land is essential to the historiography of the D annals. In his account of William's reign, the annalist invokes the literary landscape in which Anglo-Saxon lordship is imagined in order to set the scene – land becomes the textual and ideological backdrop – for the Margaret episode and the rebellion narratives. In these episodes, the annalist explores the complexities of Anglo-Saxon lordship culture, using the stories of St Margaret and Earl Waltheof to question and memorialize the lordship culture of the *Angelcynn*. In essence, then, the shape and content of the D text transform the annals into a kind of repository that simultaneously narrates and represents the Anglo-Saxon past.

These dimensions to the D conquest and settlement narrative suggest how the annals may have signified in the community in and for which they were written.[8] Inscribed in this lament for Anglo-Saxon lordship culture is a pointed discussion of post-Conquest monastic institutional identity. Scholars usually agree that the D manuscript of the *Chronicle* can be associated with the monastic house at Worcester, though they generally also note that York is a strong second possibility.[9] After the Norman Conquest, the estates and land rights of both institutions – and those of Worcester in particular – were threatened by the ways in which the Anglo-Saxons had organized their system of land tenure, a spate of monastic house rivalries, and the changes that accompanied William's new administration.[10]

Worcester faced a series of local land disputes with the neighbouring house of Evesham; the new sheriff, Urse d'Abetot, was known for his land-grabbing ways;[11] the earlier bishops' land tenure practices had resulted in land that was supposed to have reverted to the king being still held by laymen;[12] the lands of Worcester had suffered when the sees of Worcester and York were held in plurality;[13] and, finally, neighbouring institutions were being headed by Norman abbots, a practice that threatened Anglo-Saxon ecclesiastical culture.[14] For both houses, but particularly for Worcester, land is an important part of institutional culture.[15] Thus, safeguarding traditional, i.e., Anglo-Saxon, land and land rights is essential to preserving institutional identity.[16]

There are virtually no references to these local pressures in the national narrative of the D text; instead, the annalist creates an abstract meditation on culture, identity, and permanence. In his narrative of the Conquest and settlement, he invokes Anglo-Saxon lordship ideals to present both the land and the ideal of a personal and unifying relationship of man and lord as defining of Anglo-Saxon culture and identity.[17] At the same time, he also acknowledges that, as the events of history have shown, culture and identity are vulnerable. Yet even as he mourns the loss of the *Angelcynn*, his text asserts that historical narrative offers a kind of permanence that will counteract vulnerability and loss. In other words, the D text offers itself as a solution to the issues it identifies in its annals.

If reading the D text in this way highlights the differences between the D *Chronicle* and other contemporary accounts of the Conquest – the Norman and Anglo-Norman sources tend to focus on the problems of legality and lordship oaths – this interpretation also diverges from much twentieth-century historiography of the Conquest. Scholarly studies on the narratives of the Norman Conquest have explored issues such as land tenure, lordship, and the analytic value of concepts of feudalism; law, inheritance, William's justification for the invasion, and the reasons for the Anglo-Saxon defeat; the Norman empire and nationalism; and the administrative and political changes in post-Conquest England.[18]

Though the D text records the outcome of the Battle of Hastings and though the annalist laments the lost past, the annals, overall, do not supply the kind of information that would further elucidate such modern scholarly concerns. There is little information about the administrative and political changes that swept England after the Conquest, and there is no discussion of the Conquest's social and cultural consequences. Further, though he grieves over the Anglo-Saxon defeat, thereby tempting contemporary readers to place his text alongside the twelfth-century discussions of Normanness, Anglo-Saxonness, and national identity, the William annalist is just as explicit in his criticism of the Anglo-Saxons; he even goes so far as to suggest that they deserved their fate.[19] Thus the annalist's general narrative perspective runs counter to his supposed partisan nationalist sentiments. And the details of the annals fail to clarify the current historical avenues of inquiry, while the historical questions fail to explain the shape and details of the text.

Such divergence calls for a new interpretive matrix. When placed in the cultural milieu of certain eleventh-century monastic houses, houses that interpreted the function and power of written records and historical narratives in particular ways, the William annalist's narrative of lordship relations is less a vernacular discourse of Anglo-Saxon secular identity than an approach to the questions of institutional identity and cultural permanence. This new context transforms the D *Chronicle* from a nostalgic relic of the Anglo-Saxon historical and historiographical past into a vigorous piece of contemporary writing. Indeed, the agenda of the D text is closely allied to that of other well-studied, post-Conquest works like John of Worcester's *Chronicle*, Hemming's *Cartulary*, and Coleman's *Vita Wulfstani* as preserved by William of Malmesbury.

Sin, King, and the End of the *Angelcynn*

To understand both the significance of the William annalist's approach and the function of his narrative in its eleventh-century context, I begin by exploring how the other major Conquest narratives interpret the Norman invasion and Anglo-Saxon defeat. In William of Jumièges's *Gesta Normannorum ducum* (c. 1070), the Conquest is justified by Harold's broken oath. Edward appoints William as his heir,[20] and Harold swears fidelity to the duke when, having been sent by King Edward to confirm this, he is trapped by Guy of Abbeville and freed by William.[21] The legal aspect of this story is further developed in William of Poitiers's *Gesta Guillelmi* (c. 1071–7).[22] William records how Harold, ignoring the results of an election, and violating his oath,[23] takes the throne, forcing William, the adopted son of Edward, to reclaim his throne from his brother.[24] William exploits the overtones of Greek tragedy.[25] He even claims that William is ready to plead his case according to Anglo-Saxon or Norman law and shows the king offering Harold individual combat, thereby suggesting that the Conquest can be reframed as the kind of duel by which, in French and English romance texts at least, legal cases are resolved.[26] In other words, the Norman sources view the Conquest through the lens of the law:

legally, Edward makes William his heir, and Harold's failure to keep his oath of loyalty to William directly causes the invasion.

The Latin Anglo-Saxon and Anglo-Norman sources understand the Conquest differently. Again using the law, John of Worcester (writing between 1095 and 1140)[27] portrays Harold as a good king who uses both secular and canon law to bring about a better situation for his people and to protect and enhance the life of the church;[28] he offers no justification for the Norman invasion. In the *Historia novorum in Anglia*, Eadmer of Canterbury includes the story of Harold's oath, but suggests that Harold is on a private mission and that William exploits this recklessness: Harold gives his oath in order to secure the freedom of his nephew.[29] In his *Historia Anglorum*, the majority of which was written by c. 1130,[30] Henry of Huntingdon calls Harold's succession a usurpation and goes on to discuss Harold's perjury, but counters the baldness of his claim by calling the Conquest the fulfilment of a divine plan.[31]

The idea of divine control over events is repeated in Orderic Vitalis's *Ecclesiastical History*.[32] Orderic notes that it is God's will that the English leave their coast unguarded,[33] but includes the story of Harold's oath and his perjury. To these details, Orderic also adds an image of Harold as an unreasonable, arrogant, and proud king; by the conventions of salvation discourse, these sins lead directly to the loss of the kingdom.[34] In his *Gesta regum Anglorum*, William of Malmesbury uses the story of Harold's oath as a base for his account, but he also lingers over the picture of the Anglo-Saxons drinking and singing the night before the battle while the Normans pray, confess their sins, and take communion. Each behaves according to the custom of their nation, William claims.[35] The Anglo-Saxons have fallen; they are no longer zealous about learning; their monastic culture has declined; they are greedy; they drink; and they sport shaven chins, short hair, and short clothes.[36] Such delinquency justifies their defeat.

The relative consistency of these histories emphasizes the difference of the D text. As in salvation histories, the William annalist stresses that the outcome of the Battle of Hastings results from the Anglo-Saxons' transgressions, and he reaffirms the possibility of divine control over events.[37] But the Anglo-Saxons of the D text are not immoral sinners who overeat, drink too much, and engage in other kinds of depravity. Nor, in the D text at least, is Harold guilty of perjury. Rather, in a careful adaptation of the previous annals of conquest and invasion, the William annalist frames the Anglo-Saxons' sins as a lordship problem;

specifically, the Anglo-Saxons do not always act upon their obligation to be faithful to their king. Beginning by highlighting the Anglo-Saxons' disunity under Harold and Edward, the annalist shows that William's failure to keep his oath and his consequent inability to win the loyalty of his people effectively end the ideology and identity of the *Angelcynn*. In other words, the Conquest itself merely concludes a demise that began earlier.

To read the events of 1066 as part of a larger lordship narrative is to take the interpretive weight off the defeat at Hastings, to focus on the last year of Edward's reign, and to consider the events – beginning in 1065 – that ultimately make William's victory possible. In 1065, the last year of the reign of Edward the Confessor, the thanes of both Yorkshire and Northumbria rise up against Harold's brother, Tostig, kill both his Anglo-Saxon and Danish bodyguards, take his treasure, and send for Morcar, the son of Earl Ælfgar, as their next earl. Harold is sent to King Edward bearing the news and asking for permission for Morcar to remain as their earl. Edward responds positively, sending Harold back to Northampton where he delivers and guarantees the king's message and then renews Cnut's law.[38] Tostig and his wife go into exile.[39]

From reading the C text of the *Chronicle* and the *Vita Eadwardi*, modern historians of these events have reacted to the history behind the figure of Tostig and have thus produced a story of personal failure.[40] In the C text, the annalist is quite explicit: Tostig is outlawed because 'he rypte God ærost 7 ealle þa bestrypte þe he ofermihte æt life 7 æt lande' (he first robbed God and then stripped all those he overpowered of life and land).[41] The picture painted in the *Vita Eadwardi* is somewhat more complicated. Drawing explicit parallels between the Anglo-Saxon present and Theban history,[42] the author of Edward's life focuses on Tostig's character, the tension between the brothers, the pain the dispute causes the king, and the risk it poses to the kingdom.[43]

The D text has a different conceptual centre. Instead of writing Tostig's personal history, the William annalist omits the story of his brutality and injustice in order to configure the problem as one of Edward's lordship. Edward does not understand his people well enough and thus chooses the wrong lord for the people of the North.[44] And in recording Edward's responses, the annalist shows that Edward (correctly) interprets the rebellion as a problem of his lordship.[45] Instead of replying with force and engaging in what effectively would be civil war,[46] Edward acquiesces to his people's demands and proceeds to renew Cnut's laws.[47]

What this would mean in a literal sense is unclear – no particular aspect of the codes is explicitly identified, nor are there extant records that would clarify the nature of any such ceremony. But by invoking Cnut's law, the annalist suggests that Edward recalls for his people an era in which traditional enemies lived peacefully under the loyal lordship of a king, even a king who sought to protect his people from an abusive lord.[48] In other words, by having Edward renew Cnut's law, the annalist suggests that Edward symbolically promises his people in general, and the thanes of Northumbria and Yorkshire in particular, that he will be a good lord to them. That such disloyalty does not reflect negatively on Edward reinforces the conceptual importance of Edward's action: this king understands the authority and obligations implicit in his lordship bonds.

Though Edward acts appropriately, the details of the annal portray the thanes as significantly less respectful of their lordship ties. While Harold pleads their case to the king, the thanes plunder and burn the land and then compound their wrongdoing by attacking the people in Northampton: '7 fela hund manna hi naman 7 læddan norð mid heom, swa þæt seo scir 7 þa oðra scira þæ ðærneah sindon wurdan fela wintra ðe wyrsan' (And they captured many hundreds of people and took them north with them, so that the shire and the other shires that were nearby were, for many years [after that], much the worse).[49] Further, unlike the C annalist, the William annalist does not explain the reasoning for the thanes' actions,[50] and without an explanation that touches upon Tostig's brutality, the raid on Northampton registers as unmotivated violence that springs from Edward's (and not Tostig's) culture of poor lordship relations. Even though Edward agrees to their request, the men show their king no respect.[51]

Losing the Battle

The poor quality of Edward's lordship bonds is significant in itself and in the effect it has on the D conquest narrative. In the other Conquest texts, the transfer of power from Edward to Harold is freighted by the issue of legitimacy.[52] But in the D text, there is no question of Harold's right to succeed. The annal for 1065 concludes with a eulogistic poem that, ignoring the problems of the Tostig episode, rewrites history in order to commend Edward for his ideal lordship of the Anglo-Saxons. Drawing on the exile-lordship topos, the poet (who may or may not be the annalist) presents Edward in the tradition of other exiled Anglo-

Saxon kings as a lord who 'landes bereafod, wunoda wreclastum wide geond eorðan' (deprived of land, dwelled in the paths of exile far and wide throughout the earth), distributing gifts until he regains his throne.[53]

As the poet praises Edward for his lordship, his approval legitimates Harold's accession. Edward invests Harold with his glory and the kingdom as a reward for Harold's loyalty: '7 se froda swaðeah befæste þæt rice heahðungena menn, Harolde sylfum, æðelum eorle, se in ealne tid herdæ holdelice herran synum wordum 7 dædum wihte ne agælde þæs þe ðearfe wæs ðæs þeodkyngces' (And yet the wise [king] commended the kingdom to a man from an illustrious family, Harold himself, the noble earl, who at all times loyally obeyed his lord, in both word and deed, and did not neglect any task that the people's king needed).[54] Without mentioning the problems of succession on Edward's death and apparently ignoring Harold's intervention on behalf of the rebels, the poem establishes Harold as Edward's ideal and only possible successor. Because he respects and is faithful to his lord, Harold is the ideal next ruler of the Anglo-Saxons.

If, as this text suggests, Harold inherits Edward's position as lord, he also inherits the former king's problems with his thanes, problems of which formerly he was a part.[55] In the William annalist's hands, Harold is a successful lord when he is ending the threat posed by Tostig – thus redeeming his earlier behaviour – but unsuccessful at winning the support of his men in general. And, in this account of history, the continued disunity among the Anglo-Saxons lies behind the defeat at Hastings.

The annalist begins with the story of Tostig's return from exile, a story that confirms the decayed state of Anglo-Saxon lordship relations and sets up the defeat at Hastings. For other *Chronicle* kings like Alfred, Æthelred, and Edward, the return from exile is a kind of topos that functions as a precursor to winning the kingdom with strong lordship ties. The William annalist inverts this tradition by using Tostig's return to underscore the point that even before Hastings the Anglo-Saxons' lordship culture is fragmented.

At first, the annalist suggests that Harold, unlike Edward, has been able to win the loyalty of his men; he states clearly that the earls loyal to Harold are able to drive Tostig back. Their victory is symbolic: Tostig's own men desert him, and he submits to his former ally.[56] With this detail of Tostig's submission to Harold Hardrada, the annalist adds to the general narrative of dismal lordship among the Anglo-

Saxons. Not only is Tostig unable to keep his men, he is also unable to maintain his loyalty to his Anglo-Saxon lord and king. Here, Tostig abrogates his membership in the *Angelcynn*, and, in his choice of *bugan* (bow) as opposed to *cyrran* (submit), the annalist suggests that Tostig's submission is one of subjection.[57] The tie to Harold Hardrada is not the kind of tie by which a lordship bond is created and a new united people identified.

Functionally, the story of Tostig's failure underscores Harold's success, and the annalist suggests that, in the short term at least, Tostig's disloyalty and Harold's own history are counterbalanced by the ways in which Harold returns his kingdom to order.[58] When the battle at Stamford Bridge is over, Harold Hardrada and Tostig are dead; the annalist notes that the 'Engle ahton wælstowe geweald' (Anglo-Saxons had control of the field).[59] Throughout the *Chronicle* records of battle, this expression is virtually formulaic, but, for the annalists of conquest and invasion, it gains added meaning. Peace making is not about the possession or defence of territory but about the kind of lordship that unites the people. After the battle, Harold goes to Olaf, son of Harold Hardrada, to contract peace. The annalist describes Harold's peace-making ceremony in detail:

> Se kyng þa geaf gryð Olafe, þæs Norna cynges suna, 7 heora biscoppe, 7 þan eorle of Orcanege, 7 eallon þan þe on þam scypum to lafe wæron, 7 hi foron þa upp to uran kyninge, 7 sworon aðas þæt hi æfre woldon fryð 7 freondscype into þisan lande haldan.

> Then the king made peace with Olaf, the son of the Norwegian king, and with their bishop, and the earl of Orkney, and all those on the ships who had survived, and they approached our king, and swore oaths that henceforth they would always hold peace and friendship towards this land.[60]

The language of this moment sets the D text apart from all the other narratives of the Norman Conquest in the way it specifies the value and significance of a loyalty oath. In the Norman and Anglo-Norman accounts, Harold takes an oath of loyalty that later comes to bear legal significance; here, however, the power dynamic is reversed. Harold accepts others' loyalty oaths, oaths that are both personal and political – they bring about 'fryð 7 freondscype' (peace and friendship). The Norwegians and Anglo-Saxons are drawn into relationship under Harold's lordship, and this conventional lexicon places Harold's actions firmly in the tradition of Anglo-Saxon lordship and peace making. Like Alfred and Æthelred before him, Harold binds the Scandinavian invaders to him with the friendship implied in a personal lordship bond.[61] And because of the close correspondence between Anglo-Saxon discourses of lordship, political friendship, and personal friendship, the oaths do not signify primarily as part of a legal discourse.[62] Political peace, in this instance, is a product of personal lordship ties.[63]

Though the annalist portrays the Anglo-Saxons and Norwegians making peace – even becoming friends – in terms that are readily recognizable as lordship bonds, the collective identity articulated in this annal requires further study. Even as the annalist declares Harold's success, repeated references to the Anglo-Saxons' differing ethnic origins imply an ongoing awareness of the ways in which Harold has not been able to unify his kingdom; the divisions from Edward's reign continue.

In 1065, the poet proclaims the breadth of Edward's power, but a second look at his terminology shows that Edward rules not over the *Angelcynn* but over the 'Walum 7 Scottum 7 Bryttum eac ... Englum 7 Sæxum' (Welsh, and the Scots, and the Britons, as well [as] the ... Anglians, and the Saxons), a kingdom that is all too aware of ethnic difference.[64] Further and perhaps more telling examples of these differences can be found in the Tostig episode. In the entry for 1065, Tostig loses both the *Englisc* and *Denisc* men of his household.[65] After the rebellion, Morcar travels to meet Edward with a group of the people defined by their geographic origins: he goes with men from his 'scire, 7 mid Snotinghamscire, 7 Deorbyscire, 7 Lincolnascire' (shire, and with [people from] Nottinghamshire, Derbyshire, and Lincolnshire).[66] Thus, in the annal for 1066, when the annalist calls Harold 'our king,' he implies that Harold has been successful where his predecessor has not.

That said, the phrase 'ure cyning' (our king) calls into question the 'we' alongside whom the annalist positions himself. When Morcar and Eadwin are unable to resist Tostig and the Norwegians, the annalist calls Harold 'Engla cynge' (king of the Anglo-Saxons); when Harold joins battle at Stamford Bridge, he is said to arrive 'mid micclan here engliscs folces' (with a large army of the Anglo-Saxon people); when Harold and his men put the invaders to flight, he remarks that the 'engliscan' (the Anglo-Saxons) pursued them fiercely; and finally, the 'Engle' (Anglo-Saxons) take control of the battlefield.[67] This terminology invokes the unity of the Anglo-Saxons in, for example, the invasion narratives of Alfred and Cnut. But who are the people designated as *Engle*? Does *Engle*, as in previous conquest and invasion narratives, refer to the people who are the *Angelcynn* or, as in the Edward encomium, are the *Engle* separate from the Saxons and British, etc.?

The annalist never explicitly answers this question, but the division suggested by his terminology comes to the fore in his account of the Hastings battle. On one level, the Anglo-Saxons' defeat is facilitated, logistically, by Tostig's invasion: when William lands, Harold is in the wrong place at the wrong time, and his army is tired. But the William annalist does not see the Normans' success as a matter of logistics alone. His focus on lordship turns the practical aspects of the situation into a story where Harold is unable to defend the realm because he is away dealing with the lordship problems of Edward's reign. In other words, Harold's part in his brother's rebellion ultimately leads to the downfall of his own kingdom.

In the annalist's hands, it seems that Harold has not managed to win and maintain the loyalty of his men. Even as he praises Harold for his bravery, the annalist comments, 'Ac se kyng þeah him swiðe heardlice wið feaht mid þam mannum þe him gelæstan woldon' (But the king nonetheless fought very bravely against them [the Normans] alongside the men who wanted to help him).[68] In this small aside, the annalist reveals dissent among the Anglo-Saxons; Harold fights bravely, but heroic effort is insufficient because not all the men who should have supported their king wanted to do so.[69] This failure to recognize and abide by the authority invested in the king's lordship is, as the story of Tostig suggests, a long-standing difficulty that Harold, like Edward, bequeaths to his successor. Poor lordship relations are the explicit cause of the Hastings defeat.

Making William King

Though William defeats the Anglo-Saxons at Hastings, victory does not necessarily make him king. And in the *interregnum*, there is no clear line of authority and no clear leader for the Anglo-Saxons. The annalist exploits this historical situation to show how the lordship discourse that defines the *Angelcynn* finally becomes irrelevant to William's new people.

First, he suggests that the Anglo-Saxons are partly responsible for the demise of their culture. A simple defeat is not enough to remedy a long-standing problem in the culture of lordship relations; rather, the Anglo-Saxons continue to transgress by not interpreting the consequences of defeat correctly. Instead of recognizing William as their king, the Anglo-Saxons repeat the mistakes of the Tostig episode: Ealdred and the citizens of London 'woldon habban þa Eadgar cild to kynge, eallswa him wel gecynde wæs, 7 Eadwine 7 Morkere him beheton þæt hi mid him feohtan woldon' (then wanted to have Edgar Child as their king as it was certainly proper for him, and Eadwin and Morcar promised them that they would fight alongside him).[70] In recording the justification for supporting Edgar – it is 'fitting' or, perhaps, it is 'his birthright'[71] – the annalist implies that the Anglo-Saxon leaders are unable or unwilling to interpret the events at Hastings appropriately. That Morcar, Tostig's replacement, is involved is suggestive. In 1065, Morcar allowed the people, as opposed to the king, to make him an earl of the North. For the annalist, however, the decision to pursue a king by virtue of what is fitting leads to disorder: 'Ac swa hit æfre forðlicor beon sceolde, swa wearð hit from dæge to dæge lætre 7 wyrre eallswa hit æt þam ende eall geferde' (But the more things were supposed to go forward, the later they were and from day to day grew worse, exactly as it all came to pass at the end).[72]

Thus when the Anglo-Saxons are finally forced to submit, the annalist underscores the point by blaming them for the disorder: '7 bugon þa for neode þa mæst wæs to hearme gedon, 7 þæt wæs micel unræd þæt man æror swa ne dyde, þa hit God betan nolde for urum synnum' (And submitted then out of necessity [only] once the greatest damage had been done, and it was a great foolishness that they did not do so before, since God did not want to improve anything on account of our sins).[73] Explicitly, the damage in question is the ravaged landscape. Because, in Anglo-Saxon texts, the landscape is an important part of the discourse of lordship, references to the destroyed land that the Anglo-Saxons must now inhabit suggest that the 'greatest damage' is the loss of the Anglo-Saxon lordship culture. When the Anglo-Saxons yield to William, the annalist uses *bugan* ('to bow or submit,' but without the sense of a unifying lordship ceremony). The absence of the ceremony of mutual oath swearing and pledging stands in sharp contrast to the scene at Stamford Bridge. In this way, the annalist suggests, the Anglo-Saxons can be held responsible for the end of Anglo-Saxon lordship.

If the Anglo-Saxons are at fault, so too is the new king. In other *Chronicle* narratives where the kingdom is threatened, the kings – Alfred, Æthelred, Cnut, and even Harold – appear to take the defeated parties' submissions almost immediately and engage them in a ceremony of lordship that is unifying and healing.[74] But although William wins the battle, he does not enforce his authority over the Anglo-Saxons. There is no ceremony of submission and mutual pledging of oaths, and without such a scene, the king is unable to translate his military victory into lordship authority. Indeed, the annalist supplies an image of a king who, frustrated by the ongoing fighting, 'for eft ongean to Hæstingan, 7 geanbidode þær hwæðer man him to bugan wolde' (travelled again back to Hastings, and waited there [to see] if they would submit to him).[75] Again by using *bugan*, the annalist suggests that William will not participate in the kind of renewing ceremony of lordship, the ceremony by which, in other similar post-conquest or invasion scenes, the *Angelcynn* are constituted under the king's lordship.

This gap between what the annalist presents as William's expectations and *Chronicle* lexical and narrative convention informs the brief but meaningful representation of the eventual submission scene. As is traditional, the Anglo-Saxons 'gysledan 7 sworon him aðas' (gave hostages and swore him oaths).[76] In other words, the Anglo-Saxons are shown proceeding according to the dictates of their lordship culture. And, the annalist suggests, William responds in kind. The king 'heom behet þæt he wolde heom hold hlaford beon' (promised them that he would be a loyal lord to them).[77] As I argued in chapter 5, this phrase appears primarily in situations where the Anglo-Saxons are negotiating peace with their conquerors and most tellingly in the texts surrounding the Danish Conquest.[78] Thus to invoke the phrase 'hold hlaford' (loyal lord) is to explicitly pattern the settlement of the Norman Conquest after that of the Danish, a conquest in which the corrupt lordship culture of Æthelred was corrected under the reign of Cnut. In this case, then, the annalist tempts his readers into thinking that William comes to improve the poor lordship cultures of Edward and Harold.

That William and the Anglo-Saxons are not speaking the same cultural (or perhaps literal) language soon becomes clear in the clause immediately following William's promise and in the representation of his coronation. But the problem is how to understand the divide. Modern historians have suggested that in some regards Norman and Anglo-Saxon lordship practices were similar, though there were possibilities for misunderstanding the ways in which the Anglo-Saxons associated the lordship ceremony with the election to the kingship.[79] The annalist does not allow William the benefit of any kind of doubt; rather, he implies that the king deliberately contradicts his loyalty promise: '7 þeah onmang þisan hi hergedan eall þæt hi oferforon' (And yet meanwhile they [the Normans] ravaged everything that they overran).[80] The force of this interpretation rests on the '7 þeah' (and yet) by which the annalist implies that William understood the ceremony, but still decided to destroy the land despite his oath.

The annalist reinforces the deliberate nature of the king's actions in his representation of the coronation. The question of William's coronation oath is greatly discussed and turns in general on the problem of whether William was crowned according to the second or third *ordo*.[81] For the purposes of my argument, the particular rite used is not important – the *promissio regis* remains the same – unless, as has also been argued, the prelates also drew on part of the *ordo romanus*, which makes the king promise to hold the country as his predecessors had done. The latter would account for the annalist's claim that the king swore 'þæt he wolde þisne þeodscype swa wel haldan swa ænig kyngc ætforan him betst dyde' (that he would rule this kingdom as well as any king before him ever did).[82]

That said, neither rite adequately explains the second part of what the annalist claims is William's promise. William swears to rule well 'gif hi him holde beon woldon' (if they [the Anglo-Saxons] would be loyal to him).[83] The king's desire for his people to be loyal echoes the situation in 1014 when Æthelred returns to his realm, promising 'þæt he him hold hlaford beon wolde 7 ælc þæra ðinga betan þe hi ealle ascunudon, 7 ælc þara ðinga forgyfen beon sceolde þe him gedon oððe gecweden wære, wið þam ðe hi ealle anrædlice butan swicdome to him gecyrdon' (that he [Æthelred] would be a loyal lord to them, and amend each of the things that they all hated, and that everything that had been done or said against him would be forgiven, provided that they all submitted resolutely to him without any betrayal).[84] In other words, the annalist explicitly invokes the accessions (and reaccessions) of the most recent conquest situations, seeking to establish a gulf between what was expected of William and what he actually did. 'Swaþeah' (despite) these vows – again, the annalist provides interpretive guidance – the king proceeds to levy heavy taxes, leave the country with his hostages, build castles throughout the land, and oppress the people.[85] William, the annalist claims, has denied his lordship obligations.

Narrating the End of Anglo-Saxon Lordship

Once William has denied his lordship obligations, the D annals of the *Chronicle* divide. On the one hand, the annalist offers the story of

William's attempts to quell his people and secure his throne; this strand of the narrative provides an object lesson in the problems of interpreting land as a source of authority and, in so doing, traces the end of Anglo-Saxon lordship while holding the king responsible. On the other hand, the annalist uses the stories of William's rebels to show that the Anglo-Saxon nobles are also to blame. When joined with the story of Malcolm of Scotland, these narrative threads preserve the culture of Anglo-Saxon lordship.

The story of William, his lordship, and the land begins in the annal for 1067 with the story of the siege at Exeter.[86] William returns to England on St Nicholas's Day, and Christ's Church in Canterbury burns down. The two events are not causally linked, but exploiting *Chronicle* style conventions – they are linked with the conjunction 'and' – the annalist suggests, without stating, that one might be seen as a consequence of the other, and that both are symbols of an oncoming doom. The predicted misfortunes play out in the narrative of William's lordship and the land. Eadric rebels, the Welsh become 'unsehte' (hostile), the king 'sette micel gyld on earm folc, 7 þeahhwæðre let æfre herigan eall þæt hi oferforon' (laid a heavy tax on the miserable people, and nevertheless constantly had everything that they overran ravaged).[87] The message is clear: control of the land is not equivalent to possessing the authority that governs the people.

In the annalist's hands, the gulf between land and lordship means that the more William exerts his authority over the land, the greater his difficulties with the people and the greater the threat to Anglo-Saxon lordship culture. In a carefully slanted account of the siege at Exeter, the annalist suggests that the culture of lordship is now so corrupt that the people are vulnerable to treachery on the part of their thanes and the king. In his account of the same siege, Orderic Vitalis describes the king as a mild, caring leader who thought to spare his people;[88] this, however, is not the picture painted in the D text. William arrives at Exeter, where a large part of his army dies. 'Ac he heom wel behet, 7 yfele gelæste, 7 hig him þa burh ageafon, for þan þa þegenas heom geswicon hæfdon' (But he made good promises to them, and kept them badly, and they yielded the city to him because the thanes had betrayed them).[89] Echoing his comments on the coronation, the annalist again claims that William is unable to keep a promise, but he also shows that the king's disloyalty has a trickle-down effect. Explaining neither how nor why the thanes betray the people, the annalist suggests that William gains the city of Exeter because both he and his thanes fail to keep their promises to the people. Just as the king disregards the terms under which he assumed lordship of his country – notice again the 'þeahhwæðere' (nevertheless) – so the members of his nobility in turn break their promises to their own people. Nonetheless, the annalist does not criticize the Anglo-Saxon thanes; their behaviour is justified in view of the king's.

But the annal for 1067 does not conclude on this despairing note; lordship is alive, albeit beyond the territorial boundaries of the kingdom. Once the city has fallen, the annalist returns to the stories of Edgar, the former *ætheling* and candidate for the throne, and Margaret, his sister. At first it seems as though the brief *vita* of St Margaret is an inexplicable and meaningless digression. In the midst of the Norman settlement narrative, the annalist pauses to tell an almost clichéd story of an Anglo-Saxon noblewoman who was given against her will to a pagan husband; she converted him to her faith and then did great deeds for the church throughout the rest of her life. But when we consider the way in which this episode is set between images of William ravaging his land and abusing his people, the fact that the husband in question is Malcolm of Scotland, and that Margaret's marriage later enables her to fund a rebellion against the king with the resources of Scotland, a traditional enemy, the Margaret *vita* takes on a different aspect.

In the annalist's hands, Margaret becomes key to preserving the lordship culture of the *Angelcynn*. Though the Anglo-Saxons and Scots are traditional enemies, the relationship between Malcolm III, Tostig, and Edward appears to have been relatively friendly, and in contemporary historical criticism it is possible to see Tostig as a peace-maker between the Scots and the Anglo-Saxons. This story is absent from the D text where Malcolm figures primarily as an enemy until Margaret comes, embodying Anglo-Saxon lordship culture, as a peace-weaver to Scotland.[90] Unlike William's wife, who is unable to contain her husband – the juxtaposition of the two wives' stories is effective – Margaret appears to civilize her husband by converting him to the faith and indoctrinating him in the ideals of Anglo-Saxon lordship.[91] So effective is her instruction that Malcolm's respect for his lordship ties stands in sharp contrast to that of the king. When, in the annal for 1073 (*recte* 1072), William invades Scotland, Malcolm submits '7 gryðode wið Wyllelm cyngc, 7 wæs his man, 7 him gyslas salde' (and made peace with King William, and became his man, and gave him hostages).[92] At this moment, Malcolm contracts peace in the conventional language of

Anglo-Saxon peace making, and he creates the kind of lordship bond with his king that the Anglo-Saxons would have expected.

Unlike William, who the annalist insists breaks his lordship oaths, Malcolm, the traditional Anglo-Saxon enemy, understands and respects this lordship. And he abides by it, preserving a culture that is now foreign to the Anglo-Saxons. When in 1075 (*recte* 1074), Edgar returns to Malcolm's court, the Scottish king receives him and gives

> him myccla geofa 7 manega gærsama 7 eallon his mannan, on scynnan mid pælle betogen, 7 on merðerne pyleceon, 7 graschynnene, 7 hearmascynnene, 7 on pællon, 7 on gyldenan faton, 7 on seolfrenan, 7 hine 7 ealle his scyperan mid mycclan weorðscipe of his gryðe alædde.

> him and all his men great gifts and many treasures of skins covered with costly purple cloth, and of robes made from skins of martens, and of grey fur, and of ermine, and [gifts of] silk robes, and gold and silver vessels and [Malcolm] led him [Edgar] and all his men from the ship out of his domain with great honour.[93]

Though we might want to understand these gifts as symbols of support, the annalist clearly shows that this is not the case. Malcolm honours Edgar, but he does not finance this rebellion and thereby betray his lordship bond with William. When Edgar's mission goes wrong and he is captured, Malcolm advises Edgar to seek the king's peace (*gryð*) and, implicitly, the lordship bond that would accompany that peace. When compared with William, Malcolm of the Scots – a people who have consistently threatened the *Angelcynn* – is now presented as a king who respects and understands lordship relations. In other words, the ruler of the people traditionally most antagonistic to the Anglo-Saxons can now be seen as the ideal Anglo-Saxon leader.[94]

The story of Malcolm's faithfulness, evoking as it does the idea that loyalty is a principle extending beyond national boundaries, stands in sharp contrast to the narrative of domestic disregard for loyal lordship, i.e., the story of William and the Anglo-Saxon rebels. Simply put, William does not understand the people whose land he controls. In addition to the annal for 1067, the entries for 1068 and 1071 (*recte* 1070) – the year in which the king orders the monasteries to be plundered – both contain images of William (unsuccessfully) enforcing his power by destroying the land. In 1068, he quells a second rebellion by Edgar *ætheling* at York, and in the details of the brutality, the annalist continues his narrative of William's broken oaths. Specifically, the king 'þa ofsloh þa þe ætfleon ne mihton, þæt wæron fela hund manna, 7 þa burh forhergode, 7 sancte Petres mynster to bysmere macede, 7 ealle þa oðre eac forhergode 7 forhynde' (then killed all those who could not flee, that was many hundreds of men, and he plundered the town and shamed St Peter's minster, and also destroyed and humiliated all the others).[95] And, in response to another attack by Edgar and supporters, William 'þa scire mid ealle forhergode 7 aweste' (completely plundered and laid the shire to waste).[96] In 1071 (*recte* 1070), William 'let hergian ealle þa mynstra þe on Englalande wæron. 7 þæs geres wæs micel hunger' (had all the monasteries that were in England plundered, and that year, there was a great famine).[97] For the annalist, these details require no comment.

The history of Edgar and Malcolm sheds significant light on the other rebellion narratives. The stories of William's rebels are not cast in a nationalistic (and twelfth-century) discourse of Anglo-Saxon versus Norman; rather, the annalist uses their resistance as a means of charting the decline of Anglo-Saxon lordship culture. In 1066, Earls Edwin and Morcar surrender to William, but, repeating the behaviour for which the annalist criticized the Anglo-Saxons in the pre-Conquest annals, these men refuse to acknowledge their lord. Invoking the lordship topos of exile, the annalist claims that both men 'ferdon on wuda 7 on feldon' (wandered in the woods and the fields) where Edwin is killed by one of his own men.[98] In the larger narrative of disregarded lordship ties, this seems fitting.

The story of Morcar stresses the depth of this disregard. In the struggle over the land, neither William as lord nor Morcar as man abide by ideal lordship conventions. At the end of yet another rebellion, Morcar and the others are defeated and placed 'þan kyninge on hand' (into the king's hands), and William responds by taking from them the means of support for another rebellion: '7 se kyng nam heora scypa 7 wæpna 7 manega sceattas, 7 þa menn ealle he toc, 7 dyde of heom þæt he wolde' (And the king took their ships, weapons, and a lot of money, and he took all the men and did with them whatever he wanted).[99] In contrast to the terminology of the previous peace-making scenes, the annalist's language points out the futility of Morcar's submission. There is no possibility of renewal or mutual relationship in this yielding, and, further, in the final comment, the annalist hints at the danger in a king who focuses on material goods as symbols of his power. For William, money, ships, and weapons are

Writing William's Kingship 139

more important than the men; the latter, the annalist suggests, are disposable for the king.

The fullest explication of the breakdown of lordship culture comes in the story of Earl Waltheof. Immediately after his coronation, William returns to Normandy taking with him many of the remaining Anglo-Saxon nobility; Waltheof is one of these men. He participates in the 1068 rebellion by joining forces with the sons of King Swein (of Denmark), *ætheling* Edgar, Mærlswein, Earl Gospatric with the Northumbrians, and all the people in a rebellion in which the land is wasted and many Normans killed.[100] William responds by laying to waste the whole shire, and in the next year, Waltheof makes peace with William.

Waltheof, however, together with some of the remaining Anglo-Saxon nobles and some churchmen, once more plots treason. At the wedding of Ralph, earl of Norfolk, to Emma, daughter of William fitz Osbern, those gathered, including Earl Waltheof, Roger of Breteuil, and some high-ranking but nameless ecclesiastics, conspire to drive William from the kingdom with the help of Breton and Danish forces. The Danes, arriving only after William has already begun to capture the plotters, dare not challenge the king; they raid Peterborough, depart, and die at sea. The Bretons, on the other hand, are captured and either blinded, exiled, or shamed; the fate of the churchmen is not recorded. Waltheof escapes overseas, accuses himself, asks for pardon, and offers treasure. William, then abroad, 'let lihtlice' (made light) of the deed for a year, thereby suggesting that Waltheof has renegotiated himself into his lord's protection.[101] But when the king returns, Waltheof is captured and then beheaded.[102]

Though we might want to read Waltheof's rebellion as an act of resistance and thus place the annal alongside such texts as the *Gesta Herewardi*,[103] the annalist prohibits any valorization of Waltheof and his resistance. Indeed, the story of Waltheof and William is part of the general disregard for the ideals of Anglo-Saxon lordship. By using a traditional term, 'gryðode' (made peace), to describe the peace built between Waltheof and William, the annalist implies that the two are reconciled to each other and bound by a lordship tie. But neither Waltheof nor William sustain this relationship. Explicitly naming the wedding plot as a conspiracy against William's lordship – the plotters wish to drive out their 'kynehlaford' (royal lord)[104] – the annalist uses this narrative to explore the state of lordship relations in post-Conquest England. From the annalist's point of view, neither William nor Waltheof acts in accordance with the ethos of Anglo-Saxon lordship.

Waltheof breaks his peace with the king, and the king, by apparently accepting Waltheof's offer of peace and then executing him, acts in bad faith.[105]

That the Waltheof episode is not just an example of Anglo-Saxon-Norman conflict is indicated by the penultimate annal of the D text.[106] So corrupt is the culture of lordship in the new kingdom that the annals effectively conclude with a symbolic attempt at regicide that is ultimately provoked by frustration at the ways in which William performs his lordship obligations. Where in the Alfred and Æthelred-Cnut annals, Anglo-Saxon lordship culture can contain father-son disputes, William's son, Robert

> hleop fram his fæder to his eame Rotbryhte on Flandron, for þan þe his fæder ne wolde him lætan waldan his eorldomes on Normandige þe he sylf 7 eac se kyng Filippus mid his geþafunge him gegyfen hæfdon.

> deserted [lit. jumped from] his father for his uncle, Robert, in Flanders because his father did not wish him to rule his earldom in Normandy that he himself, also with the consent of King Philip, had given him.[107]

Robert attacks William and wounds him in the hand. The annalist is so repelled by the utter disregard for lordship responsibilities shown by both king and son – the giving of land is an act of lordship and William again reneges on his obligations – that he comments, 'Ne wylle we þeh her na mare scaðe awritan þe he his fæder ge ...' (Yet we do not want to write more here about the injury that he [did] to his father).[108] When a son attacks his lord, father, and king, the culture of lordship has passed.

The *Chronicle* at Worcester

The case for attributing the D annals to Worcester is unresolved, but my analysis of the significance of these annals assumes that the *Chronicle* is a Worcester text, partly because Worcester is generally accepted as the place of origin and partly because the text speaks so directly to the circumstances of the Worcester community, resonating strongly with the other extant Worcester histories.[109] The histories of Worcester, its land, and its ecclesiastical culture are long and complicated, and as they have been more fully explored elsewhere, I supply only an abbreviated version of the relevant issues.[110] My concern is the relationship between the renewed writing of historical texts at Worcester and the changes affecting the land, the minster, and Anglo-Saxon monastic culture.[111]

The post-Conquest land history of the Worcester-Evesham-York region is shaped by three men – Ealdred, Wulfstan, and Æthelwig – their relationships, rivalries, institutional positions, and desire for territory. Bishop Ealdred of Worcester understood and exploited the connection between land and authority. When he became archbishop of York, a see that is known to have been significantly less well-off than Worcester, he desired like his predecessors to hold the sees in plurality and use the wealth of Worcester to enrich York. The pope made his pallium conditional on the surrender of Worcester and, formally, Ealdred complied, but this did not mean that he ceased to be concerned with the community's estates or that his influence at Worcester did not continue. Of the two prime candidates for succession to the bishopric of Worcester, Ealdred chose the one he thought would be most obedient to him: his former prior, Wulfstan.[112] And just after his consecration Ealdred appropriated almost all the episcopal estates, once more enhancing York with the wealth of Worcester.[113]

The candidate Ealdred rejected for the bishopric was Abbot Æthelwig of Evesham.[114] According to Worcester sources at least, this was because Æthelwig appeared too worldly and too skilled in his acquisition of land and power.[115] Ealdred acted, of course, for his own reasons, but in choosing Wulfstan he furthered the long-standing rivalry between the two institutions, a rivalry that took shape over the issue of land. Æthelwig surrendered promptly to William, and William repaid him handsomely; in effect, Æthelwig governed Worcestershire, Gloucestershire, Oxfordshire, Herefordshire, Staffordshire, and Shropshire.[116] His secular authority meant that he was also potentially a powerful patron, and many committed themselves to his lordship. With this personal tie, however, also came many lands, formerly under the care of the bishop of Worcester.[117] After Æthelwig's death, Worcester was to reassert its rights in a much-discussed lawsuit.[118]

At first sight, then, the Worcester estates are embattled in many ways: by the local and geographic politics of land and by the ecclesiastical hierarchy. But these were not Wulfstan's only problems; he also had to deal with Worcester's past. The recent internal history of the community at Worcester can also be read in terms of its loss of land. Worcester had suffered during some of the battles of the Danish Conquest, and, in particular, when Cnut and Eadric Streona crossed into

Mercia. Cnut also settled three Danish earls and their followers in Herefordshire, Gloucestershire, and Worcestershire. In 1043, Swein Godwinson, threatened with excommunication for abducting a nun, yielded to the church and seized three of Worcester's estates. According to Hemming's *Cartulary*, Earl Leofric, his family, and his men held privately what was officially church land and were thus responsible for further depradations on the estates of Worcester.[119] Furthermore, Julia Barrow has argued that land politics lie behind the accounts of the changeover from secular clergy to Benedictinism. For Barrow, the discrepancies between the major sources for the conversion can be explained by the monks' recognition of a stronger diocesan authority and their consequent need to show that the Conquest did not necessarily displace local tradition and alter property ownership.[120]

The extant Worcester texts and, in particular, Hemming's *Cartulary*, reveal that, at Bishop Wulfstan's request, the community responded to these difficulties by writing history. Specifically, Hemming claims that Wulfstan asked 'cur nos, otio torpentes, res, precedenti sive nostro tempore gestas, de possessionibus dumtaxat ecclesie nostre nollemus litteris commendare' (why we, idling in our leisure, did not want to commit to writing at least the events pertaining to the possessions of our church, both those of the distant past and of our own times).[121] While Wulfstan certainly did not initiate the compilation and while there is no suggestion that he even urged the continuation of the D *Chronicle* annals, the D text nonetheless fits well into the historical culture of Worcester.[122] And though I do not contend that the D *Chronicle* can be read as a single unified text – I prefer to understand it as a text in which the same important local concerns can be felt in several different and unconnected places[123] – the importance of historical writing as, a stable means of mapping the relationship between land and culture is first indicated in the D *Chronicle* preface, a judiciously edited version of Bede's prologue to his *Historia ecclesiastica*.[124]

Like the *Historia*, the D *Chronicle* begins by marking the physical extent of the island. The land delineated by these boundaries is, for Bede, precious and holy. The D annalist does not share Bede's interest in moral and ecclesiastical history; he is interested in the land for the power it represents. The geography of Britain is transformed by the history of the people into what Henri Lefebvre calls representational space: 'Redolent with imaginary and symbolic elements, they [spaces] have their source in history – in the history of a people as well as in the history of each individual belonging to that people ... Representational space is alive: It speaks ... It embraces the loci of passion, of action, and of lived situations, and thus immediately implies time.'[125]

Thus instead of recreating and interpreting aspects of Paradise in the features of Britain, the writer of the preface moves to the settlement history and culture of the island, creating a history in which land, culture, and identity are inextricably linked. The preface opens by marking the peripheries of the island and identifying, but not interpreting, the languages of the people within those boundaries.[126] Then, for each wave of settlement, the preface author links the immigrants' history and identity to the territory they occupy and, after the first settlers, offers an extra detail by which we can know and distinguish the different people. We learn, for example, that the Britons came from Armenia (a misreading) and that they settle the South,[127] the Picts who come from Scythia via Ireland choose royal descent from the mother, and the Scots come from Ireland to Britain with a leader called Reoda.[128] Even the Romans are characterized by details. They choose not to pass through a Thames in which the Britons have scattered pointed stakes, but fight many hard battles before returning to Gaul.[129] In this account of the settlement, land and culture are unified into an identifying marker for the different people, and history, the history of the settlement, stabilizes and preserves the identity and culture of those now-lost people.

The philosophies of history and historiography indicated in the D preface and the William annals resonate with post-Conquest culture at Worcester. The commitment to Anglo-Saxon England can be read in Worcester's library, the increased interest in historical writing, Wulfstan's desires for history, Anglo-Saxon architecture, and even his desire to retain Anglo-Saxon ecclesiastical culture.[130] A chronicle that records the facts of the national, regional, and local pasts is part of this program. More significantly, a chronicle that works against the propaganda of the new king would have held much resonance for its Worcester readers. Here, the annalist preserves in his lexicon, and cultural ideals, a discourse of identity from the now-lost Anglo-Saxon England, but this seemingly nostalgic project has a function in the present. The D William annals participate in the community project of retaining Anglo-Saxon values as a way of marking Worcester's institutional identity and thus preserving its land.

CHAPTER SEVEN

Conclusion: After Lives

The *Chronicle* narratives of conquest, invasion, and settlement create a discourse of collective identity for a people known as the *Angelcynn*. Explicitly negotiating the issues that accompany invasion, defeat, conquest, and settlement as questions of the various kings' performances of their lordship obligations, the *Chronicle* annalists give new meaning to carefully selected aspects of the political and social practice of lordship.[1] By focusing on Alfred's ability to use lordship relations to bind the Danes to him in peace, the Alfred annalist narrates the foundation of a kingdom and the creation of a people. The Æthelred-Cnut annalist sets the principles of ecclesiastical kingship against the lordship ideal of mutual loyalty to explain the loss of the territorial kingdom and the simultaneous reconstitution of the *Angelcynn* under Cnut. When the *Angelcynn* do not cohere around William's lordship, the D William annalist uses his text to preserve the discourse of Anglo-Saxon collective identity and claim the cultural heritage and territorial inheritance of his monastic institution. In effect, then, the D William annalist explicitly asserts what the work of the other annalists implies: that narratives of the past create and confirm identity in the present.

That the focus on lordship and identity is maintained by multiple annalists who write over the course of three centuries is no coincidence; it is, rather, a deliberate approach to writing the history of conquest and invasion in the vernacular. Written shortly after the events at issue, each text responds to different aspects of the discourse of salvation history. The strength and power of salvation history in England is fully explored in Robert Hanning's study of early historical writing in Britain.[2] Beginning with Gildas, Hanning traces the development of a historical imagination that, as the other Alfredian historical narratives suggest, was influential and compelling for the writers of history in Alfred's circle. By contrast, the Alfred annalist reinterprets the defining tropes of the genre: sin, invasion, conquest, and settlement. Where in Bede's *Historia ecclesiastica* and Orosius's *Historiarum adversus paganos libri septem*, the sin of either the king or his people leads to conquest, now in the Alfred annals, the kingdom and the people are redeemed by the king's acts of lordship. The Danish raids no longer figure as punishments for a corrupt people, but as tests by which Alfred turns the men who submit to him into a people.

The Æthelred-Cnut annalist develops this approach. In the *Æthelred-Cnut Chronicle*, salvation historiography explains the loss of the kingdom under Æthelred. But even as the annalist tells this story, his text asserts that Cnut comes to improve the corrupt lordship relations of Æthelred's kingdom and that the king's realm is defined not by the conquest of his land but by the people with whom he contracts lordship relations. Similarly, though the D William annalist chastises the Anglo-Saxons for their sins, the people are actually undone by a series of weak lordship bonds that extends back to the reign of Edward the Confessor. Thus the Norman Conquest is less a cause of change than a cataclysm that confirms the decay of Anglo-Saxon lordship culture.

The relevance of these ideas is suggested by the Peterborough annalist's reinterpretation of the *Chronicle* discourse of lordship and identity. Given what we know of contemporary Anglo-Saxon lordship practices and given the annalists' decision to articulate identity through lordship ideals, we can assume that the readers of the early conquest and invasion narratives would immediately have recognized the significance of the *Chronicle* discourse of lordship and identity. But, over sixty years after the Norman Conquest, these ideas may have been less familiar and thus less relevant to the readers of the *Peterborough Chronicle*.[3] Nonetheless, the Peterborough annalist develops what I have identified as the D annalist's approach by retaining lordship, land, and institutional identity as the conceptual centre of his text and then exploiting the *Chronicle* discourse of identity for his present.[4] In the other conquest and invasion annals, political and cultural identity are negotiated through lordship bonds and, explicitly, not land; now, however, land is a central part of institutional identity.

In the middle of his narrative of the Norman settlement, the Peterborough annalist observes the threat of conquest by Cnut of Denmark, but he uses his entry for 1085 to criticize the king for ordering the Domesday survey. Portraying written history – *Domesday Book* – as the choice of a king who cannot form traditional (Anglo-Saxon) lordship ties, the Peterborough annalist denounces William for linking his royal authority to a written and thus tangible survey of land tenure, instead of relying on invisible personal lordship bonds. Then, in his entry for 1087, he directly links William's authority over his people to the success of this survey, effectively connecting the survey and the identity of the people.

Though he criticizes the king for using writing to assert his authority, constitute his people, and articulate their identity by claiming his power over their land, the annalist also uses his history to claim and maintain a similarly land-based identity for his home institution. As he copies the annals from his source, the Peterborough annalist inserts a series of forged charters, documents which – if interpreted as authentic – would confirm Peterborough's lands and establish the institution as one of the leading Benedictine houses.

The annalist moves from the personal lordship of the king to a more contemporary problem – the lordship of land – placing the Peterborough annals in the tradition of *Chronicle* narratives of lordship and settlement. Recognizing the presence and function of the annals' lordship ideology, the Peterborough annalist alters how the *Chronicle* discourse of identity signifies in his present. In post-Conquest Anglo-Norman England, the king's lordship is no longer a political ethos that, ignoring the shifting boundaries of land, creates and defines the people by a personal lordship tie, but this does not make lordship irrelevant to articulations of group identity. In the *Peterborough Chronicle*, the lordship of land defines the group identity of a monastic institution. In essence, then, the Peterborough annalist demonstrates the fundamental importance of the connection between lordship and expressions of collective identity.

Booking Lordship

The E annal for 1085 reports the threat of invasion. Cnut Sweinson of Denmark threatens to conquer England; William responds by settling his army throughout the country. The annalist remarks that the people were oppressed and that the king laid to waste the land closest to the sea so that the invaders should not profit from it.[5] The annalist makes no explicit link between this threat and the decision to begin the survey, but the inclusion of these details and the rationale – William desires to know 'ymbe þis land, hu hit wære gesett oððe mid hwylcon mannon' (about this land, how it might be occupied and with what sort of people) – suggests that the survey responds to the threat to William's authority.[6]

This political context accounts for the annalist's denunciation of a king who attempts to build lordship and authority through writing: 'Swa swyðe nearwelice he hit lett ut aspyrian þet næs an ælpig hide ne an gyrde landes, ne furðon – hit is sceame to tellanne, ac hit ne þuhte him nan sceame to donne – an oxe ne an cu ne an swin næs belyfon þet næs gesæt on his gewrite' (He had it searched through so very thoroughly that there was not a single hide nor quarter hide of land, nor even – it is a shame to mention, but it seemed no shame to him to do – an ox or cow or swine left over that was not placed under his writ).[7] Punning on Old English *gewrit* – this is both a technical term designating a charter, writ, book, or other official document and the word for 'writing' – the annalist invokes the notion of shame to point out William's failures in his lordship relations. In Old English lordship literature, shame is usually discussed as a failure of the man to follow his lord; shame, like disloyalty, is almost never perceived as being a problem of the lord himself.[8] This tradition and the other *Chronicle* narratives underscore William's failures. Even as the threat of conquest looms, this king does not create strong lordship ties with his men; he uses writing to secure his authority and thus his kingdom.

The question of how exactly a text enables William to secure his kingdom has long puzzled historians of the period.[9] Their question is whether the Domesday survey and the ceremonies of submission at Salisbury can be connected. For the annalist, however, the issue is whether William is an honorable and trustworthy lord. At Salisbury, 'him comon to his witan and ealle þa landsittende men þe ahtes wæron ofer eall Engleland, wæron þæs mannes men þe hi wæron; 7 ealle hi bugon to him 7 weron his menn 7 him holdaðas sworon, þet hi woldon ongean ealle oðre men him holde beon' (his *witan* and all the men occupying land who were of any account all over England came before him [the king], [no matter] whose man they were; and they all submitted to him and became his men and swore loyalty oaths to him, [saying] that they wished to be loyal to him above all other men).[10] The language and detail of this scene recall the other *Chronicle* lordship ceremonies in which the Anglo-Saxons are united and a new people created.

Though William compels the loyalty of his men in an oath-swearing ceremony, this does not redeem him from his inappropriate focus on land. The annalist goes on to explain the king's shortcomings. The king who does not see the shame in the survey also does not see the obligations brought about by these oaths: 'And þeah he dyde ærest æfter his gewunan' (And despite this [the ceremony], the king behaved first according to his wont), so he obtained money from his people regardless of whether it was right.[11] William does not follow through on his obligations to his people.

As they appear in other narratives of conquest and invasion, ceremonies of submission and lordship oaths correct the fraying social and political order by uniting the people under the lordship of the king. For the annalist, William fails in spite of the ceremony, and the depth of his failure is marked by the behaviour of *ætheling* Edgar: '7 Eadgar æþeling, Ædwardes mæg cynges, beah þa fram him, forþig he næfde na mycelne wurðscipe of him' (And Edgar *ætheling*, King Edward's kinsman, deserted him then [lit. turned or bowed from him], because he had not received much honour from him).[12] In this moment, the annalist points out the futility of Edgar's hard-won submission. In 1074, after a series of rebellions, Edgar is one of the last Anglo-Saxons to submit to William; the annalist notes that 'he wæs on þes cynges hyrede 7 nam swilce gerihta swa se cyng him geuðe' (he was accepted into the king's court and took such rights as the king granted him).[13] Edgar's decision is not treachery, but a justified reaction to William's decision not to honour his lordship obligations.

In summing up William's reign, the annalist makes the implications of the two previous entries explicit:

> He rixade ofer Englæland; 7 hit mid his geapscipe swa þurhsmeade þet næs an hid landes innan Englælande þet he nyste hwa heo hæfde, oððe hwæs heo wurð wæs, 7 syððan on his gewrit gesætt. Brytland him wæs on gewealde, 7 he þærinne casteles gewrohte 7 þet manncynn mid ealle gewealde. Swilce eac Scotland he him underþædde for his mycele strengþe. Normandige þet land wæs his gecynde; 7 ofer þone eorldom þe Mans is gehaten he rixade. 7 Gif he moste þa gyt twa gear libban, he hæfde Yrlande mid his werscipe gewunnon 7 widutan ælcon wæpnon.

> He reigned over England; and with his cleverness, he investigated it so thoroughly that there was not one hide of land in England of which he did not know the owner, or how much it was worth, and later he placed it under his writ. Wales was in his control, and he built castles in that land, and controlled that race entirely. Similarly he also subdued Scotland to his

[control] because of his great power. The land of Normandy was his by birthright; and he reigned over the earldom which is called Maine. If he had lived but two years more, he would have won Ireland with his cunning and without any weapons.[14]

Although he asserts that William ruled Normandy by right of inheritance, that he ruled Wales, Scotland, and Maine by force, and that the king would have conquered Ireland by 'werscipe' (cunning), the Peterborough annalist locates William's royal authority over England in the written results of the 1085 survey of landholdings and values. Shaped, for the Peterborough annalist at least, as a collection of facts – the record of land customs and traditions of land tenure – *Domesday Book* becomes a history or repository of the past and a record of the present. As such, *Domesday Book* has the power to structure the lordship bonds of a given community and those of the community's relationship with their king.[15] In this partially favourable encomium-like annal, writing and the decision to order the *Domesday Book* come to characterize William's reign. Lordship, as the Anglo-Saxons envisioned it and as it is written in the earlier annals, is no longer relevant.

The Peterborough annalist's rejection of writing as a way of structuring lordship ties should not be taken at face value, however.[16] Contemporary historians have shown that the lordship of land is a key issue in Anglo-Norman England and that the anxiety it generated can be detected in the writers of history at monastic houses like Durham, Canterbury, Westminster, Abingdon, and Battle Abbey. Aware of their vulnerability and seeking to assure their position in their contemporary political and ecclesiastical landscapes, these historians produce in their narratives a series of forged documents testifying to their monastery's privileges.[17] In this culture, texts such as chronicles and charters appear more binding and permanent than a personal oath or promise. The *Peterborough Chronicle* is a deliberate response to such cultural concerns and a clear part of this post-Conquest historiographical culture.

The Peterborough annals up to 1121 were written after 1116 as a unified narrative by one person – the same person who wrote the annals for 1121 to 1131.[18] In 1116, much of the abbey and surrounding village at Peterborough were destroyed by fire.[19] The annalist claims that only the chapter house and dormitory survived, suggesting that the library – the repository of the monastery's past and key to its future – had vanished, together with some of its documents.[20] While the community works at reconstructing the monastery's physical presence through its buildings, the Peterborough annalist strengthens its present position and future potential through recreating the records of its past. In other words, even as he criticizes the king for his disingenuous use of writing to assert his authority and subjugate his people, the annalist engages in similarly deceptive uses of writing.

In the Peterborough annals for 654, 656, 675, 686, 777, 852, 870, and 963, the annalist tells the history of his institution and its land grants.[21] In 654 Peterborough Abbey, then known as Medehamsted, was founded by King Peada of Mercia and King Oswy of Northumbria, brother of the later sanctified King Oswald, and then entrusted to the monk Seaxwulf. When King Peada was killed, his successor, Wulfhere, with the approval of his *witan* and Archbishop Deusdedit, decided to honour the monastery for the love of Seaxwulf, Oswy, and his brother with some generous grants of land (which the annalist lists); the king stipulates that the monastery should be free of all services and subject only to Rome.

The details of this account are relatively straightforward, if not entirely accurate. But the way in which the annalist presents them requires further consideration. In addition to the 'facts' themselves, the story of Peterborough is itself a lesson in the permanence of writing and the fragility of oaths, vows, and personal lordship relations. The annalist goes to great lengths to stress the textual tradition behind the monastery's freedoms. Thus, though in the entry for 656, he reports a series of conversations between the king and Seaxwulf and the king's oral declaration of the institution's land and privileges, the promises and declarations very quickly become text. So focused is the annalist on the necessity for writing that, throughout the *Interpolations*, there are many reproductions of important Peterborough letters and charters – in some of the latter, the manuscript even reproduces the crosses that testify to the authenticity of the signatures.

The logic behind this insistent textual history soon becomes clear. The annalist explains that Danish raiders came to Peterborough, destroyed the monastery killing all those who were in it, took all its treasures, and razed its buildings. Peterborough remained rubble for almost a hundred years, but it was resurrected in the middle of the tenth century, at the beginning of the Benedictine Reform. After his consecration, Æthelwold began to establish new monasteries and reform those that would not adhere to any rule; he asked his king, Edgar, for the monasteries that the Danes had destroyed. One such monastery was Peterborough:

Syððon com se biscop Aðelwold to þære mynstre þe wæs gehaten Medeshamstede, ðe hwilon wæs fordon fra heðene folce; ne fand þær nan þing buton ealde weallas 7 wilde wuda. Fand þa hidde in þa ealde wealle writes þet Headda abbot heafde ær gewriton, hu Wulfhere kyng 7 Æðelred his broðor hit heafden wroht, 7 hu hi hit freodon wið king 7 wið biscop 7 wið ealle weoruldþeudom, 7 hu se Papa Agatho hit feostnode mid his write, 7 se arcebiscop Deusdedit.

Afterwards Bishop Æthelwold came to the monastery that was called Medehamsted, which formerly had been destroyed by heathen people; he found nothing there but old walls and wild woods. Then he found, hidden in an old wall, the writs that Abbot Headda had written earlier, about how King Wulfhere and Æthelred his brother had founded the monastery, and how they had freed it from the king, the bishop, and from all secular services, and how Pope Agatho and Archbishop Deusdedit had sealed this in their writs.[22]

The Danes destroyed the physical, literal presence of the monastery, but its communal identity and cultural importance survive in its texts. Symbolically resurrecting the Peterborough community's foundation narrative from the foundations of its building, the annalist connects Peterborough to one of the most influential figures in the Anglo-Saxon ecclesiastical tradition. To confirm the unassailability conferred by Æthelwold's reputation, the Peterborough annalist surrounds his institution with a circle of power in which texts create privileges and privileges create texts. Upon seeing the original charters, Edgar verbally promises the monastery its exemption, lands, and all the freedoms his predecessors gave it. But the annalist records all the details of Edgar's vow as a written charter, once more stressing the primacy and importance of a textual history.[23]

The annalist's success in using his text to build an influential and unifying history for his monastery is suggested by the content of his later annals. The events of 1127–31 represent a crisis in the abbey's history. In 1127, Henry I gives the position of abbot at Peterborough to Henry of Poitou, abbot of St Jean d'Angély. Technicalities aside – canon law forbids one man from holding two abbacies at once – the monks of Peterborough do not appreciate their new abbot, particularly when, in 1130, they discover that Henry has promised Peter of Cluny that he would subject Benedictine Peterborough to Cluniac rule.[24] Angrily, the annalist declares the monastery's resistance in a proverb: '"Hæge sitteð þa aceres dæleth!"' (The hedge that separates the acres remains!)[25] If we place this proverb in the context of the annalist's work as a whole and his careful reconstruction of the abbey's history, the axiom encapsulates the annalist's work. By constructing Peterborough as a significant product of the Benedictine Reform and connecting it with the most prominent figures of that era, the annalist has so positioned his abbey in history that he can argue that Benedictine Peterborough is the hedge, the single dividing line, between Benedictine and Cluniac tradition.

But the proverb has a second field of meaning. If we interpret the 'hedge' as the annalist's narrative, then it is the annalist's text around which the Peterborough community is formed. In 1132, the narrative passes into the hands of a second annalist, and though no further mention of the abbey's place in the country or Benedictine tradition is made, Henry leaves Peterborough under a shadow of disgrace. The second annalist neither confirms nor denies the role of his monastery's 'history' in the king's decision; he merely says that the abbot accused the monks to the king, and the king sent for the monks.[26] Whether or not the first annalist's text was directly involved in settling the dispute, the fact that the monks rallied sufficiently to defend their community suggests that, within the abbey's walls, the annalist's blend of fact and fiction, national and local history has become a foundation narrative powerful enough to protect the community's culture and traditions. Peterborough survives.

As we come to recognize the agenda behind the Peterborough annalist's treatment of William's lordship bonds and to understand his attitude to written material, we must also change where we place the *Chronicle* in post-Conquest literary history. Too often, the *Peterborough Chronicle* is seen only as a source of linguistic data or as an introductory text, and its negotiation of the post-Conquest present has thus been underappreciated.[27] If we place the Peterborough annals in their twelfth-century milieu, we can see how the annalist's unhappiness with William resonates with the travails of a culture moving 'from memory to written record.'[28] This context also changes how we read the so-called *Peterborough Interpolations*. The charters and narrative digressions interspersed in the early annals are not just 'strikingly consistent with the style of historiography of the "new historians" of the twelfth century'; they are an instantiation of the conventions of Anglo-Norman historiography.[29] In other words, the project of writing history in English is not motivated by convention or nostalgia; rather, the *Peterborough Chronicle* is driven by contemporary concerns and draws upon contemporary historiographical practices. It is a history with an agenda and function in its present, and its approaches are founded upon a skilful reading of the work of the *Chronicle* annalists of invasion, conquest, and settlement.

II

In *Families of the King*, I argue that the *Chronicle* annalists consistently treat conquest, invasion, and settlement as issues of the king's practice of lordship and that the resulting narrative is central to a discourse of Anglo-Saxon collective identity and to the historiography of the annals. I conclude by examining how both the historical practice and the discourse of identity are adapted in the D and E texts to address the local needs of a monastic house. After 1154, local and national history are no longer kept in Old English at Peterborough, but the connection between lordship, identity, and historical writing does not die out.[30] In as much as the *Peterborough Chronicle* provides a legend of origins for the annalists' community while continuing the *Chronicle* ideology of lordship, it is possible to see the Peterborough annals as a hybrid text that links the historiographical practice of the *Chronicle* to the legendary originary historiography of Laʒamon's *Brut*.[31]

My consideration of Laʒamon in this context parallels Hanning's analysis of salvation history, a tradition that, as Hanning points out, culminates in Geoffrey of Monmouth's *Historia regum Britannic* with a tension between the personal and political.[32] Just as the *Chronicle* annalists rework their Latin models, so Laʒamon reworks Geoffrey. Just as the annalists put aside the universalizing motifs of salvation in order to localize their texts with specific formulations of collective identity, so Laʒamon reunites the personal and political by making individual leaders responsible for the collective identity and political integrity of their people.

The generally accepted dates for the composition of the *Brut* place it in the so-called post-Conquest 'historical revival,'[33] but Laʒamon's choice of English and distinctive treatment of Anglo-Saxon lordship ideals set him apart from his Anglo-Norman history-and romance-writing contemporaries. Taking courtly and dynastic romance as a conceptual backdrop, Laʒamon rethinks the importance of love and marriage in the protagonist's development as a knight and ruler. In courtly romances, love and marriage generally symbolize the knight's worthiness to rule his kingdom, but Laȝamon suggests that male-female passion disrupts the foundation of the state or kingdom. Thus, in his version of the Trojan foundation narrative, the mutual love of Brutus and his men enables the Trojans to flee Greece, escape Diana, overcome the inhabitants of the British Isles, and found Britain. By proceeding to narrate the Trojan invasion, conquest, and settlement of Britain as a question of Brutus's lordship and then to link the new Britons' identity to their leader's lordship, Laȝamon makes effective use of the *Chronicle* discourse of identity.

Not only does lordship lie at the conceptual centre of Brutus's Britain, it also defines Laȝamon's historiography. There is no evidence that Laȝamon knew the *Anglo-Saxon Chronicle* – he does not list it in his discussion of his sources[34] – yet, as in the *Chronicle* annals of conquest, invasion, and settlement, lordship is central to Laȝamon's historical approach. Lordship connects the preface in which Laȝamon discusses his methodology to the British foundation narrative, a connection reinforced by verbal patterning.[35] Just as in the foundation narrative where Brutus and his men are *leof* to each other, so, in the preface, Laȝamon's text and sources are *leof* to his authorial persona.

In a preface that describes the process of writing history, the idea of a loving historian may seem somewhat disconcerting. But by invoking love as a verbal and conceptual link between preface and foundation narrative, Laȝamon uses lordship to claim agency for his authorial persona. In so doing, he distances himself and his work from that of other contemporary historians. He rejects the popular contemporary historiographical convention that a patron figure inspires, motivates, and gives meaning to history, offering instead an authorial persona who, as lord of his text, accepts responsibility for his work and its meaning.[36] Indeed, as Laȝamon's authorial persona becomes his own patron, he authorizes a history that continues the Anglo-Saxon convention of narrating conquest, invasion, and settlement as tests of the king's performance of his lordship obligations. Thus, despite the Trojan content that would place the *Brut* in a different narrative tradition – one more closely related to salvation histories – Laȝamon's text can productively be read as an extension of the lordship narrative and historiography of the *Anglo-Saxon Chronicle*.

That the *Chronicle* discourse of lordship and identity and its approach to narrating the past survive beyond the *Chronicle* itself underscores the importance of this vernacular history. The narratives of conquest, settlement, and invasion, together with the theory of historiography they exemplify, transform this historical source into a cultural force that organizes carefully adapted aspects of the social and political practice of lordship into a coherent discourse of collective identity for the *Angelcynn* and for the annalists' monastic institutions.

Notes

Introduction: Reading the *Chronicle*'s Past

1 See David Dumville and Simon Keynes as excerpted in Szarmach, 'The *Anglo-Saxon Chronicle*,' 15.
2 This richness may be seen in a simple search of the *Modern Language Association* bibliography.
3 S. a. 1066 (D): Cubbin, ed., *The Anglo-Saxon Chronicle: MS D*, 81: '7 a syððan hit yflade swiðe. Wurðe god se ende þonne God wylle,' and 671 (A): Bately, ed., *The Anglo-Saxon Chronicle: MS A*, 31: 'Her wæs þæt micle fugla wel.'
4 See, for example, Keynes, 'The Declining Reputation of King Æthelred the Unready,' 236: 'It is a personal and perhaps idiosyncratic view of events ... '; and Wormald, 'Æthelred the Lawmaker,' 47: Æthelred's legislation 'has done little to restore the reputation so irreparably damaged by the Chronicler's bitter genius.'
5 For example, with the exception of the Cynewulf-Cyneheard episode, most students encounter the *Chronicle* as a link between Old and Middle English. Even in the recent Old and Middle English anthology – Treharne, ed., *Old and Middle English: An Anthology*, 254 – the requisite excerpt from the *Peterborough Chronicle* is discussed as 'one of the most important pieces of transitional writing.' But studies of the 'transitional' aspect of the *Chronicle* should not exclude consideration of agenda and meaning.
6 I discuss the complexities of translating this term in chapter 1.
7 Compelling statements of the case for the importance of Anglo-Saxon prose texts are Lees, *Tradition and Belief*, viii–ix, and her 'Working with Patristic Sources.'
8 Attribution of the manuscripts is difficult. Manuscript E is the least controversial: Clark, ed., *The Peterborough Chronicle*, xvii–xviii; in the most recent

edition of the D text, Cubbin, ed., *The Anglo-Saxon Chronicle*, lvi, lxiii–lxvi, connects D to either York or Worcester, but observes that D can most productively be associated with Ealdred, bishop of Worcester c. 1046–62 and archbishop of York 1061–9. The history of manuscript C is even more complicated. Conventionally, C has been called the *Abingdon Chronicle*, but O'Brien O'Keeffe, ed., *The Anglo-Saxon Chronicle*, lxxiv–xcii, argues that the manuscript is now more properly attributed to Canterbury (Christ Church) and not Abingdon. The most recent editor of the A manuscript, Bately, ed., *The Anglo-Saxon Chronicle*, xiii–xiv, takes no position. The cases for and against Winchester as the possible source for the first *Chronicle* and the A manuscript are made by Dumville, 'The *Anglo-Saxon Chronicle* and the Origins of English Square Minuscule Script,' who concludes that though the A manuscript might have been compiled at Winchester, the *Chronicle* itself was not composed there (98), and by Parkes, 'The Palaeography of the Parker Manuscript of the *Chronicle*,' esp. 165–6, who argues for Winchester as both the source of the A manuscript and the original compilation of the *Chronicle*.

9 Keynes, 'Declining Reputation,' 231–2.
10 On the compilation of the *Chronicle*, see Bately, 'The Compilation of the *Anglo-Saxon Chronicle* Once More,' and her 'The Compilation of the *Anglo-Saxon Chronicle*, 60 B.C. to A.D. 890.' Scholars usually associate the *Chronicle* with Alfred's court, but there is some uncertainty about how this association might be analysed. Davis, 'Alfred the Great,' suggests that the *Chronicle* was intended to function as dynastic propaganda for Alfred's court, and this perspective is argued with reference to the manuscript in Parkes, 'The Palaeography.' Most readings usually suggest only that, because the initial compilation of the annals took place during Alfred's reign, there is a connection between the court and the *Chronicle*.
11 My argument here is designed to counter the way in which palaeography is usually adduced to deny the claim that the *Chronicle* can be read with literary tools. Detractors from my position usually state that because the annals are copied without regard to content, it is hard to argue for authorial control over the material.
12 For each set of annals, I use the manuscript most contemporary to the events under discussion.
13 Goffart, *Barbarian History*, 4–5, calls this Germanic history 'barbarian,' but he carefully defines the term: 'Only in the Renaissance and afterward were some of these people [the descendants of Noah] segregated as distinctively "barbarian" or "Germanic," whereas others were assigned to the privileged antiquity of Greece and Rome.' Isidore of Seville's discussion of barbarian-

ism in this context is in Lindsay, ed., *Isidori Hispalensis episcopi Etymologiarum sive originum libri XX*, I, 32 at 59–60.
14 Goffart, *Barbarian History*, 16–17.
15 This is the title for chapter 4.4; Goffart, *Barbarian History*, 296: 'Bede's Three Models for the *Ecclesiastical History*.'
16 On the prevalence and persistence of the Anglo-Saxon migration myth, see Howe, *Migration and Mythmaking in Anglo-Saxon England*.
17 On the motif itself, see Andersson, 'The Viking Image in Carolingian Poetry'; Coupland, 'The Rod of God's Wrath or the People of God's Wrath'; and Godden, 'Apocalypse and Invasion in Late Anglo-Saxon England.' Robert W. Hanning, *The Vision of History in Early Britain*, studies the principal early historical texts from England that use this tradition. For full discussion of this tradition and relevant texts, see chapter 1.
18 My reading depends on understanding the *Æthelred-Cnut Chronicle* as a text that signifies for the reigns of both Æthelred II and Cnut. Though much of the scholarship refers to the *Æthelred Chronicle*, the proximity of the date of compilation (see Keynes, 'Declining Reputation,' 231–2) to that of the Danish Conquest suggests that the Æthelred annals might also be important to studies of the reign of Cnut. This aspect of the *Chronicle* will be recognized in Simon Keynes's forthcoming edition. For dating and the problem of where the *Æthelred-Cnut Chronicle* ends, see page 185, note 1.
19 How such a modern critical term might aptly be applied to a reading of a medieval text is discussed in chapter 1.
20 In a way, then, my argument complements that of Reynolds, 'Medieval *origines gentium* and the Community of the Realm,' and her *Kingdoms and Communities in Western Europe, 900–1300*, 250–331 esp. 256–66, in which she discusses the intersections of kingdom and regnal identity. In the introduction to her second edition that takes on some of the problems in the historiography of medieval collectivity, Reynolds agrees that 'the argument that the relation of lord and vassal was the main social bond of earlier medieval society would be weak, even if it relied on the lack of evidence of other bonds' (xlvii). But she goes on to show how lordship and a sense of collectivity are intertwined. I cannot evaluate the validity of this historical analysis: my project seeks only to explore the writing of collectivity as a problem of lordship.
21 See White, *Tropics of Discourse*, 83–5, esp. 84: 'No given set of casually recorded historical events can in itself constitute a story; the most it might offer to the historian are story *elements*. The events are *made* into a story by the suppression or subordination of certain of them and the highlighting of others, by characterization, motific repetition, variation of tone and point of

view, alternative descriptive strategies, and the like – in short, all of the techniques that we would normally expect to find in the emplotment of a novel or play' (emphasis as printed).

1. Writing Identity in *Chronicle* History

1 Geary, *The Myth of Nations*, 19. Even if they do not argue explicitly against the possibility of medieval national identity, scholars such as Anderson, *Imagined Communities*, pass quickly over the medieval period. Even in Hastings, *The Construction of Nationhood*, 38–43, a study that does examine the medieval period, identity is assumed to be less important in Anglo-Saxon England than it is after the Norman Conquest.
2 These terms are taken from Reynolds, 'What Do We Mean by "Anglo-Saxon" and "Anglo-Saxons"?' 397–8. On the use of the term *Angli* and, in particular, on its meaning in Bede's *Historia ecclesiastica*, see Wormald, 'Bede, the *Bretwaldas*, and the Origins of the *Gens Anglorum*,' and his 'The Venerable Bede and the "Church of the English",' 21–2.
3 I cannot here give a full study of all the titles used by the Anglo-Saxon kings: they vary from period to period and with the genre and function of the text involved. They are also inconsistently used. On the language of kingship, overlordship, and the question of what they designate, see Dumville, 'The Terminology of Overkingship in Early Anglo-Saxon England'; Kleinschmidt, 'Die Titularen englischer Könige im 10. und 11. Jahrhundert'; Reynolds, 'What Do We Mean'; Scharer, 'Die *Intitulationes* der angelsächsischen Könige im 7. und 8. Jahrhundert'; Wormald, 'The Venerable Bede'; and Yorke, 'The Vocabulary of Anglo-Saxon Overlordship.' Scharer, *Herrschaft und Repräsentation*, studies collective identity and royal styles of the Alfredian period, pointing out in particular the shaping influence of the works of Gregory the Great.
4 Geary, *The Myth of Nations*, 19. The significance of the Anglo-Saxon texts is underscored by Wormald, 'The Venerable Bede,' 19. Wormald argues that the collective identity articulated in Anglo-Saxon England differs from the sense of group identity in Francia, the country with which Anglo-Saxon England was most closely in dialogue and the country whose theories of ecclesiastical kingship and whose rituals and theories of lordship were well integrated into Anglo-Saxon texts and practice.
5 Smith, *The Ethnic Origins of Nations*, 22–30.
6 Ibid., 166. One salient difference between the identity articulated in the *Anglo-Saxon Chronicle* and Smith's argument at this point is that the identity of the annals is formed around and limited to the nobility.

7 For intersections of historical lordship and collective identity, see page 159, note 20.
8 I discuss lordship and its definitions more fully below. For the Continental connection, see D.H. Green, *The Carolingian Lord*, and 'Lordship'; and, problematically, Moisl, *Lordship and Tradition in Barbarian Europe*.
9 Indeed, the only clear evidence that the *Chronicle* was read by the nobility is *Æthelweard's Chronicle*, a translation of the annals into Latin. And *Æthelweard's Chronicle* is difficult; the dedicatory preface instructs the reader, Matilda, to look for a history of her family in the national narrative of the *Chronicle* past. The focus is dynastic and personal rather than ethnic. See *The Chronicle of Æthelweard*, 1–2.
10 Bhabha, 'DissemiNation,' 140. 'The concept of the "people" emerges within a range of discourses as a double narrative movement. The people are not simply historical events or parts of a patriotic body politic. They are also a complex rhetorical strategy of social reference ... We then have a contested conceptual territory where the nation's people must be thought in double-time; the people are the historical "objects" of a nationalist pedagogy, giving the discourse an authority that is based on the pre-given or constituted historical origin *in the past*; the people are also the "subjects" of a process of signification that must erase any prior or originary presence of the nation-people' (ibid., 145) [emphasis as printed].
11 Ibid., 145.
12 Ibid., 140.
13 Recent work suggesting the complexity of the annalist's account is Keynes, *The Diplomas of King Æthelred 'the Unready,'* esp. 163–231; his 'The Declining Reputation of King Æthelred the Unready'; his 'Crime and Punishment in the Reign of King Æthelred the Unready'; Stafford, 'The Reign of Æthelred II'; and Wormald, 'Æthelred the Lawmaker.'
14 For an article that brings all these issues together, see Garnett, 'Coronation and Propaganda.'
15 Bhabha, 'DissemiNation,' 145. Again, I stress that the annalists are not reporting or even foregrounding something latent in their culture; rather, they reconfigure aspects of the practice of lordship and aspects of the literary ideals of lordship as an identifying ethos.
16 Remensnyder, *Remembering Kings Past*, and Spiegel, *Romancing the Past*.
17 Reynolds, 'Medieval *origines gentium* and the Community of the Realm,' and her *Kingdoms and Communities in Western Europe, 900–1300*, esp. 256–66.
18 Howe, *Migration and Mythmaking*, 70.
19 Ibid., 32.
20 Lindsay, ed., *Isidori Hispalensis episcopi Etymologiarum*, I, 44 at 82.

21 Charles W. Jones, 'The Setting,' 10, suggests that annalistic historical writing arises from the 'discarded' material of the Easter tables. On the relationship of the Easter tables and the *Chronicle*, see Parkes, 'The Palaeography of the Parker Manuscript of the *Chronicle*, 154, and Bately, 'Manuscript Layout and the *Anglo-Saxon Chronicle*,' 35–9. It is interesting to note that Bately (36) refers to Antonia Gransden's discussion of 'living' and 'dead' chronicles. These are clearly problematic terms, but they do attempt to describe the ways in which the history of the annals is different from other contemporary examples of historical writing.

22 For a sense of the scope of the problem (currently less urgent in Anglo-Saxon studies, but a heated point of debate in Anglo-Norman studies), see Abels, *Lordship and Military Obligation in Anglo-Saxon England*; Abels studies the historical phenomenon with relation to the problems of land tenure and military service. Dalton, *Conquest, Anarchy, and Lordship*, focuses on issues of land in the county of Yorkshire; Fleming, *Kings and Lords in Conquest England*, traces the end of the Anglo-Saxon culture of lordship and the rise and problems of issues of land tenure in Anglo-Norman England; Green, *The Carolingian Lord*, examines the words for lordship trying to distinguish meaning and resonance, thus giving insight into practice; John Hudson, *Land, Law, and Lordship in Anglo-Norman England*, discusses the issues of tenure, heritability, and alienability in Anglo-Norman England; Moisl, *Lordship and Tradition in Barbarian Europe*, gives a problematic sketch of the 'Germanic' traditions of lordship; and Yorke, 'The Vocabulary of Anglo-Saxon Overlordship,' studies the terms by which we account for the different ruling structures and positions.

23 As Richard Abels observed in a personal communication (13 April 2002), the annals for the reign of Edward the Elder (Alfred's successor) are more complete in their representation of actual lordship practice.

24 For a survey of scholarship on literary representations of personal lordship, see John M. Hill, *The Anglo-Saxon Warrior Ethic*, 1–18. For readers of Old English literature, the debate is more focused on a single question: whether we can detect the presence of a Germanic lordship ideal that requires a man to die for his lord. See Frank, 'The Ideal of Men Dying with Their Lord in *The Battle of Maldon*'; Green, 'Lordship'; Harris, 'Love and Death in the *Männerbund*,' which is a careful study of whether the tradition may be said to exist at all; Woolf, 'The Ideal of Men Dying with Their Lord in the *Germania* and in *The Battle of Maldon*'; and Stephen D. White, 'Kinship and Lordship in Early Medieval England.'

25 See the Old English *Wanderer* in Muir, ed., *The Exeter Anthology of Old English Poetry*, 219, ll. 41–4: 'Þinceð him on mode þæt he his mondryhten /

clyppe ond cysse, / ond on cneo lecge / honda ond heafod' (It seems to him in his mind that he embraces and kisses his lord and lays his hands and his head on his lord's knees). Although the personal element of this moment is compelling, I should also note that Paul Hyams has argued (in person) that these scenes are equally a replication of a homage ritual and an expression of personal attachment. Harris, 'Love and Death in the *Männerbund*,' 87, suggests that this is less formal than a rite of passage.

26 If read in conjunction with other texts such as the laws or even other different annals of the *Chronicle*, however, these annals may well make notable contributions to the historical study of Anglo-Saxon lordship.

27 S. a. 443, 597, 787, 836, 866, 874, 885, 886, 896, 900, and 1001 (A): Bately, ed., *The Anglo-Saxon Chronicle: MS A*, 17, 25, 39, 43, 47, 49, 53, 53, 59, 61, and 79.

28 Wormald, 'The Venerable Bede,' and Reynolds, 'What Do We Mean,' discuss the term; Foot, 'The Making of *Angelcynn*,' takes up the significance of the compound, *Angelcynn*; and Wormald, '*Engla Lond*: The Making of an Allegiance,' explores the process of Anglo-Saxon nation formation and the significance of what the Anglo-Saxons call their land. Other approaches to the concept of an *Angelcynn* with some discussion of other meaningful terms are Kathleen Davis, 'National Writing in the Ninth Century'; Lavezzo, 'Another Country'; and Pohl, 'Ethnic Names and Identities in the British Isles.'

29 Translating this word is complicated. The 'Angel' element appears to refer to the Anglians; their history is sketched in part in Dumville, 'Essex, Middle Anglia, and the Expansion of Mercia in the South-East Midlands,' and Yorke, *Kings and Kingdoms of Early Anglo-Saxon England*, 58–71. Because of the later usage of the term and in an attempt to avoid anachronisms, I prefer to avoid the translations 'English' and 'Anglian' (unless it is clearly describing the Anglians) and translate as 'Anglo-Saxons.'

30 See *cyn* in Healey, Venezky, and Cameron, eds, *Dictionary of Old English (microform)*, 1289–91, for a summary of the full range of meanings.

31 Foot, 'The Making of *Angelcynn*,' 33, notes that Alfred used the term *Angelcynn* for a 'newly named people subject to one lord, loyalty to whom was forcibly imposed by oath.' While I do not disagree with the principle, I make no assumptions about whether this sense of a new people was a reality for the Anglo-Saxons, and I do not necessarily see Alfred as the driving force behind this new configuration of the Anglo-Saxons; I am concerned only with its meaning in the *Chronicle*.

32 Scragg, 'The *Battle of Maldon*,' 27, ll. 223–4: Me is þæt hearma mæst: / he wæs ægðer min mæg and min hlaford' (This is the greatest of all pains for me: / he was both my kinsman and my lord) [translation mine].

33 S. a. 755 (A): Bately, ed., *The Anglo-Saxon Chronicle*, 37: 'Þa cuędon hie þæt him nænig mæg leofra nære þonne hiera hlaford' (Then they said that no kinsman was dearer to them than their lord).
34 For Alfred's rebellious nobles, see Nelson, 'A King across the Sea.' Scharer, 'Zu drei Themen in der Geschichtsschreibung der Zeit König Alfreds (871–899),' 201–2, considers the problem of loyalty from the perspective of Alfred's legislation. For Alfred's legislation against treacherous subjects, see Alfred 1, 1.1, and esp. 4, 4.1, 4.2 in Liebermann, ed., *Die Gesetze der Angelsachsen*, I, 46, 46, 50, 50.
35 Foot, 'The Making of *Angelcynn*,' 33, also observes the importance of the loyalty oath, but her focus is on practice and not on the writing of such scenes in the *Chronicle*. Although no lordship oaths are preserved exactly, scholars assume that they resemble those printed as *Að* in Liebermann, ed., *Die Gesetze*, I, 464–5. Carolingian uses of the lordship oath are studied in Odegaard, 'Carolingian Oaths of Fidelity' and 'The Concept of Royal Power in Carolingian Oaths of Fidelity.' Reynolds, *Fiefs and Vassals*, 84–9, challenges the conventional understanding of the oath and its place in the contemporary historiography of the mutual relations of lord and man. Becher, *Eid und Herrschaft*, is a full study of Charlemagne's use of loyalty oaths.
36 Latin *familia* is extremely flexible. As the title of my book suggests, it frequently designates a group of non-related people. In Hincmar, *De ordine palatii*, 76 at l. 381, it designates members of the king's household; and in ecclesiastical contexts, the whole of a monastic community is also called a *familia*. See, for example, the literal and metaphorical language of the *Regularis Concordia* in which the heads of male and female monastic communities are called 'mothers and fathers' (7) and in which the king and queen 'parent' those communities (2) in Symons, ed. and trans., *Regularis Concordia*. For the idea that upon entering a monastery, a young boy should forget his blood family and claim his monastic community as family, see Coleman, *Ancient and Medieval Memories*, 129–36.
37 Foot, 'The Making of *Angelcynn*,' 29, notes that *Angelcynn* first appears in a Mercian charter from the 850s where it seems to be an equivalent for the Latin *Angli*. This is consistent with some but not all of the early *Chronicle* entries.
38 Nicholas Howe suggests, in personal conversation, that the identity of the *Angelcynn* and the Anglo-Saxons is so powerful that it can transfer to a space, the space the Anglo-Saxons inhabit while they are in Rome.
39 I take up the question of whether Alfred actually had to retake his city in chapter 2.
40 S. a. 886 (A): Bately, ed., *The Anglo-Saxon Chronicle*, 53: 'Þy ilcan geare

gesette Ælfred cyning Lundenburg, 7 him all Angelcyn to cirde þæt buton deniscra monna hæftniede was' (In the same year, Alfred occupied [lit. settled] the city of London and all the *Angelcynn* who were not imprisoned by the Danes submitted to him).

41 Bately, *The Anglo-Saxon Chronicle: Texts and Textual Relationships*, 2.
42 S. a. 896 (A): Bately, ed., *The Anglo-Saxon Chronicle*, 59: 'Næfde se here, Godes þonces, Angelcyn ealles forswiðe gebrocod ...'
43 S. a. 900 (A): Bately, ed., *The Anglo-Saxon Chronicle*, 61: 'Her gefor Ælfred Aþulfing ..., se wæs cyning ofer eall Ongelcyn butan ðæm dæle þe under Dena onwalde wæs' (Here, [in this year], died Alfred, son of Æthelwulf ... he was king over all the *Angelcynn*, except those who [lived] under Danish authority).
44 S. a. 891 (A): Bately, ed., *The Anglo-Saxon Chronicle*, 54–5. Note, however, that Asser expands this list: Asser, *Life of King Alfred*, chapter 76 at 60. This choice associates the *Anglo-Saxon Chronicle* with a number of Alfredian texts in which *Angelcynn* also appears as the preferred term for the Anglo-Saxons. As Foot, 'The Making of *Angelcynn*,' 30–2, has demonstrated, *Angelcynn* is most commonly found in late ninth-century texts, such as the letter accompanying the Old English translation of the *Regula pastoralis*, that can be associated with Alfred's court.
45 S. a. 994 (C): O'Brien O'Keeffe, ed., *The Anglo-Saxon Chronicle MS C*, 87.
46 S. a. 1011 (C): O'Brien O'Keeffe, ed., *The Anglo-Saxon Chronicle*, 96.
47 S. a. 1016 (C): O'Brien O'Keeffe, ed., *The Anglo-Saxon Chronicle*, 102: 'Þa dyde Eadric ealdorman swa swa he ær oftor dyde: astealde þæne fleam ærest mid Magesæton 7 aswac swa his cynehlaforde 7 ealre Angelcynnes þeode' (Then *ealdormann* Eadric did as he had done so often before; he was the first among the Magesæton [a local group] to start the flight. And in so doing, he betrayed his *cynehlaford* and all the people of the *Angelcynn*).
48 Ibid.
49 S. a. 1016 (C): O'Brien O'Keeffe, ed., *The Anglo-Saxon Chronicle*, 102–3.
50 S. a. 1017 (C): O'Brien O'Keeffe, ed., *The Anglo-Saxon Chronicle*, 103. That this language is a feature of the *Chronicle* is underscored by Cnut's stylization as 'ealles Engla lande ciningc' (king of all the land of the Anglo-Saxons) in I Cnut, prologue, in Liebermann, ed., *Die Gesetze*, 278.
51 S. a. 1017 (C): O'Brien O'Keeffe, ed., *The Anglo-Saxon Chronicle*, 103. For studies of how Cnut secures his kingdom using lordship relations, see chapter 5.
52 In fact, with only a few exceptions, there are few collective references to the Anglo-Saxons as a people after the Norman Conquest. For example, in the early years, the D annalist speaks of the land as *Englaland* (s. a. 1066, 1067,

and 1071 (D): Cubbin, ed., *The Anglo-Saxon Chronicle: MS D*, 81, 81, and 85), and occasionally of regional groups like the *Norðhymbrum* (83) but he uses a collective name such as *englisc* only when he needs to make a contrast with either the *Normen* (80) or the *frencisc* (86); the *Angelcynn* seem to have died with the Conquest.

53 See Dumville, 'Kingship, Genealogy, and Regnal Lists'; Moisl, 'Anglo-Saxon Royal Genealogies and Germanic Oral Tradition'; Sisam, 'Anglo-Saxon Royal Genealogies'; and Spiegel, 'Genealogy.'

54 See, most importantly, Dumville, 'The Ætheling.' Overviews of the problems of royal succession can be found in John, *Orbis Britanniae and Other Studies*, 37–43, and *Reassessing Anglo-Saxon England*, 71–4; Wormald, 'On Þa Wæpnedhealfe,' 264–71; Williams, 'Some Notes and Considerations on Problems Connected with the English Royal Succession, 860–1066'; and Yorke, *Kings and Kingdoms*, 148–54, and 167–77.

55 Spiegel, 'Genealogy.'

56 The will of Alfred's father, Æthelwulf, is not extant, but it is preserved in Asser, *Life of King Alfred*, 14–16. Alfred's will is in Harmer, ed., 'King Alfred's Will,' 15–19.

57 Keynes, *The Diplomas of King Æthelred*, 163–76.

58 S. a. 1017 (C): O'Brien O'Keeffe, ed., *The Anglo-Saxon Chronicle*, 103. On Emma's life in this period, see Stafford, *Queen Emma and Queen Edith*, 225–36.

59 William's claim is discussed by Douglas, *William the Conqueror*, 379–82; I consider this question more fully in chapter 6.

60 Parkes, 'The Palaeography,' 165.

61 Wallace-Hadrill, 'The Franks and the English in the Ninth Century.'

62 The problems of genre are nicely reformulated as an issue of audience expectation and reception in Jauss, 'Literary History as a Challenge to Literary Theory,' 22–32; the question of how this frame might be particularly productive for understanding medieval genres is explored later (76–109).

63 Clemoes, 'Language in Context,' argues that this feature is distinctively Anglo-Saxon.

64 Bhabha, 'DissemiNation,' 145.

65 Although I use it differently, I borrow this phrase from the title of Leckie Jr., *The Passage of Dominion*.

66 Goez, *Translatio imperii*, 37–62 and 62–76, is a detailed study of the *translatio* motif in the historiography of the Carolingian and migration periods.

67 Southern, 'Aspects of the European Tradition of Historical Writing: 1, The Classical Tradition from Einhard to Geoffrey of Monmouth,' 179–80, observes how this particular philosophy of causation is a break with classi-

cal tradition as represented by Sallust. For a detailed study of the historiographical tradition in which Orosius works, see Lacroix, *Orose et ses idées*, 51–69 and 87–98. Hanning, *The Vision of History in Early Britain*, studies the historical tradition in England from its beginning through to Geoffrey of Monmouth. The tradition as the annalist knew it is most likely to be from the work of Alcuin or Bede; see Howe, *Migration and Mythmaking*, 20–8, and Wallace-Hadrill, 'Charles the Bald and Alfred,' 145–6. Incidentally, this understanding of causation is similar to that articulated in Pseudo-Cyprian's ninth abuse; see Pseudo-Cyprian, *De duodecim abusivis saeculi*, 51–3; I take up the link between mirrors and salvation history in chapters 3 and 4.

68 See, for example, Bede, *Bede's Ecclesiastical History of the English People*, I, chapters 27–32, pp. 78–115. In these chapters, Bede turns from the social and political history of the English to the spiritual matters he considers necessary for the preservation of the people he has just created.

69 Interestingly, this aspect of the *Chronicle* is recognized in the composition of London, British Library, MS Cotton Tiberius B. i, the manuscript of the C text of the *Chronicle*. The manuscript begins with a copy of Orosius's *Historiarum adversus paganos libri septem*; this history is followed by two poems – the *Old English Menologium* and *Maxims II* – and these, in turn, are followed by the *Chronicle*. For descriptions and contents, see Ker, *A Catalogue of Manuscripts Containing Anglo-Saxon*, 251–3, item 191, and O'Brien O'Keeffe, ed., *The Anglo-Saxon Chronicle*, xx–xxvi. Conner, ed., *The Abingdon Chronicle, A. D. 956–1066*, xix, argues that Orosius's text was added later and was thus not copied as part of the *Chronicle*, but O'Brien O'Keeffe, 'Reading the C-Text,' 138–9, suggests that the joining of these texts was purposeful.

70 Bede, *Bede's Ecclesiastical History of the English People*, I, chapter 1, pp. 14–19.

71 Initially, the tone of Bede's *descriptio* resembles those of early encyclopedic works in which many wonders are to be found. Britain fares poorly, in Bede's text at least, when it is compared to Ireland and the Irish (18–21). The idea of the curio is also implicit in Allen Frantzen's discussion of Bede's Anglians in Rome; see Frantzen, 'Bede and Bawdy Bale,' 18–25.

72 Playing with Walter Benjamin's 'Paris: Capital of the Nineteenth Century,' Nicholas Howe points out in personal conversation that Rome is to the medieval period as Paris is to the nineteenth century.

2. Making Alfred King

1 On the way in which these readings are part of a tradition of Alfred interpretation, see Keynes, 'The Cult of King Alfred the Great.'
2 Yorke, *Wessex in the Early Middle Ages*, is a good study of the complex his-

tory of Wessex in the period. The Anglo-Saxons themselves were not consistent about their terminology; see the discussion in chapter 1 and, in particular, note 28 of that chapter for particular discussion of the word *Angelcynn*.
3 Peddie, *Alfred: Warrior King*.
4 See pages 166–7, note 67.
5 For a clear description of how the sources are used in the early annals of the *Chronicle*, see Bately, 'World History in the *Anglo-Saxon Chronicle*.
6 The one exception to this is the entry for 893 where the annalist notes that 'þa cristnan hæfdon sige' (the Christians took the victory), but this might also be the work of a separate annalist. S. a. 893 (A) in Bately, ed., *The Anglo-Saxon Chronicle: MS A*, 58. The manuscript history is discussed in full in Bately, *Texts and Textual Relationships*, 'The Compilation of the *Anglo-Saxon Chronicle* Once More,' and 'The Compilation of the *Anglo-Saxon Chronicle*, 60 B.C. to A.D. 890.'
7 Nelson, 'The Political Ideas of Alfred of Wessex,' 131, gives a precise summary of the Carolingian atmosphere in Alfred's court.
8 Both Carolingian and Anglo-Saxon lordship relations are symbolized by an oath, but the use to which the Alfred annalist puts the relationship symbolized by that oath differs from that in Carolingian accounts. The bibliography on this is vast; for introductions to the debate, page 164, note 35.
9 Explanations of this system and its implications for military service can be found in Abels, *Lordship and Military Obligation in Anglo-Saxon England*, 58–78, and *Alfred the Great*, 194–218. Details of Alfred's system can be found in the document known as the *Burghal Hidage*. The various manuscripts of this text have most recently been edited by Alexander Rumble and can be found in Hill and Rumble, eds., *The Defence of Wessex*, 14–35.
10 For example, s. a. 893 and 895 (A) in Bately, ed., *The Anglo-Saxon Chronicle*, 56 and 59.
11 Here, I distinguish my use of the term 'allegiance' from that in Wormald, '*Engla Lond*: The Making of an Allegiance.' Arguing for 'the making of *Engla lond*' as 'the making of an allegiance' based upon an oath of loyalty, Wormald's study of the state works from the principle that despite the idealism implied by oaths, land is always somewhere at issue. While I agree that 'allegiance to the new kingdom of "the English" was underwritten by oath' (7), my reading of the annalist's rhetoric challenges this understanding of the link between loyalty oaths, lordship, and land. Idealism, in my view, is precisely the point of the narrative material in the Alfred annals. I do not address the realities of land tenure; I focus specifically on the ways

in which the Alfred annalist uses the ideals of lordship and even the conventions of practice. Thus Wormald's claims – 'It is scarcely necessary to labour the significance of the fact that overriding allegiance was expected of its subjects from the very cradle of the English state. Nor will it escape notice that such an oath neatly links loyalty to a ruler with the security of ruling-class property' (7) – are profitably taken as an account of the actual mechanics of creating an Anglo-Saxon state, but they are incomplete as a matrix for reading and interpreting the *Anglo-Saxon Chronicle.*

12 Foot, 'The Making of *Angelcynn,*' also makes this point, though we arrive at it from different perspectives. That said, the relevance of Foot's approach for my argument is discussed later in the chapter. See note 82 below for discussion of the events of 886.

13 See Bately, *Texts and Textual Relationships,* 2.

14 Because the Alfred annals have a consistent theme, focus, and register of language, I would suggest that if the compiler is not the Alfred annalist, he at least read, understood, and preserved the principles of the Alfred annalist.

15 Bately, 'The Compilation of the *Anglo-Saxon Chronicle* Once More.'

16 S. a. 896 and 900 (A) in Bately, ed., *The Anglo-Saxon Chronicle,* 59 and 61. I discuss the continuator's work later in the chapter. See also Bately, *Texts and Textual Relationships,* 2.

17 My argument here is consonant with Bhabha, 'DissemiNation,' 145: 'The scraps, patches, and rags of daily life [are] repeatedly turned into the signs of a coherent national culture, while the very act of the narrative performance interpellates a growing circle of national subjects.' Given that many theories of nation also include territory and given that the history of the land is at issue in the Alfred annals, I find Bhabha's focus on the textual representations of culture productive.

18 S. a. 893 (A) in Bately, ed., *The Anglo-Saxon Chronicle,* 55: 'On þys geare ... Norþhymbre 7 Eastengle hæfdon Ælf(f)rede [sic] cyninge aðas geseald 7 Eastengle foregisla .vi. 7 þeh, ofer þa treowa, swa oft swa þa oþre hergas mid ealle herige ut foron, þonne foron hie, oþþe mid oþþe on heora healfe an' (In this year ... the Northumbrians and East Anglians gave King Alfred oaths and the East Anglians gave him six preliminary hostages; nevertheless, despite those pledges, they went out raiding quite as often as the other armies all together, and sometimes they went with them and sometimes they went on their [the other armies'] behalf).

19 S. a. 893 (A): Bately, ed., *The Anglo-Saxon Chronicle,* 57.

20 Ibid.

21 Ibid.

22 *Compaternitas* as a strategy of peace making and its significance for lordship relations are discussed in Charles-Edwards, 'Alliances, Godfathers, Treaties and Boundaries.' Lynch, *Christianizing Kinship*, 135–50, deals with *compaternitas* in Anglo-Saxon England.
23 S. a. 892 (A): Bately, ed., *The Anglo-Saxon Chronicle*, 57. Old English *cumpæder* literally means 'godfather,' and although such a relationship between Æthelred and Hásteinn is not necessarily excluded by the fact that Æthelred is also a godfather to Hásteinn's son, I have translated literally.
24 The early history of the Anglo-Saxon kingdoms can be found in a general survey like Stenton, *Anglo-Saxon England*, 32–95. More detailed studies from a variety of perspectives are Bailey, 'The Middle Saxons'; John Blair, 'Frithuwold's Kingdom and the Origins of Surrey'; Brooks, 'The Creation and Early Structure of the Kingdom of Kent,' and 'The Formation of the Mercian Kingdom'; Dumville, 'Essex, Middle Anglia, and the Expansion of Mercia in the South-East Midlands,' and 'The Origins of Northumbria'; Welch, 'The Kingdom of the South Saxons'; and Yorke, 'The Jutes of Hampshire and Wight and the Origins of Wessex.' The history of Wessex is best covered by Yorke, *Kings and Kingdoms of Early Anglo-Saxon England*, 128–56; and *Wessex in the Early Middle Ages*.
25 See note 62 below.
26 S. a. 836 (A): Bately, ed., *The Anglo-Saxon Chronicle*, 43.
27 On this division, an event that does not appear in the *Chronicle*, see Asser, *Life of King Alfred*, 13–16. See also Keynes and Lapidge, eds and trans., Introduction to *Alfred the Great*, 9–10.
28 A clear account of the impact of the Danish raids on the shape of the kingdom of Wessex is Yorke, *Wessex in the Early Middle Ages*, 107–23.
29 See Fanning, 'Bede, *Imperium*, and the Bretwaldas,' esp. 4. This has been a contentious issue in the scholarship; see Dumville, 'The Terminology of Overkingship in Early Anglo-Saxon England'; John, *Orbis Britanniae and Other Studies*, 6–8 and 35–6; Keynes, 'Rædwald the Bretwalda,' 112–14; Wormald, 'Bede, the *Bretwaldas*, and the Origins of the *Gens Anglorum*'; and Yorke, 'The Vocabulary of Anglo-Saxon Overlordship.'
30 S. a. 827 (A): Bately, ed., *The Anglo-Saxon Chronicle*, 42.
31 I am grateful to Katherine O'Brien O'Keeffe for making this clear to me.
32 Because of these difficulties – the absence of a geographically stable nation and certain kinds of unifying cultural symbols – some of the most prominent recent studies of nationalism including Anderson, *Imagined Communities* – seem leery of tackling the medieval and, in particular, the Old English period. Hastings, *The Construction of Nationhood*, 38–43, considers Anglo-Saxon England briefly, but is more interested in nationalism after the Con-

quest. The general neglect of the period seems to be a legacy of the common critical tendency to view the Middle Ages as less sophisticated than other periods. Among medieval scholars, the debate centres more clearly on a wariness about what can or cannot be called a nation and the misleading term *gens*: see Reynolds, 'Medieval *origines gentium* and the Community of the Realm.' Her *Kingdoms and Communities in Western Europe, 900–1300*, 250–6, usefully links the problems of medieval nationhood, the language of nationhood, and the roles of historical writing.

33 Moreover, the annalist's emphasis on the secular political family of lordship radically expands the meaning of *Angel*, the first semantic element, from a term for a limited ethnic group, the Anglians, to the Anglo-Saxons as a whole. In the *Historia ecclesiastica*, Bede creates a Roman Christian identity for the people who inhabit the British Isles and names them the *gens Anglorum*. Given the political history of Britain, this is certainly an interesting choice. The terminology is discussed in full in chapter 1.

34 See page 166, note 54.

35 See page 166, note 53.

36 For a rereading of the history of relations between Wessex and Mercia, see Keynes, 'King Alfred and the Mercians.' Keynes persuasively argues against the long-held idea that relations between the two neighbouring kingdoms were, by necessity, hostile. This point is also made (less fully) in Keynes and Lapidge, Introduction to *Alfred the Great*, 11. For the people at Alfred's court, see ibid., 26–7, and s. a. 890: Bately, ed., *The Anglo-Saxon Chronicle*, 54. Nelson, 'Reconstructing a Royal Family,' demonstrates the complexity of Alfred's family relations and claims for the throne.

37 See, for example, McTurk, '"Cynewulf and Cyneheard" and the Icelandic Sagas.'

38 This is also noted in Bredehoft, *Textual Histories*, 39–40. I would like to thank Tom for his great act of generosity in allowing me to read his manuscript prior to publication.

39 See, for example, Battaglia, '*Anglo-Saxon Chronicle* for 755'; Ferro, 'The King in the Doorway'; Johansen, 'Language, Structure, and Theme in the "Cynewulf and Cyneheard" Episode'; Towers, 'Thematic Unity in the Story of Cynewulf and Cyneheard'; and Wilson, 'Cynewulf and Cyneheard.' John M. Hill, *The Anglo-Saxon Warrior Ethic*, 74–88, argues that lordship is secondary to a consideration of law (*riht*).

40 Bredehoft, *Textual Histories*, 58–9, and Hill, *The Anglo-Saxon Warrior Ethic*, 58, are notable exceptions.

41 This moment and the problem of royal authority are fully discussed in Stephen D. White, 'Kinship and Lordship in Early Medieval England.'

42 White, 'Kinship and Lordship.'
43 The problem of consent, the *witan*, and the process of electing a king is complicated because the sources do not provide enough information to allow us to see any kind of established procedure in operation. I do not claim that the annalist reports the procedure exactly, but it would be helpful to understand how his comments relate to standard practice. Devisse, 'Essai sur l'histoire d'une expression qui a fait fortune,' notes that the phrase *consilium et auxilium*, often used in Carolingian texts as a formulation of the obligations of a man to his lord, was an early alternative for *consensus et consilium* (consensus and counsel). The historical use of the phrase is traced in Hannig, *Consensus fidelium*, 26–32 and 225–57. When transferred to discussions of election to the kingship, this seems to mean that consent to a candidate's accession is equivalent to acknowledging the obligations created by lordship oaths. See chapter 10 of Oleson, *The Witenagemot in the Reign of Edward the Confessor*, 82–90, and chapter 16 of Smyth, *King Alfred the Great*, 421–51. That the languages of lordship, consent, and accession to the throne all work in concert helps to explain the annalist's comment on Æthelwold's attempt to seize the throne in 901 – 'butan ðæs cyninges leafe 7 his witena' (without the leave of the king and his *witan*) s. a. 900 (A): Bately, ed., *The Anglo-Saxon Chronicle*, 61 – and the scene of submission to William I as related in the D MS entry for 1066.
44 S. a. 871 (A): Bately, ed., *The Anglo-Saxon Chronicle*, 2: 'Þa feng Ælfred ... to rice, 7 þa was agan his ielde .xxiii. wintra. 7 .ccc. 7 .xcvi. wintra þæs þe his cyn ærest Westseaxna lond on Wealum geeodon' (Then Alfred succeeded ... to the kingdom and then twenty-three years of his life had passed and three hundred and ninety-six years since his family first conquered the land of the West Saxons from the Britons). When in 552, for example, Cynric fought and won a significant battle against the Britons, the annalists, with the exception of the E annalist, write, 'Her Cynric gefeaht wiþ Brettas in þære stowe þe is genemned æt Searobyrg 7 þa Bretwalas gefliemde' (Here Cynric fought against the Britons in the place that is named Salisbury and put the Britons to flight). S. a. 552 (A): Bately, ed., *The Anglo-Saxon Chronicle*, 22.
45 Scragg, '*Wifcyþþe* and the Morality of the Cynewulf and Cyneheard Episode in the *Anglo-Saxon Chronicle*.'
46 O'Brien O'Keeffe, 'Heroic Values and Christian Ethics,' 110. Bremmer, 'The Germanic Context of "Cynewulf and Cyneheard" Revisited,' 454–6, uses Frisian texts to suggest that this is a rape scene.
47 Bredehoft, *Textual Histories*, 56–7, briefly suggests that the pivotal moment of the annal comes when Cyneheard's men refuse their offer and places this

against the usual claims that Cynewulf and his retainers are the annalists' heroes.
48 On *æthelings* as candidates for the throne, see Dumville, 'The *Ætheling*.'
49 Readers of the annal who first encounter it in any of the beginning anthologies of Old English are often surprised by its syntactical difficulty. The pronouns make it hard to distinguish between Cyneheard, Osric (Cynewulf's man), and their respective retainers. The similarity between the two leaders is further stressed by the virtually identically phrased repeated offers of safe passage for kinsmen, the loyalty demonstrated by two sets of Cynewulf's men and then by Cyneheard's own men, the presence of only one survivor after each encounter, and the honourable burial given to both Cynewulf and Cyneheard.
50 It is, of course, arguable that Cyneheard is Cynewulf's failure, but this argument might be refuted in Cynewulf's favour. Cynewulf has seen the problem and is acting to secure his position.
51 Editors focused on the heroic action assume that the annal – or at least the meaningful part – finishes with the burial of Cynewulf and Cyneheard, and they conclude their excerpts here.
52 Keynes, 'King Alfred and the Mercians.'
53 See, for an account of the land transactions and general history of Wessex in the period, Yorke, *Kings and Kingdoms*, 136–42, and *Wessex in the Early Middle Ages*, 84–93.
54 Yorke, *Kings and Kingdoms*, 141.
55 John, *Orbis Britanniae*, 14, claims that Offa would not have accepted Cynewulf as a full king on the basis of attestations in the *acta* of the ecclesiastical councils, but Keynes, 'King Alfred and the Mercians,' is more persuasive.
56 I hold this interpretation of the Cynewulf-Cyneheard episode alongside the complicated problem of Anglo-Saxon overkingship and lordship; see, most recently, Dumville, 'The Terminology of Overkingship.' My reading of the annal is not intended to shed any light on either these difficulties or their historiography, but the existence of these difficulties does add a keen relevance to the Cynewulf story.
57 Other texts support the annalist's take on Æthelbald. The Mercian king is known to have consorted with nuns, against their will, and, as a letter from Saint Boniface warns, seems to have been implicated in their possible abortions. See the letter of Boniface to Æthelbald in Whitelock, ed. and trans., *English Historical Documents c. 500–1042*, 751–6. In addition, Boniface also reprimands Æthelbald for depriving the church of certain lands and their

income. I know of no similar extant text reprimanding Cynewulf for his transactions of Cookham and though Æthelweard may seem to reprove Cynewulf for meeting a woman, this does not generally spoil his positive reputation.

58 On the use of this term and its importance to the scholarly debate on Anglo-Saxon succession, see page 166, note 54.

59 The points that follow are very much connected to de Certeau's distinction between place and space. De Certeau, *The Practice of Everyday Life*, 117: 'A space exists when one takes into consideration vectors of direction, velocities, and time variables. Thus *space* is composed of intersections of mobile elements. It is in a sense actuated by the ensemble of movements deployed within it. Space occurs as the effect produced by the operations that orient it, situate it, temporalize it and make it function in a polyvalent unity of conflictual programs or contractual proximities' [emphasis as printed]. I am grateful to Steele Nowlin for pointing this reference out to me.

60 See Lefebvre, *The Production of Space*, 41–2, on representational spaces: 'Redolent with imaginary and symbolic elements, they have their source in history – in the history of a people as well as in the history of each individual belonging to that people ... Representational space is alive: It speaks ... It embraces the loci of passion, of action, and of lived situations, and thus immediately implies time.'

61 For example, s. a. 871 (A): Bately, ed., *The Anglo-Saxon Chronicle*, 48: 'Þa Deniscan ahton wælstowe gewald' (The Danes took possession of the battlefield). Keynes, 'A Tale of Two Kings,' observes that the seriousness of the situation in the 870s is obscured by the annalist's language.

62 Both versions of the treaty of Alfred and Guthrum are available in Liebermann, ed., *Die Gesetze der Angelsachsen*, 126–9 and Hill and Rumble, eds., *The Defence of Wessex*, 14–35. A good discussion of the significance of this treaty is Dumville, 'The Treaty of Alfred and Guthrum.' The treaty and the clarity of the boundaries it draws suggest that land was very much on Alfred's mind.

63 Clemoes, 'Language in Context.' Some of the intersections of time and place are nicely expressed in Bakhtin, 'Forms of Time and Chronotope in the Novel,' 84: 'In the literary artistic chronotope, spatial and temporal indications are fused into one carefully thought-out, concrete whole. Time, as it were, thickens, takes on flesh, becomes artistically visible; likewise, space becomes charged and responsive to the movements of time, plot and history. This intersection of axes and fusion of indicators characterizes the artistic chronotope.'

64 This moment has provoked a vast amount of scholarly inquiry, usually with regard to Anglo-Saxon succession practices and, particularly in earlier

works, its plausibility. On the question of anointing, see Nelson, 'The Problem of Alfred's Royal Anointing.'
65 S. a. 871 (A): Bately, ed., *The Anglo-Saxon Chronicle*, 48.
66 Asser, *Life of King Alfred*, 32.
67 Examples abound; I quote here only a few: 'Þæs ymb .iiii. niht Eþered cyning 7 Elfred his broþur ...' (After three days, King Æthelred and Alfred, his brother ...); '7 þæs ymb .xiiii. niht gefeaht Eþered cyning 7 Elfred his broður ...' (and two weeks later, King Æthelred and Alfred, his brother, fought ...). S. a. 871 (A): Bately, ed., *The Anglo-Saxon Chronicle*, 48–9.
68 See Asser, *Life of King Alfred*, 28–9.
69 S. a. 871 (A): Bately, ed., *The Anglo-Saxon Chronicle*, 48–9.
70 Ibid., 49.
71 Ibid.
72 Ibid.
73 As further evidence of the annalist's strategy towards place, I note that Asser in his entry for the same year characterizes Reading as a royal residence, thereby ensuring that his readers understand the significance of the place. See Asser, *Life of King Alfred*, 27.
74 S. a. 874 (A): Bately, ed., *The Anglo-Saxon Chronicle*, 49.
75 Stenton, *Anglo-Saxon England*, 252–4, makes Ceolwulf a king; Keynes, 'King Alfred and the Mercians,' 12–19, comes to the same conclusion, but documents the argument better with a careful study of the evidence of the coinage and thinks more explicitly about the annalist's text.
76 S. a. 876 (A): Bately, ed., *The Anglo-Saxon Chronicle*, 50.
77 S. a. 877 (A): Bately, ed., *The Anglo-Saxon Chronicle*, 50.
78 Ibid.: '7 hie him þær foregislas saldon, swa fela swa he habban wolde 7 micle aþas sworon' (And there they gave him preliminary hostages, as many as he wanted, and swore mighty oaths).
79 S. a. 878 (A): Bately, ed., *The Anglo-Saxon Chronicle*, 50.
80 While there are many explications of otherness, I choose the following because of the explicit connection to the formation of national identity: Bhabha, 'DissemiNation,' 147–8: 'The performative intervenes in the sovereignty of the nation's *self-generation* by casting a shadow *between* the people as "image" and its signification as a differentiating sign of Self, distinct from the Other of the Outside.' (Emphasis as printed.)
81 I do not suggest that the readers of the Alfred annals would have known these poems; I list them as places where modern readers might find these topoi.
82 S. a. 878 (A): Bately, ed., *The Anglo-Saxon Chronicle*, 51: '7 þa salde se here him foregislas 7 micle aþas ...' (And then the army gave him preliminary hostages and swore mighty oaths ...).

83 For a brief description of the peace-making process as practised by both the Anglo-Saxons and Carolingians, see Keynes, 'A Tale of Two Kings,' 199. There are no surviving texts of this kind of lordship oath; scholars usually assume that they were probably fairly close to those in *Að: Eideswerth des Thegn*. See Liebermann, ed., *Die Gesetze*, 464–5.
84 Charles-Edwards, 'Alliances, Godfathers, Treaties and Boundaries.'
85 On the question of whether Alfred actually had to retake his city, see Keynes and Lapidge, eds., Introduction to *Alfred the Great*, 38–9; Keynes, 'King Alfred and the Mercians,' 24–6; and Nelson, 'The Political Ideas of Alfred of Wessex,' 154–5. Abels, *Alfred the Great*, 174–6, is more cautious. The argument depends on the numismatic evidence; see Blackburn, 'The London Mint in the Reign of Alfred.'
86 S. a. 886 (A): Bately, ed., *The Anglo-Saxon Chronicle*, 53.
87 See *gecyrran* in Healey, Venezky, and Cameron, eds, *Dictionary of Old English (microform)*, 1517. Katherine O'Brien O'Keeffe also reminds me that *cyrran* can mean 'to convert'; it is almost as if Alfred and his performance of lordship are the Anglo-Saxons' new religion.
88 This reading is supported by the phrasing of the same moment in Asser's *Vita Alfredi*. See Asser, *Life of King Alfred*, 69.
89 Foot, 'The Making of *Angelcynn*,' 33.
90 For a full discussion of usage in the *Anglo-Saxon Chronicle*, see chapter 1.
91 The exception is the entry for 874 in which the annalist writes of the 'Angelcynnes scole' (the school of the *Angelcynn*), but I discount this entry in that its unusual usage of Old English *scol* in the sense of "area" or "quarter" seems to be one of idiom; see, for example, the entry for 817. I draw my translation of Old English *scol* from Whitelock ed. and trans., *The Anglo-Saxon Chronicle: A Revised Translation*, 39, note 11. In personal conversation, Nicholas Howe has suggested that the idea of a place being associated with the name of a collective group attests to the power of their discourse of identity.
92 S. a. 871 (A): Bately, ed., *The Anglo-Saxon Chronicle*, 48, for example.
93 S. a. 896 (A): Bately, ed., *The Anglo-Saxon Chronicle*, 59.
94 S. a. 900 (A): Bately, ed., *The Anglo-Saxon Chronicle*, 61.
95 Hayden White, *The Content of the Form*, 5–9 and 14–15, and his *Tropics of Discourse*, 83–5.
96 On the compilation and sources of *The Anglo-Saxon Chronicle* for the years up to 449, see Bately, 'The Compilation of the *Anglo-Saxon Chronicle*, 60 B.C. to A.D. 890,' and her 'World History.'
97 See, for example, Howe, *Migration and Mythmaking in Anglo-Saxon England*, 28–31.

3. Proclaiming Alfred's Kingship

1 The most recent instances of the forgery argument are Smyth, *King Alfred the Great*, 271–324, and his *The Medieval Life of King Alfred the Great*, esp. 202–10. Galbraith, 'Who Wrote Asser's *Life of Alfred*?' 88–128, argues for a tenth-century date, with Leofric of Exeter as a possible author. Smyth, on the other hand, posits a late tenth- or early eleventh-century Ramsey milieu with Byrhtferth as a possible author. His argument is affirmed in part by John, *Reassessing Anglo-Saxon England*, 82, note 15.
2 The case for the authenticity of this text is made in Whitelock, *The Genuine Asser*, and Keynes, 'On the Authenticity of Asser's *Life of King Alfred*.'
3 This point is made most clearly in Campbell, 'Asser's *Life of Alfred*,' and Keynes, 'King Alfred and the Mercians.' While I agree with the general direction of these essays, I would not claim that Asser wrote primarily for his Welsh associates. Nelson, 'The Franks and the English in the Ninth Century Reconsidered,' makes a persuasive reconsideration of certain dynastically focused tensions in Anglo-Saxon and Frankish relations. This, together with the known number of Frankish visitors at Alfred's court and Asser's persistent use of Carolingian mirrors for princes, suggests the possibility of a Frankish audience. However, the lack of evidence for either country or even for both makes me reluctant to commit to an argument about the ethnicity of Asser's projected readers. For an account of how the *Vita Alfredi* might have been read outside the court, see Campbell, 'Asser's *Life of Alfred*.' By contrast, Scharer, 'The Writing of History at King Alfred's Court,' suggests how the text might have been read as a handbook for newcomers at Alfred's court.
4 Indeed, the *Vita* has not met with critical appreciation. Though Schütt, 'The Literary Form of Asser's *Vita Alfredi*,' goes a long way to pointing out the skill of the *Vita Alfredi*, Scharer, 'The Writing of History,' 203, still refers to Asser's work as a '"patchwork" of quotations, borrowed ideas and allusions.'
5 Stevenson in his edition of Asser, *Life of King Alfred*, 162–3, discusses the knowledge of Sedulius in Anglo-Saxon England, and Scharer, 'The Writing of History,' demonstrates Asser's use of Sedulius's *De rectoribus christianis* as a source.
6 Campbell, 'Asser's *Life of Alfred*,' 116–21.
7 Scharer, 'The Writing of History,' 192–204.
8 That said, I would also point out the general difficulty of genre criticism and expectations. In Jauss, 'Literary History as a Challenge to Literary Theory,' 22–32, that difficulty is productively formulated as a problem of the 'horizon of expectations.'

9 For a discussion of the problems of family and succession for Charlemagne, see Nelson, 'La famille de Charlemagne.' For the problems in the families of Charles the Bald and Louis the German and an explicit connection to the *Anglo-Saxon Chronicle*, see Nelson, 'A Tale of Two Princes'; for the problems before and after Alfred's reign, see, among others, Nelson, 'Reconstructing a Royal Family.' Though I do not see the evidence for his characterizations of Æthelwulf's personality, see Enright, 'Charles the Bald and Aethelwulf of Wessex,' who studies how these events might have impressed themselves on Æthelwulf. On Anglo-Saxon patterns of succession, see page 166, note 54. The idea that a king is to set an example and correct his people is widespread in Carolingian mirrors, see, among others, Hincmar, *De ordine palatii*, 44; Hincmar, *De regis persona et regio ministerio*, cols. 835, 850; and Sedulius Scottus, *Liber de rectoribus christianis*, 26 and 34. The most explicit emphasis on royal morality seems to be from the insular text of Pseudo-Cyprian, *De duodecim abusivis saeculi*, 43. On the influence of Pseudo-Cyprian in the Carolingian world, see Anton, 'Pseudo-Cyprian: *De duodecim abusivis saeculi* und sein Einfluß auf den Kontinent.'

10 My emphasis on the significant functions of the body counters Smyth, *King Alfred the Great*, 199–216, in which Smyth uses a chapter title to label Alfred a 'neurotic saint and invalid king.' I see the importance of Smyth's claim that the text borrows from Frankish and not Irish hagiographical topoi. Alfred's illness is indeed essential. On this topic, see David Pratt, 'The Illnesses of King Alfred the Great.'

11 Asser, *Life of King Alfred*, 54–7, esp. 57.

12 Ibid.

13 The most thorough study of this aspect of kingship is Kantorowicz, *The King's Two Bodies*. Though Kantorowicz focuses primarily on the late medieval period, much of what he says about polity-centred kingship (193–272) resonates with the texts at issue here.

14 de Certeau, *The Writing of History*, 272.

15 On the problems with and suitability of this term, see page 163, note 28.

16 On the history of the wisdom topos and its renewed importance in the mirrors for princes for Charles the Bald, see Anton, *Fürstenspiegel und Herrscherethos in der Karolingerzeit*, 255–6. For the texts, see Sedulius, *Liber de rectoribus christianis*, 30–3, and Smaragdus, *Via regia*, cols. 941–5. Because Asser uses Sedulius as a source and because the mirrors tend to repeat each other almost verbatim, I cite all following examples of the mirrors for princes topoi only from the *Liber de rectoribus christianis*.

17 S. a. 755 (A): Bately, ed., *The Anglo-Saxon Chronicle*, 36–8.

18 The bibliography for medieval prologues is extensive, but a useful account

of how prologues function is Minnis, *Medieval Theory of Authorship*, 9–72. Spivak, 'Translator's Preface,' suggests how prefatory material that is not a formal prologue might be said to 'begin' a text.

19 On the possible connections between lineage and authority, see page 166, note 53. For particular examinations of the West Saxon genealogical tradition, see Dumville, 'The West Saxon Genealogical Regnal List: Manuscripts and Texts,' and 'The West Saxon Genealogical Regnal List and the Chronology of Early Wessex.'

20 S. a. 836 (A): Bately, ed., *The Anglo-Saxon Chronicle*, 43.

21 The earliest extant manuscript of the *Anglo-Saxon Chronicle* is not Asser's source manuscript – see Asser, *Life of King Alfred*, lxxxv–lxxxviii. This textual history means that we cannot tell whether, in the version that Asser used, the reigns of Alfred and his father are in different hands. On the textual history, see Bately, *Texts and Textual Relationships*, 27–31 and 53–5. The powerful genealogy that concludes the account of Æthelwulf's reign has led some scholars to suggest that an early version of the *Chronicle* might have ended after the entry for 859. Smyth, *King Alfred the Great*, 465–9, discusses this thesis and its implications.

22 S. a. 851 (A): Bately, ed., *The Anglo-Saxon Chronicle*, 44.

23 On this incident and its implications, see Enright, 'Charles the Bald'; Stafford, 'The King's Wife in Wessex, 800–1066'; and her 'Charles the Bald, Judith, and England.'

24 Without the larger context of the *Vita Alfredi*, this remark seems incongruous. Given that the annalist's history has thus far been without evaluation, this little interpretive comment seems to suggest at best a denial of the rebellion (as narrated in the *Vita Alfredi*) or at worst its suppression.

25 Egbert is designated a *Bretwalda*, a term that in chapter 2, I argue designates a ruler of land. On the problem of the *Bretwalda* in general, see page 170, note 29.

26 On Alfred's annalist's approach to narrating the story of the land, see chapter 2.

27 Because, for the moment, I wish to distinguish only actual kings from mythical figures and gods, I collapse the more complicated and sensitive divisions of Sisam, 'Anglo-Saxon Royal Genealogies,' 299–300.

28 Ibid., 315.

29 For the possible sources of this use of the Bible, see Magoun, 'King Aethelwulf's Biblical Ancestors.' Sisam, 'Anglo-Saxon Royal Genealogies,' 314–20, uses later texts like *Beowulf* and the chronicles of Æthelweard and William of Malmesbury to discuss the extension beyond Geat. He characterizes the biblical section as 'artificial' and 'crude' (320). This tradition does appear in Nennius, but that is not a source for Asser.

30 Personal communication with Michael Lapidge, November 2001. The idea that the king and people are connected is a medieval commonplace. For a contemporary articulation of this Pauline idea, see the Old English *Regula pastoralis*: 'Forðon oft for ðæs lareowes unwisdome misfarað þa hiremen, & oft for ðæs lareowes wisdome unwisum hiremonnum bið geborgen' (Therefore, very often, the followers transgress because of their teacher's lack of wisdom and, very often, the unwise followers are spared because of their teacher's wisdom), in Sweet, ed. and trans., *King Alfred's West-Saxon Version of Gregory's Pastoral Care*, 28 [translation mine]. I discuss this convention fully in chapter 4.
31 Personal communication with Michael Lapidge, November 2001.
32 Asser, *Life of King Alfred*, 9–10; Keynes and Lapidge, eds and trans., 'Asser's *Life of King Alfred*,' 70.
33 Asser, *Life of King Alfred*, 10; Keynes and Lapidge, eds and trans., 'Asser's *Life of King Alfred*,' 70.
34 In what Asser presents as a neutral description of his wishes, Æthelwulf is seen trying to exercise control over his land even after he is dead. The king specifies that 'his sons should not quarrel unnecessarily among themselves after the death of their father,' so he arranges for the kingship to pass from son to son in order of age (Asser, *Life of King Alfred*, 14; Keynes and Lapidge, eds and trans., 'Asser's *Life of King Alfred*,' 72). His strategy asks his sons to give preference to the well-being of the kingdom, even if, in so doing, they disinherit their own sons. Because information about Anglo-Saxon succession patterns is limited and contradictory, the historical scholarship on these provisions is complex. The essential problem is the election of one of a number of eligible candidates versus a move towards patrilineal succession. Æthelwulf's will is not extant per se; we know its terms from Asser, *Life of King Alfred*, 14–16. Alfred's will has been edited and translated in Harmer, ed., 'King Alfred's Will,' 15–19.
35 Bouchard, 'Family Structure and Family Consciousness among the Aristocracy,' and Schieffer, 'Väter und Söhne im Karolingerhause.'
36 Halphen, *Charlemagne and the Carolingian Empire*, and Rosamund McKitterick, *The Frankish Kingdoms under the Carolingians, 751–987*, are good introductory studies of the Carolingians.
37 Scharer, 'The Writing of History.'
38 Bately, *Texts and Textual Relationships*, 62, argues that Asser's *Vita Alfredi* is descended from a lost MS W that, in turn, is either a direct descendant of the lost MS U or an annotated version of a lost MS V, itself a descendant of lost MS U.
39 I distinguish my work from Davis, 'Alfred the Great: Propaganda and

Truth,' and Loyn, 'The Term *Ealdorman* in the Translations Prepared at the Time of King Alfred,' in my emphasis on teaching. Loyn argues that the translators involved in Alfred's educational program use the term *ealdormann* so consistently to represent one in a subordinate position that the texts function almost as manuals for Alfred's *ealdormenn*. Davis's reading of the *Preface to the Regula pastoralis* also suggests that the translations reminded Alfred's nobility of the importance of loyalty. I do not challenge these arguments. I wish only to point out that in the *Vita Alfredi*, the responsibility for instructing the nobility is not delegated: it belongs to the king.

40 Asser, *Life of King Alfred*, 77; Keynes and Lapidge, eds., and trans., 'Asser's *Life of King Alfred*,' 101. Alfred's various claims to the throne are something of a problem in themselves. For overviews of the problems of royal succession, see page 166, note 54.

41 On the anointing of Charlemagne's sons and other Carolingian inaugurations, see Nelson, 'The Lord's Anointed and the People's Choice,' 152–9, and her 'Inauguration Rituals.' On the problems of this moment and the evidence for Alfred's anointing, see Nelson, 'The Problem of Alfred's Royal Anointing'; for the symbolism of anointing, see her 'Symbols in Context.'

42 Asser calls him 'secundarius': Asser, *Life of King Alfred*, 24, 29, and 32. On this term, see Dumville, 'The Ætheling,' 1–2 and 24.

43 Asser, *Life of King Alfred*, 9: 'illum plus ceteris filiis diligebat'; Keynes and Lapidge, eds and trans., 'Asser's *Life of King Alfred*,' 70. This explanation and, indeed, the episode are unique to Asser; in the *Anglo-Saxon Chronicle*, Æthelwulf's nobles are portrayed as honourable.

44 de Certeau, *The Writing of History*, 273: 'The Life of a Saint also points to the relation that the group holds with other groups. Thus the martyrdom tale is predominant wherever the community is very marginal, confronted with the threat of extinction, while the virtue tale represents an established church, as an epiphany of the social order in which it is inscribed.' Again, I extend de Certeau's analysis beyond its original formulation.

45 Asser, *Life of King Alfred*, 21; Keynes and Lapidge, eds and trans., 'Asser's *Life of King Alfred*,' 75.

46 Asser, *Life of King Alfred*, 32; Keynes and Lapidge, eds and trans., 'Asser's *Life of King Alfred*,' 80–1. See also chapter 2 for more discussion of this moment.

47 Asser, *Life of King Alfred*, 9: 'infamia contra morem omnium Christianorum' (a disgraceful episode – contrary to the practice of all Christian men); Keynes and Lapidge, eds and trans., 'Asser's *Life of King Alfred*,' 70.

48 The evidence for the procedure of selecting a king is scarce and difficult.

The language of accession overlaps with the language of lordship obligations. The latter is often encapsulated in the phrases *consensus et auxilium* and *consilium et auxilium*. The importance of these concepts for lordship relations and Carolingian kingship is traced in Devisse, 'Essai sur l'histoire d'une expression qui a fait fortune: *consilium et auxilium* au IXe siècle,' and explored in greater depth in Hannig, *Consensus fidelium*, esp. 26–32 and 225–57. Consenting to a candidate's accession is equivalent to acknowledging the obligations created by lordship ties. See chapter 10 of Oleson, *The Witenagemot in the Reign of Edward the Confessor*, 82–90, and chapter 16 of Smyth, *King Alfred the Great*, 421–51.

49 See, in chapter 2, the discussion of consent, lordship, and the Cynewulf-Cyneheard episode.
50 See pages 66–8.
51 Based on the numismatic evidence – Blackburn, 'The London Mint in the Reign of Alfred' – historians now usually argue that this particular moment is symbolic: see Keynes, 'King Alfred and the Mercians.' Alfred already controlled the city – he did not have to win it again. The oath of submission is what is important in both Asser and the *Chronicle*.
52 Asser, *Life of King Alfred*, 69; Keynes and Lapidge, eds and trans., 'Asser's *Life of King Alfred*,' 97–8. This is one of those passages where the text seems not to make sense. See ibid., 266n199.
53 S. a. 827 (A): Bately, ed., *The Anglo-Saxon Chronicle*, 42. On the complexities of this problem and the concomitant question of overkingship, see page 170, note 29 and page 171, note 36. For the Danish victory over Mercia, see Asser, *Life of King Alfred*, 34–5; Keynes and Lapidge, eds and trans., 'Asser's *Life of King Alfred*,' 82.
54 The *Anglo-Saxon Chronicle* records two further attacks in 892 and 896, raids that Asser, because he makes the argument through a more startling comparison with Francia, does not mention here. Further reference to the persistence of the Danish raids is made in Asser, *Life of King Alfred*, 76. See Keynes and Lapidge, eds and trans., 'Asser's *Life of King Alfred*,' 101.
55 Charles the Fat was deposed by Arnulf, his brother's illegitimate son (though Asser does not record this either). Considering the history of Alfred's succession to the West Saxon throne, it seems likely that Alfred, too, feared his family: see Nelson, 'A King across the Sea.' Alfred's father had used a testamentary document to determine that the throne would pass from son to son in order of age. He thereby disinherited the children of his older sons. Indeed, accounts of Alfred's accession in the king's own will and in Asser suggest the difficulties Alfred faced when disinheriting Æthelred's children and later gaining their loyalty. Ultimately, however, Alfred

seems to have succeeded: Æthelred's children do not rebel until the reign of Alfred's son, Edward the Elder. See, Wormald, 'On Þa Wæpnedhealfe.'
56 Asser, *Life of King Alfred*, 19; Keynes and Lapidge, eds and trans., 'Asser's *Life of King Alfred*,' 74.
57 Curtius, *European Literature and the Latin Middle Ages*, 128–30.
58 Asser, *Life of King Alfred*, 19–20; Keynes and Lapidge, eds and trans., 'Asser's *Life of King Alfred*,' 74.
59 Asser, *Life of King Alfred*, 19–20; Keynes and Lapidge, eds and trans., 'Asser's *Life of King Alfred*,' 74–5.
60 As in other saints' lives, Alfred suffers physically, but Asser is not interested in the virtues and graces of the physical body. Nonetheless, the connection between the book and the political body is significant. Asser's history is performative; the collective identity it conveys is a form of textual affiliation.
61 See note 16 above.
62 Æthelgifu is consigned to a monastery, and Æthelflæd marries Æthelred, *ealdormann* of Mercia.
63 Keynes and Lapidge, eds and trans., 'Asser's *Life of King Alfred*,' 90; Asser, *Life of King Alfred*, 58: 'Æthelweard ... ludis literariae disciplinae ... cum omnibus pene totius regionis nobilibus infantibus et etiam multis ignobilibus sub diligenti magistrorum cura traditus est.' Note that Asser does not go as far as we might expect, given the prescriptions of the *Preface to the Regula pastoralis*.
64 Keynes and Lapidge, eds and trans., 'Asser's *Life of King Alfred*,' 90; Asser, *Life of King Alfred*, 58: 'ut antequam aptas humanis artibus vires haberent, venatoriae scilicet et ceteris artibus, quae nobilibus conveniunt, in liberalibus artibus studiosi et ingeniosi viderentur.'
65 Keynes and Lapidge, eds and trans., 'Asser's *Life of King Alfred*,' 90; Asser, *Life of King Alfred*, 58: 'ad omnes indigenas et alienigenas humilitate, affabilitate et etiam lenitate, et cum magna patris subiectione huc usque perseverant.'
66 For an account of Alfred's 'misbehaving' noblemen, see Nelson, 'A King across the Sea,' 52–3.
67 Nicholas Howe here reminds me of the Old English poem *Precepts* in Muir, ed., *The Exeter Anthology of Old English Poetry*, 228–31.
68 Asser, *Life of King Alfred*, 60; Keynes and Lapidge, eds and trans., 'Asser's *Life of King Alfred*,' 91.
69 Lerer, *Literacy and Power in Anglo-Saxon Literature*, 63–4, combines questions of genealogy, paternity, and cultural production in his analysis of Alfred as a king and teacher.

70 Among these children, the equalizing experience of education promotes a sense of community, shared experience, and thence the moral virtues which discourage rebellion.
71 Asser, *Life of King Alfred*, 59–60; Keynes and Lapidge, eds and trans., 'Asser's *Life of King Alfred*,' 91.
72 Asser, *Life of King Alfred*, 60; Keynes and Lapidge, eds and trans., 'Asser's *Life of King Alfred*,' 91.
73 Asser *Life of King Alfred*, 60; Keynes and Lapidge, eds and trans., 'Asser's *Life of King Alfred*,' 91.
74 Asser, *Life of King Alfred*, 77: 'nullum aut parvum voluntarie pro communi regni necessitate vellent subire laborem' (Keynes and Lapidge, eds and trans., 'Asser's *Life of King Alfred*,' 101).
75 Asser, *Life of King Alfred*, 77–8; Keynes and Lapidge, eds and trans., 'Asser's *Life of King Alfred*,' 101–2.
76 In this regard, the *Vita Alfredi* resembles the many chapter headings of the Old English *Regula pastoralis*, many of which suggest that there are a variety of different ways to 'encourage' a people to live out a faith-filled life. For example, Sweet, ed., *King Alfred's West-Saxon Version of Gregory's Pastoral Care*, 178: 'Ða weras mon sceal hefiglicor & stiðlicor læran, & ða wif liohtlicor; forðæm ðæt ða weras higien to maran byrðene & ða wif mid oleccunga weorðen on gebrohte' (One should instruct men more intensely and firmly, and women more lightly, in order that men strive towards greater burdens and women be brought on with flattery) [translation mine].
77 Asser's narrative does not close formally, and the entries stop in the middle of Alfred's life.
78 See, for example, the title of the recent volume in honour of Janet Bately: Roberts and Nelson with Godden, eds, *Alfred the Wise*.
79 Arngart, ed., *The Proverbs of Alfred*, 72: 'Alured. he wes in englene lond. / an king. wel swiþe strong. / He wes king. and he wes clerek. / wel he luuede godes werk. / he wes wis on his word. / and war on his werke. / he wes þe wysuste mon: / þat wes englelonde on.'
80 Sweet, ed. and trans., *King Alfred's West-Saxon Version of Gregory's Pastoral Care*, 9: 'Be ðære byrðenne ðæs reccenddomes' (Concerning the Burden of Government).
81 Sweet, ed. and trans., *King Alfred's West-Saxon Version of Gregory's Pastoral Care*, 3.
82 I am deeply influenced by Jennifer Morrish, 'King Alfred's Letter as a Source on Learning in England,' in which Morrish shows the rhetorical nature of Alfred's letter. This approach lies behind my wish to interrogate Alfred's assertion here.

4. Undoing Æthelred

1 Earlier scholarship tended to take the dates 983–1016 as the dates for the *Æthelred-Cnut Chronicle*, but in the publication of the prospectus for the new *Anglo-Saxon Chronicle* editions, the annals for 983–1022 are announced as the *Chronicle of Æthelred and Cnut*. I use this dating throughout chapters 4 and 5. See the excerpt published in Szarmach, 'The *Anglo-Saxon Chronicle*,' 16. Though Æthelred begins to rule in 979, the *Æthelred-Cnut Chronicle* comprises only those annals that are identifiably written by a single annalist writing at a single time; see Keynes, 'The Declining Reputation of King Æthelred the Unready,' 229–31; Keynes (232) goes on to suggest that the account was written by a Londoner.
2 S. a. 1011 (C): O'Brien O'Keeffe, ed., *The Anglo-Saxon Chronicle: MS C*, 95.
3 See Keynes, 'Declining Reputation.'
4 I borrow the phrase 'royal action' from Stafford, 'The Reign of Æthelred II.' Stafford studies the domestic and foreign political situations of Æthelred's reign, analyses the diplomatic measures the king tried to take, and accounts for his successes and failures.
5 Godden, 'Apocalypse and Invasion in Late Anglo-Saxon England,' 130–42.
6 The contemporary relevance of the language of sin is indicated in the titles of the texts at issue: Pseudo-Cyprian's work is edited in Pseudo-Cyprian, *De duodecim abusivis saeculi*. Ælfric's translation of the *De duodecim* retains the notion of abuse; see Ælfric, *De octo uiciis et de duodecim abusiuis huius seculi*. Wulfstan's formulation of the question suffuses his *Sermo Lupi ad Anglos*. Throughout this chapter I will quote from the tradition represented by MSS E and I. See Wulfstan, *Sermo Lupi ad Anglos*. Wulfstan clearly articulates the obligations of a Christian king in his *Institutes of Polity*, II Polity 4 and 5, p. 41: 'Cristenum cyninge gebyreð swyðe rihte, þæt he cristen folc rihtlice healde, and þæt he sy, swa hit riht is, folces frofer and rihtwis hyrde cristenre heorde. And him gebyreð þæt he eallum mægene christendom rære and Godes cyrcan æghwar georne fyrðrige and friðige.' (It is most befitting for a Christian king that he justly rule the Christian people, and that he be, as it is right [for him to be], the comforter of the people and a righteous shepherd of the Christian herd. And it is fitting for him to raise up Christendom with all his might and zealously promote and protect God's church everywhere). I quote from II Polity because the text is slightly more detailed.
7 The importance of homiletic writing is seen in the works of both Ælfric and Wulfstan. Hagiographic writing of the period is a vast topic; Lapidge and Love, 'England and Wales (600–1550),' and Whately, 'Late Old English

Hagiography,' are full surveys of Latin and vernacular writings respectively.

8 For a full discussion of salvation historiography, see pages 166–7, note 67.
9 On Æthelred, peace making, and his councillors, see Damon, 'Advisors for Peace in the Reign of Æthelred Unræd.' Some accounts of the king's policy are Andersson, 'The Viking Policy of Ethelred the Unready'; Stafford, 'The Reign of Æthelred II'; and, in the greatest detail, Keynes, *The Diplomas of King Æthelred 'the Unready,' 978–1016*, 163–228.
10 In accordance with the *Chronicle* manuscript entries for 978 and 979 (C) and the historiography of Æthelred's reign, I separate accession and coronation. On the significance of this delay for Æthelred, see Keynes, *The Diplomas of King Æthelred*, 174 and 233 note 7. On the *ordo* in use in the tenth century, see Nelson, 'The Second English *ordo*,' and on the problem of delayed consecrations, see her 'Inauguration Rituals,' 63–70. That by the time of the Norman Conquest, the delay and separation are routine is suggested in Garnett, 'Coronation and Propaganda.' I take up the implications of this delay in chapter 6.
11 S. a. 1011 (C): O'Brien O'Keeffe, ed., *The Anglo-Saxon Chronicle*, 95.
12 Æthelred's culpability is furthered by the annalist's style. As is customary throughout the *Anglo-Saxon Chronicle*, the Æthelred-Cnut annalist links events with the coordinating conjunction 'and.' While this does not necessarily impose a causal relationship between the events he describes, the juxtaposition of these happenings and the word 'and' itself is suggestive.
13 This and the other blindings of Æthelred's reign are discussed in context in Keynes, 'A Tale of Two Kings,' 211–13, and in more detail in his *The Diplomas of King Æthelred*, 183–4. Bührer-Thierry, '"Just Anger" or "Vengeful Anger"?' argues that in a Carolingian context, blinding is a punishment for disloyalty to the king.
14 The annalist is quite explicit about this. S. a. 999 (C): O'Brien O'Keeffe, ed., *The Anglo-Saxon Chronicle*, 88: '7 þonne æt ðam ende ne beheold hit nan þing seo scypfyrding ne seo landfyrding buton folces geswinc ...' (And then, finally, it availed nothing – neither the fleet nor the territorial army – except hardship for the people).
15 Given that the common account of Æthelred's reign begins in 983 and that the entries of MS C from 979 to 82 are unique, the account of Æthelred's accession and the Otto episode are not usually included as part of the *Æthelred-Cnut Chronicle*. This is not to say that the Æthelred-Cnut annalist did not write them, only that the uniqueness of these entries makes his authorship of the annals seem unlikely.
16 Although, as suggested above, the Æthelred-Cnut annalist probably did

not write the entries for 979–82, I do work with the assumption that he had access to them or entries very similar to them. That is, I do not think that the annalist was working with a source from the 'northern' tradition of the *Chronicle*.

17 S. a. 982 (C): O'Brien O'Keeffe, ed., *The Anglo-Saxon Chronicle*, 85: '7 se casere ahte wælstowe geweald, 7 hwæðere he þær wæs miclum geswenced ær he þanon hwurfe' (And the emperor had control of the battlefield; however, he was very hard pressed there before he [could] leave there).

18 For a more detailed account of the problems of this annal, see Plummer, ed., *Two of the Saxon Chronicles Parallel*, II, 169.

19 On the Anglo-Saxon genealogies, see page 166, note 53.

20 This is not to say that Otto is without connections to the West Saxon royal family and, strangely, to the tradition of *Chronicle* historiography. Campbell, 'England, France, Flanders, Germany in the Reign of Ethelred II, 194 and note 19, observes that Æthelweard, for whom *Æthelweard's Chronicle* is named, was related to Otto I distantly and, citing L. Whitbread, 'Æthelweard and the *Anglo-Saxon Chronicle*,' remarks that the C text account of Otto's campaign might have come from a communication from Matilda (the dedicatee of *Æthelweard's Chronicle*) to Æthelweard.

21 Anglo-Saxon succession practices are complicated and contradictory. For overviews of the problems of royal succession, see page 166, note 54.

22 de Certeau, *The Writing of History*, 272.

23 Ibid.

24 One of the implications of this succession pattern and the wills of Æthelwulf and Alfred is the possibility that the kingdom might be considered inheritable property. Æthelwulf's will is not extant per se; Alfred's will is in Harmer, ed., 'King Alfred's Will,' 15–19.

25 Actually, the story is not as simple as it might seem. The A and C annalists report the rebellion of Æthelwold, Edward's cousin, as a direct consequence of Edward's succession, stating that Æthelwold acted 'without the leave of the king or his *witan*.' They both thus suggest that the *witan* had accepted Edward's accession as lawful. S. a. 900 (A): Bately, ed., *The Anglo-Saxon Chronicle*, 61–2, and 901 (C): O'Brien O'Keeffe, ed., *The Anglo-Saxon Chronicle*, 71. Edward responds by trapping Æthelwold in a siege at Badbury. After declaring his willingness to fight to the death, Æthelwold, acting again 'without the king's leave,' takes a nun hostage and flees to the Danish army in Northumbria. At this point, the other manuscripts note that the Danes accepted Æthelwold as king (s. a., for example, 901 (D): Cubbin, ed., *The Anglo-Saxon Chronicle*, 36); MS A merely says that Edward ordered him to be pursued, but that he could not overtake the rebel. Æthelwold

188   Notes to pages 76–8

goes to ground, reappearing in 901 with a fleet that he had apparently collected overseas. Again, other manuscripts suggest that submission was made and Æthelwold accepted as some form of ruler; A observes only that Æthelwold came to Essex. This reticence suggests not only partisanship, but that the A annalist cannot allow Æthelwold to be seen as any form of legitimate ruler. In 902 (s. a. 904 A), Æthelwold persuades an East Anglian army to break the peace and harry Mercia; Edward responds by destroying their lands. There follows a battle which the Danes officially win, and though the terms on which the rebellion was settled are unknown, Edward's succession was not directly contested again.

26 In the years leading up to 918, Edward fights for and gradually wins the loyalty of many of the Anglo-Saxons. In 905 A/906 C, Edward declares peace with the East Anglians and Northumbrians; in 911 A/912 C, Edward gains London, Oxford, and the lands belonging to these cities; in 912 A/913 C, Edward wins some of the Anglo-Saxons who had been loyal to the Danes; in 917 A/915 C, Edward wins the loyalty of many of the principal Danes; in 918 A only, 'him cierde eall þæt folc to þe on Mercna lande geseten wæs, ægþer ge denisc ge englisce' (to him [Edward] submitted all the people who were settled in the land of the Mercians, both Danish and Anglo-Saxon): Bately, ed., *The Anglo-Saxon Chronicle*, 69.

27 But even though this claim depends on the idea that the unknown annalist has read and understood the annals of Alfred's reign, I do not mean to suggest that he claims for Otto the same kind of lordship that defined the narrative of Alfred's reign. The Æthelred-Cnut annalist is not the only tenth-century reader of the *Chronicle* history. The only copy of Asser's *Vita Alfredi* known to have survived past the medieval period was made at this time, and Byrhtferth's historical writing suggests that there was substantial interest in the annals for Alfred's reign. On Byrhtferth's treatment of Asser's *Vita Alfredi* and its relationship to the text now incorporated in Symeon of Durham's *Historia regum*, see the essays by Hart, 'Byrhtferth's Northumbrian Chronicle,' and Lapidge, 'Byrhtferth of Ramsey and the Early Sections of the *Historia regum* attributed to Symeon of Durham.'

28 Wormald, 'Æthelred the Lawmaker,' 47.

29 S. a. 1004 (C): O'Brien O'Keeffe, ed., *The Anglo-Saxon Chronicle*, 90–1.

30 In the entry for 1003 (C): O'Brien O'Keeffe, ed., *The Anglo-Saxon Chronicle*, 90, the annalist comments, 'Þonne se heretoga wacað þonne bið eall se here swiðe gehindrad' (When the general is cowardly, then all the army is greatly hindered). Plummer, ed., *Two of the Saxon Chronicles*, 2: 183, notes that a similar expression is found in one of Alcuin's letters, but, as Thomas D. Hill, '"When the Leader is Brave ...,"' notes, the proverb can be found in

the *Regula pastoralis* and there is also a parallel expression in I Corinthians 14:8. Hill argues that the translation into Old English begins a vernacular tradition specifically associated with Alfred's resistance to the Danes and that an eleventh-century manifestation of this idea is found in the *Durham Proverbs* manuscript. I discuss the proverb more fully in chapter 5.

31 S. a. 986, 994, 1002 (St Brice's Day massacre), 1004 (Ulfcytel), 1008, 1009, 1012, 1016, and 1017 (Cnut's accession) (C): O'Brien O'Keeffe, ed., *The Anglo-Saxon Chronicle*, 85, 87, 89, 91, 92, 92–4, 96, 100–3.

32 The history of the East Anglians is particularly associated with the question of kingship in Anglo-Saxon England. A general survey of East Anglian history is Yorke, *Kings and Kingdoms of Early Anglo-Saxon England*, 58–71. More detailed studies of Anglian kingship are Carver, 'Kingship and Material Culture in Early Anglo-Saxon East Anglia'; Dumville, 'Essex, Middle Anglia, and the Expansion of Mercia in the South-East Midlands'; and Keynes, 'Rædwald the Bretwalda.' Dumville, 'The Anglian Collection of Royal Genealogies and Regnal Lists,' discusses the East Anglian genealogical material. On the *Bretwalda*, see page 170, note 29.

33 It is not just that Ælfheah becomes a cult figure, it is also that Cnut, Æthelred's Danish successor, saw the value of the cult. See Lawson, *Cnut: The Danes in England in the Early Eleventh Century*, 140–2 and 181–2.

34 See Osbern, *Vita Sancti Elphegi Archiepiscopi Cantuariensis et martyris*, cols 371b–93 at col. 380a. The text of Ælfheah's *passio* and *translatio* has been reedited in Osbern, 'Life and Passion of St Ælfheah.'

35 On the *Chronicle* account of Osbern's *Life*, see the introduction to Osbern, 'Life and Passion of St Ælfheah,' 285–7. For a full *Chronicle* account of his translation, see s. a. 1023 (D): Cubbin, ed., *The Anglo-Saxon Chronicle*, 64; the entry for 1023 (C) merely records the event: O'Brien O'Keeffe, ed., *The Anglo-Saxon Chronicle*, 104.

36 On contemporary fighting ecclesiastics, see Abels, *Lordship and Military Obligation in Anglo-Saxon England*, 122–3 and 183. On religious culture and war in the period, see John, 'War and Society in the Tenth Century,' and 'The World of Abbot Ælfric'; Stafford, 'Church and Society in the Age of Ælfric'; and Yorke, 'Æthelwold and the Politics of the Tenth Century.'

37 S. a. 1011 (C): O'Brien O'Keeffe, ed., *The Anglo-Saxon Chronicle*, 96.

38 de Certeau, *The Writing of History*, 276.

39 Ibid., 272.

40 Stafford, 'The Reign of Æthelred II,' is a strong and convincing discussion of Æthelred's actions and options. I borrow my phrase from her title.

41 Whether or not the king might fight and the consequences of waging war are important issues for Carolingian theorists of kingship; see Hincmar, *De*

regis persona et regio ministerio, cols 833–56 at cols 840c–44b, chapters 7–15. Sedulius Scottus, *Liber de rectoribus christianis*, 70, observes that divine help is always more effective than military strength, but this implies that the king may, indeed, fight. While there are many surveys of the philosophy of war, I prefer Cross, 'The Ethic of War in Old English,' for the way in which it traces the ideas through the sources.

42 On tenth- and eleventh-century connections with the Continent, see Bullough, 'The Continental Background of the Reform'; Ortenberg, *The English Church and the Continent in the Tenth and Eleventh Centuries*; and Wormald, 'Æthelwold and His Continental Counterparts. For a study of one particularly contemporary journey to Rome, see Ortenberg, 'Archbishop Sigeric's Journey to Rome in 990.' Ortenberg reprints London, British Library, MS Cotton Tiberius B. v, 23v–4r, the *Itinerary of Archbishop Sigeric*. Of particular interest, is the work of Abbo of Fleury; Ælfric translates his *Life of Edmund* and the version of Pseudo-Cyprian, *De duodecim abusivis saeculi*, included in his *Collectio canonum*. Brief statements of the intellectual connection between Ælfric and Abbo are given by John, 'The World of Abbot Ælfric,' and Lawson, 'Archbishop Wulfstan and the Homiletic Element in the Laws of Æthelred II and Cnut,' 566–7.

43 Hincmar, *De regis persona*, col. 834a.

44 Pseudo-Cyprian, *De duodecim abusivis saeculi*, 51–3.

45 Wulfstan, *Institutes of Polity*, II Polity, chapters 13–14, p. 47. The quote is taken from Ælfric, 'Feria secunda. Letania maiore,' 183: 'Þæt folc bið gesælig þurh snoterne cyning. sigefæst. and gesundful. ðurh gesceadwisne reccend; And hi beoð geyrmede ðurh unwisne cyning. on manegum gelimpum. for his misræde' (The people are blessed in a wise king, victorious and prosperous through a discerning ruler. And they are made miserable on many occasions by a foolish king, because of his misguidance).

46 Ælfric, *Dominica post ascensionem Domini*, 380–1, ll. 46–7. Carolingian thinkers are unanimous on the importance of councillors and the fact that a king should look to his council for wisdom (second, of course, to divine wisdom). Hincmar, *De regis persona*, cols 837c–9b, discusses the kind of councillors a king should have; Hincmar, *De ordine palatii*, 50–2, ll. 176–203, citing Pseudo-Cyprian, is a more practical discussion of the king's officers; Pseudo-Cyprian, *De duodecim abusivis saeculi*, 51, merely says that the king's councillors should be sober; Smaragdus, *Via regia*, cols 959a–60b, chapter 20, discusses the kind of counsel a king should have.

47 On Carolingian learning as a virtue, see Anton, *Fürstenspiegel und Herrscherethos in der Karolingerzeit*, 255–6. For the texts with particular discussions, see Sedulius, *Liber de rectoribus christianis*, 30–3, and Smaragdus, *Via regia*, cols 941–5.

48 Ælfric, *The Maccabees*, 121, ll. 812–18. The motif is studied more fully in Duby, *The Three Orders*, and Powell, 'The "Three Orders" of Society.'
49 Ælfric, *On the Old and New Testament*, 71, ll. 1207–20. For a consideration of the letter in context, see Powell, 'The "Three Orders" of Society,' 112.
50 Wulfstan, *Institutes of Polity*, I Polity, chapters 24–9, and II Polity, chapters 31–6, pp. 55–6, repeats these distinctions.
51 Ælfric, *On the Old and New Testament*, 71, ll. 1204–7.
52 For an explanation of the traditional typological interpretation of the kingships mentioned in *Wyrdwriteras*, particularly that of David, see Anton, *Fürstenspiegel*, 419–36.
53 Ælfric, *Wyrdwriteras*, 728, ll. 4–5.
54 Ibid., 730, ll. 47–50.
55 Ælfric, *De octo viciis*, 115.
56 Ibid., Pseudo-Cyprian, *De duodecim abusivis saeculi*, 52–3.
57 Ælfric, *De octo viciis*, 117.
58 By adopting a strategy of baptism, Æthelred appears to repeat Alfred's successful strategy with Guthrum. Keynes, 'A Tale of Two Kings,' 199, suggests that baptism is a traditional peace-making strategy. For a fuller discussion of this possibility, see chapter 2.
59 See note 14 above.
60 S. a. 1011 (C): O'Brien O'Keeffe, ed., *The Anglo-Saxon Chronicle*, 96.
61 The following brief sketch of Æthelred's reign is drawn from my reading of four essays on different aspects of Æthelred's rule. Fleming, *Kings and Lords in Conquest England*, 3–52, provides an analysis of the alliances among members of the aristocracy and the king that were sealed by obligations of kinship and landholding and traces their demise in the reign of Cnut. Keynes, *The Diplomas of King Æthelred*, 163–231, considers diplomatic activity and social context. Keynes, 'The Historical Context of the Battle of Maldon,' provides an overview of the reign, centring on the Battle of Maldon. Stafford, 'The Reign of Æthelred II,' focuses on the king's political responses to key events and the political and social context in which the king worked.
62 The text of the peace treaty is edited and translated in Keynes, 'Historical Context,' 104–7.
63 Keynes, *The Diplomas of King Æthelred*, 176–86, discusses what he calls 'the period of youthful indiscretions'; Æthelred's actions in the early 990s are part of this period.
64 Given the larger context of the Carolingian mirrors for princes, this actuality might also serve as a metaphor for the blighted state of the realm.
65 Keynes, *The Diplomas of King Æthelred*, 178–9.
66 Keynes, 'Historical Context,' 93, and Stafford, 'The Reign of Æthelred II,' 30.

67 Wilcox, 'The St. Brice's Day Massacre and Archbishop Wulfstan.' The problems associated with this massacre and Æthelred's rationale are taken up more fully in chapter 5.
68 S. a. 1002 (C): O'Brien O'Keeffe, ed., *The Anglo-Saxon Chronicle*, 89.
69 As Wilcox, 'The St. Brice's Day Massacre,' 82–3, comments, the evidence for Danish settlement outside the boundaries of the Danelaw is complicated, but Oxford, outside the boundaries of the Danelaw as defined in Hart, *The Danelaw*, 3–19, seems to be the only location in which the massacre was actually carried out. Full surveys of the historiography of the Danish settlement can be found in Hadley, *The Northern Danelaw*, 1–41, and Trafford, 'Ethnicity, Migration Theory, and the Historiography of the Scandinavian Settlement of England.' Recent studies of the Danelaw and Scandinavian settlement are Hadley, '"And They Proceeded to Plough and to Support Themselves,"' and '"Cockles Amongst the Wheat"'; Sawyer, *Kings and Vikings*, 98–112; and Williams, '"Cockles Amongst the Wheat."'
70 For an account of Æthelred's 'Viking policy,' see note 9 above.
71 Keynes, *The Diplomas of King Æthelred*, 186–201, and Stafford, 'The Reign of Æthelred II,' 29.
72 Unlike the other men, however, Ulfcytel seems not to have held the rank of *ealdormann*: Stafford, 'The Reign of Æthelred II,' 33.
73 The annals for 1006, 1015, and 1016 (C): O'Brien O'Keeffe, ed., *The Anglo-Saxon Chronicle*, 99–103, show that Æthelred's trust was misplaced. Fleming, *Kings and Lords*, 32, notes the relevant marriages. Even Cnut, though he at first appointed him to Mercia, distrusted Eadric; he had him killed the very same year. On the other hand, Uhtræd was so loyal to Æthelred that Cnut was not able to gain his surrender. Fleming, *Kings and Lords*, 34, citing the author of *De obsessione Dunelmi*, translates Uhtræd's response as follows: 'I shall serve King Æthelred faithfully as long as he shall live. *He is my lord and also my father-in-law*, by whose gift I have riches and honor enough. I will never betray him' (emphasis as printed). As the *Chronicle* annals suggest, the personal tie Uhtræd feels to Æthelred is rare; in 1016, Uhtræd is murdered at Cnut's command (40). Ulfcytel's relationship to his king is the subject of discussion below.
74 For more on the lives of these women, see Stafford, 'The King's Wife in Wessex, 800–1066.'
75 Wulfstan, *Sermo Lupi ad Anglos*, 274.
76 That Wulfstan should read the story of Gildas and the Britons in this way is highlighted by Dorothy Whitelock's point that Wulfstan is actually translating from one of Alcuin's letters: Whitelock, 'Archbishop Wulfstan, Homilist and Statesman,' 43.
77 Wulfstan, *Sermo Lupi ad Anglos*, 274–5: '7 soþ is þæt ic secge, wyrsan dæda

we witan mid Englum þonne we mid Bryttan ahwar gehyrdan' (And, I tell [you] the truth, we know of worse deeds among the Anglo-Saxons than we ever heard about anywhere among the Britons).

78 S. a. 1014 (C): O'Brien O'Keeffe, ed., *The Anglo-Saxon Chronicle*, 98.
79 Lawson, 'Archbishop Wulfstan and the Homiletic Element,' 565, finds it 'odd ... that Æthelred's subjects would only accept his return from exile on condition that he ruled more lawfully (*rihtlicor*)' [emphasis as printed]. But the comment is only odd if interpreted outside the discourse of Carolingian kingship. Nevertheless, 1014 can be associated with some literal legislation on Æthelred's part: VIII Æthelred. On the possible function of this code, the extant version of which can be dated to 1014, see Keynes, 'Crime and Punishment,' 74–5 and note 47; and Wormald, 'Æthelred the Lawmaker,' 59–60, and *The Making of English Law*, 341–2.
80 Stafford, 'The Reign of Æthelred II,' 35–6.
81 S. a. 1016 (C): O'Brien O'Keeffe, ed., *The Anglo-Saxon Chronicle*, 100.
82 Ibid., 102–3.
83 Ibid.
84 Keynes, 'Declining Reputation.'
85 Ibid., 236: 'it is a personal and perhaps idiosyncratic view of events.'
86 Ibid., 236–40.
87 Ibid., 236.

5. Unmaking Æthelred but Making Cnut

1 Æthelred's reign begins in 979, but the *Æthelred-Cnut Chronicle* is usually considered to begin in 983. See page 185, note 1.
2 S. a. 1014 (C): O'Brien O'Keeffe, ed., *The Anglo-Saxon Chronicle: MS C*, 98. I quote and discuss this promise in full below.
3 Examples are too numerous to cite, but a careful and compelling analysis of how Æthelred came to develop this reputation can be found in Keynes, 'The Declining Reputation of King Æthelred the Unready,' 227–35.
4 I do not claim that loyal lordship defines these texts in their entirety or that it is characteristic of Cnut's entire body of legislation; such a claim would underestimate the complexity of Cnut's laws.
5 This text has most recently been edited and translated in Kennedy, 'Cnut's Law Code of 1018.' Discussions of Cambridge, Corpus Christi College, MS 201 (also known as D) and its importance are found in Kennedy, 'Cnut's Law Code of 1018'; Whitelock, 'Wulfstan and the Laws of Cnut,' 433–44, and 'Wulfstan's Authorship of Cnut's Laws'; and Wormald, *The Making of English Law*, 206–10 and 346–7.

6 The letter for 1020 and II Cnut 69–83 are edited, respectively, in Liebermann, ed., *Die Gesetze der Angelsachsen*, 273–5 and 356–67.
7 Without such specification, the historical questions of how these ideas affect other issues in lordship scholarship – absolute loyalty versus limited commitment, service requirements, and obligations of protection – cannot be answered. Abels, *Lordship and Military Obligation in Anglo-Saxon England*, 132–45 and 146–84, offers several clear discussions of different aspects of the relevant issues.
8 See Fleming, *Kings and Lords in Conquest England*, 21–52; Keynes, 'Cnut's Earls'; Larson, 'The Political Policies of Cnut as King of England'; and Mack, 'Changing Thegns.' Richardson, 'Making Thanes,' is an exploration of how the imaginative world of literature can be part of this process.
9 For a discussion of the *Angelcynn*, see page 163, note 28.
10 For a full exposition of the Æthelred-Cnut annals as salvation history, see chapter 4.
11 S. a. 1014 (C): O'Brien O'Keeffe, ed., *The Anglo-Saxon Chronicle*, 98.
12 Ibid., 99. The language of friendship and the acts of oath swearing reinforce the idea that this is a kingship defined by the lordship bond. Some of the very different connections between friendship and Anglo-Saxon lordship are worked out in Althoff, 'Friendship and Political Order,' 93, and Barrow, 'Friends and Friendship in Anglo-Saxon Charters.'
13 S. a. 1015 (C): O'Brien O'Keeffe, ed., *The Anglo-Saxon Chronicle*, 99.
14 Ibid., 99–100.
15 Ibid., 100.
16 When the *witan* sent to Æthelred in exile, Edmund was sent in return with his father's response. Æthelred may well have felt threatened. When Swein died, Cnut, Æthelred himself, and his sons Athelstan and Edmund, were all possible candidates for the throne: Stafford, 'The Reign of Æthelred II,' 35–6. Keynes, 'The Æthelings in Normandy,' 173–81, discusses, with a Continental perspective, Æthelred's marriage, his alliance with the Normans through Emma, his exile in Normandy, the fate of her children after Æthelred's return in 1014, and Cnut's accession (185–6). Anglo-Saxon succession is a complicated subject with an extensive bibliography: see page 166, note 54.
17 Stafford, 'The Reign of Æthelred II,' 36, notes that all 'tenth century rival claimants for the throne' went to the North, exploiting the separatist feelings in these areas. How Tostig, Harold, and northern separatism play into the D text narratives of the Norman Conquest and settlement is explored in Barlow, *The Godwins*, 83–8; DeVries, *The Norwegian Invasion of England in 1066*, 168–92; and in chapter 6. Some north-south tensions with particular

significance for the Danish Conquest are surveyed in Kapelle, *The Norman Conquest of the North*, 10–20.

18 S. a. 900, 903, 904 (A): Bately, ed., *The Anglo-Saxon Chronicle*, 61–2.
19 S. a. 900 (A): Bately, ed., *The Anglo-Saxon Chronicle: MS A*, 61; Asser, *Life of King Alfred*, 10; Keynes and Lapidge, eds and trans., 'Asser's *Life of King Alfred*,' 70.
20 On the *ætheling* and succession, see page 166, note 54.
21 S. a. 1016 (C): O'Brien O'Keeffe, ed., *The Anglo-Saxon Chronicle*, 101.
22 S. a. 1015 (C): O'Brien O'Keeffe, ed., *The Anglo-Saxon Chronicle*, 100.
23 S. a. 1016 (C): O'Brien O'Keeffe, ed., *The Anglo-Saxon Chronicle*, 102–3.
24 A brief search of the fragments *hlafordswice* (treachery) and *hlafordsearu* (high treason) and *hlaford* and *swican* in reasonably close context using the *Old English Corpus*, sponsored by Healey, Venezky, and Cameron, eds, *Dictionary of Old English (microform)* – online at PSU only at http://80-ets.umdl.umich.edu.ezproxy.libraries.psu.edu/o/oec/, accessed April 2004 – suggests that the crime is generally envisaged in this way. It is significant that this perspective is, as Wulfstan's *Sermo Lupi ad Anglos* suggests, both widespread and contemporary. Abandoning the positions Wulfstan articulates in the *Sermo* and his *Institutes of Polity*, the Cnut legal texts deal with the potential for a lord to betray his men. I am grateful to Tom Hill who, in sharing his *hlafordswice* file with me, launched my thinking in this area.
25 Even in the Cynewulf-Cyneheard episode of the *Chronicle*, the relevant issue is whether the men will betray their lord; there is little and sometimes no explicit consideration of whether the lords' actions are tantamount to a betrayal of their men. I here emphasize the distinction between the language of the texts with which I am working and the historical problems of governance and social reality. What we know of lordship ceremonies in Francia seems to suggest that there is precedent for a king expressing his obligation to his men, but that conventionally in Anglo-Saxon England and particularly in the texts cited as sources of lordship ideology, loyalty is only expressed by a man to his lord. Stafford, 'The Laws of Cnut and the History of Anglo-Saxon Royal Promises,' 184, notes that at Coulaines in 843 Charles the Bald 'promised to honour his *fideles* and treat them with justice and equity, just as his *fideles* were to promise to honour and serve him.' Stafford comments on the similarity of the situation of ninth-century Francia and early eleventh-century England – the raids and the internal defections – and finds it 'hardly surprising' (185) that Wulfstan and Hincmar might use ritual and ceremony to bind their kings to their responsibilities. For the texts of general Carolingian oaths, see Odegaard, 'Carolingian Oaths of

Fidelity.' For a possible Old English text, see *Að* in Liebermann, ed., *Die Gesetze*, 464.

26 S. a. 1016 (C): O'Brien O'Keeffe, ed., *The Anglo-Saxon Chronicle*, 102–3.
27 Ibid., 100.
28 In the historiography of King Alfred's reign and in studies of the raids on the Continent, tribute payments seem relatively uncontroversial. For a brief survey and discussion, see Abels, 'Paying the Danegeld,' and Keynes, 'A Tale of Two Kings,' 199–203. Æthelred's lack of success and the sheer amount of money involved has generated much discussion: see, in particular, Lawson, '"Those Stories Look True,"' 'Danegeld and Heregeld Once More,' and 'The Collection of Danegeld and Heregeld in the Reigns of Æthelred II and Cnut'; and Gillingham, '"The Most Precious Jewel in the English Crown,"' and 'Chronicles and Coins as Evidence for Levels of Tribute and Taxation.'
29 The annals from 979–82 are not usually considered part of the *Æthelred-Cnut Chronicle* (983–1022); the account of Æthelred's reign common to MSS C, D, and E begins in 983 and these entries, as we have them from MS C, are unique. Nonetheless, given the coherence of the overall account, I do think that the Æthelred-Cnut annalist was working with either these entries or some that resembled them.
30 For a fuller exposition of *compaternitas* as acts of lordship and peace making, see chapter 2.
31 S. a. 994 (C): O'Brien O'Keeffe, ed., *The Anglo-Saxon Chronicle*, 87.
32 S. a. 997 (C): O'Brien O'Keeffe, ed., *The Anglo-Saxon Chronicle*, 88.
33 S. a. 998 (C): O'Brien O'Keeffe, ed., *The Anglo-Saxon Chronicle*, 88.
34 That said, even though he does not call the king to account, the annalist's irritation is quite visible. See s. a. 999 (C): O'Brien O'Keeffe, ed., *The Anglo-Saxon Chronicle*, 88: '7 swencte þæt earme folc þæt on ðam scipon læg' (And oppressed the wretched people who were aboard the ships).
35 S. a. 1000 (C): O'Brien O'Keeffe, ed., *The Anglo-Saxon Chronicle*, 88.
36 S. a. 1001 (C): O'Brien O'Keeffe, ed., *The Anglo-Saxon Chronicle*, 89.
37 S. a. 1002 (C): O'Brien O'Keeffe, ed., *The Anglo-Saxon Chronicle*, 89.
38 Here, Keynes, 'A Tale of Two Kings,' 212, takes on both James Campbell, 'England, France, Flanders, Germany in the Reign of Ethelred II,' 200, and Henry Loyn, 'Ethelred the Unready.'
39 Keynes, *The Diplomas of King Æthelred 'the Unready,' 978–1016*, 204–5, note 188. General discussions are Keynes, *The Diplomas of King Æthelred*, 203–5, and his 'A Tale of Two Kings,' 211–12.
40 S. a. 1001 (A): Bately, ed., *The Anglo-Saxon Chronicle*, 80. More details are supplied in William of Malmesbury, *Gesta regum Anglorum*, vol. 1, ii.166.i, p. 276 and ii.177.1, pp. 300–1.

41 See page 163, note 28, for discussion of the *Angelcynn*.
42 On the Danelaw in general and the difficulties of making a distinction between Danes and Anglo-Saxons, see Innes, 'Danelaw Identities'; Lund, 'King Edgar and the Danelaw'; Reynolds, 'What Do We Mean by "Anglo-Saxon" and "Anglo-Saxons"?' and Stenton, *Anglo-Saxon England*, 502–25.'
43 S. a. 1003 (C): O'Brien O'Keeffe, ed., *The Anglo-Saxon Chronicle*, 90.
44 This is made quite clear by the syntax: 'Þa Swegen geseah ... þa lædde he' (When Swein saw ... then he led).
45 Following Klaeber and Plummer, Thomas D. Hill, '"When the Leader is Brave ..."', traces out the Latin and Old English analogues for this maxim, focusing in particular on *Durham Proverb no. 31*: 'Eall here bið hwæt þonne se lateow byþ hwæt' and its corresponding proverbs in the *Chronicle* and the Old English *Regula pastoralis* (234).
46 S. a. 1004 (C): O'Brien O'Keeffe, ed., *The Anglo-Saxon Chronicle*, 90–1.
47 I discuss this moment more fully in chapter 4.
48 S. a. 1006 (C): O'Brien O'Keeffe, ed., *The Anglo-Saxon Chronicle*, 91.
49 See Bührer-Thierry, '"Just Anger" or "Vengeful Anger"?' I am grateful to Katherine O'Brien O'Keeffe for this reference.
50 Keynes, 'A Tale of Two Kings,' 212, and *The Diplomas of King Æthelred*, 183–4, show how these actions might be incorporated into the political history of Æthelred's reign.
51 S. a. 1009 (C): O'Brien O'Keeffe, ed., *The Anglo-Saxon Chronicle*, 92.
52 Ibid.
53 Ibid., 93.
54 Ibid.
55 Ibid.
56 S. a. 1011 (C): O'Brien O'Keeffe, ed., *The Anglo-Saxon Chronicle*, 96.
57 Ibid., 95: '7 hi into coman þuruh syruwrencas forðan Ælmær hi becyrde, þe se arcebisceop Ælfeah ær generede æt his life' (And they gained entry by tricks for Ælfmær betrayed it, he who previously had had his life saved by Archbishop Ælfheah).
58 S. a. 1003 and 1011 (C): O'Brien O'Keeffe, ed., *The Anglo-Saxon Chronicle*, 90 and 95.
59 S. a. 1011 (C): O'Brien O'Keeffe, ed., *The Anglo-Saxon Chronicle*, 96. I discuss what it might mean for Ælfheah to be head of the *Angelcynn* in chapter 4.
60 Although *bugan* and *cyrran* can have similar meanings, the annalist does distinguish between them. Both words can mean to 'submit,' 'yield,' and 'convert,' but the appropriate entries in Healey, Venezky, and Cameron, eds, *Dictionary of Old English*, suggest that there are some semantic differences between *bugan* and *cyrran*. *Cyrran* has a more generally sustained transformative sense, and historians have traded upon this resonance to

argue that – as it is used in the Alfred annals – *cyrran* means to 'submit' with the expectation that the ceremony of submission is also one that creates a lordship tie (see chapter 2). Interestingly, this distinction is maintained throughout the Alfred annals, the *Æthelred-Cnut Chronicle*, and, also, the D Conquest entries (see chapter 6).

61 S. a. 1013 (C): O'Brien O'Keeffe, ed., *The Anglo-Saxon Chronicle*, 97.
62 Ibid., 97–8.
63 Ibid., 98.
64 Ibid.
65 Ibid. In stating that the people now take Cnut as their 'fulne' (full) king, the annalist both communicates his disapproval of the arrangement of dividing the kingdom and assures us of the legitimacy of Cnut's succession.
66 S. a. 1009 (C): O'Brien O'Keeffe, ed., *The Anglo-Saxon Chronicle*, 92.
67 Though it says nothing about the Æthelred-Cnut annalist's work, the anachronism reinforces the importance of this topos in the *Chronicle* annals.
68 S. a. 1065 (C): O'Brien O'Keeffe, ed., *The Anglo-Saxon Chronicle*, 119. The topos of exile as an important part of kingship in early Anglo-Saxon historical writing and, in particular, Bede's *Historia ecclesiastica* has been explored in Damon, '*Wadan Wræclastas*: Bede, Cadwalla of Wessex, and the Exile's Path to Kingship.'
69 S. a. 1065 (C): O'Brien O'Keeffe, ed., *The Anglo-Saxon Chronicle*, 118–19. This is of course literal family, but the larger context of my analysis also suggests how the notion of family may resonate with the king's lordship family. For full discussion of this overlap, see chapter 1 and Fleming, *Kings and Lords*, 24.
70 S. a. 1014 (C): O'Brien O'Keeffe, ed., *The Anglo-Saxon Chronicle*, 98. What we know about the process of election to the kingship is focused through a series of other problems such as the role of the *witan*, the issue of consent, and the importance and similarity of lordship ritual. For overviews of the problem, see Smyth, *King Alfred the Great*, 421–51, and the discussion on page 172, note 43. That the languages of lordship, consent, and accession to the throne all work in concert helps to explain the scene of submission to William I. S. a. 1066 (D): Cubbin, ed., *The Anglo-Saxon Chronicle: MS D*, 81. This is discussed more fully in chapter 6.
71 S. a. 1014 (C): O'Brien O'Keeffe, ed., *The Anglo-Saxon Chronicle*, 98. Old English *gecynde* in this context can mean 'natural' (by birthright), but I prefer to translate with 'proper' or 'fitting,' because my argument as a whole moves away from legitimate succession by birthright towards a kingship defined by deeds.
72 Ibid.

73 I am aware of the anachronism implied by using terms such as 'charter' and 'promise' and of the scholarly difficulties of separating them from the more easily recognized coronation oaths; see Stafford, 'The Laws of Cnut,' for a full discussion of the issues. I take no position on how Æthelred's promise, if actually made, might have functioned; nor do I discuss what it might have meant for Cnut to make the same promise in his 1020 letter. My interest here is in how the Æthelred-Cnut annalist suggests the promise should be seen: as a defining moment for the king's rule and as the performative articulation (and thus creation) of an alternative identifying culture.
74 S. a. 1014 (C): O'Brien O'Keeffe, ed., *The Anglo-Saxon Chronicle*, 99.
75 The annalist then proceeds to define Cnut's accession by his loyal lordship, and the difficulties of this betrayal are put aside.
76 S. a. 1015 (C): O'Brien O'Keeffe, ed., *The Anglo-Saxon Chronicle*, 99–100.
77 Stafford, 'The Reign of Æthelred II,' 36.
78 Ibid., 36–7.
79 S. a. 1015 (C): O'Brien O'Keeffe, ed., *The Anglo-Saxon Chronicle*, 100.
80 S. a. 1016 (C): O'Brien O'Keeffe, ed., *The Anglo-Saxon Chronicle*, 100.
81 Ibid., 102.
82 Interestingly, none of the extant sources mentions Cnut's coronation. Lawson, *Cnut: The Danes in England*, 82–3, claims he was crowned by Archbishop Lyfing while Stafford, 'The Laws of Cnut,' 185, mentions Wulfstan.
83 S. a. 1017 (C): O'Brien O'Keeffe, ed., *The Anglo-Saxon Chronicle*, 103. Exactly what it might have meant for Emma to be 'fetched' as Cnut's wife is discussed in Keynes, 'The Æthelings in Normandy,' 182–5.
84 The importance of this distinction is made doubly clear when we compare the Æthelred-Cnut annals to the D manuscript account of the Norman Conquest and settlement.
85 Fleming, *Kings and Lords*, 21–52, and Mack, 'Changing Thegns,' analyse the changeover in power as a change in lordship relations.
86 Stafford, 'The Laws of Cnut,' suggests that this and other such royal promises (particularly those in the later medieval period) might actually function as coronation charters.
87 I use the word 'associated' advisedly. Wulfstan's authorship for Cambridge, Corpus Christi College, MS 201 is argued in Whitelock, 'Wulfstan and the Laws of Cnut'; Whitelock's case is reviewed and augmented in Kennedy, 'Cnut's Law Code of 1018.' Wulfstan's authorship for Cnut's laws is argued in Whitelock, 'Wulfstan's Authorship of Cnut's Laws.' Authorship of the 1020 letter is more complicated; only the latter part of the letter is in Wulfstan's style. See Keynes, 'The Additions in Old English,' 95–6, and Wormald, *The Making of English Law*, 347.

88 I stress the difference between the *Sermo Lupi* and the laws because it is a commonplace of historical scholarship that Wulfstan's work can be used as a guide to the historical reality of post-Conquest England; this small contradiction in his positions is thus generally overlooked. A notable exception and sensitive guide to some of these difficulties is Loomis, '*Regnum* and *sacerdotium* in the Early Eleventh Century.' For Wulfstan's prominence and some scepticism, see Wormald, 'Archbishop Wulfstan and the Holiness of Society,' 225–6 and 247–51.
89 Text and translation from Kennedy, 'Cnut's Law Code of 1018,' 72.
90 Cnut's 1020 letter to his people in Liebermann, ed., *Die Gesetze*, 273.
91 Healey, Venezky, and Cameron, eds, *Dictionary of Old English: Old English Corpus*.
92 I discuss this moment more fully in chapter 6.
93 Prologue to IV Edgar in Liebermann, ed., *Die Gesetze*, 206. In IV Edgar, Edgar takes personal responsibility, if not for the wrongdoing at least for directing its remedy; the frequent use of the first person pronoun suggests the extent to which Edgar acknowledges his responsibility for the plague.
94 IV Edgar 16 in Liebermann, ed., *Die Gesetze*, 214.
95 Indeed, the 1018 peace treaty literally invokes the laws of Edgar as a necessary part of the peace. On Edgar's laws as a symbol of continuity, see, among others, Wormald, *The Making of English Law*, 131–4.
96 Whitelock, 'Archbishop Wulfstan, Homilist and Statesman,' 32, and Wormald, *The Making of English Law*, 317–20 (on the rhetoric and content of IV Edgar) and 210–12 (the manuscript connection).
97 Wormald, *The Making of English Law*, 356–60, Table 5.4.
98 Whitelock, 'Archbishop Wulfstan, Homilist and Statesman,' 32.
99 Lawson, 'Archbishop Wulfstan and the Homiletic Element in the Laws of Æthelred II and Cnut,' and Wormald, *The Making of English Law*, 197–210, 339–41, and 352–5.
100 Reynolds, *Kingdoms and Communities in Western Europe, 900–1300*, 250–6.
101 Butler, *Excitable Speech*, 152.
102 Ibid., 155.
103 In other words, in addition to providing insight into Anglo-Saxon society, the Anglo-Saxon law codes also supply an ideology of social and cultural order that shapes their readers' perceptions of what it means to be a citizen. O'Brien O'Keeffe, 'Body and Law in Late Anglo-Saxon England,' 209–18, is a compelling analysis of how an entry from the C text of the *Anglo-Saxon Chronicle* and law texts interact in their production of an Anglo-Saxon subject who can succeed to the throne. This analysis of law and legal discourse is particularly important to Anglo-Saxon studies, because

although historians assume that the Anglo-Saxons lived by the texts that are extant to us, there is no external evidence that this is the case.
104 I realize that 'charter' can also be a technical term, but I here rely on the second sense of the word; I do not mean to suggest that these texts should literally be read as charters. For a more literal use of this term and its implications, see Stafford, 'The Laws of Cnut.' On the importance of IV Edgar, see Lund, 'King Edgar and the Danelaw.'
105 Stafford, 'The Laws of Cnut,' 178–80.
106 Ibid., 180–1. On the likely content of this section of VIII Æthelred, see Wormald, 'Æthelred the Lawmaker,' 59–60, and on VIII Æthelred in general, see his *The Making of English Law*, 336 and 457.
107 Stafford, 'The Laws of Cnut,' 184. Lawson, 'Archbishop Wulfstan and the Homiletic Element,' 579, reading John of Worcester, also associates the oath with a coronation ceremony. That said, the *promissio regis* in the extant *ordines* does not resemble this oath.
108 In this sense, then, Cnut's vow is a perlocutionary speech act, one that brings about a particular effect. In this case, speech creates a new society characterized by loyal lordship on the part of the king. See Butler, *Excitable Speech*, 3.
109 All quotations and translations are taken from Alistair Campbell, ed., and trans., *Encomium Emma Reginae*. Discussions of authorship are in Simon Keynes's new introduction (xxxix–xli) and Campbell's introduction (ci–cv). With good reason, Keynes prefers the scenario by which the encomiast is located in England.
110 The encomiast's discussion of his material can be found in his *argumentum*; Alistair Campbell, ed., and trans., *Encomium Emmae Reginae*, 6–9.
111 I take up the themes of loyalty, family relations, and succession explicitly in chapters 1 and 2. Fleming, *Kings and Lords*, 24, presents a genealogical table showing the interrelationships of tenth-century Anglo-Saxon kings and their *ealdormenn*; the complexity of these relations suggests the problems of family and succession.
112 Alistair Campbell, ed., and trans., *Encomium Emma Reginae*, 8–9.
113 Ibid., 8–11.
114 Ibid., 10–11.
115 Ibid. Before tracing the impact Thorkell has on Anglo-Saxon England, Simon Keynes refers to Thietmar's account in which Thorkell's decision to join with Æthelred arises from his failure to prevent his men from murdering Ælfheah: Keynes, *The Diplomas of King Æthelred*, 221–5 and note 241. An outline of Thorkell's activities, as they appear in the *Encomium*, can be found in John, 'The *Encomium Emmae Reginae*,' 65–76; Larson, 'Political

Policies,' 725–31, offers a brief survey of the earls; Keynes, 'Cnut's Earls,' is more detailed and considers Thorkell in relationship to the Danish raids and to his position in Cnut's reign (54–6). Without deeper discussion of loyalty as a central theme in the *Encomium*, the prominence of Thorkell's story can make the text seem somewhat loosely organized.
116 Alistair Campbell, ed., and trans., *Encomium Emma Reginae*, 14–15.
117 Ibid., 16–17.
118 Ibid., 16–21.
119 Ibid., 30–1.
120 I analyse the overlapping languages of lordship and the annalist's consistent presentation of conquest as a lordship problem in chapter 6.
121 The debate over continuity is usually framed as one of land tenure, which I consider more fully in chapter 6 and the Conclusion. Nationalist readings of the Conquest usually focus on the entry for 1066. S. a. 1066 (D): Cubbin, ed., *The Anglo-Saxon Chronicle*, 79–81. In particular, they emphasize the D annalist's epithet for William – Wyllelm Bastard (79) – the phrase, 'Harold ure cyng' (Harold, our king) (80), and the bitter comment that concludes the annal: '7 a syððan hit yflade swiðe. Wurðe god se ende þonne God wylle' (And always after that it got very much worse. May the end be good when God wills) (81).

6: Writing William's Kingship

1 The use of *Angelcynn* in this context is traced most fully in the introduction and page 163, note 28.
2 The D annalist is not the only Anglo-Saxon writer to interpret the Conquest as a moment of irreversible change; see Otter, '1066: The Moment of Transition,' on the *Vita Wulfstani* and *Vita Eadwardi Regis*. Historically speaking, the question of change is difficult to answer. In many ways, the Normans continued some of the practices and conventions of Anglo-Saxon life and government and changed others; thus the degree of change may be correlated with the area under examination. In the introductory discussion to an extensive exploration of the post-Conquest church, for example, Barlow, *The English Church 1066–1154*, 57–8, summarizes some of the most rapid personnel changes, but (29–53) suggests that structural changes were slower. By contrast, discussions of post-Conquest land tenure frequently highlight the differences in system and the rapidity of change. See, controversially, Fleming, *Kings and Lords in Conquest England*, 107–44, on the systemic changes. Nevertheless, the symbolism of William's coronation and his claim to the throne by right of law depend on a certain notion of continuity.

3 Because we usually define the Conquest by the Battle of Hastings, the annal for 1065, an entry for the reign of Edward the Confessor, is not conventionally included in the conquest narrative. If, however, we look beyond the military history offered in the annals, different boundaries emerge.
4 For my purposes, the relationship of culture and identity is aptly described in Bhabha, 'DissemiNation,' 145: 'As the scraps, patches, and rags of daily life' are 'turned into the signs of a coherent national culture ... the very act of the narrative performance interpellates a growing circle of national subjects. In the production of the nation as narration there is a split between the continuist accumulative temporality of the pedagogical, and the repetitious, recursive strategy of the performative.'
5 On the king's castle-building program as a means of settlement, see Le Patourel, *The Norman Empire*, 316–18, and, more generally, Judith Green, *The Aristocracy of Norman England*, 172–93, esp. 75–8. Orderic Vitalis, *The Ecclesiastical History of Orderic Vitalis*, IV (ii.185), 218, explains how essential castles were to defeating the Anglo-Saxons.
6 There is no evidence that the D annalist knew these particular poems, but the consistent presentation of lordship in these texts suggests a widespread literary and cultural imagination – which the annalist may well have shared – that linked lordship and land in this way.
7 As discussed below, the annalist consistently portrays William's actions as deliberately hostile, as opposed to the result of a cultural misunderstanding or an example of political change.
8 The palaeography of the D manuscript in general and the William annals in particular is different. See note 123 below.
9 See note 109 below.
10 Kapelle, *The Norman Conquest of the North*, 105–57, is a general history of the North in this period, while Dalton, *Conquest, Anarchy, and Lordship*, 9–12 and 19–78, is more focused on York, with full discussions of land tenure (79–112) and monastic culture (134–42).
11 The most recent histories of the community at Worcester are Barrow, 'The Community of Worcester, 961–c.1100'; Emma Mason, 'Change and Continuity in Eleventh-Century Mercia,' and *Saint Wulfstan of Worcester*, 108–55; and Williams, 'The Spoliation of Worcester.' Mason, 'Change and Continuity,' 157, suggests that Æthelwig, abbot of Evesham, was actually more of a threat to Worcester's land than Urse.
12 Mason, *Saint Wulfstan of Worcester*, 209–16; the crucial text here is Hemming, *Hemingi Chartularium ecclesiae Wigorniensis*, 282–6. On Oswald's leases, see Barrow, 'Community of Worcester.'
13 The tension between Worcester and York seems to have influenced Wulf-

stan's appointment: see William of Malmesbury, *The Vita Wulfstani of William of Malmesbury*, 18–19; Swanton, ed. and trans., *Three Lives of the Last Englishmen*, 105.

14 Wulfstan addressed this practice by forming a confraternity of monastic houses in which all the institutions were, no matter what the origins of their abbots, dedicated to Anglo-Saxon Benedictinism: Mason, *Saint Wulfstan of Worcester*, 196–201.
15 I offer here no detailed discussion about the community of York, because it does not have the same post-Conquest historical tradition as Worcester. Though, in some ways, the survival of the many Worcester texts might be an accident of history, the composition and compilation of so many pieces of historical writing both advances and supports my cultural arguments about the function of history.
16 See, especially, Rampolla, 'A Vision of the Past.'
17 Unlike my earlier chapters, where land has figured either as an absent presence or wholly in the negative, this chapter reveals that land is now a central part of Anglo-Saxon monastic identity at Worcester.
18 The scholarly debate on the Norman Conquest and the kinds of answers historians have provided are summarized in Barlow, 'William I and the Norman Conquest,' 137–40, and Chibnall, *The Debate on the Norman Conquest*.
19 S. a. 1066 (D): Cubbin, ed., *The Anglo-Saxon Chronicle: MS D*, 81: '7 þæt wæs micel unræd þæt man æror swa ne dyde, þa hit God betan nolde for urum synnum' (And it was a great foolishness that they did not do so before, since God did not want to improve anything on account of our sins).
20 William of Jumièges, 'Gesta Normannorum ducum,' in *The Gesta Normannorum ducum of William of Jumièges*, vii 13 (31), 158–9.
21 Ibid., 160–1.
22 These are the outermost limits for the dates; see William of Poitiers, *The Gesta Guillelmi of William of Poitiers*, xx–xxi.
23 Ibid., ii.1, 100–1.
24 Ibid., 112–15.
25 Ibid., ii.7, 110–13 and ii.22, 136–7. He may well have been reading Statius.
26 Ibid., ii.12, 118–23.
27 John of Worcester, *The Chronicle of John of Worcester*, xix.
28 S. a. 1066: John of Worcester, *The Chronicle of John of Worcester*, 600–1.
29 Eadmer, *Eadmeri Historia novorum in Anglia*, 6–8.
30 Henry of Huntingdon, *Historia Anglorum*, lxi.
31 S. a. 1066: Henry of Huntingdon, *Historia Anglorum*, vi.27, 384–5.

32 Orderic Vitalis, *The Ecclesiastical History of Orderic Vitalis*. Book III appears to have been written c. 1125 (xv).
33 Ibid., III (ii.144), 168–9.
34 Ibid., III (ii.145–6), 172–3.
35 William of Malmesbury, *Gesta regum Anglorum*, iii, 241–2, 452–5.
36 Ibid., 245, 456–61.
37 S. a. 1066 (D): Cubbin, ed., *The Anglo-Saxon Chronicle*, 81: 'Wurðe god se ende þonne God wylle' (May the end be good when God wills).
38 A similar symbolic understanding of Cnut's law in this context is suggested in Wormald, *The Making of English Law*, 133.
39 S. a. 1065 (D): Cubbin, ed., *The Anglo-Saxon Chronicle*, 78: '7 he nywade þær Cnutes lage ... 7 Tostig eorl 7 his wif, 7 ealle þa ðe woldon þæt he wolde, faran suð ofer sæ' (And there he [the king] renewed Cnut's law ... And Earl Tostig and his wife, and all those who wanted what he wanted, went south, over the sea).
40 See the perspectives offered in Barlow, *The Godwins*, 83–8; DeVries, *The Norwegian Invasion of England in 1066*, 168–92; and Kapelle, *The Norman Conquest of the North*, 86–119.
41 S. a. 1065 (C): O'Brien O'Keeffe, ed., *The Anglo-Saxon Chronicle*, 118.
42 Barlow, ed., and trans., *The Life of King Edward*, i.5, 58–61.
43 Ibid., i.5, 46–52, i.7, 76–83.
44 On the reasons that make Tostig a poor (and sound) choice for Edward, see DeVries, *Norwegian Invasion*, 177–8, and Kapelle, *The Norman Conquest of the North*, 86–8.
45 Interestingly, Barlow, ed., and trans., *Life of King Edward*, 80–1, suggests that the pain of not being able to save his earl stayed with Edward until he died and that Edward was saddened by the disobedience of his men.
46 Not engaging in civil war is an explicit part of the Latin text; ibid: 'Et quia in eadem gente horrebat quasi bellum ciuile' (And because in that race horror was felt at what seemed civil war).
47 S. a. 1065 (D): Cubbin, ed., *The Anglo-Saxon Chronicle*, 78: '7 he nywade þær Cnutes lage' (And there he [the king] renewed Cnut's law).
48 This claim is developed more extensively in chapter 5.
49 S. a. 1065 (D): Cubbin, ed., *The Anglo-Saxon Chronicle*, 78. Harold's role in this episode is significant: in supporting the rebels, he effectively betrays his king. That Harold's lordship is not perfect in this regard anticipates the kinds of difficulties he will have in the annalist's account of his brief reign.
50 S. a. 1065 (C): O'Brien O'Keeffe, ed., *The Anglo-Saxon Chronicle*, 118.
51 In this regard, the annal for 1065 evokes the Æthelred-Cnut annalist's

approach to narrating the king's brutality (s. a. 1002 (C): O'Brien O'Keeffe, ed., *The Anglo-Saxon Chronicle*, 89), while simultaneously prefiguring the narrative of the Norman settlement.

52 This is one of the central issues in Norman Conquest historiography; I supply only a brief introduction. The problem turns on the closely linked problems of Harold's oath (discussed below), Godwin's rebellion, and William's arrival. S. a. 1051 (D): Cubbin, ed., *The Anglo-Saxon Chronicle*, 71. For discussion of these interrelated issues, see Barlow, *The Godwins*, 40–9 (Godwin); Barlow, *Edward the Confessor*, 214–55 (Edward and Harold); Miles W. Campbell, 'A Pre-Conquest Norman Occupation of England?' 'Earl Godwin of Wessex and Edward the Confessor's Promise of the Throne to William of Normandy,' and 'The Anti-Norman Reaction in England in 1052'; Douglas, *William the Conqueror*, 159–80 (William); and John, 'Edward the Confessor and the Norman Succession.'

53 S. a. 1065 (D): Cubbin, ed., *The Anglo-Saxon Chronicle*, 79.

54 Ibid., 79.

55 This is deeply ironic, given that Harold's support of the northern rebels is one of the problems Edward must face.

56 S. a. 1066 (D): Cubbin, ed., *The Anglo-Saxon Chronicle*, 80: '7 þa butsacarlas hine forsocan ... 7 Tostig him to beah 7 his man wearð' (And the seamen deserted him ... And Tostig submitted to him [Harold] and became his man).

57 The differences between *bugan* and *cyrran* are more fully documented in chapter 5. *Cyrran* is discussed in the introduction and chapter 1.

58 Reading from the hitherto understudied Norwegian sources, DeVries, *Norwegian Invasion*, 284–6, observes how the battle narratives play up the relationship between the brothers and cites, in particular, the scenes of verbal bargaining, scenes which for readers of Old English invoke both the poem on the battle of Maldon and the Cynewulf-Cyneheard episode of the *Chronicle*.

59 S. a. 1066 (D): Cubbin, ed., *The Anglo-Saxon Chronicle*, 80.

60 Ibid.

61 Though there is no baptismal ceremony, this scene compares with the images of peace making between Alfred and Guthrum (s. a. 878 (A): Bately, ed., *The Anglo-Saxon Chronicle*, 51: '7 þa salde se here him foregislas 7 micle aþas ...' (And then the army gave him preliminary hostages and swore strong oaths ...), and the scenes between Æthelred and Olaf: s. a. 994 (C): O'Brien O'Keeffe, ed., *The Anglo-Saxon Chronicle*, 87.

62 In this regard, the peace Harold contracts with the Norwegians differs slightly from Cnut's peace with the Anglo-Saxons.

63 This is fully consonant with what we know of Anglo-Saxon friendship: Althoff, 'Friendship and Political Order,' and Barrow, 'Friends and Friendship in Anglo-Saxon Charters.'
64 S. a. 1065 (D): Cubbin, ed., *The Anglo-Saxon Chronicle*, 78–9.
65 Ibid., 77.
66 Ibid., 78.
67 S. a. 1066 (D): Cubbin, ed., *The Anglo-Saxon Chronicle*, 80.
68 Ibid.
69 John of Worcester takes this one step further: s. a. 1066: John of Worcester, *The Chronicle of John of Worcester*, 604–5: 'Sed quia arto in loco constituti fuerant Angli, de acie se multi subtraxere et cum eo perpauci constantes corde remansere' (But because the English were drawn up in a narrow place many slipped away from the battlefield, and very few of a constant heart remained with him).
70 S. a. 1066 (D): Cubbin, ed., *The Anglo-Saxon Chronicle*, 80–1. On Edgar's career, see Nicholas Hooper, 'Edgar the Ætheling.'
71 See page 198, note 71.
72 S. a. 1066 (D): Cubbin, ed., *The Anglo-Saxon Chronicle*, 81.
73 Ibid.
74 Compare, for example, the ceremonies of Alfred at Edington, Æthelred and Olaf, the language of Cnut's legal texts, and, most pointedly, the scene between Harold Godwinson and Olaf.
75 S. a. 1066 (D): Cubbin, ed., *The Anglo-Saxon Chronicle*, 81.
76 Ibid.
77 Ibid.
78 Healey, Venezky, and Cameron, eds, *Dictionary of Old English: Old English Corpus*. See chapter 5 for full discussion. To read the oath in this way is to see a scenario quite different from the one articulated in Nelson, 'The Rites of the Conqueror,' 387–8.
79 On the differences of the two systems for choosing a king and the potential for misunderstanding, see Garnett, 'Coronation and Propaganda,' esp. 93–9, and Nelson, 'The Rites of the Conqueror.'
80 S. a. 1066 (D): Cubbin, ed., *The Anglo-Saxon Chronicle*, 81.
81 Nelson, 'The Rites of the Conqueror,' 382, shows that the third *ordo* is a 'splicing together of forms from the *Second English Ordo* with forms from the king's *ordo* in the *Pontificale Romano-Germanicum*, compiled at St. Alban's, Mainz.' Lapidge, 'Ealdred of York and MS Cotton Vitellius E. XII,' explains how the material arrived in England: through Ealdred, archbishop of York and the man who crowned William.
82 S. a. 1066 (D): Cubbin, ed., *The Anglo-Saxon Chronicle*, 81.

83 Ibid.
84 S. a. 1014 (C): O'Brien O'Keeffe, ed., *The Anglo-Saxon Chronicle*, 98. And it further resonates with the legal texts legitimating Cnut's accession.
85 S. a. 1066 (D): Cubbin, ed., *The Anglo-Saxon Chronicle*, 81.
86 These events are not correctly assigned; this may be deliberate.
87 S. a. 1067 (D): Cubbin, ed., *The Anglo-Saxon Chronicle*, 81.
88 Orderic Vitalis, *The Ecclesiastical History of Orderic Vitalis*, IV (ii. 179–81), 210–15. Orderic even comments on how the king's behaviour was effective in winning the people's loyalty.
89 S. a. 1067 (D): Cubbin, ed., *The Anglo-Saxon Chronicle*, 82. In this way, the D annalist elides the story of Gytha, Harold's mother. On which see John of Worcester, *The Chronicle of John of Worcester (1067–1140)*, 6–7, and, for Gytha in Exeter, see Williams, *The English and the Norman Conquest*, 19–23.
90 See Barlow, ed. and trans., *Life of King Edward*, 66–7; this moment and the sworn brotherhood between Tostig and Malcolm are discussed in DeVries, *Norwegian Invasion*, 172–6, and Kapelle, *The Norman Conquest of the North*, 91–2. The absence of this story contrasts with the entry for 1031 in which the D manuscript notes the submission of Malcolm II to Cnut: s. a. 1031 (D): Cubbin, ed., *The Anglo-Saxon Chronicle*, 65.
91 The ideal behaviour of St Margaret, her position as a role model, and the educational purposes of her other Latin *vitae* are discussed in Huneycutt, 'The Idea of the Perfect Princess.' In context, however, the story of Margaret contrasts with the failure of William's wife to similarly control and 'civilize' her husband.
92 S. a. 1073 (D): Cubbin, ed., *The Anglo-Saxon Chronicle*, 85.
93 S. a. 1075 (D): Cubbin, ed., *The Anglo-Saxon Chronicle*, 86.
94 In the discourses of Anglo-Saxon identity, the Scots frequently serve as an Other. Homi Bhabha directly connects otherness and discourses of national identity: Bhabha, 'DissemiNation,' 147–8: 'The performative intervenes in the sovereignty of the nation's self-generation by casting a shadow between the people as "image" and its signification as a differentiating sign of Self, distinct from the Other of the Outside.'
95 S. a. 1068 (D): Cubbin, ed., *The Anglo-Saxon Chronicle*, 83–4.
96 Ibid., 84.
97 S. a. 1071 (D): Cubbin, ed., *The Anglo-Saxon Chronicle*, 84–5. D is one year ahead of the actual date and remains that way until the entry for 1079.
98 S. a. 1072 (D): Cubbin, ed., *The Anglo-Saxon Chronicle*, 85. The episode evokes the Cynewulf-Cyneheard episode; s. a. 755 (A): Bately, ed., *The Anglo-Saxon Chronicle*, 36–8.

99 S. a. 1072 (D): Cubbin, ed., *The Anglo-Saxon Chronicle*, 85.
100 S. a. 1068 (D): Cubbin, ed., *The Anglo-Saxon Chronicle*, 83–4.
101 S. a. 1076 (D): Cubbin, ed., *The Anglo-Saxon Chronicle*, 87.
102 Gillingham, '1066 and the Introduction of Chivalry into England,' is concerned with the difference between the punishment for Waltheof, the punishment of the Bretons, the freedom permitted Edgar, and William's general willingness to be reconciled with the rebels. Gillingham, pointing out the secondary conflicts and Waltheof's record, suggests (41–3) that William treats the other rebels as if they were Norman, but, sending a message, punishes Waltheof according to English law.
103 Van Houts, *Gender and Memory*, 128–31, argues that the *Gesta Herewardi* negotiates the present and remembers the past by valorizing rebellion in a narrative of the epic, heroic tradition.
104 Compare the account in the *Peterborough Chronicle* where the annalist simply writes 'king.' S. a. 1075 (E): Clark, ed., *The Peterborough Chronicle*, 5. Judith Green, *The Aristocracy of Norman England*, 257–60, discusses the rebellion with regard to notions of loyalty, and Williams, *The English and the Norman Conquest*, 60, offers some discussion of motivation.
105 The D annalist is not alone in ascribing this particular fault to William. Writing in Old Norse and in Waltheof's service, Þorkill Skallason composes a poem that accuses William of betrayal, neatly reversing the Norman charges.
106 That it is the penultimate annal is certainly an accident of manuscript history, but one that registers alongside my discussion of lordship. However, the last annal also concludes with a commentary on broken oaths: s. a. 1080 (D): Cubbin, ed., *The Anglo-Saxon Chronicle*, 89: 'Her werþ Anagus ofsleien fram Scotta eere 7 þer werþ micel weell ofsleigen mid him. Þer wes codes riþt gesochen on him for þet he wes all forswoorn' (Here Angus was killed by the Scottish army and many others were killed with him. There God's justice was done [on him] for he had broken all his oaths). Cubbin, ed., *The Anglo-Saxon Chronicle*, xi, notes that this annal is entered fifty years too early.
107 S. a. 1079 (D): Cubbin, ed., *The Anglo-Saxon Chronicle*, 88.
108 Ibid., 89.
109 The argument for placing the D text at York is made in Whitelock et al., ed. and trans., *The Anglo-Saxon Chronicle*, xv–xvi; her case is more fully laid out in Cubbin, ed., *The Anglo-Saxon Chronicle*, esp. lxiii–lxv. However, there is also a significant amount of evidence for Worcester: Cubbin, ed., *The Anglo-Saxon Chronicle*, lxv–lxxviii, and it is on the basis of such evidence

that the D text is conventionally assigned to Worcester. Cubbin, ed., *The Anglo-Saxon Chronicle*, lxxx–lxxxi, refines the generally accepted argument by linking the text to Archbishop Ealdred. Reading from the problem of Cnut's laws, Wormald, *The Making of English Law*, 130–1, makes a similar but independent case for Ealdred. Dumville, 'Some Aspects of Annalistic Writing at Canterbury,' 34–5, suggests that D was most likely compiled no later than 1100, with 1080 and 1130 as the most extreme points.

110 On Worcester, its church, community, land, and history, see, among others, Atkins, 'The Church of Worcester: Part One,' and 'The Church of Worcester: Part Two'; John, *Orbis Britanniae*, 234–48; A.E.E. Jones, *Anglo-Saxon Worcester*; Keller, *Die litterarischen Bestrebungen von Worcester in angelsächsischer Zeit*; King, 'Ealdred, Archbishop of York;' Emma Mason, 'Change and Continuity,' and *Saint Wulfstan of Worcester*; Robinson, *St. Oswald and the Church of Worcester*; and Williams, 'The Spoliation of Worcester.'

111 The diversity and significance of historical writing at Worcester is discussed in Brett, 'John of Worcester and his Contemporaries,' and Rampolla, 'A Vision of the Past.' Keller, *Die litterarischen Bestrebungen*, is a more wide-ranging survey that attempts to contextualize and account for literary production at Worcester throughout the entire Old English period. Wulfstan, Anglo-Saxon values, and historical narrative are discussed in Emma Mason, *Saint Wulfstan of Worcester*, 206–9. McIntyre, 'Early Twelfth-Century Worcester Cathedral Priory,' 91–3, 98–101, 109, 113, 195, and 198, is a full study of the Worcester manuscripts from Wulfstan's time.

112 William of Malmesbury, *Vita Wulfstani*, 16; Swanton, ed. and trans., *Three Lives of the Last Englishmen*, 103. For discussion, see Vanessa King, 'Ealdred, Archbishop of York,' 130–7, and Mason, *Saint Wulfstan of Worcester*, 84–7.

113 William of Malmesbury, *Vita Wulfstani*, 19–20; Swanton, ed. and trans., *Three Lives of the Last Englishmen*, 105–6.

114 See Darlington, 'Æthelwig, Abbot of Evesham, Part I,' and 'Æthelwig, Abbot of Evesham, Part II.'

115 William of Malmesbury, *Vita Wulfstani*, 18; Swanton, ed. and trans., *Three Lives of the Last Englishmen*, 105.

116 Emma Mason, *Saint Wulfstan of Worcester*, 125–27.

117 See Williams, 'The Spoliation of Worcester,' 393–4.

118 The Evesham and Worcester perspectives are printed side by side in van Caenegem, ed., *English Lawsuits from William I to Richard I*, 10, A, B, C, D, pp. 29–32.

119 Williams, 'The Spoliation of Worcester.' The narrative of plundering is of

course based on Hemming's *Cartulary*; Williams casts a critical eye over Hemming's claims, consistently pointing out the inaccuracies that derive from institutional bias.

120 Barrow, 'The Community of Worcester.'
121 Hemming, *Hemingi Chartularium ecclesiae Wigorniensis*, 284. More general discussions of the writing of history and the history of the lands are Brett, 'John of Worcester'; Rampolla, 'A Vision of the Past'; and Southern, 'Aspects of the European Tradition of Historical Writing: 4, The Sense of the Past,' 246–56.
122 If Wulfstan had not cared, the *Chronicle* might well have lapsed sooner.
123 The difficulty of reading the D text is exacerbated by the number of hands. Cubbin, ed., *The Anglo-Saxon Chronicle*, xi–xv, detects as many as eighteen possible hands; this opinion is not shared by Ker, *A Catalogue of Manuscripts Containing Anglo-Saxon*, 254–5, who acknowledges five clear hands and then notes a series of breaks and possible changes. For my purposes, the number of hands is not important: I highlight the sustained language and focus of the annals.
124 Scholars know neither whether the manuscripts from which the D annalist worked had a prologue nor whether the prologue that currently prefaces the manuscript is original to the annalist who compiled these annals into the D manuscript. Palaeographically, the same hand copies (or adapts) the preface and the annals up to 261 (most of which are blank). See Cubbin, ed., *The Anglo-Saxon Chronicle*, x–xi, and Ker, *A Catalogue of Manuscripts Containing Anglo-Saxon*, 254.
125 See Lefebvre, *The Production of Space*, 41–2. An equally helpful definition of space is de Certeau, *The Practice of Everyday Life*, 117: 'A *space* exists when one takes into consideration vectors of direction, velocities, and time variables. Thus space is composed of intersections of mobile elements. It is in a sense actuated by the ensemble of movements deployed within it. Space occurs as the effect produced by the operations that orient it, situate it, temporalize it and make it function in a polyvalent unity of conflictual programs or contractual proximities' [emphasis as printed].
126 Bede, questing for the holy, reads linguistic diversity in the context of sacred writing (Bede, *Bede's Ecclesiastical History of the English People*, 16–17). By contrast, the D text simply reads, 'Brytene igland is ehta hund mila lang 7 twa hund mila brad, 7 her synd on þam iglande fif geþeodu' (The island of Britain is eight hundred miles long and two hundred miles wide, and there are five languages on the island). See Cubbin, ed., *The Anglo-Saxon Chronicle*, 1.
127 Cubbin, ed., *The Anglo-Saxon Chronicle*, 1. This is, of course, an error.

128 Ibid.
129 The manuscript layout is key to understanding how the coming of the Romans becomes part of the preface. In the A, B, and C manuscripts, the annals proper begin in 60 B.C. with the coming of the Roman army. D includes the narrative of the Roman invasion in the preface – Cubbin, ed., *The Anglo-Saxon Chronicle*, 1, note 3, observes that there is no gap between the preface and the beginning of the Roman narrative and that the initial S is slightly bigger than its surrounding letters – thereby suggesting that the Romans are one of the founding peoples of the Anglo-Saxon realm.
130 In the *Vita Wulfstani*, Wulfstan is shown resisting rebuilding the minster: William of Malmesbury, *Vita Wulfstani*, 52; Swanton, ed. and trans., *Three Lives of the Last Englishmen*, 134–5. Rebuilding the Anglo-Saxon churches seems to have been a large-scale Norman project; see Emma Mason, *Saint Wulfstan of Worcester*, 201–3.

7. Conclusion: After Lives

1 I stress here that the lordship in the *Chronicle* annals of conquest and invasion is less a reflection of reality than a careful representation of selected aspects of lordship practice. How lordship is presented and what aspects of this relationship are stressed varies according to the historical circumstances of the different annalists. For full discussion, see the introduction and chapter 1.
2 Hanning, *The Vision of History in Early Britain*.
3 As a way of highlighting the difference between the pre-and post-Conquest periods, I note that John Hudson, *The Formation of the English Common Law*, 86–9, argues that the Normans interpreted land as a marker of social identity. Previously, land was to be avoided in discussions of collective identity; now, land is crucial.
4 I do not mean to imply that the Peterborough annalist saw the D text; that is not supported by the manuscript history. The relationship between the D and E manuscripts of the *Chronicle* is complicated. Clark, ed., *The Peterborough Chronicle*, xix, notes that D and E are broadly similar up to 1031; after 1057, in a very general sense, D shares some entries with E. Dumville, 'Some Aspects of Annalistic Writing at Canterbury,' 34–8, though embarked on a different project, discusses the relationship between the two texts, beginning with the principle that D is based on an ancestor of E for the text up to 1063.
5 S. a. 1085 (E): Clark, ed., *Peterborough Chronicle*, 8.

6 Ibid. Historians have also posited this link; see note 9 below.
7 Ibid., 9.
8 In the Cynewulf-Cyneheard episode of the *Chronicle* and in poems such as *Beowulf* and the *Battle of Maldon*, it is shameful for the men not to die with their lord (but see also Frank, 'The Ideal of Men Dying with Their Lord in *The Battle of Maldon*'; Harris, 'Love and Death in the *Männerbund*'; and Woolf, 'The Ideal of Men Dying with Their Lord in the *Germania* and in *The Battle of Maldon*'). There is little or no explicit discussion of whether it might be shameful of the lord to have put his men in this position in the first place; for this, see chapter 5.
9 Although they have frequently connected the threat of Cnut Sweinson's invasion, the commissioning of the Domesday survey, and the oath taking at Salisbury, historians have tended to disagree about how to bring these events into relationship with each other. Douglas, *William the Conqueror*, 351–3, suggests that the king, always in need of money, found that the best way to gain it was to discover the resources of his new land and formalize the changes that occurred during the Conquest. Harvey, 'Domesday Book and Anglo-Norman Governance,' seeking to locate *Domesday Book* in its administrative and political contexts, demonstrates how the survey could have been used as a resource for king and tenants. Applying logistical arguments, Holt, '1086,' suggesting that the submission and oath taking were planned as the conclusion to the survey, argues that the barons cooperated in the survey because its results assured them of their landholdings, that William conducted the survey because he could use it to secure their loyalty, and that the bargain was confirmed on both sides with the oath of loyalty in 1086. Higham, 'The Domesday Survey,' painting a picture of an aging, isolated, besieged monarch, suggests from a study of the circumstances surrounding its commission that though *Domesday Book* provided William with a tool to strengthen his control over his nobility, it was also a concession on his part. Using the now available information, the king agreed to shoulder more equally the costs of billeting a large army. Income and the threat of conquest are taken up in Roffe, *Domesday: The Inquest and the Book*, 67–70. Though telling in their analysis of scenarios and rationales for *Domesday Book*, none of these interpretations explains an equally salient issue: the annalist's reaction to *Domesday Book* as text. This omission is partially rectified in Roffe, *Domesday*, 1–10, esp. 7–10.
10 S. a. 1086 (E): Clark, ed., *Peterborough Chronicle*, 9.
11 Ibid.
12 Ibid. On Edgar's life and career, see, in brief, Hooper, 'Edgar the Ætheling.'
13 S. a. 1074 (E): Clark, ed., *Peterborough Chronicle*, 5. The various *Chronicle*

treatments of the Anglo-Saxon rebels is one of the places where the different agendas of D and E are most tangible.

14 S. a. 1087 (E): Clark, ed., *Peterborough Chronicle*, 12. E is one year in advance.

15 How *Domesday Book* might have been used is a point of contention. The evidence has been interpreted as suggesting that *Domesday Book* was not used as a general source of reference until much later; Clanchy, *From Memory to Written Record*, 33–4, 181–4. Fleming, *Domesday Book and the Law*, 11–35 and 68–85, argues that *Domesday Book* is a legal text and that the inquest was undertaken specifically to help resolve land disputes. Contra Fleming, Roffe, *Domesday*, 165–8, argues that William did not intend to use the book as a legal text for resolving disputes.

16 For two very different studies of literacy after the conquest, see Clanchy, *From Memory to Written Record*, and Stock, *The Implications of Literacy*.

17 On forgery at Westminster, see Mason, Bray, and Murphy, eds, *Westminster Abbey Charters*; for Durham, see Offler, *Durham Episcopal Charters*; for Canterbury, see Emms, 'The Historical Traditions of St. Augustine's Abbey, Canterbury,' and Southern, 'The Canterbury Forgeries.' On the career of a master forger, see Foliot, *The Letters and Charters of Gilbert Foliot*; Fleming, *Domesday Book and the Law*, 53–67, sets the context for these kinds of historical forgeries. The Battle Abbey forgeries are discussed in Searle, 'Battle Abbey and Exemption.' A good introductory survey of the issues is Chibnall, 'Forgery in Narrative Charters.'

18 Clark, ed., *Peterborough Chronicle*, xv–xviii. Clark divides the *Chronicle* into three parts: annals up to 1121 in a homogeneous hand and ink; 1121–31, written by the same scribe in blocks of 1122, 1123, 1124, 1125–6/11, 1126/12–1127, and 1128–31; a second scribe writes the entries for 1132–54.

19 The history of the Peterborough community in the post-Conquest years is studied by Edward King, *Peterborough Abbey, 1086–1310*, and Mackreth, 'Peterborough, from St. Aethelwold to Martin de Bec.'

20 Hugh Candidus, writing perhaps between fifteen and thirty years after the fire, states that the destruction was marginally less complete, suggesting that the Peterborough annalist exaggerates for reasons more fully explained below. See Hugo Candidus, *The Peterborough Chronicle of Hugh Candidus*, 97.

21 This is not all the Peterborough-specific material, simply the entries relevant to the foundation and refoundation narratives. The authenticity of the charters is recorded (with Sawyer numbers) in Sawyer, *Anglo-Saxon Charters*, no. 68 (88), no. 72 (89–90), and no. 787 (251–2). The other extant Peterborough charters are not preserved in the *Chronicle*.

22 S. a. 963 (E): Clark, ed., *Peterborough Chronicle*, 123. In her edition, Clark

places the *Interpolations* after the main text and after the commentary, thus reinforcing the scholarly view that, as their name suggests, the *Interpolations* are 'not really' part of the *Chronicle*.

23 The Peterborough annalist does not fear losing the monastery's endowments as a result of the Conquest; he seeks rather to assure his monastery's land for the future. King, *Peterborough Abbey*, 9, notes that the gifts in the third and most recent period of endowment (including gifts of land from Brand, the last Anglo-Saxon abbot) were confirmed by William I in 1067. On the textual problems of William's charters, see Bates, 'The Conqueror's Charters.'

24 For a fuller study of this trend and of post-Conquest monastic history in general, see Knowles, *The Monastic Order in England*, esp. 283.

25 S. a. 1130 (E): Clark, ed., *Peterborough Chronicle*, 52.

26 S. a. 1132 (E): Clark, ed., *Peterborough Chronicle*, 54.

27 Scholars of Old English in the twelfth century usually focus on religious works, historians focus on the increasing production of Latin chronicles, and scholars of early Middle English usually look to religious works or texts like Laȝamon's *Brut* and the *Owl and the Nightingale*. A significant case in point is Treharne, ed., *Old and Middle English: An Anthology*, 254, where the *Chronicle* is noted as 'transitional.'

28 I borrow the phrase from the title of Clanchy, *From Memory to Written Record*; relevant discussion is at 1–43.

29 Galloway, 'Writing History in England,' 260.

30 The history of Peterborough is continued in Latin in Hugo Candidus, *The Peterborough Chronicle of Hugh Candidus*.

31 I make this argument more completely in my 'Love Rewritten.'

32 Hanning, *The Vision of History*, 174. Though I agree with Hanning's analysis here, I would also wish to complicate his history of romance.

33 Southern, 'Aspects of the European Tradition of Historical Writing: 4, The Sense of the Past,' 246–50.

34 Laȝamon, *Laȝamon: Brut*, 2–3: the relevant sources are Bede, a Latin text by Saint Albin (this is a much-discussed attribution), and the *Roman de Brut* of Wace.

35 Laȝamon, *Laȝamon: Brut*, 2–3: London, British Library MS Cotton Caligula A.ix begins with the chapter heading, 'Incipit hystoria Brutonum' (Here begins the History of the Britons). In this manuscript, the lines I read as a preface form part of the narrative itself. By contrast, the other extant manuscript, London, British Library MS Cotton Otho C.xiii, begins, 'Incipit Prologus libri Brutonum' (Here begins the Prologue to the Book of the Britons); it formally separates the preface from the remainder of the narrative.

36 For brief discussion, see Gransden, 'Prologues in the Historiography of Twelfth-Century England.' Good examples of the genre are Henry of Huntingdon, *Historia Anglorum*, 2–9; and William of Malmesbury, *Gesta regum Anglorum*, 2–13. The *Gesta regum* is a particularly interesting example of the genre: William issued a series of dedicatory letters.

Bibliography

Primary Sources

Ælfric. *On the Old and New Testament*. Edited and translated by S.J. Crawford. EETS o.s. 160. London: Oxford University Press, 1960.
- *The Maccabees*. In *Ælfric's Lives of Saints*. 2 vols. Edited and translated by W.W. Skeat, 2:66–124. EETS o.s. 94 and 114. London: Oxford University Press, 1966.
- *Dominica post ascensionem Domini*. In *Homilies of Ælfric: A Supplementary Collection*. 2 vols. Edited by J.C. Pope, 1:378–89. EETS o.s. 259. London: Oxford University Press, 1967.
- *Wyrdwriteras*. In *Homilies of Ælfric: A Supplementary Collection*. 2 vols. Edited by J.C. Pope, 2:728–32. EETS o.s. 260. London: Oxford University Press, 1968.
- *Feria secunda. Letania maiore*. In *Ælfric's Catholic Homilies: The Second Series*. Edited by Malcolm Godden, 180–9. EETS s.s. 5. London: Oxford University Press, 1979.
- *De octo uiciis et de duodecim abusiuis huius seculi*. Edited and translated by Richard Morris. EETS o.s. 29 and 34. Millwood, NY: Kraus Reprint, 1988.

Æthelweard. *The Chronicle of Æthelweard*. Edited and translated by Alistair Campbell. London: Thomas Nelson and Sons, 1962.

Alcuin. *De clade Lindisfarnensis monasterii*. In *Poetae Latini Aevi Carolini*. Edited by E. Dümmler, 229–35. Monumenta Germaniae Historica: Rerum Germanicarum medii aevi 1. Berlin: Weidmann, 1881.
- 'Letter #16 to Ethelred of Northumbria.' In *Epistolae Karolini Aevi II*. Edited by E. Dümmler, 42–4. Monumenta Germaniae Historica: Epistolarum 4. Berlin: Weidmann, 1895.

Arngart, O., ed. *The Proverbs of Alfred*. 2 vols. Lund: C.W.K. Gleerup, 1942, 1955.

Asser. *Life of King Alfred: Together with the Annals of Saint Neots Erroneously Ascribed to Asser*. Edited by William Henry Stevenson. 2nd ed. Oxford: Clarendon Press, 1959.

Barlow, Frank, ed. and trans. *The Life of King Edward Who Rests at Westminster*. 2nd ed. Oxford: Clarendon Press, 1992.

Bately, Janet, ed. *The Old English Orosius*. EETS s.s. 6. London: Oxford University Press, 1980.

– *The Anglo-Saxon Chronicle: MS A. The Anglo-Saxon Chronicle: A Collaborative Edition*. Vol. 3. Cambridge: D.S. Brewer, 1986.

Bede. *Bede's Ecclesiastical History of the English People*. Edited and translated by Bertram Colgrave and R.A.B. Mynors. Reprint with corrections. Oxford: Clarendon Press, 1991.

Campbell, Alistair, ed. and trans. *Encomium Emma Reginae*. Reprint, with a supplementary introduction by Simon Keynes. Cambridge: Cambridge University Press, 1998.

Clark, Cecily, ed. *The Peterborough Chronicle, 1070–1154*. 2nd ed. Oxford: Clarendon Press, 1970.

Conner, Patrick W., ed. *The Abingdon Chronicle, AD 956–1066: (MS C with reference to BDE). The Anglo-Saxon Chronicle: A Collaborative Edition*. Vol. 10. Cambridge: D.S. Brewer, 1996.

Cross, James E., and Jennifer Morrish Tunberg, eds. *The Copenhagen Wulfstan Collection: Copenhagen Kongelige Bibliotek Gl. kgl. sam. 1595*. Early English Manuscripts in Facsimile 25. Copenhagen: Rosenkilde and Bagger, 1993.

Cubbin, G.P., ed. *The Anglo-Saxon Chronicle: MS D. The Anglo-Saxon Chronicle: A Collaborative Edition*. Vol. 6. Cambridge: D.S. Brewer, 1996.

Eadmer. *Eadmeri Historia novorum in Anglia*. Edited by Martin Rule. Rolls Series 81. London: Longman and Trübner, 1884.

Foliot, Gilbert. *The Letters and Charters of Gilbert Foliot, Abbot of Gloucester (1139–48), Bishop of Hereford (1148–63), and London (1163–87)*. Edited by Z.N. Brooke, Adrian Morey, Christopher Nugent, and Lawrence Brooke. Cambridge: Cambridge University Press, 1967.

Gildas. *Liber querulus de excidio Britanniae*. Edited and translated by Michael Winterbottom. London: Phillimore, NJ: 1978.

Harmer, F.E., ed. 'King Alfred's Will.' In *Select English Historical Documents of the Ninth and Tenth Centuries*, 15–19. Cambridge: Cambridge University Press, 1914.

Healey, Antonette diPaolo, Richard L. Venezky, and Angus Cameron, eds. *Dictionary of Old English (microform)*. Toronto: Pontifical Institute of Mediaeval Studies, 1986–.

Healey, Antonette diPaolo, et al. *Dictionary of Old English: Old English Corpus*. Dictionary of Old English Project, Centre for Medieval Studies, University of Toronto: http://www.hti.umich.edu/english/oec, 2000.

Hemming. *Hemingi Chartularium ecclesiae Wigorniensis*. Edited by Thomas Hearne. Oxford: Sheldonian Theatre, 1723.

Henry, Archdeacon of Huntingdon. *Historia Anglorum: The History of the English*. Edited and translated by Diana E. Greenway. Oxford: Clarendon Press, 1996.

Hincmar. *De regis persona et regio ministerio*. Edited by J.P. Migne, cols 833–56. Patrologiae Cursus Completus. Series Latina 125. Paris, 1852.

– *De ordine palatii*. Edited and translated (German) by Thomas Gross and Rudolf Schieffer. 2nd ed. Monumenta Germaniae Historica. Fontes Iuris Germanici Antiqui 3. Hanover: Hahnsche Buchhandlung, 1980.

Hugo Candidus. *The Peterborough Chronicle of Hugh Candidus*. Edited by W.T. Mellows. 2nd revised ed. Peterborough: Museum Society, 1966.

John of Worcester. *The Chronicle of John of Worcester: The Annals from 450 to 1066*. Edited by R.R. Darlington and P. McGurk, and translated by Jennifer Bray and P. McGurk. Vol. 2. Oxford: Clarendon Press, 1995.

– *The Chronicle of John of Worcester: The Annals from 1067 to 1140 with the Gloucester Interpolations and the Continuation to 1141*. Edited and translated by P. McGurk. Vol. 3. Oxford: Clarendon Press, 1998.

Keynes, Simon, and Michael Lapidge, eds and trans. 'Asser's *Life of King Alfred*.' In *Alfred the Great: Asser's Life of King Alfred and Other Contemporary Sources*. Harmondsworth: Penguin, 1983.

– *Alfred the Great: Asser's Life of King Alfred and Other Contemporary Sources*. Harmondsworth: Penguin, 1983.

Klaeber, F., ed. *Beowulf and the Fight at Finnsburg*. 3rd ed. Lexington, MA: Heath, 1950.

Laȝamon. *La amon: Brut*. 2 vols. Edited by G.L. Brook and R.F. Leslie. EETS o.s. 250, 251. London: Oxford University Press, 1963.

Legg, J. Wickham, ed. *Three Coronation Orders*. Henry Bradshaw Society 29. London: Harrison and Sons, 1900.

Liebermann, Friedrich, ed. *Ungedruckte Anglo-Normannische Geschichtsquellen*. Strasbourg: Trübner, 1879.

– *Die Gesetze der Angelsachsen*. 3 vols. Halle: Max Niemeyer, 1903–16.

Lindsay, W.M., ed. *Isidori Hispalensis episcopi Etymologiarum sive originum libri XX*. Oxford: Clarendon Press, 1911.

Mason, Emma, Jennifer Bray, and Desmond J. Murphy, eds. *Westminster Abbey Charters, 1066–c.1214*. London Record Society 25. London: London Record Society, 1988.

Muir, Bernard J., ed. *The Exeter Anthology of Old English Poetry.* 2 vols. Exeter: University of Exeter Press, 1994.
O'Brien O'Keeffe, Katherine, ed. *The Anglo-Saxon Chronicle: MS C. The Anglo-Saxon Chronicle: A Collaborative Edition.* Vol. 5. Cambridge: D.S. Brewer, 2001.
Offler, H.S. *Durham Episcopal Charters, 1071–1152.* Surtees Society 179. Gateshead: Northumberland Press, 1968.
Orderic Vitalis. *The Ecclesiastical History of Orderic Vitalis.* Edited and translated by Majorie Chibnall. Vol. 2. Oxford: Clarendon Press, 1969. Reprint, 1990.
Orosius. *Orose: Histoires (Contre les Païens).* 3 vols. Edited and translated (French) by Marie-Pierre Arnaud-Lindet. Paris: Les Belles Lettres, 1990.
Osbern. *Vita Sancti Elphegi Archiepiscopi Cantuariensis et martyris.* Edited by J.P. Migne, cols 371b–93. Patrologiae Cursus Completus. Series Latina 149. Paris, 1882.
– 'Life and Passion of St Ælfheah.' In *The Reign of Cnut: King of England, Denmark, and Norway.* Edited and translated by Alexander R. Rumble, 294–315. London: Leicester University Press, 1994.
Plummer, Charles, ed. *Two of the Saxon Chronicles Parallel with Supplementary Extracts from the Others.* 2 vols. Oxford: Clarendon Press, 1892, 1899.
Pseudo-Cyprian. *De duodecim abusivis saeculi.* Edited by S. Hellmann. Texte und Untersuchungen zur Geschichte der altchristlichen Literatur 34. Leipzig: J.C. Hinrichs, 1909.
Sedulius Scottus. *Liber de rectoribus christianis.* Edited by S. Hellmann. Quellen und Untersuchungen zur lateinischen Philosophie des Mittelalters 1. Munich: Beck, 1906.
– *On Christian Rulers and the Poems.* Translated by E.G. Doyle. Binghamton: State University of New York Press, 1983.
Scragg, D.G. 'The Battle of Maldon.' In *The Battle of Maldon AD 991.* Edited by D.G. Scragg, 15–36. Oxford: Blackwell, 1991.
Smaragdus. *Via regia.* Edited by J.P. Migne, cols 931–70. Patrologiae Cursus Completus. Series Latina 102. Paris, 1851.
Smyth, Alfred P. *The Medieval Life of King Alfred the Great: A Translation and Commentary on the Text Attributed to Asser.* Houndmills, Basingstoke, Hampshire: Palgrave, 2002.
Swanton, Michael, ed. and trans. *The Anglo-Saxon Chronicle.* New York: Routledge, 1998.
– ed. and trans. *Three Lives of the Last Englishmen.* New York: Garland, 1984.
Sweet, Henry, ed. and trans. *King Alfred's West-Saxon Version of Gregory's Pastoral Care.* EETS o.s. 45 and 50. London: Humphrey Milford and Oxford University Press, 1871.

Symons, Thomas, ed. and trans. *Regularis Concordia: Anglicae nationis monachorum sanctimonialiumque.* London: Thomas Nelson and Sons, 1953.
Treharne, Elaine, ed. *Old and Middle English: An Anthology.* Oxford: Blackwell, 2000.
van Caenegem, R.C., ed. *English Lawsuits from William I to Richard I.* Vol. 1. Selden Society 106. London: Selden Society, 1991 (for 1990).
Whitelock, Dorothy, ed. and trans. *English Historical Documents c. 500–1042.* Vol. 1. New York: Oxford University Press, 1979.
Whitelock, Dorothy, M. Brett, and C.N.L. Brooke, eds. *Councils and Synods with Other Documents Relating to the English Church: Part I, 871–1066.* Vol. 1. Oxford: Clarendon Press, 1981.
Whitelock, Dorothy, with David C. Douglas, and Susie I. Tucker, eds and trans. *The Anglo-Saxon Chronicle: A Revised Translation.* New Brunswick, NJ: Rutgers University Press, 1961.
William of Jumièges. *Gesta Normannorum ducum.* Edited by Jean Marx. Rouen: A. Lestringant, 1914; Paris: A. Picard, 1914.
– 'Gesta Normannorum ducum.' In *The* Gesta Normannorum ducum *of William of Jumièges, Orderic Vitalis, and Robert of Torigni.* Vol. 2. Edited and translated by Elisabeth M.C. van Houts. Oxford: Clarendon Press, 1995.
William of Malmesbury. *The* Vita Wulfstani *of William of Malmesbury.* Edited by Reginald R. Darlington. Camden Society, 3rd ser. 40. London: Royal Historical Society, 1928.
– *Gesta regum Anglorum: The History of the English Kings.* Edited and translated by R.A.B. Mynors, R.M. Thomson, and M. Winterbottom. Vol. 1. Oxford: Clarendon Press, 1998.
– *Gesta regum Anglorum: The History of the English Kings.* Edited and translated by R.M. Thomson and M. Winterbottom. Vol. 2. Oxford: Clarendon Press, 1999.
William of Poitiers. *The* Gesta Guillelmi *of William of Poitiers.* Edited and translated by R.H.C. Davis and Marjorie Chibnall. Oxford: Clarendon Press, 1998.
Wulfstan. *Sermo Lupi ad Anglos.* In *The Homilies of Wulfstan.* Edited by Dorothy Bethurum, 267–75. Oxford: Clarendon Press, 1957.
– *Die 'Institutes of Polity, Civil and Ecclesiastical.'* Edited and translated by Karl Jost. Bern: Francke Verlag, 1959.

Secondary Sources

Abels, Richard. *Lordship and Military Obligation in Anglo-Saxon England.* Berkeley and Los Angeles: University of California Press, 1988.
– 'English Tactics, Strategy, and Military Organization in the Late Tenth

Century.' In *The Battle of Maldon, AD 991*, edited by D.G. Scragg, 143–55. Oxford: Blackwell, 1991.
- 'Sheriffs, Lord-Seeking, and the Norman Settlement of the South-East Midlands.' *Anglo-Norman Studies* 19 (1996): 19–50.
- *Alfred the Great: War, Kingship, and Culture in Anglo-Saxon England*. London: Longman, 1998.
- 'Paying the Danegeld: Anglo-Saxon Peacemaking with the Vikings.' In *War and Peace in Ancient and Medieval Europe*, edited by P. DeSouza and J. France. Cambridge: Cambridge University Press, forthcoming.

Airlie, Stuart. 'Bonds of Power and Bonds of Association in the Court Circle of Louis the Pious (814–840).' In *Charlemagne's Heir: New Perspectives on the Reign of Louis the Pious*, edited by Peter Godman and Roger Collins, 191–204. Oxford: Clarendon Press, 1990.

Althoff, Gerd. 'Friendship and Political Order.' In *Friendship in Medieval Europe*, edited by Julian Haseldine, 91–105. Stroud: Sutton, 1999.

Althusser, Louis. 'Ideology and Ideological State Apparatuses: Notes Towards an Investigation.' In *Lenin and Philosophy and Other Essays*, translated by Ben Brewster, 127–86. New York: Monthly Review Press, 1971.

Anderson, Benedict. *Imagined Communities: Reflections on the Origin and Spread of Nationalism*. Revised ed. London: Verso, 1991.

Andersson, Theodore M. 'The Viking Image in Carolingian Poetry.' In *Les relations littéraires franco-scandinaves au moyen âge: Actes du Colloque de Liège*, 217–46. Paris: Les Belles Lettres, 1975.
- 'The Viking Policy of Ethelred the Unready.' *Scandinavian Studies* 59 (1987): 284–95.

Anton, Hans Hubert. *Fürstenspiegel und Herrscherethos in der Karolingerzeit*. Bonn: Ludwig Röhrscheid Verlag, 1968.
- 'Pseudo-Cyprian: *De duodecim abusivis saeculi* und sein Einfluß auf den Kontinent, insbesondere auf die karolingischen Fürstenspiegel.' In *Die Iren und Europa im früheren Mittelalter*, edited by Heinz Löwe, 2:568–617. Stuttgart: Klett-Cotta, 1982.
- 'Gesellschaftsspiegel und Gesellschaftstheorie in Westfranken/Frankreich: Spezifik, Kontinuitäten, und Wandlung.' In *Ius Commune: Veröffentlichungen des Max-Planck-Instituts für Europäische Rechtsgeschichte, Frankfurt am Main*, edited by Angela De Benedictis and Annamaria Pisapia, 51–120. Frankfurt am Main: Vittorio Klostermann, 1999.

Atkins, Ivor. 'The Church of Worcester from the Eighth to the Twelfth Century: Part One.' *Antiquaries Journal* 17 (1937): 371–91.
- 'The Church of Worcester from the Eighth to the Twelfth Century: Part Two.' *Antiquaries Journal* 20 (1940): 1–38, 203–29.

Bailey, Keith. 'The Middle Saxons.' In *The Origins of Anglo-Saxon Kingdoms*, edited by Steven Bassett, 108–22 and 265–69.

Bakhtin, M.M. 'Forms of Time and Chronotope in the Novel.' In *The Dialogic Imagination: Four Essays*, edited by Michael Holquist, translated by Caryl Emerson and Michael Holquist, 84–258. Austin: University of Texas Press, 1981.

Banton, Nicholas. 'Monastic Reform and the Unification of Tenth-Century England.' In *Religion and National Identity: Papers Read at the Nineteenth Summer Meeting and the Twentieth Winter Meeting of the Ecclesiastical History Society*, edited by Stuart Mews, 71–85. Oxford: Blackwell, 1982.

Barlow, Frank. *Edward the Confessor*. Berkeley and Los Angeles: University of California Press, 1970.

– *The English Church 1000–1066: A History of the Later Anglo-Saxon Church*. 2nd ed. London: Longman, 1979.

– *The English Church 1066–1154*. London: Longman, 1979.

– 'The Effects of the Norman Conquest.' In his *The Norman Conquest and Beyond*, 151–87. London: Hambledon Press, 1983.

– 'William I and the Norman Conquest.' In his *The Norman Conquest and Beyond*, 129–50. London: Hambledon Press, 1983.

– 'Domesday Book: An Introduction.' In *Domesday Essays*, edited by Christopher Holdsworth, 17–28. Exeter: University of Exeter Press, 1986.

– *The Feudal Kingdom of England, 1042–1216*. 5th ed. London: Longman, 1999.

– *The Godwins: The Rise and Fall of a Noble Dynasty*. London: Longman, 2002.

Barnett, T. Ratcliffe. *Margaret of Scotland: Queen and Saint, Her Influence on the Early Church in Scotland*. London: Oliver and Boyd, 1926.

Barrow, Julia. 'How the Twelfth-Century Monks of Worcester Perceived their Past.' In *The Perception of the Past*, edited by Paul Magdalino, 53–74. London: Hambledon Press, 1992.

– 'The Community of Worcester, 961–c.1100.' In *St Oswald of Worcester: Life and Influence*, edited by Nicholas Brooks and Catherine Cubitt, 84–99. London: Leicester University Press, 1996.

– 'Friends and Friendship in Anglo-Saxon Charters.' In *Friendship in Medieval Europe*, edited by Julian Haseldine, 106–23. Stroud: Sutton, 1999.

Barthes, Roland. 'The Death of the Author.' In *Image, Music, Text*, translated by Stephen Heath, 142–8. New York: Hill and Wang, 1977.

Bassett, Stephen, ed. *The Origins of Anglo-Saxon Kingdoms*. London: Leicester University Press, 1989.

Bately, Janet. 'King Alfred and the Old English Translation of *Orosius*.' *Anglia* 88 (1970): 433–60.

- 'The Relationship between Geographical Information in the *Old English Orosius* and Latin Texts Other Than *Orosius*.' *Anglo-Saxon England* 1 (1972): 45–62.
- 'The Compilation of the *Anglo-Saxon Chronicle*, 60 B.C. to A.D. 890: Vocabulary as Evidence.' *Proceedings of the British Academy* 64 (1978): 93–129.
- 'World History in the *Anglo-Saxon Chronicle*: Its Sources and its Separateness from the *Old English Orosius*.' *Anglo-Saxon England* 8 (1979): 177–94.
- 'The Literary Prose of King Alfred's Reign: Translation or Transformation?' *Old English Newsletter Subsidia* 10 (1980): 1–26.
- 'The Compilation of the *Anglo-Saxon Chronicle* Once More.' *Leeds Studies in English* n.s. 16 (1985): 7–26.
- 'Manuscript Layout and the *Anglo-Saxon Chronicle*.' *Bulletin of the John Rylands Library* 70 (1988): 21–43.
- 'Old English Prose before and during the Reign of Alfred.' *Anglo-Saxon England* 17 (1988): 93–138.
- *The* Anglo-Saxon Chronicle: *Texts and Textual Relationships*. Reading: University of Reading Press, 1991.

Bates, David. 'Domesday Book, 1086–1986.' In *Domesday Essays*, edited by Christopher Holdsworth, 1–15. Exeter: University of Exeter Press, 1986.
- 'Normandy and England after 1066.' *English Historical Review* 104 (1989): 851–80.
- *William the Conqueror*. London: George Philip, 1989.
- 'The Conqueror's Charters.' In *England in the Eleventh Century: Proceedings of the 1990 Harlaxton Symposium*, edited by Carola Hicks, 1–15. Stamford, CT: Paul Watkins, 1992.

Battaglia, Francis Joseph. '*Anglo-Saxon Chronicle* for 755: The Missing Evidence for a Traditional Reading.' *PMLA* 81 (1966): 173–8.

Baxter, Stephen. 'The Earls of Mercia and Their Commended Men in the Mid-Eleventh Century.' *Anglo-Norman Studies* 23 (2000): 23–46.

Becher, Matthias. *Eid und Herrschaft: Untersuchungen zum Herrscherethos Karls des Großen*. Sigmaringen: Jan Thorbecke Verlag, 1993.

Beckerman, John S. 'Succession in Normandy, 1087, and in England, 1066: The Role of Testamentary Custom.' *Speculum* 47 (1972): 258–60.

Berg, Dieter. '"Regnum Norm-Anglorum" und englisches Königtum: Zur Entwicklung der anglonormannischen Herrschaftsideologie im 11. und 12. Jahrhundert.' In *Historiographia mediaevalis: Studien zur Geschichtsschreibung und Quellenkunde des Mittelalters*, edited by Dieter Berg and Hans-Werner Goetz, 168–80. Darmstadt: Wissenschaftliche Buchgesellschaft, 1988.

Bhabha, Homi K. 'Introduction: Narrating the Nation.' In *Nation and Narration*, edited by Homi K. Bhabha, 1–7. London: Routledge, 1990.
– 'DissemiNation: Time, Narrative and the Margins of the Modern Nation.' In *The Location of Culture*, 139–70. New York: Routledge, 1994.
Biddle, M., H.T. Lambrick, and J.N.L. Myres. 'The Early History of Abingdon, Berkshire, and its Abbey.' *Medieval Archaeology* 12 (1969): 26–69.
Blackburn, Mark A.S. 'The London Mint in the Reign of Alfred.' In *Kings, Currency, and Alliances: History and Coinage of Southern England in the Ninth Century*, edited by Mark A.S. Blackburn and David N. Dumville, 105–23. Woodbridge, Suffolk: Boydell Press, 1998.
Blair, John. 'Frithuwold's Kingdom and the Origins of Surrey.' In *The Origins of Anglo-Saxon Kingdoms*, ed. Bassett, 97–107 and 263–5.
Bouchard, Constance B. 'Family Structure and Family Consciousness among the Aristocracy in the Ninth to Eleventh Centuries.' *Francia* 14 (1986): 639–58.
Bourdieu, Pierre. *Outline of a Theory of Practice*. Translated by Richard Nice. Cambridge: Cambridge University Press, 1977.
Bredehoft, Thomas. *Textual Histories: Readings in the* Anglo-Saxon Chronicle. Toronto: University of Toronto Press, 2001.
Brehe, S.K. 'Reassembling the *First Worcester Fragment*.' *Speculum* 65 (1990): 521–36.
Bremmer, Rolf. 'The Germanic Context of "Cynewulf and Cyneheard" Revisited.' *Neophilologus* 81 (1997): 445–65.
Brett, Martin. 'John of Worcester and his Contemporaries.' In *The Writing of History in the Middle Ages*, edited by R.H.C. Davis and J.M. Wallace-Hadrill, 101–26. Oxford: Clarendon Press, 1981.
Brooks, Nicholas. 'The Development of Military Obligations in Eighth- and Ninth-Century England.' In *England Before the Conquest: Studies in Primary Sources Presented to Dorothy Whitelock*, edited by Peter Clemoes and Kathleen Hughes, 69–84. Cambridge: Cambridge University Press, 1971.
– *The Early History of the Church of Canterbury: Christ Church from 597 to 1066*. London: Leicester University Press, 1984.
– 'The Creation and Early Structure of the Kingdom of Kent.' In *The Origins of Anglo-Saxon Kingdoms*, edited by Steven Bassett, 55–74 and 250–4.
– 'The Formation of the Mercian Kingdom.' In *The Origins of Anglo-Saxon Kingdoms*, ed. Bassett, 159–70 and 275–7.
Bührer-Thierry, Geneviève. '"Just Anger" or "Vengeful Anger"? The Punishment of Blinding in the Early Medieval West.' In *Anger's Past: The Social Uses of an Emotion in the Middle Ages*, edited by Barbara H. Rosenwein, 75–91. Ithaca, NY: Cornell University Press, 1998.

Bullough, Donald A. 'The Continental Background of the Reform.' In *Tenth-Century Studies: Essays in Commemoration of the Millennium of the Council of Winchester and* Regularis Concordia, edited by David Parsons, 20–36 and 210–14. London: Phillimore, 1975.

Burton, Janet. *Monastic and Religious Orders in Britain, 1000–1300*. Cambridge: Cambridge University Press, 1994.

Butler, Judith. *Gender Trouble: Feminism and the Subversion of Identity.* New York: Routledge, 1990.

– *Excitable Speech: A Politics of the Performative*. New York: Routledge, 1997.

Campbell, James. 'Observations on English Government from the Tenth to the Twelfth Century.' *Transactions of the Royal Historical Society* 5th series, 25 (1975): 39–54.

– 'Bede's *reges* and *principes*.' In his *Essays in Anglo-Saxon History*, 85–98.

– 'England, France, Flanders, Germany in the Reign of Ethelred II: Some Comparisons and Connections.' In his *Essays in Anglo-Saxon History*, 191–207.

– 'Some Twelfth-Century Views of the Anglo-Saxon Past.' In his *Essays in Anglo-Saxon History*, 209–28.

– 'Asser's *Life of Alfred*.' In *The Inheritance of Historiography, 350–900*, edited by Christopher Holdsworth and T.P. Wiseman, 115–35. Exeter: University of Exeter Press, 1986.

Campbell, James, ed. *Essays in Anglo-Saxon History.* London: Hambledon Press, 1986.

Campbell, Miles W. 'A Pre-Conquest Norman Occupation of England?' *Speculum* 46 (1971): 21–31.

– 'Earl Godwin of Wessex and Edward the Confessor's Promise of the Throne to William of Normandy.' *Traditio* 28 (1972): 141–58.

– 'Note sur les déplacements de Tostig Godwinson en 1066.' *Annales de Normandie* 22 (1972): 3–9.

– 'The Anti-Norman Reaction in England in 1052: Suggested Origins.' *Mediaeval Studies* 38 (1976): 428–41.

– 'The Rise of an Anglo-Saxon "Kingmaker": Earl Godwin of Wessex.' *Canadian Journal of History* 13 (1978): 17–33.

Carver, Martin. 'Kingship and Material Culture in Early Anglo-Saxon East Anglia.' In *The Origins of Anglo-Saxon Kingdoms*, ed. Bassett, 141–58 and 270–5.

Charles-Edwards, Thomas. 'Alliances, Godfathers, Treaties and Boundaries.' In *Kings, Currency, and Alliances: History and Coinage of Southern England in the Ninth Century,* edited by Mark A.S. Blackburn and David N. Dumville, 47–62. Woodbridge, Suffolk: Boydell Press, 1998.

Chibnall, Marjorie. 'Forgery in Narrative Charters.' In *Fälschungen im Mittelalter: Internationaler Kongreß der Monumenta Germaniae Historica, München, 16th–19th September 1986*, edited by Horst Fuhrmann, 4:331–46. Hanover: Hahnsche Buchhandlung, 1988.
- 'Anglo-French Relations in the Work of Orderic Vitalis.' In *Documenting the Past: Essays in Medieval History Presented to George Peddy Cuttino*, edited by J.S. Hamilton and Patricia J. Bradley, 5–19. Woodbridge, Suffolk: Boydell Press, 1989.
- *The Debate on the Norman Conquest*. New York: St Martin's Press, 1999.
Clanchy, M.T. *From Memory to Written Record: England, 1066–1307*. 2nd ed. Oxford: Blackwell, 1993.
Clark, Cecily. 'The Narrative Mode of *The Anglo-Saxon Chronicle* Before the Conquest.' In *England Before the Conquest: Studies in Primary Sources Presented to Dorothy Whitelock*, edited by Peter Clemoes and Kathleen Hughes, 215–35. Cambridge: Cambridge University Press, 1971.
Clarke, Peter A. *The English Nobility under Edward the Confessor*. Oxford: Clarendon Press, 1994.
Clemoes, Peter. 'Language in Context: *Her* in the 890 *Anglo-Saxon Chronicle*.' *Leeds Studies in English* n.s. 16 (1985): 27–36.
- 'Loyalty as a Responsibility of the Individual.' In *Interactions of Thought and Language in Old English Poetry*, 409–37. Cambridge: Cambridge University Press, 1995.
Coates, Simon. 'Perceptions of the Anglo-Saxon Past in the Tenth-Century Mo-nastic Reform Movement.' In *The Church Retrospective: Papers Read at the 1995 Summer Meeting and the 1996 Winter Meeting of the Ecclesiastical History Society*, edited by R.N. Swanson, 61–74. Woodbridge, Suffolk: Boydell Press, 1997.
Coleman, Janet. *Ancient and Medieval Memories: Studies in the Reconstruction of the Past*. Cambridge: Cambridge University Press, 1992.
Coupland, Simon. 'The Rod of God's Wrath or the People of God's Wrath: The Carolingian Theology of the Viking Invasions.' *Journal of Ecclesiastical History* 42 (1991): 535–54.
Cownie, Emma. *Religious Patronage in Anglo-Norman England, 1066–1135*. Bury St Edmonds, Suffolk: St Edmundsbury Press, 1998.
Cross, James E. 'The Ethic of War in Old English.' In *England Before the Conquest: Studies in Primary Sources Presented to Dorothy Whitelock*, edited by Peter Clemoes and Kathleen Hughes, 269–82. Cambridge: Cambridge University Press, 1971.
Cunliffe, Barry. *Wessex to A.D. 1000*. London: Longman, 1993.

Curtius, Ernst Robert. *European Literature and the Latin Middle Ages*. Translated by William Trask. London: Routledge and Kegan Paul, 1953.
Cutler, Kenneth E. 'The Godwinist Hostages: The Case for 1051.' *Annuale Mediaevale* 12 (1971): 70–7.
Dalton, Paul. *Conquest, Anarchy, and Lordship: Yorkshire 1066–1154*. Cambridge: Cambridge University Press, 1994.
Damon, John Edward. 'Advisors for Peace in the Reign of Æthelred Unræd.' In *Peace and Negotiation: Strategies for Coexistence in the Middle Ages and the Renaissance*, edited by Diane Wolfthal, 57–78. Turnhout: Brepols, 2000.
– '*Wadan Wræclastas*: Bede, Cædwalla of Wessex, and the Exile's Path to Kingship' (forthcoming).
Darlington, R.R. 'Æthelwig, Abbot of Evesham, Part I.' *English Historical Review* 48 (1933): 1–22.
– 'Æthelwig, Abbot of Evesham, Part II.' *English Historical Review* 48 (1933): 177–98.
Davies, Wendy. 'St. Mary's Worcester and the *Liber Landavensis*.' *Journal of the Society of Archivists* 4 (1972): 459–85.
Davis, Craig R. 'Cultural Assimilation in the Anglo-Saxon Royal Genealogies.' *Anglo-Saxon England* 21 (1992): 23–36.
Davis, Kathleen. 'National Writing in the Ninth Century: A Reminder for Postcolonial Thinking about the Nation.' *Journal of Medieval and Early Modern Studies* 28 (1998): 611–37.
Davis, R.H.C. 'The Norman Conquest.' *History* 51 (1966): 279–86.
– 'Alfred the Great: Propaganda and Truth.' *History* 56 (1971): 169–82.
– 'The *Carmen de Hastingae Proelio*.' *English Historical Review* 93 (1978): 241–61.
– 'William of Poitiers and His History of William the Conqueror.' In *The Writing of History in the Middle Ages*, edited by R.H.C. Davis and J.M. Wallace-Hadrill, 71–100. Oxford: Clarendon Press, 1981.
– 'Alfred and Guthrum's Frontier.' *English Historical Review* 97 (1982): 803–10.
– 'Domesday Book: Continental Parallels.' In *Domesday Studies: Papers Read at the Novocentenary Conference of the Royal Historical Society and the Institute of British Geographers, Winchester, 1986*, edited by J.C. Holt, 15–39. Woodbridge, Suffolk: Boydell Press, 1987.
Dawtry, Anne. 'The Benedictine Revival in the North: The Last Bulwark of Anglo-Saxon Monasticism?' In *Religion and National Identity: Papers Read at the Nineteenth Summer Meeting and the Twentieth Winter Meeting of the Ecclesiastical History Society*, edited by Stuart Mews, 87–98. Oxford: Blackwell, 1982.
de Certeau, Michel. *The Practice of Everyday Life*. Translated by Steven Rendall. Berkeley and Los Angeles: University of California Press, 1984.

- *The Writing of History.* Translated by Tom Conley. New York: Columbia University Press, 1988.
Deshman, Robert. '*Christus rex et magi reges:* Kingship and Christology in Ottonian and Anglo-Saxon Art.' *Frühmittelalterliche Studien* 10 (1976): 367–405.
Devisse, J. 'Essai sur l'histoire d'une expression qui a fait fortune: *consilium et auxilium* au IXe siècle.' *Le moyen âge* 74 (1968): 179–205.
DeVries, Kelly. *The Norwegian Invasion of England in 1066*. Woodbridge, Suffolk: Boydell Press, 1999.
Douglas, David C. *William the Conqueror: The Norman Impact upon England*. Berkeley and Los Angeles: University of California Press, 1964.
Duby, Georges. *The Three Orders: Feudal Society Imagined*. Translated by Arthur Goldhammer. Chicago: University of Chicago Press, 1980.
Dumville, David N. 'The Anglian Collection of Royal Genealogies and Regnal Lists.' *Anglo-Saxon England* 5 (1976): 23–50.
- 'Kingship, Genealogy, and Regnal Lists.' In *Early Medieval Kingship*, edited by P.H. Sawyer and Ian N. Wood, 72–104. Leeds: University of Leeds Press, 1977.
- 'The *Ætheling*: A Study in Anglo-Saxon Constitutional History.' *Anglo-Saxon England* 8 (1979): 1–33.
- 'Some Aspects of Annalistic Writing at Canterbury in the Eleventh and Early Twelfth Centuries.' *Peritia* 2 (1983): 23–57.
- 'The West Saxon Genealogical Regnal List and the Chronology of Early Wessex.' *Peritia* 4 (1985): 21–66.
- 'The West Saxon Genealogical Regnal List: Manuscripts and Texts.' *Anglia* 104 (1986): 1–32.
- 'English Square Minuscule Script: The Background and Earliest Phases.' *Anglo-Saxon England* 16 (1987): 147–79.
- 'Essex, Middle Anglia, and the Expansion of Mercia in the South-East Midlands.' In *The Origins of Anglo-Saxon Kingdoms*, ed. Bassett, 123–40 and 270.
- 'The Origins of Northumbria: Some Aspects of the British Background.' In *The Origins of Anglo-Saxon Kingdoms*, ed. Bassett, 213–22 and 284–6.
- 'The Treaty of Alfred and Guthrum.' In *Wessex and England from Alfred to Edgar*, 1–27.
- 'The *Anglo-Saxon Chronicle* and the Origins of English Square Minuscule Script.' In *Wessex and England from Alfred to Edgar*, 55–139.
- 'King Alfred and the Tenth-Century Reform of the English Church.' In *Wessex and England from Alfred to Edgar*, 185–205.

- *Wessex and England from Alfred to Edgar: Six Essays on Political, Cultural, and Ecclesiastical Revival.* Woodbridge, Suffolk: Boydell Press, 1992.
- 'English Square Minuscule Script: The Mid-Century Phases.' *Anglo-Saxon England* 23 (1994): 133–64.
- 'The Terminology of Overkingship in Early Anglo-Saxon England.' In *The Anglo-Saxons from the Migration Period to the Eighth Century: An Ethnographic Perspective*, edited by John Hines, 345–73. Woodbridge, Suffolk: Boydell Press, 1997.

Dunbabin, Jean. 'Discovering a Past for the French Aristocracy.' In *The Perception of the Past in Twelfth Century Europe*, edited by Paul Magdalino, 1–14. London: Hambledon Press, 1992.

Eberhardt, Otto. *Via regia: Der Fürstenspiegel Smaragds von St. Mihiel und seine literarische Gattung.* Munich: Wilhelm Fink, 1977.

Edelstein, Wolfgang. *Eruditio und sapientia: Erziehung und Weltbild in der Karolingerzeit. Untersuchungen zu Alcuins Briefen.* Freiburg im Breisgau: Verlag Rombach, 1965.

Elias, Norbert. 'State Formation and Civilization.' In *The Civilizing Process*, translated by Edmund Jephcott, 257–524. Oxford: Blackwell, 1994.

Emms, Richard. 'The Historical Traditions of St. Augustine's Abbey, Canterbury.' In *Canterbury and the Norman Conquest: Churches, Saints, and Scholars, 1066–1109*, edited by Richard Eales and Richard Sharpe, 159–68. London: Hambledon Press, 1995.

Enright, Michael J. 'Charles the Bald and Aethelwulf of Wessex: The Alliance of 856 and Strategies of Royal Succession.' *Journal of Medieval History* 5 (1979): 291–302.

Fanning, Steven. 'Bede, *Imperium*, and the Bretwaldas.' *Speculum* 66 (1991): 1–26.

Fell, Christine E. 'Edward King and Martyr and the Anglo-Saxon Hagiographic Tradition.' In *Ethelred the Unready*, ed. Hill, 1–13.

Ferro, Karen. 'The King in the Doorway: The *Anglo-Saxon Chronicle*, A.D. 755.' *Kings and Kingship, Acta* 11 (1986): 17–30.

Fisher, D.J.V. 'The Anti-Monastic Reaction in the Reign of Edward the Martyr.' *Cambridge Historical Journal* 10 (1950–2): 254–70.

- 'The Church in England between the Death of Bede and the Danish Invasions.' *Transactions of the Royal Historical Society* 5th series, 2 (1952): 1–19.

Fleischman, Suzanne. 'On the Representation of History and Fiction in the Middle Ages.' *History and Theory* 22 (1983): 278–310.

Fleming, Robin. *Kings and Lords in Conquest England.* Cambridge: Cambridge University Press, 1991.

- 'Rural Elites and Urban Communities in Late-Saxon England.' *Past and Present* 141 (1993): 3–37.
- 'Oral Testimony and the Domesday Inquest.' *Anglo-Norman Studies* 17 (1994): 101–22.
- *Domesday Book and the Law: Society and Legal Custom in Early Medieval England*. Cambridge: Cambridge University Press, 1998.

Foot, Sarah. 'The Making of *Angelcynn*: English Identity before the Norman Conquest.' *Transactions of the Royal Historical Society* 6th series, 6 (1996): 25–49.
- 'Remembering, Forgetting and Inventing: Attitudes to the Past in England at the End of the First Viking Age.' *Transactions of the Royal Historical Society* 6th series, 9 (1999): 185–200.

Foreville, Raymonde. 'Le sacre des rois anglo-normands et angevins et le serment du sacre (XIe–XIIe siècles).' *Anglo-Norman Studies* 1 (1978): 49–62 and 202–7.

Foucault, Michel. 'What Is an Author?' In *Language, Counter-Memory, Practice*, edited by Donald F. Bouchard, translated by Donald F. Bouchard and Sherry Simon, 113–38. Ithaca, NY: Cornell University Press, 1977.

Frame, Robin. *The Political Development of the British Isles, 1100–1400*. Oxford: Oxford University Press, 1990.

Frank, Roberta. 'The Ideal of Men Dying with Their Lord in *The Battle of Maldon*: Anachronism or *Nouvelle Vague*.' In *People and Places in Northern Europe, 500–1600*, edited by Ian Wood and Niels Lund, 95–106. Woodbridge, Suffolk: Boydell Press, 1991.
- '*The Battle of Maldon*: Its Reception, 1726–1906.' In *Heroic Poetry in the Anglo-Saxon Period: Studies in Honor of Jess B. Bessinger, Jr*, edited by Helen Damico and John Leyerle, 29–46. Kalamazoo, MI: Medieval Institute Publications, Western Michigan University, 1993.

Frantzen, Allen J. 'Bede and Bawdy Bale: Gregory the Great, Angels, and the *Angli*.' In *Anglo-Saxonism and the Construction of Social Identity*, edited by Allen J. Frantzen and John D. Niles, 17–39. Gainesville: University Press of Florida, 1997.

Galbraith, V.H. 'Who Wrote Asser's *Life of Alfred*?' In *An Introduction to the Study of History*, 88–128. London: C.A. Watts, 1964.

Galloway, Andrew. 'Writing History in England.' In *The Cambridge History of Medieval English Literature*, edited by David Wallace, 255–83. Cambridge: Cambridge University Press, 1999.

Gameson, Richard. 'Book Production and Decoration at Worcester in the Tenth and Eleventh Centuries.' In *St Oswald of Worcester: Life and Influence*, edited by Nicholas Brooks and Catherine Cubitt, 194–243. London: Leicester University Press, 1996.

Garnett, George. '"Franci et Angli": The Legal Distinctions between Peoples after the Conquest.' *Anglo-Norman Studies* 8 (1985): 109–37.
- 'Coronation and Propaganda: Some Implications of the Norman Claim to the Throne of England in 1066.' *Transactions of the Royal Historical Society* 5th series, 36 (1986): 91–116.
- 'The Origins of the Crown.' *Proceedings of the British Academy* 89 (1996): 171–214.

Garrison, Mary. 'Letters to a King and Biblical Exempla: The Examples of Cathuulf and Clemens Peregrinus.' *Early Medieval Europe* 7 (1998): 305–28.

Geary, Patrick. *The Myth of Nations: The Medieval Origins of Europe.* Princeton, NJ: Princeton University Press, 2001.

Gerchow, Jan. 'Prayers for King Cnut: The Liturgical Commemoration of a Conqueror.' In *England in the Eleventh Century: Proceedings of the 1990 Harlaxton Symposium,* edited by Carola Hicks, 219–38. Stamford, CT: Paul Watkins, 1992.

Gillingham, John. '"The Most Precious Jewel in the English Crown": Levels of Danegeld and Heregeld in the Early Eleventh Century.' *English Historical Review* 104 (1989): 373–84.
- 'Chronicles and Coins as Evidence for Levels of Tribute and Taxation in Late Tenth- and Early Eleventh-Century England.' *English Historical Review* 105 (1990): 939–50.
- 'The Context and Purposes of Geoffrey of Monmouth's *History of the Kings of Britain.*' *Anglo-Norman Studies* 13 (1990): 99–118.
- 'Conquering the Barbarians: War and Chivalry in Twelfth-Century Britain.' *Haskins Society Journal* 4 (1992): 67–84.
- '1066 and the Introduction of Chivalry into England.' In *Law and Government in Medieval England and Normandy: Essays in Honour of Sir James Holt,* edited by George Garnett and John Hudson, 31–55. Cambridge: Cambridge University Press, 1994.
- 'Thegns and Knights in Eleventh-Century England: Who Was Then the Gentleman?' *Transactions of the Royal Historical Society* 6th series, 5 (1995): 129–53.
- 'The Beginnings of English Imperialism.' In his *The English in the Twelfth Century,* 3–18.
- *The English in the Twelfth Century: Imperialism, National Identity, and Political Values.* Woodbridge, Suffolk: Boydell Press, 2000.
- 'The Foundations of a Disunited Kingdom.' In his *The English in the Twelfth Century,* 93–109.
- 'Henry of Huntingdon and the Twelfth-Century Revival of the English Nation.' In his *The English in the Twelfth Century,* 123–44.

Godden, Malcolm. 'Ælfric and Anglo-Saxon Kingship.' *English Historical Review* 102 (1987): 911–15.
- 'Apocalypse and Invasion in Late Anglo-Saxon England.' In *From Anglo-Saxon to Early Middle English*, edited by Malcolm Godden, Douglas Gray, and Terry Hoad, 130–62. Oxford: Clarendon Press, 1994.

Goetz, Hans-Werner. '"Beatus homo qui invenit amicum." The Concept of Friendship in Early Medieval Letters of the Anglo-Saxon Tradition on the Continent (Boniface, Alcuin).' In *Friendship in Medieval Europe*, edited by Julian Haseldine, 124–36. Stroud: Sutton, 1999.

Goez, Werner. *Translatio imperii: Ein Beitrag zur Geschichte des Geschichtdenkens und der politischen Theorien im Mittelalter und in der frühen Neuzeit*. Tübingen: J.C.B. Mohr (Paul Siebeck), 1958.

Goffart, Walter. *The Narrators of Barbarian History (A.D. 550–800): Jordanes, Gregory of Tours, Bede, and Paul the Deacon*. Princeton, NJ: Princeton University Press, 1988.

Gransden, Antonia. 'Traditionalism and Continuity during the Last Century of Anglo-Saxon Monasticism.' *Journal of Ecclesiastical History* 40 (1989): 159–207.
- 'Prologues in the Historiography of Twelfth-Century England.' In *England in the Twelfth Century: Proceedings of the 1988 Harlaxton Symposium*, edited by Daniel Williams, 55–81. Woodbridge, Suffolk: Boydell and Brewer, 1990.

Green, D.H. *The Carolingian Lord: Semantic Studies on Four Old High German Words: balder, frô, truhtin, hêrro*. Cambridge: Cambridge University Press, 1965.
- 'Lordship.' In *Language and History in the Early Germanic World*, 102–20. Cambridge: Cambridge University Press, 1998.

Green, Judith. 'Aristocratic Loyalties on the Northern Frontier of England, c. 1100–1174.' In *England in the Twelfth Century: Proceedings of the 1988 Harlaxton Symposium*, edited by Daniel Williams, 83–100. Woodbridge, Suffolk: Boydell Press, 1990.
- *The Aristocracy of Norman England*. Cambridge: University of Cambridge Press, 1997.

Hadley, Dawn. M. '"And They Proceeded to Plough and to Support Themselves": The Scandinavian Settlement of England.' *Anglo-Norman Studies* 19 (1996): 69–96.
- '"Cockles Amongst the Wheat": The Scandinavian Settlement of England.' In *Social Identity in Early Medieval Britian*, edited by William O. Frazer and Andrew Tyrrell, 111–35. London: Leicester University Press, 2000.
- '"Hamlet and the Princes of Denmark": Lordship in the Danelaw, c. 860–954.' In *Cultures in Contact: Scandinavian Settlement in England in the Ninth and*

Tenth Centuries, edited by Dawn M. Hadley and Julian D. Richards, 107–32. Turnhout: Brepols, 2000.
– *The Northern Danelaw: Its Social Structure, c. 800–1100*. London: Leicester University Press, 2000.
Halphen, Louis. *Charlemagne and the Carolingian Empire*. Translated by Giselle de Nie. Amsterdam: North-Holland Publishing, 1977.
Hannig, Jürgen. *Consensus fidelium: Frühfeudale Interpretationen des Verhältnisses von Königtum und Adel am Beispiel des Frankenreiches*. Stuttgart: Anton Hiersemann, 1982.
Hanning, Robert W. *The Vision of History in Early Britain: From Gildas to Geoffrey of Monmouth*. New York: Columbia University Press, 1966.
Harris, Joseph. 'Love and Death in the *Männerbund*: An Essay with Special Reference to the *Bjarkamál* and *The Battle of Maldon*.' In *Heroic Poetry in the Anglo-Saxon Period: Studies in Honor of Jess B. Bessinger, Jr*, edited by Helen Damico and John Leyerle, 77–114. Kalamazoo, MI: Medieval Institute Publications, Western Michigan University, 1993.
Hart, Cyril. 'Byrhtferth and his Manual.' *Medium Ævum* 41 (1972): 95–109.
– 'The East Anglian Chronicle.' *Journal of Medieval History* 7 (1981): 249–82.
– 'The B Text of the *Anglo-Saxon Chronicle*.' *Journal of Medieval History* 8 (1982): 241–99.
– 'Byrhtferth's Northumbrian Chronicle.' *English Historical Review* 97 (1982): 558–82.
– 'The Early Section of the *Worcester Chronicle*.' *Journal of Medieval History* 9 (1983): 251–315.
– *The Danelaw*. London: Hambledon Press, 1992.
Harvey, Sally P.J. 'Domesday Book and Anglo-Norman Governance.' *Transactions of the Royal Historical Society* 5th series, 25 (1975): 175–93.
Hastings, Adrian. *The Construction of Nationhood: Ethnicity, Religion and Nationalism*. Cambridge: Cambridge University Press, 1997.
Higham, N.J. 'The Domesday Survey: Context and Purpose.' *History* 78 (1993): 7–21.
Hill, David, ed. *Ethelred the Unready: Papers from the Millenary Conference*. British Archaeological Reports, British Series 59. Oxford: British Archaeological Reports, 1978.
Hill, David, and Alexander R. Rumble, eds. *The Defence of Wessex: The Burghal Hidage and Anglo-Saxon Fortifications*. Manchester: Manchester University Press, 1996.
Hill, Joyce. 'Monastic Reform and the Secular Church: Ælfric's Pastoral Letters in Context.' In *England in the Eleventh Century: Proceedings of the 1990 Harlax-*

ton Symposium, edited by Carola Hicks, 103-17. Stamford, CT: Paul Watkins, 1992.
- *Bede and the Benedictine Reform*. Jarrow: St Paul's Church, 1999.

Hill, John M. *The Cultural World in Beowulf*. Toronto: University of Toronto Press, 1995.
- *The Anglo-Saxon Warrior Ethic*. Gainesville: University Press of Florida, 2000.

Hill, Thomas D. 'The Myth of the Ark-Born Son of Noe and the West-Saxon Royal Genealogical Tables.' *Harvard Theological Review* 80 (1987): 379-83.
- 'Woden as "Ninth Father": Numerical Patterning in Some Old English Royal Genealogies.' In *Germania: Comparative Studies in the Old Germanic Languages and Literatures*, edited by Daniel G. Calder and T. Craig Christy, 161-74. Wolfeboro, NH: D.S. Brewer, 1988.
- 'The *Liber Eliensis* "Historical Selections" and the Old English *Battle of Maldon*.' *Journal of English and Germanic Philology* 96 (1997): 1-12.
- '"When the Leader is Brave ...": An Old English Proverb and Its Vernacular Context.' *Anglia* 119 (2001): 232-6.

Holdsworth, Christopher. 'Peacemaking in the Twelfth Century.' *Anglo-Norman Studies* 19 (1996): 1-17.

Hollister, C. Warren. *Anglo-Saxon Military Institutions: On the Eve of the Norman Conquest*. Oxford: Clarendon Press, 1962.
- 'Normandy, France and the Anglo-Norman *regnum*.' *Speculum* 51 (1976): 202-42.

Holt, J.C. 'Feudal Society and the Family in Early Medieval England: II, Notions of Patrimony.' *Transactions of the Royal Historical Society* 5th series, 33 (1983): 193-220.
- '1086.' In *Domesday Studies: Papers Read at the Novocentenary Conference of the Royal Historical Society and the Institute of British Geographers, Winchester, 1986*, edited by J.C. Holt, 41-64. Woodbridge, Suffolk: Boydell Press, 1987.

Hooper, Nicholas. 'Edgar the Ætheling: Anglo-Saxon Prince, Rebel, and Crusader.' *Anglo-Saxon England* 14 (1985): 197-214.

Howe, Nicholas. *Migration and Mythmaking in Anglo-Saxon England*. New Haven: Yale University Press, 1989.

Hudson, Benjamin T. 'The Family of Harold Godwinsson and the Irish Sea Province.' *Journal of the Royal Society of Antiquaries of Ireland* 109 (1979): 92-100.
- 'Cnut and the Scottish Kings.' *English Historical Review* 107 (1992): 350-60.

Hudson, John. 'Administration, Family, and Perceptions of the Past in Late Twelfth-Century England: Richard FitzNigel and the Dialogue of the Exche-

quer.' In *The Perception of the Past in Twelfth-Century Europe*, edited by Paul Magdalino, 74–98. London: Hambledon Press, 1992.
- *Land, Law, and Lordship in Anglo-Norman England*. Oxford: Clarendon Press, 1994.
- 'The Abbey of Abingdon, Its *Chronicle* and the Norman Conquest.' *Anglo-Norman Studies* 19 (1996): 181–202.
- *The Formation of the English Common Law: Law and Society in England from the Norman Conquest to Magna Carta*. London: Longman, 1996.

Huneycutt, Lois L. 'The Idea of the Perfect Princess: The *Life of St. Margaret* in the Reign of Matilda II (1100–1118).' *Anglo-Norman Studies* 12 (1989): 81–97.

Hunter, Michael. 'Germanic and Roman Antiquity and the Sense of the Past in Anglo-Saxon England.' *Anglo-Saxon England* 3 (1974): 29–50.

Hyams, Paul. 'Feud and the State in Late Anglo-Saxon England.' *Journal of British Studies* 40 (2001): 1–43.
- 'Homage and Feudalism: A Judicious Separation.' In *Die Gegenwart des Feudalismus*, edited by Natalie Fryde, Pierre Monet, and Otto Gerhard Oexle, 13–49. Göttingen: Vandenhoeck and Ruprecht, 2002.
- 'Approaches to the Understanding of Feud and Friendship.' In *Rancor and Reconciliation: Wrong and Its Redress from the Tenth to the Thirteenth Centuries*. Ithaca, NY: Cornell University Press, forthcoming.

Ingledew, Francis. 'The Book of Troy and the Genealogical Construction of History: The Case of Geoffrey of Monmouth's *Historia regum Britanniae*.' *Speculum* 69 (1994): 665–704.

Innes, Matthew. 'Danelaw Identities: Ethnicity, Regionalism, and Political Allegiance.' In *Cultures in Contact: Scandinavian Settlement in England in the Ninth and Tenth Centuries*, edited by Dawn M. Hadley and Julian D. Richards, 65–88. Turnhout: Brepols, 2000.

Jauss, Hans Robert. 'Literary History as a Challenge to Literary Theory.' In *Towards an Aesthetic of Reception*, translated by Timothy Bahti, 3–45. Minneapolis: University of Minnesota Press, 1982.

Johansen, John G. 'Language, Structure, and Theme in the "Cynewulf and Cyneheard" Episode.' *English Language Notes* 31 (1993): 3–7.

John, Eric. *Orbis Britanniae and Other Studies*. Leicester: Leicester University Press, 1966.
- 'War and Society in the Tenth Century: The Maldon Campaign.' *Transactions of the Royal Historical Society* 5th series, 27 (1977): 173–91.
- 'Edward the Confessor and the Norman Succession.' *English Historical Review* 94 (1979): 241–67.
- 'The *Encomium Emmae Reginae*: A Riddle and a Solution.' *Bulletin of the John Rylands Library* 63 (1980): 58–94.

- 'The World of Abbot Ælfric.' In *Ideal and Reality in Frankish and Anglo-Saxon Society*, edited by Patrick Wormald, Donald Bullough, and Roger Collins, 300–16. Oxford: Blackwell, 1983.
- *Reassessing Anglo-Saxon England*. Manchester: Manchester University Press, 1996.

Jones, A.E.E. *Anglo-Saxon Worcester*. Worcester: Ebenezer Baylis and Son, 1958.

Jones, Charles W. 'The Setting.' In *Saints' Lives and Chronicles in Early England*. 2–15. Ithaca, NY: Cornell University Press, 1947.

Kantorowicz, Ernst H. *The King's Two Bodies: A Study in Mediaeval Political Theology*. Princeton, NJ: Princeton University Press, 1957.

Kapelle, William E. *The Norman Conquest of the North: The Region and Its Transformation, 1000–1135*. Chapel Hill: University of North Carolina Press, 1979.

Keller, Wolfgang. *Die litterarischen Bestrebungen von Worcester in angelsächsischer Zeit*. Strasbourg: Trübner, 1900.

Kennedy, A.G. 'Cnut's Law Code of 1018.' *Anglo-Saxon England* 11 (1983): 57–81.

Ker, N.R. *A Catalogue of Manuscripts Containing Anglo-Saxon*. Revised ed. Oxford: Clarendon Press, 1990.

Kershaw, Paul. 'The Alfred-Guthrum Treaty: Scripting Accommodation and Interaction in Viking Age England.' In *Cultures in Contact: Scandinavian Settlement in England in the Ninth and Tenth Centuries*, edited by Dawn M. Hadley and Julian D. Richards, 43–64. Turnhout: Brepols, 2000.

Keynes, Simon. 'The Declining Reputation of King Æthelred the Unready.' In *Ethelred the Unready*, ed. Hill, 227–53.
- *The Diplomas of King Æthelred 'the Unready,' 978–1016: A Study in their Use as Historical Evidence*. Cambridge: Cambridge University Press, 1980.
- 'The Additions in Old English.' In *The York Gospels: A Facsimile*, edited by N. Barker, 81–99. London: Roxburghe Club, 1986.
- 'A Tale of Two Kings: Alfred the Great and Æthelred the Unready.' *Transactions of the Royal Historical Society* 5th series, 36 (1986): 195–217.
- 'The Æthelings in Normandy.' *Anglo-Norman Studies* 13 (1990): 173–205.
- 'Crime and Punishment in the Reign of King Æthelred the Unready.' In *People and Places in Northern Europe, 500–1600: Essays in Honour of Peter Hayes Sawyer*, edited by Ian Wood and Niels Lund, 67–81. Woodbridge, Suffolk: Boydell Press, 1991.
- 'The Historical Context of the Battle of Maldon.' In *The Battle of Maldon, AD 991*, edited by D.G. Scragg, 81–113. Oxford: Blackwell, 1991.
- 'Rædwald the Bretwalda.' In *Voyage to the Other World: The Legacy of Sutton Hoo*, edited by Calvin B. Kendall and Peter S. Wells, 103–23. Minneapolis: University of Minnesota Press, 1992.

- 'Cnut's Earls.' In *The Reign of Cnut: King of England, Denmark, and Norway*, edited by Alexander R. Rumble, 43–88. London: Leicester University Press, 1994.
- 'On the Authenticity of Asser's *Life of King Alfred*.' *Journal of Ecclesiastical History* 47 (1996): 529–51.
- 'King Alfred and the Mercians.' In *Kings, Currency, and Alliances: History and Coinage of Southern England in the Ninth Century*, edited by Mark A.S. Blackburn and David N. Dumville, 1–45. Woodbridge, Suffolk: Boydell Press, 1998.
- 'The Cult of King Alfred the Great.' *Anglo-Saxon England* 28 (1999): 225–356.

King, Edward. *Peterborough Abbey, 1086–1310: A Study in the Land Market*. Cambridge: Cambridge University Press, 1973.

King, Vanessa. 'Ealdred, Archbishop of York: The Worcester Years.' *Anglo-Norman Studies* 18 (1995): 123–37.

Kleinschmidt, Harald. 'Die Titularen englischer Könige im 10. und 11. Jahrhundert.' In *Intitulatio III: Lateinische Herrschertitel und Herrschertitularen vom 7 bis zum 13 Jahrhundert*, edited by Herwig Wolfram and Anton Scharer, 75–129. Mitteilungen des Instituts für Österreichische Geschichtsforschung. Supplementary volume 29. Cologne: Böhlau Verlag, 1988.
- '*Nomen* and *gens*: The Germanic Settlement in Britain and the Genesis of the English.' *Archives: Journal of the British Records Association* 26 (2001): 97–111.
- 'What does the *Anglo-Saxon Chronicle* Tell Us about "Ethnic" Origins?' *Studi Medievali* 3rd series, 42 (2001): 1–40.

Knowles, David. *The Monastic Order in England: A History of its Development from the Times of St. Dunstan to the Fourth Lateran Council, 940–1216*. 2nd ed. Cambridge: Cambridge University Press, 1963.

Lacroix, Benoit. *Orose et ses idées*. Montréal: Institut d'Études Médiévales and Librairie Philosophique; Paris: J. Vrin, 1965.

Lapidge, Michael. 'Ealdred of York and MS Cotton Vitellius E. XII.' *The Yorkshire Archaeological Journal* 55 (1983): 11–26.
- 'Byrhtferth of Ramsey and the Early Sections of the *Historia regum* attributed to Symeon of Durham.' In *Anglo-Latin Literature, 900–1066*, 317–42. London: Hambledon Press, 1993.
- 'Æthelwold as Scholar and Teacher.' In *Bishop Æthelwold: His Career and Influence*, edited by Barbara Yorke, 89–117. Woodbridge, Suffolk: Boydell Press, 1997.

Lapidge, Michael, and R. Love. 'England and Wales (600–1550).' In *Hagiographies: Histoire internationale de la littérature hagiographique latine et vernaculaire en Occident des origines à 1550*, edited by Guy Philippart, vol. 3, 203–325. Turnhout: Brepols, 1994.

Larson, Laurence M. 'The Political Policies of Cnut as King of England.' *The American Historical Review* 15 (1910): 720–43.

Lavelle, Ryan. 'Towards a Political Contextualization of Peacemaking and Peace Agreements in Anglo-Saxon England.' In *Peace and Negotiation: Strategies for Coexistence in the Middle Ages and the Renaissance*, edited by Diane Wolfthal, 39–55. Turnhout: Brepols, 2000.

Lavezzo, Kathy. 'Another Country: Ælfric and the Production of English Identity.' *New Medieval Literatures* 3 (1999): 67–93.

Lawson, M.K. 'The Collection of Danegeld and Heregeld in the Reigns of Æthelred II and Cnut.' *English Historical Review* 99 (1984): 721–38.

– '"Those Stories Look True": Levels of Taxation in the Reigns of Æthelred II and Cnut.' *English Historical Review* 104 (1989): 385–406.

– 'Danegeld and Heregeld Once More.' *English Historical Review* 105 (1990): 951–61.

– 'Archbishop Wulfstan and the Homiletic Element in the Laws of Æthelred II and Cnut.' *English Historical Review* 107 (1992): 565–86.

– *Cnut: The Danes in England in the Early Eleventh Century*. London: Longman, 1993.

Leckie Jr., R. William. *The Passage of Dominion: Geoffrey of Monmouth and the Periodization of Insular History in the Twelfth Century*. Toronto: University of Toronto Press, 1981.

Lees, Clare. 'Working with Patristic Sources: Language and Context in Old English Homilies.' In *Speaking Two Languages: Traditional Disciplines and Contemporary Theory in Medieval Studies*, edited by Allen J. Frantzen, 157–80 and 264–76. Albany: State University of New York Press, 1991.

– *Tradition and Belief: Religious Writing in Late Anglo-Saxon England*. Minneapolis: University of Minnesota Press, 1999.

Lefebvre, Henri. *The Production of Space*. Translated by Donald Nicholson-Smith. Oxford: Blackwell, 1991.

Le Goff, Jacques. 'The Symbolic Ritual of Vassalage.' In *Time, Work, and Culture in the Middle Ages*, 237–87 and 354–67. Chicago: University of Chicago Press, 1982.

Le Patourel, John. *The Norman Empire*. Oxford: Clarendon Press, 1976.

Lerer, Seth. *Literacy and Power in Anglo-Saxon Literature*. Lincoln: University of Nebraska Press, 1991.

Lewis, C.P. 'The Early Earls of Norman England.' *Anglo-Norman Studies* 13 (1990): 207–23.

Loomis, Dorothy Bethurum. '*Regnum* and *sacerdotium* in the Early Eleventh Century.' In *England Before the Conquest: Studies in Primary Sources Presented to Dorothy Whitelock*, edited by Peter Clemoes and Kathleen Hughes, 129–45. Cambridge: Cambridge University Press, 1971.

Loud, G.A. 'The "gens Normannorum": Myth or Reality?' *Anglo-Norman Studies* 4 (1981): 104–16.

Loyn, Henry. 'The Term *Ealdorman* in the Translations Prepared at the Time of King Alfred.' *English Historical Review* 68 (1953): 513–25.

– 'Gesiths and Thegns in Anglo-Saxon England from the Seventh to the Tenth Century.' *English Historical Review* 70 (1955): 529–49.

– 'Kinship in Anglo-Saxon England.' *Anglo-Saxon England* 3 (1974): 197–209.

– 'Ethelred the Unready.' In *Ethelred the Unready*, ed. Hill, 271–3.

– 'Bede's Kings: A Comment on the Attitude of Bede to the Nature of Secular Kingship.' *Trivium* 26 (1991): 54–64.

– '*De Iure Domini regis*: A Comment on Royal Authority in Eleventh-Century England.' In *England in the Eleventh Century: Proceedings of the 1990 Harlaxton Symposium*, edited by Carola Hicks, 17–24. Stamford, CT: Paul Watkins, 1992.

– 'Abbots of English Monasteries in the Period Following the Norman Conquest.' In *England and Normandy in the Middle Ages*, edited by David Bates and Anne Curry, 95–103. London: Hambledon Press, 1994.

Lund, Niels. 'King Edgar and the Danelaw.' *Mediaeval Scandinavia* 9 (1976): 181–95.

Lynch, Joseph H. *Christianizing Kinship: Ritual Sponsorship in Anglo-Saxon England*. Ithaca, NY: Cornell University Press, 1998.

Mack, Katharin. 'Changing Thegns: Cnut's Conquest and the English Aristocracy.' *Albion* 16 (1984): 375–87.

Mackreth, D.F. 'Peterborough, from St. Aethelwold to Martin de Bec, c. 970–1155.' In *Monasteries and Society in Medieval Britain: Proceedings of the 1994 Harlaxton Symposium*, edited by Benjamin Thompson, 137–56. Stamford, CT: Paul Watkins, 1999.

Magennis, Hugh. 'Treatments of Treachery and Betrayal in Anglo-Saxon Texts.' *English Studies* 76 (1995): 1–19.

Magoun, F.P. 'King Aethelwulf's Biblical Ancestors.' *Modern Language Review* 46 (1951): 249–50.

Mason, Emma. 'Pro statu et incolumnitate regni mei: Royal Monastic Patronage, 1066–1154.' In *Religion and National Identity: Papers Read at the Nineteenth Summer Meeting and the Twentieth Winter Meeting of the Ecclesiastical History Society*, edited by Stuart Mews, 99–117. Oxford: Blackwell, 1982.

– 'Change and Continuity in Eleventh-Century Mercia: The Experience of St Wulfstan of Worcester.' *Anglo-Norman Studies* 8 (1985): 154–76.

– *Saint Wulfstan of Worcester, c. 1008–1095*. Oxford: Blackwell, 1990.
Mason, J.F.A. 'Barons and Their Officials in the Later Eleventh Century.' *Anglo-Norman Studies* 13 (1990): 243–62.
Matthew, D.J.A. 'The English Cultivation of Norman History.' In *England and Normandy in the Middle Ages*, edited by David Bates and Anne Curry, 1–18. London: Hambledon Press, 1994.
McIntyre, Elizabeth A. 'Early Twelfth-Century Worcester Cathedral Priory, with Special Reference to the Manuscripts There.' DPhil dissertation. University of Oxford, 1978.
McKitterick, Rosamund. *The Frankish Kingdoms under the Carolingians, 751–987*. London: Longman, 1983.
McTurk, R.W. '"Cynewulf and Cyneheard" and the Icelandic Sagas.' *Leeds Studies in English* n.s. 12 (1981): 81–127.
Meaney, Audrey. 'D: An Undervalued Manuscript of the *Anglo-Saxon Chronicle*.' *Parergon* 1 (1983): 13–38.
Miller, William Ian. *Bloodtaking and Peacemaking: Feud, Law, and Society in Saga Iceland*. Chicago: University of Chicago Press, 1990.
Minnis, A.J. *Medieval Theory of Authorship: Scholastic Literary Attitudes in the Later Middle Ages*. 2nd ed. Philadelphia: University of Pennsylvania Press, 1988.
Moisl, Hermann. 'Anglo-Saxon Royal Genealogies and Germanic Oral Tradition.' *Journal of Medieval History* 7 (1981): 215–48.
– *Lordship and Tradition in Barbarian Europe*. Lewiston, NY: Edwin Mellen Press, 1999.
Morrish, Jennifer. 'King Alfred's Letter as a Source on Learning in England.' In *Studies in Earlier Old English Prose*, edited by Paul E. Szarmach, 87–107. Albany: State University of New York, 1986.
Mostert, Marco. *The Political Theology of Abbo of Fleury: A Study of the Ideas about Society and Law of the Tenth-Century Monastic Reform Movement*. Hilversum: Verloren, 1987.
Nelson, Janet L. 'National Synods, Kingship as Office, and Royal Anointing: An Early Medieval Syndrome.' In *Councils and Assemblies: Papers Read at the Eighth Summer Meeting and the Ninth Winter Meeting of the Ecclesiastical History Society*, edited by G.J. Cuming and Derek Baker, 41–59. Cambridge: Cambridge University Press, 1971.
– 'Inauguration Rituals.' In *Early Medieval Kingship*, edited by Ian N. Wood and P.H. Sawyer, 50–71. Leeds: University of Leeds, 1977.
– 'The Earliest Surviving Royal *ordo*: Some Liturgical and Historical Aspects.' In *Authority and Power: Studies on Medieval Law and Government Presented to Walter Ullmann on His Seventieth Birthday*, edited by Brian Tierney and Peter Linehan, 29–48. Cambridge: Cambridge University Press, 1980.

- 'A King across the Sea: Alfred in Continental Perspective.' *Transactions of the Royal Historical Society,* 5th series, 36 (1986): 45–68.
- *Politics and Ritual in Early Medieval Europe.* London: Hambledon Press, 1986.
- 'The Problem of Alfred's Royal Anointing.' In her *Politics and Ritual in Early Medieval Europe,* 309–28.
- 'The Rites of the Conqueror.' In her *Politics and Ritual in Early Medieval Europe,* 375–401.
- 'Ritual and Reality in the Early Medieval *ordines.*' In her *Politics and Ritual in Early Medieval Europe,* 329–40.
- 'The Second English *ordo.*' In her *Politics and Ritual in Early Medieval Europe,* 361–74.
- 'Symbols in Context: Rulers' Inauguration Rituals in Byzantium and the West in the Early Middle Ages.' In her *Politics and Ritual in Early Medieval Europe,* 259–82.
- 'Wealth and Wisdom: The Politics of Alfred the Great.' *Kings and Kingship, Acta* 11 (1986): 31–52.
- 'The Lord's Anointed and the People's Choice: Carolingian Royal Ritual.' In *Rituals of Royalty: Power and Ceremonial in Traditional Societies,* edited by David Cannadine and Simon Price, 137–80. Cambridge: Cambridge University Press, 1987.
- 'A Tale of Two Princes: Politics, Text, and Ideology in a Carolingian Annal.' *Studies in Medieval and Renaissance History* n.s. 10 (1988): 103–41.
- 'Hincmar of Rheims on King-Making: The Evidence of the *Annals of St. Bertin,* 861–882.' In *Coronations: Medieval and Early Modern Monarchic Ritual,* edited by János M. Bak, 16–34. Berkeley and Los Angeles: University of California Press, 1990.
- 'La famille de Charlemagne.' *Byzantion* 61 (1991): 194–212.
- 'Reconstructing a Royal Family: Reflections on Alfred, From Asser, Chapter Two.' In *People and Places in Northern Europe, 500–1600: Essays in Honour of Peter Hayes Sawyer,* edited by Ian Wood and Niels Lund, 47–66. Woodbridge, Suffolk: Boydell Press, 1991.
- 'History-Writing at the Courts of Louis the Pious and Charles the Bald.' In *Historiographie im frühen Mittelalter,* edited by Anton Scharer and Georg Scheibelreiter, 435–42. Vienna: Oldenbourg, 1993.
- 'The Political Ideas of Alfred of Wessex.' In *Kings and Kingship in Medieval Europe,* edited by Anne J. Duggan, 125–58. London: King's College, Centre for Late Antique and Medieval Studies, 1993.
- 'The Franks and the English in the Ninth Century Reconsidered.' In *The Preservation and Transmission of Anglo-Saxon Culture,* edited by Paul E. Szarmach

and Joel T. Rosenthal, 141–58. Kalamazoo, MI: Medieval Institute Publications, Western Michigan University Press, 1997.
Noble, Thomas F.X. 'The Monastic Ideal as a Model for Empire: The Case of Louis the Pious.' *Revue Bénédictine* 86 (1976): 235–50.
North, Richard. 'Getting to Know the General in the *Battle of Maldon*.' *Medium Ævum* 60 (1991): 1–15.
O'Brien, Bruce R. *God's Peace and King's Peace: The Laws of Edward the Confessor*. Philadelphia: University of Pennsylvania Press, 1999.
O'Brien O'Keeffe, Katherine. 'Heroic Values and Christian Ethics.' In *The Cambridge Companion to Old English Literature*, edited by Malcolm Godden and Michael Lapidge, 107–25. Cambridge: Cambridge University Press, 1991.
– 'Body and Law in Late Anglo-Saxon England.' *Anglo-Saxon England* 27 (1998): 209–32.
– 'Reading the C-Text: The After-Lives of London, British Library, Cotton Tiberius B. i.' In *Anglo-Saxon Manuscripts and Their Heritage*, edited by Phillip Pulsiano and Elaine M. Treharne, 137–60. Aldershot: Ashgate, 1998.
Odegaard, Charles E. 'Carolingian Oaths of Fidelity.' *Speculum* 16 (1941): 284–96.
– 'The Concept of Royal Power in Carolingian Oaths of Fidelity.' *Speculum* 20 (1945): 279–89.
Oleson, Tryggvi J. *The Witenagemot in the Reign of Edward the Confessor: A Study in the Constitutional History of Eleventh-Century England*. Toronto: University of Toronto Press, 1955.
– 'Edward the Confessor's Promise of the Throne to Duke William of Normandy.' *English Historical Review* 72 (1957): 221–8.
Ortenberg, Veronica. 'Archbishop Sigeric's Journey to Rome in 990.' *Anglo-Saxon England* 19 (1990): 197–246.
– *The English Church and the Continent in the Tenth and Eleventh Centuries: Cultural, Spiritual, and Artistic Exchanges*. Oxford: Clarendon Press, 1992.
Otter, Monika. '1066: The Moment of Transition in Two Narratives of the Norman Conquest.' *Speculum* 74 (1999): 565–86.
Parkes, M.B. 'The Palaeography of the Parker Manuscript of the *Chronicle*, Laws and Sedulius, and Historiography at Winchester in the Late Ninth and Tenth Centuries.' *Anglo-Saxon England* 5 (1976): 149–71.
Peddie, John. *Alfred: Warrior King*. Thrupp, Stroud, Gloucestershire: Sutton, 1999.
Peters, Edward. 'Gregory VII's Concept of the *rex inutilis* and Its Antecedents in Law and Historiography, 751–1100.' In *The Shadow King: rex inutilis in Medieval Law and Literature, 751–1327*. 30–80. New Haven, CT: Yale University Press, 1970.

Pohl, Walter. 'Ethnic Names and Identities in the British Isles: A Comparative Perspective.' In *The Anglo-Saxons from the Migration Period to the Eighth Century: An Ethnographic Perspective*, edited by John Hines, 7–40. Woodbridge, Suffolk: Boydell Press, 1997.

Poole, Russell. 'Skaldic Verse and Anglo-Saxon History: Some Aspects of the Period 1009–1016.' *Speculum* 62 (1987): 265–98.

Potts, Cassandra. '*Atque unum ex diversis gentibus populum effecit:* Historical Tradition and the Norman Identity.' *Anglo-Norman Studies* 18 (1995): 139–52.

Powell, Timothy E. 'The "Three Orders" of Society in Anglo-Saxon England.' *Anglo-Saxon England* 23 (1994): 103–32.

Pratt, David. 'The Illnesses of King Alfred the Great.' *Anglo-Saxon England* 30 (2001): 39–90.

Pulsiano, Phillip. '"Danish Men's Words Are Worse than Murder": Viking Guile and *The Battle of Maldon*.' *Journal of English and Germanic Philology* 96 (1997): 13–25.

Rampolla, Mary Lynn. 'A Vision of the Past: Crisis and Historical Consciousness in Worcester, 1095 to c. 1140.' PhD dissertation. University of Toronto, 1985.

Raraty, David G.J. 'Earl Godwine of Wessex: The Origins of his Power and his Political Loyalties.' *History* 74 (1989): 3–19.

Remensnyder, Amy G. *Remembering Kings Past*. Ithaca, NY: Cornell University Press, 1995.

Reynolds, Susan. 'Eadric *Silvaticus* and the English Resistance.' *Bulletin of the Institute of Historical Research* 54 (1981): 102–5.

– 'Medieval *origines gentium* and the Community of the Realm.' *History* 68 (1983): 375–90.

– 'What Do We Mean by "Anglo-Saxon" and "Anglo-Saxons"?' *Journal of British Studies* 24 (1985): 395–414.

– *Fiefs and Vassals: The Medieval Evidence Reinterpreted*. Oxford: Clarendon Press, 1994.

– *Kingdoms and Communities in Western Europe, 900–1300*. 2nd ed. Oxford: Oxford University Press, 1997.

Richardson, Peter R. 'Making Thanes: Literature, Rhetoric, and State Formation in Anglo-Saxon England.' *Philological Quarterly* 78 (1999): 215–32.

Roberts, Jane, and Janet L. Nelson, with Malcolm Godden, eds. *Alfred the Wise: Studies in Honour of Janet Bately on the Occasion of Her Sixty-fifth Birthday*. Cambridge: D.S. Brewer, 1997.

Robinson, J. Armitage. *St. Oswald and the Church of Worcester*. British Academy Supplemental Papers 5. London: Oxford University Press, 1919.

Roffe, David. *Domesday: The Inquest and the Book*. Oxford: Oxford University Press, 2000.

Rumble, Alexander R., ed. *The Reign of Cnut: King of England, Denmark and Norway*. London: Leicester University Press, 1994.

Sahlins, Marshall. *Islands of History*. Chicago: University of Chicago Press, 1985.

Sawyer, P.H. 'The Wealth of England in the Eleventh Century.' *Transactions of the Royal Historical Society* 5th series, 15 (1965): 145–64.

– *Anglo-Saxon Charters: An Annotated List and Bibliography*. London: Royal Historical Society, 1968.

– *Kings and Vikings: Scandinavia and Europe A.D. 700–1100*. London: Methuen, 1982.

– '1066–1086: A Tenurial Revolution?' In *Domesday Book: A Reassessment*, edited by Peter Sawyer, 71–85. London: Edward Arnold, 1985.

Scharer, Anton. 'Die *Intitulationes* der angelsächsischen Könige im 7. und 8. Jahrhundert.' In *Intitulatio III: Lateinische Herrschertitel und Herrschertitularen vom 7 bis zum 13 Jahrhundert*, edited by Herwig Wolfram and Anton Scharer, 9–74. Mitteilungen des Instituts für Österreichische Geschichtsforschung. Supplementary volume 29. Cologne: Böhlau Verlag, 1988.

– 'Zu drei Themen in der Geschichtsschreibung der Zeit König Alfreds (871–899).' In *Ethnogenese und Überlieferung: Angewandte Methoden der Frühmittelalterforschung*, edited by Karl Brunner and Brigitte Merta, 200–8. Vienna: R. Oldenbourg, 1994.

– 'König Alfreds Hof und die Geschichtsschreibung: Einige Überlegungen zur *Angelsachsenchronik* und zu Assers *De rebus gestis Aelfredi*.' In *Historiographie im frühen Mittelalter*, edited by Anton Scharer and Georg Scheibelreiter, 443–58. Vienna: R. Oldenbourg, 1994.

– 'The Writing of History at King Alfred's Court.' *Early Medieval Europe* 5 (1996): 177–206.

– *Herrschaft und Repräsentation: Studien zur Hofkultur König Alfreds des Großen*. Vienna: R. Oldenbourg, 2000.

Schieffer, Rudolf. 'Väter und Söhne im Karolingerhause.' In *Beiträge zur Geschichte des Regnum Francorum. Referate beim Wissenschaftlichen Colloquium zum 75 Geburtstag von Eugen Ewig*, edited by Rudolf Schieffer, 149–64. Sigmaringen: Jan Thorbecke, 1990.

Schütt, Marie. 'The Literary Form of Asser's *Vita Alfredi*.' *English Historical Review* 72 (1957): 209–20.

Scragg, D.G. '*Wifcyþþe* and the Morality of the Cynewulf and Cyneheard Episode in the *Anglo-Saxon Chronicle*.' In *Alfred the Wise: Studies in Honour of Janet Bately on the Occasion of Her Sixty-Fifth Birthday*, edited by Jane Roberts, Janet L. Nelson, and Malcolm Godden, 179–85. Cambridge: D.S. Brewer, 1997.

Searle, Eleanor. 'Battle Abbey and Exemption: The Forged Charters.' *English Historical Review* 83 (1968): 449–80.

Sheppard, Alice. 'The King's Family: Securing the Kingdom in Asser's *Vita Alfredi*.' *Philological Quarterly* 80 (2001): 409–39.

– 'Love Rewritten: Patronizing Meaning and Authorizing History in the Prologue to Laʒamon's *Brut*.' *Mediaevalia* 23 (2002): 99–121.

Shippey, T.A. 'Wealth and Wisdom in King Alfred's *Preface* to the Old English *Pastoral Care*.' *English Historical Review* 94 (1979): 346–55.

Short, Ian. '*Tam Angli quam Franci*: Self-Definition in Anglo-Norman England.' *Anglo-Norman Studies* 18 (1995): 153–75.

Silverman, M.J. 'Ælfric's Designation of the King as "Cristes Sylfes Speligend."' *Review of English Studies* n.s. 35 (1984): 332–4.

Sims-Williams, Patrick. 'The Settlement of England in Bede and the *Chronicle*.' *Anglo-Saxon England* 12 (1983): 1–41.

Sisam, Kenneth. 'Anglo-Saxon Royal Genealogies.' *Proceedings of the British Academy* 39 (1953): 287–348.

Smith, Anthony D. *The Ethnic Origins of Nations*. Oxford: Blackwell, 1986.

Smyth, Alfred P. *King Alfred the Great*. Oxford: Oxford University Press, 1995.

Southern, R.W. 'The Canterbury Forgeries.' *English Historical Review* 73 (1958): 193–226.

– 'Aspects of the European Tradition of Historical Writing: 1, The Classical Tradition from Einhard to Geoffrey of Monmouth.' *Transactions of the Royal Historical Society* 5th series, 20 (1970): 173–96.

– 'Aspects of the European Tradition of Historical Writing: 2, Hugh of St. Victor and the Idea of Historical Development.' *Transactions of the Royal Historical Society* 5th series, 21 (1971): 159–79.

– 'Aspects of the European Tradition of Historical Writing: 3, History as Prophecy.' *Transactions of the Royal Historical Society* 5th series, 22 (1972): 159–80.

– 'Aspects of the European Tradition of Historical Writing: 4, The Sense of the Past.' *Transactions of the Royal Historical Society* 5th series, 23 (1973): 243–63.

Spiegel, Gabrielle M. 'Genealogy: Form and Function in Medieval Historical Narrative.' *History and Theory* 22 (1983): 43–53.

– *Romancing the Past: The Rise of Vernacular Prose Historiography in Thirteenth-Century France*. Berkeley and Los Angeles: University of California Press, 1993.

Spivak, Gayatri Chakravorty. 'Translator's Preface.' In Jacques Derrida, *Of Grammatology*. ix–xc. Baltimore: Johns Hopkins University Press, 1976.

Stafford, Pauline. 'Church and Society in the Age of Ælfric.' In *The Old English*

Homily and its Backgrounds, edited by Paul E. Szarmach and Bernard F. Huppé, 11–42. Albany: State University of New York Press, 1978.
- 'The Reign of Æthelred II: A Study in the Limitations on Royal Policy and Action.' In *Ethelred the Unready*, edited by David Hill, 15–46.
- 'Charles the Bald, Judith, and England.' In *Charles the Bald: Court and Kingdom, Papers Based on a Colloquium Held in London in April 1979*, edited by Margaret Gibson, Janet L. Nelson, with the assistance of David Ganz, 137–51. British Archaeological Reports, International Series 101. Oxford: British Archaeological Reports, 1981.
- 'The King's Wife in Wessex, 800–1066.' *Past and Present* (1981): 3–27.
- 'The Laws of Cnut and the History of Anglo-Saxon Royal Promises.' *Anglo-Saxon England* 10 (1982): 173–90.
- *Unification and Conquest: A Political and Social History of England in the Tenth and Eleventh Centuries*. London: Edward Arnold, 1989.
- 'Women and the Norman Conquest.' *Transactions of the Royal Historical Society* 6th series, 4 (1994): 221–49.
- *Queen Emma and Queen Edith: Queenship and Women's Power in Eleventh-Century England*. Oxford: Blackwell, 1997.

Stenton, F.M. *The Early History of the Abbey of Abingdon*. Reading: University College, 1913. Reprint, Stamford, CT: Paul Watkins, 1989.
- 'The Supremacy of the Mercian Kings.' *English Historical Review* 33 (1918): 433–52.
- *Anglo-Saxon England*. 3rd ed. Oxford: Clarendon Press, 1971.

Stock, Brian. *The Implications of Literacy: Written Language and Models of Interpretation in the Eleventh and Twelfth Centuries*. Princeton, NJ: Princeton University Press, 1983.

Sturdy, David. *Alfred the Great*. London: Constable, 1995.

Szarmach, Paul E. 'The Meaning of Alfred's *Preface* to the *Pastoral Care*.' *Mediaevalia* 6 (1980): 57–86.
- 'The *Anglo-Saxon Chronicle*: A Collaborative Edition.' *Old English Newsletter* 15 (1982): 15–17.

Taviani-Carozzi, Huguette. 'De l'histoire au mythe: la généalogie royale anglo-saxonne.' *Cahiers de civilisation médiévale* 36 (1993): 355–73.

Taylor, A.R. 'The Academic and the Devil.' *Leeds Studies in English* n.s. 12 (1981): 3–11.

Thacker, Alan. 'Æthelwold and Abingdon.' In *Bishop Æthelwold: His Career and Influence*, edited by Barbara Yorke, 43–64. Woodbridge, Suffolk: Boydell Press, 1997.

Thundyil, Zacharias P. *Covenant in Anglo-Saxon Thought: The Influence of the Bible, Church Fathers, and Germanic Tradition on Anglo-Saxon Laws, History, and* the Poems The Battle of Maldon and Guthlac. Madras: Macmillan of India, 1972.

Towers, Tom H. 'Thematic Unity in the Story of Cynewulf and Cyneheard.' Journal of English and Germanic Philology 62 (1963): 310–16.

Townend, Matthew. 'Pre-Cnut Praise-Poetry in Viking Age England.' Review of English Studies n.s. 51 (2000): 349–70.

– 'Contextualising the Knútsdrápur: Skaldic Praise-Poetry at the Court of Cnut.' Anglo-Saxon England 30 (2001): 145–79.

Trafford, Simon. 'Ethnicity, Migration Theory, and the Historiography of the Scandinavian Settlement of England.' In Cultures in Contact: Scandinavian Settlement in England in the Ninth and Tenth Centuries, edited by Dawn M. Hadley and Julian D. Richards, 17–39. Turnhout: Brepols, 2000.

van Houts, Elisabeth M.C. 'The Norman Conquest through European Eyes.' English Historical Review 110 (1995): 832–53.

– 'The Memory of 1066 in Written and Oral Traditions.' Anglo-Norman Studies 19 (1996): 167–79.

– Memory and Gender in Medieval Europe, 900–1200. Toronto: University of Toronto Press, 1999.

Vollrath, Hanna. Die Synoden Englands bis 1066. Paderborn: Ferdinand Schöningh, 1985.

Wallace-Hadrill, J.M. 'The Franks and the English in the Ninth Century: Some Common Historical Interests.' History n.s. 35 (1950): 202–18.

– 'Charles the Bald and Alfred.' In Early Germanic Kingship in England and on the Continent: The Ford Lectures Delivered in the University of Oxford in Hilary Term 1970, 124–51. Oxford: Clarendon Press, 1971.

Warren, Michelle R. History on the Edge: Excalibur and the Borders of Britain, 1100–1300. Minneapolis: University of Minnesota Press, 2000.

Welch, Martin. 'The Kingdom of the South Saxons: The Origins.' In The Origins of Anglo-Saxon Kingdoms, ed. Bassett, 75–83 and 254–6.

West, Francis James. 'The Colonial History of the Norman Conquest?' History 84 (1999): 219–36.

Whately, Gordon. 'Late Old English Hagiography.' In Hagiographies: Histoire internationale de la littérature hagiographique latine et vernaculaire en Occident des origines à 1550, edited by Guy Philippart, 2:429–99. Turnhout: Brepols, 1996.

Whitbread, L. 'Æthelweard and the Anglo-Saxon Chronicle.' English Historical Review 74 (1959): 577–89.

White, Hayden. Tropics of Discourse: Essays in Cultural Criticism. Baltimore: Johns Hopkins University Press, 1985.

– The Content of the Form: Narrative Discourse and Historical Representation. Baltimore: Johns Hopkins University Press, 1987.

White, Stephen D. 'Kinship and Lordship in Early Medieval England: The Story of Sigeberht, Cynewulf, and Cyneheard.' *Viator: Medieval and Renaissance Studies* 20 (1989): 1–18.

Whitelock, Dorothy. 'Wulfstan and the So-Called Laws of Edward and Guthrum.' *English Historical Review* 56 (1941): 1–21.

– 'Archbishop Wulfstan, Homilist and Statesman.' *Transactions of the Royal Historical Society* 4th series, 24 (1942): 25–45.

– 'Wulfstan and the Laws of Cnut.' *English Historical Review* 63 (1948): 433–52.

– 'Wulfstan's Authorship of Cnut's Laws.' *English Historical Review* 70 (1955): 72–85.

– 'Wulfstan at York.' In *Franciplegius: Medieval and Linguistic Studies in Honor of Francis Peabody Magoun, Jr*, edited by Jess B. Bessinger and Robert P. Creed, 214–31. New York: New York University Press, 1965.

– 'The Prose of Alfred's Reign.' In *Continuations and Beginnings: Studies in Old English Literature*, edited by E.G. Stanley, 67–103. London: Nelson, 1966.

– *The Genuine Asser*. Reading: University of Reading Press, 1968.

Wilcox, Jonathan. 'The *Battle of Maldon* and the Anglo-Saxon Chronicle, 979–1016: A Winning Combination.' *Proceedings of the Medieval Association of the Midwest* 3 (1996): 31–50.

– 'The St. Brice's Day Massacre and Archbishop Wulfstan.' In *Peace and Negotiation: Strategies for Coexistence in the Middle Ages and the Renaissance*, edited by Diane Wolfthal, 79–91. Turnhout: Brepols, 2000.

Williams, Ann. 'Some Notes and Considerations on Problems Connected with the English Royal Succession, 860–1066.' *Anglo-Norman Studies* 1 (1978): 144–67.

– 'Land and Power in the Eleventh Century: The Estates of Harold Godwineson.' *Anglo-Norman Studies* 3 (1980): 171–87.

– '"Cockles Amongst the Wheat": Danes and the English in the Western Midlands in the First Half of the Eleventh Century.' *Midland History* 11 (1986): 1–22.

– *The English and the Norman Conquest*. Woodbridge, Suffolk: Boydell Press, 1995.

– 'The Spoliation of Worcester.' *Anglo-Norman Studies* 19 (1996): 383–408.

Wilson, James H. 'Cynewulf and Cyneheard: The Falls of Princes.' *Papers on Language and Literature* 13 (1977): 312–17.

Wood, Ian. 'Before and After the Migration to Britain.' In *The Anglo-Saxons from the Migration Period to the Eighth Century: An Ethnographic Perspective*, edited by John Hines, 41–54. Woodbridge, Suffolk: Boydell Press, 1997.

Woolf, Rosemary. 'The Ideal of Men Dying with Their Lord in the *Germania* and in *The Battle of Maldon*.' *Anglo-Saxon England* 5 (1976): 63–81.

Wormald, Patrick. 'The Uses of Literacy in Anglo-Saxon England and its Neighbours.' *Transactions of the Royal Historical Society* 5th series, 27 (1977): 95–114.
- 'Æthelred the Lawmaker.' In *Ethelred the Unready*, ed. Hill, 47–80.
- 'Bede, the *Bretwaldas*, and the Origins of the *Gens Anglorum*.' In *Ideal and Reality in Frankish and Anglo-Saxon Society: Studies Presented to J.M. Wallace-Hadrill*, edited by Patrick Wormald, Donald Bullough, and Roger Collins, 99–129. Oxford: Blackwell, 1983.
- 'The Venerable Bede and the "Church of the English".' In *The English Religious Tradition and the Genius of Anglicanism*, edited by Geoffrey Rowell, 13–32. Wantage: Ikon, 1992.
- '*Engla Lond*: The Making of an Allegiance.' *Journal of Historical Sociology* 7 (1994): 1–24.
- 'Æthelwold and His Continental Counterparts: Contact, Comparison, Contrast.' In *Bishop Æthelwold: His Career and Influence*, edited by Barbara Yorke, 13–42. Woodbridge, Suffolk: Boydell Press, 1997.
- 'Archbishop Wulfstan and the Holiness of Society.' In *Legal Culture in the Early Medieval West: Law as Text, Image and Experience*, 225–51. London: Hambledon Press, 1999.
- *The Making of English Law: King Alfred to the Twelfth Century.* Vol. 1, *Legislation and Its Limits*. Oxford: Blackwell, 1999.
- 'On Þa Wæpnedhealfe: Kingship and Royal Property from Æthelwulf to Edward the Elder.' In *Edward the Elder, 899–924*, edited by N.J. Higham and D.H. Hill, 264–79. London: Routledge, 2001.

Yorke, Barbara. 'The Vocabulary of Anglo-Saxon Overlordship.' In *Anglo-Saxon Studies in Archaeology and History*, edited by David Brown, James Campbell, and Sonia Chadwick Hawkes, 171–200. British Archaeological Reports, British Series 2. Oxford: British Archaeological Reports, 1981.
- 'The Jutes of Hampshire and Wight and the Origins of Wessex.' In *The Origins of Anglo-Saxon Kingdoms*, ed. Bassett, 84–96 and 256–63.
- *Kings and Kingdoms of Early Anglo-Saxon England*. London: Seaby, 1990.
- *Wessex in the Early Middle Ages*. London: Leicester University Press, 1995.
- 'Æthelwold and the Politics of the Tenth Century.' In *Bishop Æthelwold: His Career and Influence*, edited by Barbara Yorke, 65–88. Woodbridge, Suffolk: Boydell Press, 1997.
- 'Political and Ethnic Identity: A Case Study of Anglo-Saxon Practice.' In *Social Identity in Early Medieval Britain*, edited by William O. Frazer and Andrew Tyrrell, 69–89. London: Leicester University Press, 2000.

Index

Manuscripts of the *Anglo-Saxon Chronicle*

Note: years are indicated in bold type; page numbers in italics denote reference or single-word citations; page numbers in roman type denote substantive citations.

Manuscript A of the *Anglo-Saxon Chronicle*: **443**, *16*, *17*; **552**, *172n44*; **597**, *16*, *17*; **671**, 3–4/*157n3*; **755**, *16*/*164n33*, 54, *208n98*; **787**, *16*, *17*; **827**, 31, 62; **836**, *16*, *17*, 30, 54; **851**, 55; **866**, *16*; **871**, 39/*174n61*, 40, 41/*175n67*, 42, 48/*176n92*, *172n44*; **874**, *16*, 43; **876**, 39, 44; **877**, 43, 44, 45, *175n80*; **878**, 45, 46/*175n82*, *206n61*; **885**, *16*; **886**, *16*, 18/*164–5n40*, 47; **891**, 18; **892**, 30, *182n54*; **893**, 26/*168n6*, 27/*168n10*, 28/*169n18*, 29, 30; **895**, 27/*168n10*; **896**, *16*, 18/*165n42*, 28, 49, *182n54*; **900**, *16*, 18/*165n43*, 28, 49, 76/*187–8n25*, 97/*195nn18*, 19, *172n43*; **903**, 97/*195n18*; **904**, 76/*187–8n25*, 97/*195n18*; **905**, *188n26*; **911**, *188n26*; **912**, *188n26*; **917**, *188n26*; **918**, *188n26*; **1001**, *16*, 102/*196n40*

Manuscript C of the *Anglo-Saxon Chronicle*: **597**, *17*; **787**, *17*; **816**, *17*; **836**, *17*; **875**, *17*; **901**, 76/*187–8n25*; **906**, *188n26*; **912**, *188n26*; **913**, *188n26*; **915**, *188n26*; **978**, 73/*186n10*; **979**, 73/*186n10*; **982**, *187n17*; **986**, 78/*189n31*; **994**, 18, 78/*189n31*, 100–1; **997**, 101/*196n32*; **998**, 101; **999**, 74/*186n14*, 101/*196n34*; **1000**, *101*; **1001**, 101; **1002**, 18, 78/*189n31*, 87, 102, 127/*205–6n51*; **1003**, 103–4, *107*, *188n30*; **1004**, 18, 77, 78/*189n31*, 104–5; **1006**, 88/*192n73*, 105; **1008**, 78/*189n31*; **1009**, 18, 78/*189n31*, 106–7, 109; **1011**, 18, 71, 73, 80, 85–6, *107*, *107*/*197n57*, *107*/*197n59*; **1012**, 78/*189n31*; **1013**, 108; **1014**, 90, 94/*193n2*, 96–7, 99, 109, 109/*198n70*, 110, *134*; **1015**, 88/*192n73*, 91, 97, 98/*195n22*, 99, 110/*199n76*, 111; **1016**, 19, 19/*165n47*, 78/*189n31*, 88/

192n73, 91/193n81, 98, 99/196nn26–
7, 111, 112; **1017**, 19, 19/165n50, 20,
78/189n31, 112; **1023**, 79/189n35;
1065, 109, 109/198nn68–9, 126, 127
Manuscript D of the *Anglo-Saxon
Chronicle*: **816**, 17; **874**, 17; **901**, 76/
187–8n25; **1023**, 79/189n35; **1031**,
136/208n90; **1051**, 127/206n52;
1065, 127–8, 127/205–6n51; 130,
205nn39, 47; **1066**, 3–4/157n3,
129, 130–1, 132, 133–4, 134, 138,
165–6n52, 172n43, 198n70,
202n121, 204n19, 205n37, 206n56;
1067, 135, 165–6n52; **1068**, 137–8,
139/209n100; **1071**, 138, 165–6n52;
1072, 138; **1073**, 136; **1075**, 137;
1076, 139/209n101; **1079**, 140; **1080**,
209n106
Manuscript E of the *Anglo-Saxon
Chronicle*: **443**, 17; **597**, 17; **654**, 150;
656, 150; **675**, 150; **686**, 150; **777**,
150; **787**, 17; **815**, 17; **836**, 17; **852**,
150; **870**, 150; **963**, 150–1; **1074**, 148;
1075, 139/209n104; **1085**, 145–6,
146/212n5; **1086**, 146–8; **1087**, 148–
9; **1130**, 152; **1132**, 152/215n26

General Index

Abbo, author of poem on the siege of
Paris, 52
Abels, Richard, 162n23
Abingdon, 149
Aclea, 55–6
Ælfgar, son of *ealdormann* Ælfric, 74.
See also blindings
Ælfgifu, first wife of Æthelred II, 97.
See also Emma, queen, wife of
Æthelred and Cnut

Ælfheah, archbishop of Canterbury,
18, 76, 79–80, 100, 107–8, 189n33
Ælfhelm, *ealdormann* of Northumbria, 74, 105
Ælfmær, abbot of St Augustine's,
Canterbury, 79, 107–8
Ælfric, abbot of Eynsham: *Dominica
post ascensionem Domini*, 82–3;
homilies and saints' lives, 71–2 (*see
also* hagiographic discourse; homiletic discourse); *Letter to Sigeweard*,
83; *Maccabees*, 83; pastoral letter to
Wulfstan, 83; translation of *Old
English Heptateuch*, 83; translation
of Pseudo-Cyprian, 22, 81–2, 84–5;
Wyrdwriteras fragment, 83–4
Ælfric, *ealdormann* of Hampshire, 73,
77, 103–4
Ælfstan, bishop of Rochester, 86
Ælle, king of the South Saxons, 31
Æthelbald, king of Mercia, 33–4, 37,
173n57
Æthelbald, son of King Æthelwulf,
king of Wessex, 56, 59–60, 62, 97
Æthelmær, *ealdormann* of Hampshire
and thane, 108
Æthelmær the Fat, *ealdormann* of the
West, 112
Æthelred I, king of Wessex: accession of, 60, 62–3; death of, 59–60; as
effective lord, 40–1
Æthelred II, king of Anglo-Saxon
England: abuse of royal power (*rex
iniquus*), 84–6, 90–1; accession of,
73, 186n10, 186–7n15, 194nn16–17;
accountability of, 71; betrayal of
lordship, 99–100; called to resist,
79; compared to Cnut, 96; defeat
and lordship ritual, 132–3; early
years of, 74–5, 86; exile, 90, 96–7,

108–9, 114–15, 194n16; fall of kingdom, 11, 19–20; genealogy of, 20, 75; poor lordship of, 97–9; portrayed as incompetent, 87–8; reign as one of chaos, 73–4, 186n14; responsible for loss of kingdom, 96–7; treachery by, 110–11; treachery in reign of, 102–6; as unjust, 86–7, 90–1, 191n64, 193n79; wives of, 97

II Æthelred, 102. *See also* St Brice's Day massacre

VI Æthelred, 116

VIII Æthelred, 117

Æthelred, *ealdormann* of Mercia, 29–30, 61–2

Æthelred-Cnut Chronicle: Æthelred's culpability in, 72–3; betrayal central to, 107; conceptual preface to, 74; culture of disloyalty in, 91–2, 100, 103–4, 117; dates of, 71, 185n1, 193n1, 196n29; depiction of lordship in, 14–15, 18–19, 114, 119–20; discourse of collective identity, 96, 144; figure of king in, 79–80; focus on fighting in, 71–2, 76; genealogical references, 75; historical context of, 86–8, 105–6; as history for Æthelred and Cnut, 94–5, 159n18; as history of a people, 6–7, 100; homiletic discourse in, 81; importance of continuity to, 96; inaccuracy of, 92–3; intertextuality of, 106–7, 109; king not held responsible, 100–2, 196n34; king's unwillingness to fight, 98; language of Æthelred's return, 109–10; legal texts in context of, 95–6, 113–18; metonymic link between king and kingdom, 78–9; narration of history, 13; narrating the loss of identity, 72–3, 76; narrative strategy of, 100–2, 112, 119–20, 205–6n51; new culture of shared lordship, 94–5; relationship to other texts, 90, 95–6, 193n79; as salvation historiography, 21, 85–8, 92–3, 145; salvation historiography transformed, 96–9; scholarly studies of, 72–3; 1016 victory of Cnut, 19, 92; use of Christian ideology, 7; writer of, 74, 186–7nn15–16

Æthelstan, king of Kent, Surrey, Essex, Sussex, son of King Æthelwulf, 54

Æthelweard, *ætheling*, son of Alfred, 64

Æthelweard, *ealdormann* of the West, 35, 100

Æthelwig, abbot of Evesham, 141–2

Æthelwold, St, bishop of Winchester, 150–1

Æthelwold, rebel, son of Æthelred I, 76, 97, 187–8n25

Æthelwulf, king of Wessex, 30, 41–2, 54–7, 59, 180n34

Æthelwulf, *ealdormann*, 40–1

Agatho, Pope, 151

Alcuin: Danish raids on Lindisfarne, 23; letter to Æthelred of Northumbria, 23; narration of history, 6–7

Alfred, king of Wessex and Anglo-Saxon England: and Æthelred I, 60; baptism of Guthrum, 47, 191n58; betrayed by brother, 41–2; body and power in Asser, 52–3; compared to Æthelred II, 100–1; and compilation of *Chronicle*, 6–7; defeat and lordship ritual, 132–3; education of sons, 64–5; exile of,

254 Index

45–6, 109; genealogy of, 20; illnesses of, 53; journey to kingship, 58–63; king of the *Angelcynn*, 49; land tenure and lordship, 27; learns to read, 64, 183n60; lordship obligations of, 41; military service, 27; as noble brother, 41, 60; occupies London, 47–8, 61–2; peace making, 44–5; *Preface to the Regula pastoralis*, 69–70; size of kingdom, 30–1; symbolic act of lordship, 182n51; takes throne, 59–60; youth of, 63–9. *See also* Asser, bishop of Sherborne, *Vita Alfredi*

Alfred annals: Alfred wins kingdom (878), 47; Asser's use of, 58; created a political family, 70; Danish duplicity in, 44–5; Danish occupation in, 28–30, 38–9; distinctiveness of, 50; ecclesiastical kingship in, 40, 52; genealogy in, 32; Guthrum (peace treaty), 7, 39, 174n62; the 'here' of, 39–40; identity creation of, 49, 51–2, 68–9, 144; interpretations of, 26; loss of land in, 42–3, 45–6; languages of power in, 30–2, 45, 48; liturgical calendar in, 46; London's significance in, 61–2, 182n51; lordship ceremony (886), 28, 47–8; lordship as defining, 42; lordship focus of, 50; military history in, 29–30, 48–9; narration of history, 13; narrative strategy of, 27–8, 38–9, 41–7, 49; performance of lordship, 26–8; philosophy of lordship, 18, 29–30, 38, 49, 60; rhetoric of lordship, 49–50; unreliable representation of lordship, 27–8; use of *Angelcynn* in, 17–19; use of the past in, 6–7; vocabulary of defeat and victory, 39–40, 44. *See also* A Manuscript of the *Anglo-Saxon Chronicle*

A Manuscript of the *Anglo-Saxon Chronicle*: Æthelwulf's reign, 54–5, 179n24; composition of, 5; genealogy in, 19–20, 32, 55–6; inclusion of biblical history, 55; rebellion of Æthelwold, 187–8n25; recent editions of, 3; use of *Angelcynn* in, 19–20. *See also Anglo-Saxon Chronicle*

Andover, 100

Angelcynn: in Æthelred-Cnut annals, 78–80; after the Norman Conquest, 19, 165–6n52; in Alfred annals, 48–9, 176n91; Anglo-Saxon identity, 80; in Asser's *Vita Alfredi*, 53; attacked from within, 103; Cnut as legitimate inheritor of, 96, 108–9, 198n65; collective identity, 155; Danish members of, 19, 87, 91–2; defined by, 94; demise of, 19, 76, 121; in discourse of identity, 4, 13, 15; historic use of, 17–18; leader of, 79–80, 107–8; lordship definitive of, 18–19, 28, 32, 100, 106–7; meaning of term, 16–20, 31–2, 163n31, 164nn36–8, 171n33; preserving the lordship culture of, 136; recognized by Danes, 100, 105; role of the Scots, 137, 208n94; under Cnut, 144; used in peace-making tactics, 100–1. *See also* Anglo-Saxon identity

Anglo-Danish peace treaty, 113–14

Anglo-Norman literary tradition, 153

Anglo-Saxon Chronicle: Alfred's symbolic act of lordship, 61–2; attribution of, 157–8n8; audience for, 10, 161n9; common stock, 18, 33, 58;

Index 255

compared to Carolingian mirrors, 22–3; compilation of, 5–7, 17, 28, 121–4, 142, 157–8n8, 169n14, 211n122; Continental influence on, 20–3, 50; genealogical discourse in, 54–5, 75; genealogical prefaces of, 19–20; identity in, 32, 79 (*see also* Anglo-Saxon identity); as an ideological text, 50; land-based authority, 146; Latin translation of, 35; lordship, annalists' depiction of, 14–15 (*see also* lordship); narrative strategy of, 15, 21, 24, 39–40, 42–3, 167n69 (*see also* narrative strategies); pedagogical role of, 11–13, 24; place in post-Conquest history, 152–3; reediting of, 3; relationship among manuscripts, 212n4, 212n129; role of salvation history, 24, 88–92 (*see also under* historical narrative, salvation historiography); scholarly study of, 5, 157–8n8, 158n11; significance in community, 122–3; specificity of, 23; syntax of, 39–40, 186n12. *See also* A Manuscript of the *Anglo-Saxon Chronicle*; *Æthelred-Cnut Chronicle*; B Manuscript; C Conquest narrative; D Manuscript; E Manuscript; *Peterborough Chronicle*; *Peterborough Interpolations*

Anglo-Saxon homilists, 82–3. *See also* Ælfric, abbot of Eynsham; homiletic discourse; Wulfstan, archbishop of York

Anglo-Saxon identity: as collective, 9–10, 51–2, 68–9, 96, 144, 155, 160nn3–4; culture of leadership, 79–80; 'Eastengla folces' (the East Anglian people), 28–30, 78–9, 104, 107, 189n32; focus of discourse on, 4–5; includes Danes, 19, 91–2, 102–3; lament for, 122; land and culture as, 106, 142–3; language of peace making, 130–1; link with fighting, 75–6; lordship as defining component of, 4, 7–8, 25, 28, 32–8, 48–9, 95, 146, 161nn10, 15; loss of, 72–3, 76, 90, 123–5; loss of kingdom, 108; in naming, 9, 160n3; narration of history of, 100, 153; rituals of lordship in, 29–30, 100–1; role of historical narrative in, 11–13, 123; role of law codes in, 117, 200–1n103; role of leader in, 79; role of legal discourse, 116–18; shift of symbol of, 80–1; told through salvation history, 88–92; Ulfcytel and Archbishop Ælfheah as emblems of, 76–80. *See also* identity

Anglo-Saxon kingship, 82, 123. *See also* Carolingian kingship texts / Carolingian mirrors; succession

Anglo-Saxon religious culture, 79, 81–2, 143, 151

Anglo-Saxons (selective references): *adventus Saxonum*, 12; landscape in texts of, 46, 122; myth of origins, 12–13; transgressions leading to defeat, 131–4; use of the term, 163nn29, 31

Anglo-Scandinavian identity, 95, 118, 130. *See also* Danes; Danish Conquest; Danish raids; identity

Annals of St Bertin, 21, 50

Asser, bishop of Sherborne, *Vita Alfredi*: Æthelwulf (father of Alfred) story in, 54–7; Alfred betrayed by brother Æthelred in, 41–2; audience for, 51; authenticity

of, 51; and Carolingian texts, 53–4; comparisons to, 52; ideals of kingship in, 57; identity in, 51–2; importance of family relations in, 64–6, 182–3n55; inclusion of will's details, 57; interpretation of King Æthelwulf in, 56–7; London in, 61–2; metaphorical crownings in, 57–63, 67–8; narrative of anointing in, 58–9; narrative strategy of, 54, 57, 68; public dimension of lordship in, 52–3; ship metaphor in, 63, 66–7; sources for, 51–2, 58, 60, 62–3, 69; teaching key to Alfred's authority in, 68–70, 180–1n39, 184nn70, 76; transfer of power in, 61; use of Orosius, 56; virtue in a king in, 59–60. *See also* Alfred, king of Wessex and Anglo-Saxon England
'Astronomer' (anon), 52

baptism. *See under* peace making, baptism's role in
Barrow, Julia, 142
Bately, Janet, 28
Battle Abbey, 149
Battle of Maldon, 6, 15–16, 34, 99
Bede the Venerable, monk: *descriptio*, 25, 142, 167n71; and discourse of sin, 50, 70; *Historia ecclesiastica*, 5–6, 23–5, 31–2, 37, 142, 145, 171n33; historical models of, 6; narration of history, 6–7; not innocent historian, 5–6
Benedictinism, 81, 150–2
Beornred, king of Mercia, 37
Beowulf, 6, 15, 34, 99
betrayal, 91–2, 97–100, 103–5, 110–12, 195n24

Bhabha, Homi K., 10–12, 24, 161n10, 169n17, 203n4, 208n94
blindings, 74, 105, 139, 186n13
B Manuscript of the *Anglo-Saxon Chronicle*, 3, 20. See also *Anglo-Saxon Chronicle*
Bourdieu, Pierre, 116
Bretwalda, 31, 49, 170n29, 179n25
Brihtric, son of Ælfheah of Devonshire, 112
Britons, 89–90, 143, 172n44
Brutus, 154
Burgred, king of Mercia, 56
Butler, Judith, 116–17
Byrhtnoth, *ealdormann* of Essex (in *Battle of Maldon*), 16

Cambridge, Corpus Christi College, MS 201, 113–14
Campbell, James, 52
Canterbury, 37, 79, 107, 135, 149
Carolingian kingship texts/Carolingian mirrors: Anglo-Saxon adaptations of, 81–2, 84–6, 191n64; borrowings from, 51–2; central texts for this study, 22; ecclesiastical kingship, 52–3; evident in Æthelred-Cnut annals, 81; *familia regis*, 17; iconography of King David, 83–4; ideals of kingship, 57; king as example of faith life, 52; significance of fighting in, 74–80, 189–90n41; traits of genre, 22; value of learning in, 64, 66; virtue in kings, 59, 66; wisdom in, 82–3, 190n46
Carolingians: Christian tradition of historical narratives, 27; influence on Anglo-Saxons, 10; relations with Anglo-Saxons, 20–3, 82; style of text (narratives), 21

Index 257

Cartulary. See Hemming, Cartulary
C Conquest narrative of the Anglo-Saxon Chronicle: composition of, 5; rebellion of Æthelwold, 187–8n25; recent editions of, 3; Tostig, 126–7; use of Angelcynn in, 17–18; use of 'hold hlaford' in, 114–15. See also Anglo-Saxon Chronicle
Ceawlin, king of Wessex, 31
Ceolwulf, king of Mercia, 43–4
Cerdic, king of Wessex, 33, 55
Charlemagne, emperor, king of the Franks, 57–8
Charles-Edwards, Thomas, 46–7
Charles the Bald, emperor, king of the Franks, 55
Charles the Fat, emperor, king of the Franks, 182–3n55
Christian ideology: kingship, 22–5; morality, 24; teaching role of ruler, 69; use of baptism, 46–7 (see also under peace making, baptism's role in). See also sin
citizen, 10, 25, 117, 200–1n103
C Manuscript. See Æthelred-Cnut Chronicle; C Conquest narrative of the Anglo-Saxon Chronicle
Cnut, king of England: accession justified, 102; becomes king, 91–3, 97; betrays his people, 110; ceremony of lordship, 132–3; coronation of, 112–13, 199n83; Danish raids, 110–11; defeats the Anglo-Saxons, 19, 94–5; elected as king, 90; founding principle of reign, 114; genealogy of, 20; ideal lordship of, 14–15, 19, 112–18; into Mercia, 141–2; law code (1018), 95, 116–18, 126–7, 193n4, 195–6n24; Letter to the People (1020), 114

II Cnut, 95, 117. See also Wulfstan, archbishop of York
Cnut Sweinson, king of Denmark, 146
Coleman, Vita Wulfstani, 124
compaternitas, 30. See also peace making
conquest and invasions in narrative: analysis of, 11; and Angelcynn, 19; depicted as problems of government, 24; and failure of loyalty oaths, 148; language of, 48; as less important, 41, 65; and limits set, 17; and lordship as type of leadership, 21; the practice of, 6–7, 15; and transfer of power motif, 23; and use of Engle, 130–1; as written in the vernacular, 144–5. See also historical narrative
coronation oath, 110, 117–18, 133–4, 199n73. See also oaths of loyalty
coward, 104
Cumberland, 74, 86
Cynewulf-Cyneheard episode: bravery's role in, 40; Cynewulf killed in, 35; historical context absent in, 35–8; ideal lordship in, 99; kinship in, 16; lordship and identity in, 32–8; lordship ideology in, 6, 15; relationship to Alfred annals, 33, 38; role in historical narrative, 54; scholarly commentary on, 33–4; similarity of the two Anglo-Saxon leaders, 173n49
Cynric, king of Wessex, 172n44

Danelaw, 87, 115
Danes: of Anglo-Saxon England, 87; crisis of succession, 118; as Deniscan, 48; and Guthrum baptism, 46; as keepers of mutual loyalty, 118–

258 Index

19; and narrative of loyalty, 118–19; as Other, 45; slaughter of, 74 (*see also* St Brice's Day massacre)

Danish Conquest: Æthelred as corrupt, 74; failure of Anglo-Saxon lordship, 98–100; narrative of loyalty, 118–20; no single event, 113; Norman interpretation of, 114–15; representations of, 120; role of disloyalty in, 98–9; as a series of accessions, 94

Danish raids (selective references): Æthelred's attempts to halt, 87; in Alfred annals, 28–30, 38–40, 44–5; of Canterbury (1011), 79; Cnut as king, 109; from Dublin, 86; monastery at Tavistock, 101; and peace making, 43–5; reactions to, 73; relationship to Anglo-Saxon sins, 88–90; represented in historical narrative, 145; response to, 100; taking Reading, 43, 175n73; Ulfcytel's failure with, 76–8

de Certeau, Michel, 53, 75, 80, 181n44

D Manuscript of the *Anglo-Saxon Chronicle*: compilation of, 121–4, 127, 211nn123–4; recent editions of, 3; use of *Angelcynn* in, 17–19; use of 'hold hlaford' in, 114–15, 120; a Worcester text, 140–3. See also *Anglo-Saxon Chronicle*; William annals

Deor, 122

Derbyshire, 130

Deusdedit, archbishop, 150

Domesday Book, 145–9, 213n9. *See also* William I, king of Anglo-Norman England, the Conqueror

Dublin, 86

Durham, 149

Eadmer of Canterbury, chronicler, *Historia novorum in Anglia*, 125

Eadric (*silvaticus*), rebel, 135

Eadric Streona, *ealdormann* of Mercia: betrayal, 19, 91–2, 97–100, 110–12, 119; control of Mercia, 88; killed, 112; into Mercia, 141–2, 192n73

Eadwig, *ætheling*, son of Æthelred II, 112

Eadwin, earl, 130

Ealdgyth, wife of Sigeferth, 110–11

Ealdred, bishop of Worcester, archbishop of York, 141. See also *under* D Manuscript, compilation of

East Anglia: councillors of, 77; Danes violate peace of, 47; loss of chief men, 77–8, 104–5; loss of king, 43; Thorkell succeeds, 112. See also Ulfcytel Snilling

East Anglian people, 48, 78. See also Anglo-Saxon identity

Easter tables, 13, 162n21

ecclesiastical culture, 40, 52–3, 84–5, 123

Ecgbryht, king of Wessex, Alfred's grandfather, 17, 31, 54, 179n25

Edgar, king of Anglo-Saxon England, 115, 117, 150–1

IV Edgar, 115–17, 200n93

Edgar, *ætheling*, 132, 136–9, 148

Edmund Ironside, *ætheling*, king of Anglo-Saxon England, 91–2, 97–8, 111, 119

education: affirming authority of king, 53–4, 63, 67–70, 180–1n39, 184nn70, 76; connection between loyalty and the book, 64–7; emphasized in Alfredian texts, 69; loyalty by, 58; pedagogical role of *Chronicle*, 11–3, 24, 53–4

Edward annals: hagiographic reading of, 76; threats to throne, 75–6, 187–8nn25–6
Edward the Confessor, king of Anglo-Saxon England, 124, 126–9, 133–4, 136, 205n45
Edward the Elder, king of Wessex, 75–6
Edwin, earl of Mercia, 138
Egbert, king. *See* Ecgbryht, king of Wessex, Alfred's grandfather
Einhard, *Vita Karoli*, 52, 70
E Manuscript of the *Anglo-Saxon Chronicle*: Æthelred's return from exile, 114–15; authority through writing, 146–8; discourse of identity in, 153; Edgar *ætheling*, 148–9; recent editions of, 3; use of *Angelcynn* in, 17–19. *See also Anglo-Saxon Chronicle; Peterborough Chronicle; Peterborough Interpolations*
Emma, queen, wife of Æthelred and Cnut, 20, 87, 97, 118
Emma, daughter of William fitz Osbern, 139
Encomium Emmae Reginae, 118–19
Eric, earl of Northumbria, 112
Ermoul, author of praise poem of Louis the Pious, 52
ethnie, 9–10
Evesham, 141
Evesham, house of, 122–3
Exeter, 39, 135–6
exile, lordship topos of, 45–6, 90, 96–7, 108–9, 114–15, 126–8, 138, 194n16, 198n67

'feng to rice,' 19, 42, 60–1, 91, 98, 108
Foot, Sarah, 17, 164n35
Fræna, Anglo-Saxon leader, 73

Francia, 20, 47, 62
Frankish annalists, 21
Frankish mirrors, 53. *See also* Carolingian kingship texts / Carolingian mirrors
Frankish succession, 57, 60, 62
Frythegyst, Anglo-Saxon leader, 73

Gainsborough, 108
Geary, Patrick, 9
Geat, legendary West Saxon ancestor, 55
genealogical discourse: in Æthelred-Cnut annals, 75; in Asser's *Vita Alfredi*, 58–60; authorizing power of, 19–20, 32, 40; or political family, 34; use of by Asser, 54; use of in *Chronicle*, 54–6
Geoffrey of Monmouth, *Historia regum Britannie*, 153
Gesta Herewardi, 139
Gildas: *De excidio et conquestu Britannie*, 6, 23, 144–5; in Wulfstan's *Sermo Lupi*, 89–90
Gloucestershire, 141–2
Godden, Malcolm, 72, 81
Godwin, Anglo-Saxon leader, 73
Goffart, Walter, 5–6
Greater Wessex, 26
Gregory the Great, Pope, *Regula pastoralis*, 5, 27, 53, 69–70
Grimbald of St Bertin, 20, 27
Guthrum, Danish king in East Anglia, 7, 39, 46–7, 191n58
Guy of Abbeville, 124

hagiographic discourse: in Æthelred-Cnut annals, 72; in Alfred and Edward annals, 76; Anglo-Saxon identity, 80–1; importance of, 185–

6n7; link with national identity, 75–6, 170–1n32; question of should the king fight, 74–80, 189–90n41
Hampshire, 34
Hanning, Robert, 144–5, 153
Harold II, king of Anglo-Saxon England: ceremony of lordship, 132–3; lordship culture of, 133–4; loyalty oath, 124–5, 129–30; loyalty of his men, 131; succession of, 125–31; support of rebels, 127, 205n49
Harold Hardrada, 128–9
Hásteinn (OE Hæsten), Danish leader, 28–30, 48–9
Hastings, Battle of, 121, 125–31
Headda, abbot of Peterborough, 151
Hemming, *Cartulary*, 124, 142, 210–11n119
Henry I, king of Anglo-Norman England, 117, 151
Henry of Huntingdon, *Historia Anglorum*, 92–3, 125
Henry of Poitou, abbot of St Jean d'Angély, 151–2
Herefordshire, 141–2
Hill, Thomas, 104
Hincmar of Rheims: *De ordine palatii*, 22; *De regis persona et regio ministerio*, 22, 57, 82
historians: importance at Alfred's court, 51; innocence of, 5–6; mainstream medieval, 92–3; philosophy of causation, 23–4
historical narrative: contemporary agenda of, 152–3; in context of others, 6–7, 54, 106; conventions of Christian historiography, 57; of Danish Conquest, 118–20, 145; foundation narratives, 12, 144, 151–2, 154; of Germanic history, 5–6; homiletic, 85; as identity creators, 4, 8, 10–13, 15–17, 68–9, 72–3, 76, 100, 120, 123, 144; land and culture in, 142–3 (*see also* land); lordship central to, 11–12, 154; lordship of land, 149; of Norman Conquest, 7, 19, 127–8, 206n52; power of, 68, 124; readers of the *Chronicle*, 188n27; rebellion narratives, 122, 138–40; role in identity, 123; salvation historiography, 21, 23–7, 56, 72–3, 85–8, 92–3, 115, 144–5, 153 (*see also* sin); salvation historiography, role of, 88–92; salvation historiography transformed, 96–9; West Saxon history, 35. *See also* narrative strategies

'hold hlaford,' 114–15, 117–18, 120, 133, 195n24. *See also* coronation oath

homiletic discourse: in Æthelred-Cnut annals, 72, 80–4; in Cnut's legislation, 116; of ecclesiastic kingship, 84–5; function of, 81–2; importance of, 185–6n7; king not fighting in, 84–5; links to salvation historiography, 85

homiletic understanding of sin, 89–90

honour in military success (*wyrðscype*), 106–7. *See also* militarism

Howe, Nicholas, 12–13, 50, 164n38

identity: culture and, 121, 203n4; *Denisc*, 130; discourse of, 4, 8, 28, 120; *Englisc*, 130; from historical narrative, 15–17, 68–9, 123, 144; land and, 106, 142–3; language of, 130–1; legal discourse and, 113,

116–18; medieval national, 9, 160n1; monastic institutional, 122–3; national, 9–10, 31–2, 75–6, 120, 137–8, 170–1n32; not a historical phenomenon, 10, 161n10; political and cultural through lordship, 145–6; as textual community, 10–12. *See also* Anglo-Saxon identity; Anglo-Scandinavian identity

Isidore of Seville, *Etymologiae*, 13

Isle of Man, 86

John of Worcester: *Chronicle*, 124; Harold as a good king, 125; historical accuracy of writings, 92–3

Jonas d'Orléans, *De institutione regia*, 22

Jordanes, 5

Kennet, 73

Keynes, Simon, 5, 36, 86, 92, 102

Laȝamon, *Brut*, 153–4

land: authority in, 135, 146; landscape in Old English literature, 46, 122, 132, 203n6; linked to identity, 106, 142–3; linked to lordship, 27, 43–4, 57, 122–3, 149, 203n6, 204n17, 212n3; loss of, 42–3, 45–6; in oaths of loyalty, 27, 168–9n11

language: for Danes as Other, 45, 175n80; of distinct people, 143; of family or kinship, 16–17, 198n69; of friendship, 96–7, 194n12; of identity, 130–1; of kingship, 9, 160n3; lack of subordinating conjunctions, 47–8, 98, 186n12; legal discourse, 129–30; of lordship, 17; of lordship culture, 133–4; of marginalization, 4; of passive accession, 108; of peace making (*friþ niman*), 44; of place (*her*), 38–40; for prostitute or wife (Cynewulf-Cyneheard episode), 35; *Regula pastoralis*, 53; of request and promise, 90–1; of royal authority (*Bretwalda*), 31–2, 49, 170n29, 179n25; of royal election, 57, 60; salvation discourse, 115; shame in lordship literature, 147, 213n8; shaped by lord's loyalty, 109–10; in significance of loyalty oath, 129; of sin, 72, 185n6; of submission (*(ge)cyrran*), 48; of succession, 92, 98, 109, 181–2n48, 198nn70–1; of succession/accession, 60–1; *unrædas*, 71, 73, 86, 87–8; use of *bugan* and *cyrran*, 108, 110, 129, 133, 197–8n60; use of *gryðian*, 139; vocabulary of defeat and victory, 39–40, 44; vocabulary of war, 56; *(syru)wrenc*, 79, 107–8

Lapidge, Michael, 56

Lawson, Malcolm, 116

Lefebvre, Henri, 39, 142–3

Leofric, earl of Mercia, 142

Leofwine, *ealdormann*, 112

Lincolnshire, 130

Lindsey, 110

London, 18, 29, 47–8, 61–2, 98, 111

lordship: acts as generative, 62; authority through writing, 146–53; conceptual centre of text, 11–12, 15, 145–6; culture of corrupt, 139–40; culture of disloyalty, 91–2, 100, 103–4, 107; culture of loyalty, 109–10, 115, 118–19, 137–8; culture of mutual loyalty, 95, 99, 114, 117–18, 194n7, 195–6nn24–5; death of culture of, 121–2, 125–6, 140; defining of, 7, 13–15, 119–20, 159n20; depic-

tion of, 14–15, 18, 162n23, 163n26; and honour, 106–7; ideal, 99, 105; identity linked to, 4, 7–8, 25, 28, 32, 48, 95, 146, 161n15; ideology of, 6, 20, 36, 94, 96; land linked to, 27, 43–4, 57, 122–3, 149, 203n6, 204n17, 212n3; and morality of kings, 57; of Normans and Anglo-Saxons, 133–4; notion of shame, 147; and peace making, 31–2, 40, 43–4, 47, 129; in political and legal culture, 17, 115; practices of, 6, 11–14, 23, 34–5, 38, 50, 58, 74; public dimension of, 28, 52–3; rhetoric of, 118; role in authority of king, 19–20, 27, 95, 112–13, 115, 127, 139–40, 193n4, 209n102; and spiritual kinship, 47; teaching/education linked to, 53–4, 63–70, 180–1n39, 184nn70, 76
Lyfing, archbishop of Canterbury, 112

Magna Carta, 117
Maine, 149
Malcolm III of Scotland, 135–9
Maldon, Battle of, 73
Malmesbury, 110
Margaret, St, sister of *ætheling* Edgar, wife of Malcolm III, 122, 136
Mercia: Alfred ruler of, 62; Cnut's succession, 91, 98–9; under Danes, 38, 45; *ealdormann* Eadric, 88, 112; Edmund loses, 98; kings of, 34, 37; relations with Wessex, 36–8; suffers battle in Danish Conquest, 141; weakness of, 43
Mercians: in Alfred's court, 66; separate from West Saxons, 48
militarism: honour in military success (*wyrðscype*), 106–7; military history in Alfred annals, 27, 29–30; narrow focus of, 49–50
monastic communities: destruction of buildings of, 150–1; institutional identity of, 122–3; and lordship of land, 146; and privileges, 149; plundered by William, 137–8; and production of manuscripts, 5; as threatened, 123, 203nn13, 14; and use of textual history, 11, 150–2
Morcar, earl of Northumbria, son of Earl Ælfgar, 126, 130, 132, 138
Morcar, thane, 91, 97, 110–11

narrative strategies: authority through writing, 146–53; basis of study, 6–8; conceptual functions of, 57–9, 68, 112, 119–20, 205–6n51; literary context of, 15, 21, 24; lordship as metaphor for realm, 50; metaphorical crownings, 58–63, 67–8; metaphor of ship, 63, 66–7; omissions of context in, 5–6, 35, 37–43, 86–8, 100–2, 105–6, 127; omissions of textual traditions, 41; of people over land, 45–6; rhetoric of lordship, 49; syntax of, 38–40, 47–8, 98, 186n12; unreliable representations, 27–8, 73–4; use of vernacular, 50–1, 144–5. *See also* historical narrative
Nennius, *Historia Brittonum*, 6, 23
Nithard, *Histories*, 21
Norman Conquest: comparison of interpretations of, 124–7, 202n2; dates of, 203n3; and lordship practices, 15; as patterned after Danish Conquest, 114–15, 133–4; and practice of narrating conquests, 7;

scholarly concerns of, 123–4; transfer of power in, 123, 199n84
Norman Conquest narratives: no issue of legitimacy, 127–8, 206n52; no longer *Angelcynn*, 19
Normandy, 87, 149
Northampton, 126–7
Northman, son of *ealdormann* Leofwine, 112
Northumbria, 43, 97–8, 112, 126–7
Northumbrians as separate from West Saxons, 48
Norway, 129–30
Norwich, 76–7
Notker of St Gall, stories of Charlemagne, 52
Nottinghamshire, 130

oaths of loyalty: absence of, 132–3; broken, 124–5; with Danes, 44, 118, 133–4; failure of, 96–7, 137–8, 147–8; link to land, 27, 168–9n11; with purchasing peace, 91–2; significance of, 17, 114–15, 129–30, 164n35, 168n8, 194n12. *See also* coronation oath
O'Brien O'Keeffe, Katherine, 35
Offa, king of Mercia, 34, 37
Olaf, king of Norway, son of Harold Hardrada, 129
Olaf Tryggvason, king of Norway, 73, 85–6, 100–2, 105
Old English Bede, 24, 31, 51
Old English heroic literature: barren landscape in, 46, 122, 203n6; Christian tradition in, 27; emotionality of, 15; exile in, 109; ideal lordship in, 99; intertextuality of, 6, 106–7, 109; literary studies of personal lordship, 16, 34. *See also* Cynewulf-Cyneheard episode

Old English Orosius, 24, 51
Orderic Vitalis, *Ecclesiastical History*, 125, 135
Orkney, earl of, 129
Orosius: *Historiarum adversus paganos libri septem*, 6–7, 23–5, 50–1, 56, 70, 145, 167n69
Oswy, king of Northumbria, 150
Otto, Emperor, 74–6, 186n15, 187n20
Oxfordshire, 141

Pallig, possible traitor, 102–3
Parker Manuscript. *See* A Manuscript of the *Anglo-Saxon Chronicle*
Parkes, Malcolm, 20
Paul the Deacon, 5
peace making: baptism's role in, 18, 47, 100, 191n58, 206n61; in code of lordship, 31–2; comparisons of, 21; *compaternitas*, 30; extending of lordship to enemies, 40; with Guthrum, 46–7; honour in face of treachery, 29–30; ideals of personal lordship, 43–4; importance in Alfred annals, 27; language of (*friþ niman*), 44; as lordship, 129; with Malcolm of Scotland, 136–7; with Olaf, 105; policy over tactics, 100–1; purchased with the army, 91–2; and rituals of lordship, 43–4; similarity in rituals of, 43; tribute payments in, 47, 72, 100, 196n28; use of *gryðian*, 139. *See also* oaths of loyalty
Peada, king of Mercia, 150
Peterborough, 139
Peterborough Abbey (Medehamsted), 150
Peterborough Chronicle: authority through writing, 145–8; fire at

Peterborough, 149–50, 214n20; hedge proverb in, 151–2; recreating the records of the past, 149–51; summary of William's reign, 148–9. See also E Manuscript of the Anglo-Saxon Chronicle
Peterborough Interpolations, 150, 152–3
Peter of Cluny, 151–2
philosophy of causation, 23–5. See also under historical narrative, salvation historiography
Picts, 143
power: authority through writing, 145–6, 149–50; and the book, 68; in loyalty oath, 129–30, 133–4, 147–8; responsibility for text, 154; succession rights, 127–8, 187n24; transfer of (translatio imperii), 23–4, 61–2, 113
proverb: about cowardly general, 104, 188–9n30; about hedge, 151–2
Proverbs of Alfred, 69
Pseudo-Cyprian, De duodecim abusivis saeculi, 22, 81–2, 84–5

Ralph, earl of Norfolk, 139
Reading, 43
reading: of the Chronicle's history, 5–7; difficulty of, 4–5; scholarly practices of, 3
Regula pastoralis. See Gregory the Great
Remensnyder, Amy, 12
Reynolds, Susan, 12, 116, 159n20
Richard I, duke of Normandy, 112
Richard II, duke of Normandy, 87
Robert, duke of Normandy, father of William I, 20
Robert, duke of Normandy, son of William I, 140

Rochester, 47, 74, 86
Roger of Breteuil, earl of Hereford, 139
Romans, 25, 32, 143
Royal Frankish Annals, 21, 50
Ruin, 122
rule of law and punishment: constructing the Anglo-Saxon subject, 117, 200–1n103; lordship and king's authority, 95, 115, 127, 139–40, 193n4, 209n102

St Brice's Day massacre, 18, 74, 86–7, 102–3, 105, 192n69
Salisbury, 147–8
salvation history. See under historical narrative, salvation historiography
Scharer, Anton, 52
Scotland, 136, 143, 148–9
Scragg, D.G., 35
Seafarer, 46, 109, 122
Seaxwulf, abbot of Peterborough, 150
Sedulius Scottus: and context of Asser's Vita Alfredi, 52; Liber de rectoribus christianis, 22, 57
Shropshire, 141
Sidroc, Danish earl, 39–40
Sigebryht, king of Wessex, 33–4, 36–7
Sigeferth, thane, 91–2, 97, 110–11
sin: conquest and invasion as the outcome of, 6–7, 23, 72–3, 185n6; and Danish raids, 88–90; as indicator of political change, 56; and loss of identity, 90; and loss of kingdom, 84; reinterpretation of discourse of, 26–7, 145, 168n6; secular misdeed as, 84. See also under historical narrative, salvation historiography

Smaragdus, *Via regia*, 22
Smith, Anthony, 9–10, 160n6
social order, duties of men, 83
Spiegel, Gabrielle, 12
Stafford, Pauline, 91, 110, 117–18
Staffordshire, 141
Stamford Bridge, 132
Strathclyde, 86
succession: crisis when Cnut elected king, 90–2, 98–9, 118; Frankish, 57; fraternal, 57; of Harold II, 125–31; and power, 127–8, 187n24. *See also* genealogical discourse; language
Swein Forkbeard, king of Denmark and Anglo-Saxon England, 76–7, 90, 104, 108, 118–19
Swein Godwinson, earl, 142

Tavistock, 101
Thegan, author of life of Louis the Pious, 52
Thetford, 73, 77
Thorkell the Tall, earl of East Anglia, 112, 119
Þurcytel Myranheafod (Mare's Head), 107
Tostig, earl of Northumbria, 126–32, 136
Trojans, 154

Ufegeat, 74, 105. *See also* blindings
Uhtræd of Bamborough, earl of Northumbria, 87, 108, 192n73
Ulfcytel Snilling, East Anglian leader, 18, 76–8, 87, 104–5
Urse d'Abetot, sheriff of Worcestershire, 122–3

virtue of king, 59, 66

Vita Alfredi. *See* Asser, bishop of Sherborne, *Vita Alfredi*
Vita Eadwardi, 126, 205n45. *See also* Edward the Confessor, king of Anglo-Saxon England

Wales, 148
Waltheof, earl of Northumbria, 122, 139–40, 209nn102, 105
Wanderer, 15, 46, 109, 122
Wessex: Alfred as king of, 27–8, 30, 44–5; Cnut succeeds, 112; Edmund's succession, 98–9; under King Edmund, 91; linked to Mercia, 36–8, 62
Westminster, 149
West Saxon, royal descent, 75. *See also* genealogical discourse
West Saxon history, 20, 28, 31, 35–8, 49, 68–9. *See also* historical narrative
West Saxons (selective references): in Alfred's court, 66; conquered by Danes, 44–5; genealogy of, 55; return of land lost to Danes, 46; rivalry with Mercians, 36–7, 62; separate from other Saxon groups, 48; submission to Cnut, 91–2
White, Hayden, 50
Whitelock, Dorothy, 116
William I, king of Anglo-Norman England, the Conqueror: coronation of, 132–4; disloyalty of, 133–8, 209–10n106; and the *Domesday Book*, 145–53, 213n9; failure of lordship, 11, 135–6; genealogy of, 20; and the Norman invasion, 124–5; relationship with Scotland, 136–7; use of writing authority, 148–9; wife of, 136
William annals: Anglo-Saxon culpa-

bility in, 121, 124–7, 131–4; Anglo-Saxon lordship culture in, 121–2, 125–6; civil war in, 126, 205n46; Cnut's law in, 127; comparisons to other interpretations, 124–7; compilation of, 142, 211n124; defeat in, 126–7; Edward's lordship in, 126–7, 205n45; eulogistic poem of, 127–8; and function of historical narrative, 144; historical context omitted from, 127; land and lordship in, 135–40; literary landscape in, 122; loss of Anglo-Saxon identity in, 123–4; Margaret episode, 122, 136; and narration of history, 6–8, 13, 153; preface of, 142–3, 211nn124, 126, 212n129; rebellion narratives, 122, 138–40; significance of loyalty oath in (Harold) 129, (William), 133; symbolic regicide in, 140; weak lordship bonds in, 145. *See also* D Manuscript of the *Anglo-Saxon Chronicle*

William of Jumièges, *Gesta Normannorum ducum*, 124

William of Malmesbury: and Coleman's *Vita Wulfstani*, 124; *Gesta regum Anglorum*, 125; historical accuracy of, 92–3

William of Poitiers, *Gesta Guillelmi*, 124

wisdom of just councillors, 82–3, 190n46

witan (selective references), 11, 34, 60, 73, 82–3, 109, 115, 172n43, 198n70

Woden, legendary West Saxon ancestor, 55

Worcester lands, 122–3, 140–3, 203–4n13

Worcestershire, 141–2

Wormald, Patrick, 116, 160n4, 168n11

Wulfgeat, thane, 105

Wulfheah, son of *ealdormann* Ælfhelm, 74, 105. *See also* blindings

Wulfhere, king of Mercia, 150–1

Wulfnoth of Sussex, 73, 106–7

Wulfstan, archbishop of York: access to IV Edgar, 115–16; homilies of, 113; *Institutes of Polity*, 81–3, 113; letter from Ælfric to, 83; rhetoric of, 113; *Sermo Lupi ad Anglos*, 81, 88–90, 92, 113, 200n88; story of Gildas (*Sermo Lupi*), 89–90, 192n76; 1018 law code, 95–6, 113–18, 127, 193n4, 195n24; 1020 Letter to the People, 95, 199n87; and II Cnut, 95, 117

Wulfstan, St, bishop of Worcester: continuation of *Chronicle*, 142, 211n122; post-Conquest land history, 141; and Worcester lands, 141–2, 203n13, 212n130

York, 137, 141
Yorkshire, 126–7

Toronto Old English Series

General Editor
ANDY ORCHARD

Editorial Board
ROBERTA FRANK
THOMAS N. HALL
ANTONETTE DIPAOLO HEALEY
MICHAEL LAPIDGE

1 *Computers and Old English Concordances* edited by Angus Cameron, Roberta Frank, and John Leyerle
2 *A Plan for the Dictionary of Old English* edited by Roberta Frank and Angus Cameron
3 *The Stowe Psalter* edited by Andrew C. Kimmens
4 *The Two Versions of Waerferth's Translation of Gregory's Dialogues: An Old English Thesaurus* David Yerkes
5 *Vercelli Homilies IX–XXIII* edited by Paul E. Szarmach
6 *The Dating of Beowulf* edited by Colin Chase
7 *Eleven Old English Rogationtide Homilies* edited by Joyce Bazire and James E. Cross
8 *Old English Word Studies: A Preliminary Author and Word Index* Angus Cameron, Allison Kingsmill, and Ashley Crandell Amos
9 *The Old English Life of Machutus* edited by David Yerkes
10 *Words and Works: Studies in Medieval English: Language and Literature in Honour of Fred C. Robinson* edited by Peter S. Baker and Nicholas Howe
11 *Old English Glossed Psalters: Psalms 1–50* edited by Phillip Pulsiano
12 *Families of the King: Writing Identity in the Anglo-Saxon Chronicle* Alice Sheppard
13 *Verbal Encounters: Anglo-Saxon and Old Norse Studies for Roberta Frank* edited by Antonina Harbus and Russell Poole
14 *Latin Learning and English Lore: Studies in Anglo-Saxon Literature for Michael Lapidge* edited by Katherine O'Brien O'Keeffe and Andy Orchard
15 *Early English Metre* by Thomas A. Bredehoft

16 *Source of Wisdom: Old English and Early Medieval Latin Studies in Honour of Thomas D. Hill* edited by Charles D. Wright, Frederick M. Biggs, and Thomas N. Hall
17 *The Narrative Pulse of Beowulf: Arrivals and Departures* John M. Hill
18 *Verse and Virtuosity: The Adaptation of Latin Rhetoric in Old English Poetry* Janie Steen
19 *Finding the Right Words: Isidore's Synonyma in Anglo-Saxon England* Claudia Di Sciacca
20 *Striving with Grace: Views of Free Will in Anglo-Saxon England* Aaron J Kleist
21 *Klaeber's Beowulf and the Fight at Finnsburg, 4th edition* edited by R.D. Fulk, Robert E. Bjork, and John D. Niles

www.ingramcontent.com/pod-product-compliance
Lightning Source LLC
Chambersburg PA
CBHW030310080526
44584CB00012B/508